# No More Masks!

# No More Masks!

An Anthology of
Twentieth-Century
American Women Poets

NEWLY REVISED AND EXPANDED

Edited with an Introduction by

Florence Howe

HarperPerennial
*A Division of HarperCollinsPublishers*

HarperCollins books may be purchased for educational, business, or sales promotional use. For information please write: Special Markets Department, HarperCollins Publishers, Inc., 10 East 53rd Street, New York, NY 10022.

*Designed by Jessica Shatan*

Library of Congress Cataloging-in-Publication Data

No more masks! : an anthology of twentieth-century American women poets, newly revised and
    expanded / edited with an introduction by Florence Howe. — 1st ed.
        p.   cm.
    Includes index.
    ISBN 0-06-096517-7 (paper)
    1. American Poetry—Women authors.   2. American poetry—20th century.   3. Women—
United States—Poetry.      I. Howe, Florence.
PS589.N58   1993
811'.50809287—dc20                                                                                   92-54843

94 95 96 97 ❖/HC 10 9 8 7 6 5 4      (pbk.)

*To Ellen Bass*
*a true partner*

*and for Muriel Rukeyser*
*a true muse*

# Contents

## PART ONE

*. . . we're a queer lot*
*We women who write poetry.* —AMY LOWELL

## PART THREE
*Loving in the War Years* —CHERRIE MORAGA

# PREFACE

Twenty-two years ago, Ellen Bass and I began to collect poems by women, "about" women. At first it was a lark, a game, entertainment to while away a summer at the Cape. But the early poems caught us, especially Amy Lowell's lines about women poets being "queer"; Elinor Wylie's mysterious narrative about the two sisters, "Loneliness" and "Solitude"; Muriel Rukeyser's "Not Sappho, Sacco"; and Louise Bogan's "Medusa," in which the dreaded snake-haired figure became muse. But would we find poets (and poems) enough to fill a volume?

In the early seventies, it was still possible to use a card catalog under the word "women" and find "poets," though we could not have known then that many poets had slipped away, out of that net into invisibility. A quartet of women poets were known to us personally and through their books: Denise Levertov, Anne Sexton, and Marianne Moore had been part of a poetry series I directed at Goucher College through the nineteen sixties, and Adrienne Rich had come, uninvited, along with Robert Lowell.

Through a library search we found Maxine Kumin, Margaret Walker, Carolyn Kizer, and fifty others, almost none of whom were also to be found in anthologies of American poetry. And the younger poets found us: Word spread quickly in the early seventies through women's liberation newspapers and newsletters. We received three hundred submissions through the mail, some in manuscript and some in books already published. And how did we choose? What criteria did we use? Were we ideological?

The last question is the easiest, for our feminism was inchoate. We could not have articulated a political position—except, perhaps, inclusiveness. As I look back now, we were in possession of the kind of ideological blank slate that such pioneering work requires. We chose what interested us. We followed our curiosity. We insisted that the poem tell us something we didn't already know about women: about women's experience, women's dreams, women's thoughts. We insisted that the poem please us aesthetically—as a shape, as a signifier. We asked that the poem communicate openly. We asked that the poems all together be exciting to read, an adventure for the uninitiated.

We organized the volume into three sections: poets born between 1875 and 1920; those born between 1920 and 1940; those born after 1940. And we insisted on dating each poem.[1] Thus we had poems in the volume from the twenties through the first years of the seventies. Dates seemed very important to us, though we never explained why. Looking back, I think it was that we were finding our way through uncharted territory, without guides. We had no body of literary criticism, no literary history of these women poets. And so dates were our anchors, our starting places.

Without fanfare, with few reviews and most of those hostile, the volume stayed in print until 1987, chiefly because of the interest of feminist teachers, scholars, and critics, some of whom are also poets. When Ellen Bass and I began to work on a second edition of *No More Masks!* we faced a formidable challenge: how to represent both the enormous number—and often generous output—of new poets published since the early seventies and the new work produced by those poets included in the first edition who are still writing. Would we find the same themes that we had unwittingly collected earlier? The answers to this question must await the Introduction. Here I want only to express my regret that Ellen Bass could not continue to work on this new edition with me, and to add that the dedication to her is only a small sign of my gratitude. It is rare and lovely when a student turns teacher and mentor for the person who has been that to her.

It is also rare that a teacher and scholar has the opportunity to revise an anthology two decades on in her own lifetime. I want to thank many individuals and several institutions for the opportunity to have enjoyed firsthand the amazing production of poets through these past twenty years.

The Board of Directors of The Feminist Press at The City University of New York allowed me to take three months in the middle of 1992 to complete the selection of poems and draft the Introduction to the volume. Poets House opened its library's doors to me, even during days and weeks when they were presumably closed. There I could read, as in the comfort of my living room—but also with a photocopy machine handy—books published within the year, as well as whole collections

---

1. The date following each poem is usually the date of publication in a volume by the poet, although for poets Genevieve Taggard, Adrienne Rich, and Audre Lorde, who have dated their poems within a single volume, the dates are of composition. In addition, the dates of several poems published here for the first time are dates of composition.

of particular poets. The New York Public Library's holdings—both in the giant reference division and in the smaller but very accessible borrower's library across the street—was, despite budget cuts, extraordinary. Thanks to that collection, I was able to read all day, then cross the street and borrow a dozen books to read that evening, returning the next day to continue the process.

A handful of scholarly books on modern women poets and a few anthologies of their work produced since 1973, when *No More Masks!* first appeared, were especially useful. Among them, of most importance were *An Asian American Women's Anthology* (1989), edited by Shirley Geok-lin Lim, Mayumi Tsutakawa, and Margarita Donnelly; William Drake's *Women Poets in America, 1915–1945* (1987); J. Lee Greene's introduction to *Time's Unfading Garden: Anne Spencer's Life and Poetry* (1977); Gloria T. Hull's introductions to *Give Us Each Day: The Diary of Alice Dunbar-Nelson* (1984) and *The Works of Alice Dunbar-Nelson* (1988); Alicia Ostriker's *Stealing the Language: The Emergence of Women's Poetry in America* (1986); Deborah Pope's *A Separate Vision: Isolation in Contemporary Women's Poetry* (1984); Marta Ester Sanchez's *Contemporary Chicana Poetry: A Critical Approach to an Emerging Literature* (1985); Erlene Stetson's *Black Sister: Poetry by Black American Women, 1746–1980* (1981); and Cheryl Walker's *Masks Outrageous and Austere: Culture, Psyche, and Persona in Modern Women Poets* (1991).

My process was a simple one: I read and photocopied all the poems that seemed to be potentially of use in the anthology. I read more than two hundred poets and read or reread, in three months of intensive work, more than five hundred separate volumes of poetry, eventually creating a stack of poems that measured 25 inches high. Making the first cut—from 2,000 poems to 750—took one seven-day week. Making the second cut took longer. While all final choices (and necessary cuts) are my responsibility, I want to acknowledge the advice (I didn't always take) of the following friends and to thank them for their generosity: Ellen Bass, Liza Fiol-Matta, Marilyn Hacker, Nancy Porter, Tillie Olsen, Elaine Hedges, and William Hedges. The research assistance of Louise Murray and the computer genius of Liza Fiol-Matta were invaluable. Jacqueline Brown cheerfully copied poems from books in my collection and from those I could take out of the public library. I want to acknowledge also the quick and helpful responses of more than two scores of agents, permissions managers, editors, and small press publishers.

How can I acknowledge those poets whose precious work could not be included? Obviously, it would be wonderful to be able to produce, perhaps next time, *two* volumes covering twentieth-century U.S. women poets.

But I *can* thank the poets who wrote of their pleasure that a new edition of *No More Masks!* was about to appear. Adrienne Rich has been cheering me on for several years now. Maxine Kumin sent me a copy of a note telling her agent that this was "*the* anthology." Ruth Stone wrote, "What a joy to hear that a new enlarged edition of *No More Masks!* is on the way." Diane Wakoski, who had declined to be in the first edition, wrote, "Now that I live in the context of the academy, I see how useful it is to perceive poets first through their social relationships." And many others, some too young for the first edition, wrote that they were honored to be included. From my perspective, all the poets honor me.[2]

Finally, no volume would have been begun except for the imagination and persistence of Ellen Bass and Charlotte Raymond, our literary agent, and no volume would have been produced except for the same qualities in the hands of two editors, Janet Goldstein and Peternelle van Arsdale. A writer also needs the kindness and generosity of friends. I want to thank especially Mariam Chamberlain, Helene D. Goldfarb, and Joanne Markell for loving care.

NEW YORK CITY
*December 1992*

---

2. In the first edition of this anthology, three poets declined my invitation to be included in a "segregated" volume. Twenty years later, I extended the invitation once again. Elizabeth Bishop's publisher wrote, regretting that the poet had left instructions in her will that forced such a decline once again. She is present in the volume, nevertheless, in a selection of poems chosen from among her students and admirers. I regret also that, at the very last moment, after a lengthy and courteous correspondence, Mary Oliver changed her mind again and withdrew her poems. Finally, I deeply regret that Maya Angelou and her publisher were not able to accept the fees established for the volume as a whole. Similarly, the estate of Audre Lorde, for financial reasons, chose effectively to cut her selections in half.

## THE POEM AS MASK
### Orpheus

When I wrote of the women in their dances and wildness, it
    was a mask,
on their mountain, god-hunting, singing, in orgy,
it was a mask; when I wrote of the god,
fragmented, exiled from himself, his life, the love gone down
    with song,
it was myself, split open, unable to speak, in exile from myself.

There is no mountain, there is no god, there is memory
of my torn life, myself split open in sleep, the rescued child
beside me among the doctors, and a word
of rescue from the great eyes.

No more masks! No more mythologies!

Now, for the first time, the god lifts his hand,
the fragments join in me with their own music.

—MURIEL RUKEYSER, 1968

# INTRODUCTION

Many of us who grew up reading British male romantic poets remember the visionary Wordsworth's "Intimations of Immortality" and Shelley's line about poets as the true "legislators of the world." But what about women poets? Twenty years ago, we named the first edition of this volume for a line in Muriel Rukeyser's visionary "The Poem as Mask," in which she insists that the fragments and the invisibility that control women's lives will, at last, come to wholeness and vision. Twenty years ago, we could see the outlines of a fifty-year pattern of women's poems in the United States, particularly on the subject of female identity. We found a stream of poems that queried even the idea of woman as poet; we found a stream of poems that, consciously or not, mirrored the division women poets experienced in their lives, especially if they were both nurturing wives and mothers and creative artists; and we found a new stream among very young poets, identifying themselves with witches and other "wild" women, eager to leave domesticity behind them. We also found a gulf separating the seventy-three white poets in the volume from the fourteen black poets, especially with regard to portraits of mother-daughter relations. That, then, was 1973.

This edition reconceives and expands the first edition of *No More Masks!* asking especially, What has changed? What difference has the women's movement (now in its third decade) made to the themes of poets? To the visibility of women poets? Who are the Wordsworths and Shelleys of our time?

We open still with Muriel Rukeyser's "The Poem as Mask," in part because her living presence in the early seventies directly nurtured this volume, in part because her vision of wholeness is still, for most, a vision. New differences now divide women's poetic consciousness, among them race and age, and no one has yet solved the marshalling of energies necessary for the woman who would be wife and mother as well as artist. We close with a poem by Adrienne Rich, probably the best poet writing today in the United States, and a significant theoretician of and activist in the women's movement. Rich's poem "Final Notations" is the concluding poem in *An Atlas of the Difficult World.* The volume encompasses every painful dilemma of human beings— especially those in the United States—wanting to live the good life but aware of the needs, rights, and misery of others on a planet ultimately small and vulnerable to the destructive energies of the West. Rich's vision extends Rukeyser's beyond the individual poet to the "you" who are readers, everywhere in the world. "You," she is saying, have the "will" to survive the destruction; you may even make a difference in its course.

If these two poems bridge the decades between the old volume and the new, they also lead back to the poets who precede them and forward to the younger (or newer) poets in the volume. The period covered by the selections is now seventy-five years; the number of poets is 104, not 87. In each of the three sections are new or newly recovered poets as well as new poems by poets present in the first edition. Therefore, the book has necessarily become larger, though it needs to be said at the outset that the size masks the number of poets and poems that could not be included. To control the size of the volume, we not only used as guide the quality of each poet included but required that each poet have published at least two volumes.

But what of the vision? What of the "legislation" proffered by these poems? What has altered in poetry during these two decades of rapid change and discovery for all areas of women's life and history? The poets themselves have changed. This is not a volume of white women poets with a handful of black poets; rather, the collection mirrors the poetic quality of a multicultural universe in which women of color are at least as numerous as white women. Further, the specificity of identity has become especially important, in life and in art. Some poets identify themselves as lesbian, as working-class, as ethnically Jewish or Slavic, Chinese or Chicana, or some combination of these and other elements.

The differences between poems of white women and black women in the first edition may be found, intensified, in the early part of this one. But beyond that first section and despite the specificity of identity throughout, similar thematic concerns permeate all segments of the female poetic population. And what is new is new for all; controlled, furious poems on incest and child abuse, on rape and other forms of violence against women, for example, could fill an entire volume. Poems about caring for children—from every imaginable perspective, in every emotional tone—could fill another. Poems on the Holocaust, an entirely new subject of these decades, come also from poets who are neither Jewish nor white. Poems on the so-called small wars—in El Salvador and Nicaragua, for example—follow in the lines of earlier poems on Vietnam. Newer poems on the environmental wars that destroy whales, forests, even the air we breathe may be found in all three sections. Poems on father-daughter relationships have joined the flood of poems about mother-daughter relationships. Poems about aging are almost as numerous as poems about growing up. Sexuality— lesbian and heterosexual—is celebrated, sometimes with humor. Poems about women's bodies—menstruation, pregnancy, birthing, breast- feeding—are often cheerful and witty. Such poems exude confidence, as do those that celebrate late love affairs, lesbian partnerships, marriages, or even the single life of the woman poet.

An elegiac note comes through as well, especially in mourning the early deaths—from cancer, AIDS, and rape and other forms of brutali- ty—of sisters and brothers, of husbands or lovers, as well as the deaths of parents or of other poets and friends. But always in control of the pain and even of the painful vision are the poets' language and rhythms.

These poems are carefully wrought. They have also the energy and confidence of a women's movement, perhaps nurtured by some of these poets, and that nurtures in turn. For readers today, the question "What is it to be a woman?" can be answered only by the statement that to be a woman is to be fully human, to love and to work, to care not only for the children in the family but the children in the world, and the air and water as well. To be a woman poet, further, is to encompass, as Adrienne Rich has put it, "the difficult world."


## PART ONE


*. . . we're a queer lot*
*We women who write poetry.* —AMY LOWELL


The poets in this section are the pioneers, the women who first tried, often with the consciousness of gender, to be poets, and who succeeded despite a society generally hostile to them. Often invisible even to one another, they attempted themes sometimes attributed only to later generations. Poems about lesbian love, racism, pregnancy and nursing, childlessness, and aging, for example, may be found before the 1940s. A selection from "The Ghetto" (1918) by Lola Ridge, a long narrative poem about working-class immigrant Jews in New York City, opens Part One; a lesbian love poem published in 1991 after May Swenson's death closes it.

The first fifteen poets in this section were born before the turn of the century, most of them dead or no longer writing poetry by the 1930s. Whether women should be poets at all was still a question in the early 1900s. Though Hawthorne had railed against that "female horde of [nineteenth-century] scribblers," and though Frances Ellen Watkins Harper was the most famous black poet of the nineteenth century, two informal "groups" of women poets—one white and one black—knew little of each other and seemed also not to acknowledge their forebears. The consciousness of Amy Lowell admitted only Emily Dickinson into the (male) company of Poetry, along with a woman who never forgot that she was also a wife—Elizabeth Barrett Browning—and, of course, Sappho, "a burning birch tree/All tall and glittering fire." In "Letter to My Sister," African-American Anne Spencer, without mentioning Harper, warns:

It is dangerous for a woman to defy the gods;
To taunt them with the tongue's thin tip,
Or strut in the weakness of mere humanity,
Or draw a line daring them to cross. . . .

By the twenties, according to Gloria Hull and William Drake, a "small circle of black women poets . . . were attracted . . . to the home of Georgia Douglas Johnson in Washington, D.C.," a home that served also as "Washington locus of the Harlem Renaissance." They included, in addition to Johnson and Anne Spencer, Angelina Weld Grimké, Alice Ruth Moore Dunbar-Nelson, and Clarissa Scott Delaney. By the twenties, up north, a handful of white women knew each other as poets: Amy Lowell, H.D., Sara Teasdale, Elinor Wylie, Gertrude Stein. The contemporary male literary figures—Richard Aldington (H.D.'s husband) and Ezra Pound, for example, or Paul Lawrence Dunbar (Alice Dunbar-Nelson's husband) and Langston Hughes—were not only more visible than the women; they were Poets, not merely women poets. But there is still one significant difference between the two groups: Lowell and her peers were published in their day, and often to acclaim. Few black women published volumes in their lifetime; their poems were known to peers chiefly through publication in *Opportunity* and *Crisis* and in the several anthologies of black poetry published in the twenties.

If race separates these two groups of poets, then, gender connects them. A handful of poems treat the subject directly:

> . . . I was, being human, born alone;
> I am, being woman, hard beset;
> I live by squeezing from a stone
> The little nourishment I get.
> —ELINOR WYLIE, *"Let No Charitable Hope"*

> The heart of a woman falls back with the night,
> And enters some alien cage in its plight,
> And tries to forget it has dreamed of the stars
> While it breaks, breaks, breaks on the sheltering bars.
> —GEORGIA DOUGLAS JOHNSON, *"The Heart of a Woman"*

But what of the woman poet? In "The Wind" (1914), Sara Teasdale assumes that her poems have the "freedom" she does not:

> I am a woman, I am weak,
>    And custom leads me as one blind,
> Only my songs go where they will
>    Free as the wind.

In "The Sisters" (1925), Amy Lowell asks and answers the key question: Why do women write poetry at all?

> Taking us by and large, we're a queer lot
> We women who write poetry. And when you think
> How few of us there've been, it's queerer still.
> I wonder what it is that makes us do it,
> Singles us out to scribble down, man-wise.
> The fragments of ourselves.

Women poets were "queer" not only in relation to men who were poets but to women who were not. For a woman to feel chosen enough to take on an allegedly male activity has, in the past, meant that she was separated from other women and had to make some adjustment in order to survive in a male world. She might have to deny her sexuality and her human need for family, for instance—as Amy Lowell did—and live out her days as a spinster. Lowell could be comfortable in neither world; nor could Sara Teasdale and Louise Bogan.

But several other poets of this generation, including the very different Gertrude Stein and Marianne Moore, managed other kinds of lives—lesbian and single, respectively—in more equanimity than some of their peers. Wit controls their treatment of gendered themes. Stein's long poem *Patriarchal Poetry* is a dazzling satire. Placed alongside Lowell's contemporary "The Sisters," which locates the "problem" in the gender of women who try to be "man-wise," Stein's poem challenges the patriarchal order controlling women poets as "other" and "lesser" than men. With the humor of her sometimes obtuse-seeming repetition of basic phrases, startlingly clear when read aloud, Stein speaks slyly in some lines directly to male poets: "Let her let her try to be let her try. . . ." And to the women, and those for whom her poem might be considered too lengthy, a slyer line still: "Patriarchal poetry might be finished tomorrow. . . ."

But the white poets of this first generation also chide women for their lack of "wilderness"—Louise Bogan's word: their acceptance of the privileged safety of gendered middle-class lives. Lola Ridge, Genevieve Taggard, Muriel Rukeyser, and Kay Boyle cross these first two generations, urging women to march out of their complacent or long-suffering lives. Their poems raise questions of justice and decency for recent immigrants, for the poor of all races, for workers who would unionize, for young black males in a white racist South, and for the black men who fought on the losing side in the battle for Spain's freedom. And for women? Their poems are curiously reminiscent of some modern responses to the recent women's movement: One should fight for the poor, the black, the helpless—male or female—first, and only then for the more privileged class of women. Even Muriel Rukeyser, the favorite poet of many students and poets today, could be critical, as in "More of a Corpse Than a Woman": ". . . destroy the leaden heart," she says to women, " we've a new race to start."

In the rare, openly autobiographical "Poem Out of Childhood," she tells us two pieces of information about herself. In a phrase naming the source of her "rebellion" as "Not Sappho, Sacco," she disposes of Greek culture in favor of the injustice of the Sacco-Vanzetti case, in which two working-class Italians were condemned to death for their beliefs. And when she turns to her "adolescence," she remembers her father shaving:

"Oh, and you," he said, scraping his jaw, "What will you be?"
"Maybe—something—like—Joan—of—Arc . . . "

One can see Rukeyser, as well as Ridge, Taggard, and Boyle, as lifelong Joans of Arc, working pens-not-swords on behalf of justice and with a vision to make things right. Genevieve Taggard, for example, celebrates the black soldiers of the Abraham Lincoln Brigade who went to fight in the thirties for freedom in Spain. Kay Boyle, in her nineties, wrote in memory of the men who died in the Attica uprising. And Rukeyser, before her untimely death, stood vigil before a North Korean poet's prison.

Few of Rukeyser's contemporaries have been as prolific as she. Of them, only Boyle, Gwendolyn Brooks, Josephine Jacobsen, and May Swenson have had relatively long publishing lives as poets. Margaret Walker and Naomi Replansky were one-volume poets until relatively recently. Ruth Stone, whose first book appeared when she was in her mid-forties, is now publishing regularly.

The "silences" of many others, who lived as closet poets or whose poetic lives ceased after the twenties or the thirties, are painful to enumerate. Among them is Anne Spencer, whose garden was part of her poetic life and who left the poem "1975" for her biographer to publish after her death:

Turn an earth clod
Peel a shaley rock
In fondness molest a curly worm
Whose *familiar* is everywhere
Kneel
And the curly worm    sentient *now*
Will *light* the word that tells the poet what a poem is

As isolated as Anne Spencer from the world of publishing poets were two women who lived, respectively, in Portland, Oregon, and near the shore of Lake Michigan in Wisconsin. Lorine Niedecker and Hazel Hall may seem worlds apart, but they were both self-taught working-class women whose chief joy in life was writing poetry. Hall, who died in 1924 at age thirty-nine and who was confined to a chair in her room for almost all of her life, had earned her living by doing fine sewing. She left a small body of lyrics that remind us of the indomitable human spirit and of the human desire to record, through poetry, the life of that spirit. From Niedecker, who says she "worked the print shop," we have a small body of mischievous, witty poems that also hint at the irresistible lure of writing poetry. Here is a sample from "In the great snowfall before the bomb":

> . . . The women hold jobs—
> clean house, cook, raise children, bowl
> and go to church.
>
> What would they say if they knew
> I sit for two months on six lines
> of poetry?

The presence of these poems suggests that the effort to restore the "lost" voices of women poets may not yet have ended. That these last-named writers were self-taught rather than college educated may also give special heart to working-class writers today.

## PART TWO

### The Will to Change—ADRIENNE RICH

The heart of this book, these poems testify not only to the will to change one's perception of self but to the willingness to work on changing the world. Many of the poets in this section have been social activists for two decades, fighting for civil rights, for an end to the war in Vietnam, and ultimately for women's rights, including the rights of lesbians. During the past twenty years, they have gone from being young poetic stars on the horizon to becoming the poets well known to readers and to audiences eager to hear poets read. While their poems reflect their social concerns, their poetry has also won significant awards: Among this group of thirty-eight poets are five Yale Younger Poets, one Lamont winner, five holders of Academy of American Poets Fellowships, eight Pulitzer winners; and two holders of MacArthurs and one winner of the Lila Wallace Reader's Digest Literary Award.

Unlike previous generations, half of these women are mothers, many of them teachers as well. Now between the ages of fifty-two and seventy-two, some have also experienced caring for aged parents. Along with some of the women in Part One, these poets have not only opened poetry to the dailiness of housework and gardening, to the joy and grief of caring for family, to explorations of sexuality, to the politics of a starving world, and to the pleasures of a creative life, they have made such poetry popular. Their books sell, when they can be found in bookstores. Their appearances on the reading circuits and at literary conferences draw crowds of readers.

As teachers and political activists, these poets confirm American values, perhaps most significantly the value of merit, the flip side of the coin of racism. In their segregrated Washington D.C. world, the women of the Harlem Renaissance wrote of racism and heroism, but only in the past decade has their poetry found a somewhat enlarged audience. Writing from segregated Mississippi and Chicago decades later, neither Margaret Walker nor Gwendolyn Brooks found an easy place in the published world of poets. It is not that the cities and towns of the United States today are, in general, less segregated socially. But simple racial lines no longer rule publishing. And the poets of this generation, whatever their race, live somewhat differently from their elders. Significant friendships between poets now cross racial lines; some poets live in racially mixed heterosexual marriages or lesbian unions. And poets who spend time at writers' colonies, on college campuses, or at conferences find themselves in racially mixed company.

The effect of such "mixing" on poetry is complex. Denise Levertov's "The Long Way Round," *for Alice Walker and Carolyn Taylor,* narrates the poet's taking "lessons" about color "from distant Asia" first and only afterward "from near-as-my-hand persons, Black sisters," learning what it must be to wake each day

> to the sense of one's own beautiful
> human skin, hair, eyes, one's
> whole warm sleep-caressed body
> as something that others
> hated,
>     hunted,
>         haunted by its otherness,
> something they wanted to see disappear.

At the poem's close, Levertov uses the image of the swimming pool filled with women of all races and a man, "some fool of a coach,/strutting the pool's edge" and "shouting":

"If you're White
*you* have
the right of way!"

Levertov leaves us with the possibility that we are not only swimming for our lives but potentially *drowning* in the chlorine's racism "stinging our eyes."

In "Foul Line—1987," a poem written a decade after Levertov's, Colleen McElroy captures a still commonplace experience. In a restaurant, a white waitress cannot meet the poet's African-American eyes even for an instant, though she gives focused attention to a white male customer. "Nothing personal," McElroy says,

But all she sees is color
Black, a shadow, something dark . . .

And I wonder vaguely if I might
Have met her in Selma
Or later opposite some other picket
Lines—we're the right age
For such encounters
     And despite laws to the contrary
     Neither of us has ever lost
     Our sense of misplacement
     And can say politely
     We both know how far we've come

Clearly, the dream of sisterhood has far to go with respect to race relations. The dream itself has not kept women from criticizing other women, though, including themselves. "Hypocrite women," Denise Levertov opens a poem of the early sixties, "how seldom we speak/of our own doubts." Three years into the new decade of the women's, movement, in *Pro Femina,* Carolyn Kizer is more "impolite" still:

Our masks, always in peril of smearing or cracking,
In need of continuous check in the mirror or silverware,
Keep us in thrall to ourselves, concerned with our surfaces.

"Have you used your mind today?" Kizer asks "maimed" women. What she wants for independent women, especially for those who are also writers, is nothing less than freedom. For after all, she writes, women

> . . . are the custodians of the world's best-kept secret:
> Merely the private lives of one-half of humanity.

Like Amy Lowell's "The Sisters," Kizer's is a relatively loose, discursive poem, quite unlike much that the two poets wrote on other subjects. If both are intimate in tone, Kizer's is deliberately antipoetic and breezy, written in a loose jargon and long, loping anapests. The chief difference between them, however, is ideological. In Kizer's poem, gone is the assumption that poetry is male work and that the woman who writes it, therefore, must be part of "a queer lot." When Lowell asked why women, "Already mother-creatures," were also given brains sufficient to the making of poems, she concluded that women poets were bound to be few because the task of combining the two kinds of lives was so impossible:

> The strength of forty thousand Atlases
> Is needed for our every-day concerns.

For Kizer, who assumes (and has experienced) motherhood, the question is different: How can the woman poet be herself in a world in which her poems may be admired only if "*she writes like a man*"?

Adrienne Rich's "Snapshots of a Daughter-in-Law," written at about the same time as *Pro Femina,* begins to answer that question. Choosing for her title a primary limiting definition for the adult woman, Rich also criticizes women for complacency:

> Our blight has been our sinecure:
> mere talent was enough for us—
> glitter in fragments and rough drafts.

And of course she acknowledges male power that judges women writers' "crime" as

> only to cast too bold a shadow
> or   smash the mould straight off.

Her solution: A vision of an androgynous new "she":

Well,

she's long about her coming, who must be
more merciless to herself than history.
Her mind full to the wind, I see her plunge
breasted and glancing through the currents,
taking the light upon her
at least as beautiful as any boy
or helicopter,
poised, still coming,
her fine blades making the air wince
but her cargo
no promise then:
delivered
palpable
ours.

The "cargo . . . delivered/palpable/ours" is nothing less than the
body of poetry, which takes on the changing of consciousness about
women, men, families, and the world. In Rich's work, the questions
become *"With whom do you believe your lot is cast?/From where does your
strength come?"* She answers *from other women,* and in "Hunger," to take
but one example, she frames her politics and her poems accordingly:

The decision to feed the world
is the real decision. No revolution
has chosen it. For that choice requires
that women shall be free . . .
Until we find each other, we are alone.

Still only a "dream," the ideal of *racial* sisterhood beyond national
boundaries appears also in poems about Vietnam written during the
seventies. After experiencing the extraordinary strength and kindness
of "The Women in Vietnam," even to her, an American "enemy," Grace
Paley concludes:

I said is it true? We are sisters?
They said, Yes, we are of one family

In "Sisters in Arms," a poem of the eighties, Audre Lorde records the
voice of a South African woman speaking directly to her, as though
thinking about the sisterhood dream:

"Someday you will come to *my* country
and we will fight side by side?"

The vision of women fighting side by side is a subtext through the
poems that testify to male violence against women—in the family or
on the streets. The enormous stream of poems on this theme touches all
aspects of human life. June Jordan's "Poem About My Rights," for
example, begins by answering the question why she can't take a walk
at night in the city or "on the beach/or far into the woods." The poem's
torrential language explores rape laws, national and international rapes,
and focuses ultimately on "the problems" of being black and female. "I
am the history of rape," she writes, an obvious allusion to the experi-
ence of slavery for African-American women; "this poem/is not consent
I do not consent." The poem's conclusion fairly leaps off the page:

*I am not wrong: Wrong is not my name*
My name is my own my own my own
and I can't tell you who the hell set things up like this
but I can tell you that from now on my resistance
my simple and daily and nightly self-determination
may very well cost you your life

As new as poems describing the rape of children or adult women are
those depicting incest. Lucille Clifton's "to my friend, jerina" opens
quietly:

listen,
when i found there was no safety
in my father's house
i knew there was none anywhere.

Other poems record incest by a brother (Diane Wakoski's "Justice Is
Reason Enough") and a mother (Sharon Olds's "What If God"). Incest
poems may offer what Edmund Wilson called, in an entirely different
context, the "shock of recognition," ameliorating, through openness,
the painful experience, and allowing the healing to begin.
    Similarly, poems about wife-battering break old taboos. A recent
poem by Mitsuye Yamada, "The Club," tells the story of a wife able to
free herself from a husband who beats her using one of his "overseas
treasures/I was never to touch." Yamada's heroine frees herself by "dar-
ing" to pick up the statue one morning:

"Well, my sloe-eyed beauty," I said
"have you served him enough?"

The battered wife dares further: she wraps the statue "in two sheets of paper towels": "We're leaving," she whispers, "you and I/together." Other poems offer glimpses of battered mothers who stayed in marriages because of the children, of children who remember their mothers crying or who themselves remember the battering of angry and sometimes drunken fathers. This theme only deepens among the younger poets in Part Three.

At the same time, the poets of this generation write lovingly of other family relations, or with delightful humor, as in Lucille Clifton's recent poem to male children, "wishes for sons":

i wish them cramps.
i wish them a strange town
and the last tampon.
i wish them no 7-11.

One may read Sylvia Plath's "Daddy" or "The Disquieting Muses," two negative poems about her parents, beside Diane Wakoski's "Thanking My Mother for Piano Lessons" or a recent poem by Patricia Goedicke that portrays her mother with her small girl children "In the Ocean":

We would rub against her like minnows
We would flow between her legs, in the surf

Smooth as spaghetti she would hold us
Close against her like small polliwogs climbing

All over her as if she were a hill,
A hill that moved, our element

But hers also, safe
In the oval of each other's arms.

Not surprisingly, the poets of this generation write openly and movingly about the care of aged parents, sometimes in nursing homes—see especially Mona Van Duyn's "The Stream"—and about their deaths—see Jean Valentine's "My Mother's Body, My Professor, My Bower" and

Wanda Coleman's "Dear Mama (2)." This generation of poets also writes more openly than before of aging and illness and even of physical impairment; see poems by Vassar Miller, Marie Ponsot, and Muriel Rukeyser.

A few poets of this generation write generously of heterosexual marriage, especially in light of their own aging. If we know Mona Van Duyn's devastating portrait of a marriage called "The Fear of Flying" (not included in this volume), we may compare it to a newer poem called "Late Loving." Or consider Diane Di Prima's early poem, "The Quarrel," beside the more recent "Poem in Praise of My Husband." Patricia Goedicke's "Lucky" describes a late marriage, and Maxine Kumin's loving and comic "The Rendezvous," a late love affair:

> . . . How I meet a male bear.
> How I am careful not
> to insult him. I unbutton
> my blouse. He takes out
> his teeth. I slip off
> my skirt. He turns
> his back and works his way
> out of his pelt,
> which he casts to the ground
> for a rug.

But many of the poets of this generation now write, like Denise Levertov, of "A Woman Alone." In some poems, women have not chosen that path—see Vassar Miller's "Trimming the Sails" or Yamada's "Homecoming"—but there is also the special joy in Molly Peacock's "So, When I Swim to the Shore" (see Part Three). In Marie Ponsot's "Love Is Not Love," the poet reaches out to other women, even those far back in the past who may have had similar troubles:

> . . . I reach for comfort
> to the left-out lives of women here and gone.
> They lend them willingly. They know my need.
> They do not hate me for crying. It beats despair.

As distinctly new as the poems about violence are those about love between women. Adrienne Rich's "(The Floating Poem)," part of a sonnet sequence called *Twenty-one Love Poems* dated 1974–1976, contains one of the earliest, and perhaps still the loveliest, lines of lesbian sexuality:

Whatever happens with us, your body
will haunt mine—tender, delicate
your lovemaking, like the half-curled frond
of the fiddlehead fern in forests
just washed by sun.

This and other more recent poems of Rich remind us of a tradition of
lesbian poets, stretching back to Grimké's "Caprichosa" (1901) and to
poems by Muriel Rukeyser and May Swenson (see Part One), and allow
us to look ahead to the blossoming of lesbian poetry among the poets
of the next generation.

## PART THREE

*Loving in the War Years* — CHERRIE MORAGA

The oldest poets of the generation born after 1940 were in their twenties
when the women's movement began in the 1960s; the youngest ones were ado-
lescent, some of them learning that they were "free to be." They are the poets
of the future. Their poems and their lives are freer than the generations that
preceded them: in style, with language, about women's bodies, about sexu-
ality, and about difference. More of these poets are openly lesbian than in
any previous generation. Twenty of the forty poets included here are women
of color; it would have been possible to add another forty poets and main-
tain that proportion or, among younger poets still, increase it.

What does that tell us? Optimistically, one might rejoice to see
poetry truthfully reflect a multi-ethnic, multiracial society. And still,
in addition to hope, there is a warning in Nellie Wong's questions (see
Part Two) at the end of "Toward a 44th Birthday":

. . . How far, how near will sisters talk?
Will art atrophy, will it become the tools in our hands?

Ironically, though the younger poets are more numerous and often
exceedingly productive, their selections here are of necessity too brief
to indicate their individual virtuosity and the variety of subjects on
which each writes. Among them are six winners of the Lamont Poetry

Award (Marilyn Hacker, Ai, Carolyn Forché, Sharon Olds, Mary Jo Salter, and Minnie Bruce Pratt), one Pulitzer prize-winner (Rita Dove), a MacArthur (Jorie Graham) and two winners of the new Lila Wallace Readers Digest Literary Awards (Sharon Olds and Ntozake Shange). If they are as skilled as previous generations—many of them having been taught by older women poets, as some of the poems indicate—they are also no less burdened. For the "change" envisioned by Adrienne Rich in her early poems is long in coming, and Audre Lorde's mid-eighties incantatory prayer in "Call" continues to demand repeating:

> Mother    loosen my tongue or adorn me
> with a lighter burden

The ideology and euphoria of the seventies, captured in a few poems here (see, for example, Robin Morgan's "The Invisible Woman" and Susan Griffin's "An Answer to a Man's Question, 'What Can I Do About Women's Liberation?'") have given way to the vision expressed best in the title to Part Three, "Loving in the War Years." The battle for women's liberation, joined as it must be with all other battles for human justice and the survival of the planet, has, in fact, only begun.

The poets of this generation meet some of these burdens with humor about their bodies and sexuality. While the poets of the first two generations never mentioned sexual organs, and at least two poets of the previous generation referred to vaginas as ugly (see Denise Levertov's "Hypocrite Women" and Colette Inez's "Warrior Daughters"), Ellen Bass sees them quite differently:

> Vaginas of women, all the clusters
> of vulva, clitoris, labia,
> all the shades of coral and persimmon
> peach, tulip, and carnelian . . .

As does Rita Dove ("After Reading *Mickey in the Night Kitchen* for the Third Time Before Bed"):

> My daughter spreads her legs
> to find her vagina. . . .
> . . . She demands
> to see mine and momentarily
> we're a lopsided star
> among the spilled toys,

my prodigious scallops
exposed to her neat cameo.

Several other aspects of female bodies receive fresh and sometimes humorous treatment at the hands of these feisty poets. Remember Edna St. Vincent Millay's serious, even pained "Menses" (Part One)? Or even Marge Piercy's vision of menopause as "Something to Look Forward To" (Part Two)? Here, Alta's humorous working-class woman's voice turns the occasion into a funny story of blood on the sheets after a night of sex. For Molly Peacock, in "Smell," "The smoky smell of menses—Ma always left the bathroom door open"—reminds her of the elephant house at the zoo, and her sympathetic portrait of elephants' "wise eyes," their "majesty and benignity," are also humorous homage to her mother and other women. The poem concludes:

God, what animals we are, huge of haunch,
bloody and wise in the stench of bosk.

For Alma Luz Villanueva, menses is "Witches' Blood," celebrated as a "power," a "secret/wrapped in ancient tongues": "O woman/you dare birth/yourself." She too ends humorously:

. . . call me witch
call me hag
call me sorceress
call me mad
call me woman.　 do not
call me goddess.
I do not want the position.

In "Tampons," a long tour-de-force on the subject, Ellen Bass describes a bit of her own experience, "when my uterus lets/go and I am an open anemone," and more of the history of tampons, sanitary napkins, tassaways, diaphragms, menstrual extraction, and mosses, concluding that there is no safe and sanitary way to control the monthly bleeding of much of half the population. The last third of this poem is a comic vision:

. . . For a little while cleaning products will boom,
409, Lysol, Windex. But
the executives will give up. The cleaning woman is leaving a

red wet rivulet, as she scrubs down the previous stains.
It's no use. The men would have to
do it themselves, and that will never come up
for a vote at the Board.

Sexuality in the poems of this generation is also freer, distinctively direct, and often playful, even humorous. In these poems, heterosexual or lesbian, women are active: Ntozake Shange's "its happenin/but you dont know abt it" describes a woman's bodily reactions to a man's presence: "i am naked & wantin/to be explored . . . i am all lips & thigh." Nikki Giovanni's "Seduction" describes a woman undressing a man even as he lectures her on "The revolution." Poems by Ellen Bass and Sharon Olds describe women making love to men. Bass's "In Celebration" opens:

Last night I licked
your love, you love,
like a cat. . . .

Olds ends "First Sex" triumphantly:

. . . and the actual
flood like milk came out of his body, I
saw it glow on his belly,
. . . I rubbed it into my
hands like lotion, I signed on for the duration.

While lesbian poems also may treat sexuality with humor (see, for example, Pat Parker's "For Willyce") Marilyn Hacker's sonnet sequences and longer poems often mix high spirits and outrageous images with tenderness, as in "Nearly a Valediction":

You happened to me. I was happened to
like an abandoned building by a bull-
dozer, like the van that missed my skull
happened a two-inch gash across my chin.
You were as deep down as I've ever been.
You were inside me like my pulse. . . .

At least a single antecedent may be found to the new larger flow of poems about pregnancy (and the pain of not being able to bear children), childbirth, and breast-feeding. See, for example, in Part One, Genevieve Taggard's "With Child" (1921) or Amy Lowell's "The Garden by Moonlight" (1919) or Muriel Rukeyser's "Night Feeding" (1935). Or, from Part Two, Jane Cooper's "Waiting" (1971), Linda Pastan's "Notes from the Delivery Room" (1971), and Alicia Ostriker's "Propaganda Poem: Maybe for Some Young Mamas" (1975–1979). But the proportion of mothers among these younger poets is higher than in earlier generations, and some of them write of pregnancy or birth with particular triumph—and humor. Here is Sandra McPherson in "Pregnancy":

It is the best thing.
I should always like to be pregnant.

Tummy thickening like a yoghurt,
Unbelievable flower.

And Sharon Olds, "The Language of the Brag":

I have done what you wanted to do, Walt Whitman,
Allen Ginsberg, I have done this thing,
I and the other women this exceptional
act with the exceptional heroic body,
this giving birth, this glistening verb,
and I am putting my proud American boast
right here with the others.

Poems about the care of children, about trying to be good mothers, sometimes alone, without partners of either sex, form the largest new group of family poems. Violence-filled childhoods provide one subtext. Thus, in the pleasure-filled poems about Sharon Olds's children, one may find also a sense of urgency, of escape from danger, or of the fragility of the moment. In one of many poems about mothering her daughter Iva, Marilyn Hacker portrays the struggle, as Muriel Rukeyser once put it, "to be non-violent in the violent day." Hacker describes the mother locked into the bathroom, separated from the child: "We cry on both sides of the door."

For some of these younger poets, a different kind of fear emerges when they look at their children. Here is Linda Hogan's "Daybreak":

. . . Her innocence is my guilt.
In her dark eyes
the children of Hiroshima
are screaming
and her skin is
their skin
falling off.
How quickly we could vanish. . . .

Like other poets of their generation, Hacker and Hogan are writing about "Loving in the War Years," the effort to be human in a world dangerous to all life. As Pat Parker writes in one of her last poems, "Love isn't" these days purely "joyful," bright, warm; "I come cloudy," she says, "I come rage," "I come sad," and with the world's troubles. But her conclusion reminds us of some of the other, earlier, poets in this volume:

. . . I care for you
I care for our world
if I stop
caring about one
it would be only
a matter of time
before I stop
loving
the other.

How does one continue to love and live productively in a dangerous world? This generation of poets looks to the past for strength, as well as to the future. They look to poets who have taught them, to Muriel Rukeyser and Elizabeth Bishop, for example. Or to poets or others whose lives offer them monuments of encouragement. Thus Sandra McPherson looks back to Hazel Hall; Lucha Corpi, Rachel Hadas, and Mary Jo Salter to Emily Dickinson; Joy Harjo (and Diane Di Prima before her) to Audre Lorde; Carolyn Forché to Claribel Allegría; Alta to Pat Parker; Susan Griffin to Harriet Tubman and Barbara Deming.

Another source of strength comes from the poems about grandmothers. In these poems, ethnic identity and family history are especially important. Part Three opens with "Beneath the Shadow of the Freeway" by Lorna Dee Cervantes and includes Alma Luz Villanueva's "To Jesus Villanueva, with Love," Marilyn Nelson Waniek's "The House on

Moscow Street" (one of a series of poems on her family's history), and Carolyn Forché's "Burning the Tomato Worms."

More than a single snapshot of a woman, these poems offer a series of images, even in some cases the narrative of a life. The grandmother may be strong, but she is also a flawed, rounded character, sometimes in conflict with other family members. Forché's and Villanueva's poems are elegies, Forché's written across the distance of years; Villanueva's still a fresh loss. For both poets, the grandmother is irrevocably linked to their childhoods; Villanueva enjoys breaking hospital rules to make the last days of her grandmother joyous, remembering the rules broken by her grandmother to help her survive a difficult childhood. And for those interested in family history or to those who know little of their own ethnic backgrounds—in the polyglot that is the United States—these poems offer what Marilyn Waniek names "the homeplace," "generations lost to be found/to be found."

Lorna Dee Cervantes's "Poem for the Young White Man Who Asked Me How I, an Intelligent, Well-Read Person, Could Believe in the War Between Races," written in 1981, names another one of the "wars" that continues to govern the lives and the poems of the younger generation of poets. As Cherrie Moraga sees it ("Loving in the War Years") there are many wars, especially for lesbians of color who would love:

> I've got to take you as you come
> to me, each time like a stranger
> all over again. Not knowing
> what deaths you saw today
> I've got to take you
> as you come, battle bruised
> refusing our enemy, fear.

How, then, do women in wartime live every day? Olga Broumas writes about touching. Tess Gallagher describes the difficulty of being "On Your Own" at work in a man's world:

>                              . . . It's hard work
> having your way, even
> half the time, and having it,
> know what not to do with it. Who
> hasn't thrown away a life or two
> at the mercy of another's passion,
> spite or industry.

In "Soul Food," Janice Mirikitani describes the difficulty of living in an interracial marriage:

> We prepare
> the meal together.
> I complain,
> hurt, reduced to fury
> again by their
> subtle insults
> insinuations
> because I am married to you.
> Impossible autonomy, no mind
> of my own.

Perhaps Judy Grahn has said it best for her generation when she envisions the distinctions among sex, love, and romance—in a time of war for women. In "My name is Judith," she says, early in the poem, "I want to be called The Power of Love."

> . . . not until we have ground we call our own
> to stand on
> & weapons of our own in hand
> & some kind of friends around us
> will anyone ever call our name Love,
> & then when we do we will all call ourselves
> grand, muscley names:
> the Protection of Love,
> the Provision of Love & the
> Power of Love.
> until then, my sweethearts,
> let us speak simply of
> romance, which is so much
> easier and so much less
> than any of us deserve.

The militant poems of the eighties and nineties follow in the tradition of Grahn's seventies poem above but with a vision of a far longer and more difficult war in view than women had imagined a generation ago. Rachel Hadas's "Pass It On, II" evokes "twin gestures, teaching/mothering: two tasks" that contain echoes of guns ("barrels") and fires. The image of burning is especially strong, for it concludes the poem:

*Carry on the torch* was what they told me
in high school, i.e. teach; be like your father.
Knowledge, it seemed, was like a relay race.
                    I didn't know
the torch would have to pass through my own body.

One may remember Muriel Rukeyser's father shaving and asking her what she wanted to be when she grew up, and her answer: Joan of Arc. Here, the force of the poem reminds us of the shift over half a century between the lives of women of Rukeyser's and Hadas's generations. This generation of women, freed to be like their fathers, not restricted to their mother's lives, are, nevertheless, women. As Hadas puts it "A body passes/through a body, changing it forever."Hadas reminds us of the responsibility of women, freshened by the past twenty-five years to include an entirely new vision of women's freedom and power. Hadas is also reminding us of the cost of such a battle and of the poet's language as weapon. Similarly, and with some ambiguity also, the final stanza of "Winter Song," a new poem by Lucha Corpi, points to the function of poetry in the wartime life on the planet:

Nothing is fixed or perpetual
not rain
or seed
or you
or I
or our grief
in this world that is bleeding
because we're forever cutting paths
opening our way along unfamiliar roads
conquering the fury of oblivion verse by verse.

## TWO THEMES AND THE QUESTION OF MUSE

Two themes insist on special—and separate—recognition. First, the theme of the divided self extends from Elinor Wylie to recent poems by Colleen McElroy, Linda Hogan, and Lucille Clifton. Second, I group together a series of narratives from Holocaust history and from biblical and classical myth whose theme is the search for justice through the recognition (and elimination) of violence. These two themes may help answer another question: Who is the (woman) poet's muse? Certainly, they refocus attention on the opening question of this Introduction: the function of women poets in the modern world.

### The Poet's Search for the Wholeness of Identity

Eleven poems in this volume (and many more I have collected) attempt a definition of a woman by splitting her into two (occasionally three) "sisters" or women. Often, the poem consists of static characterizations: in Adrienne Rich's "Women," two women are sewing, each quite different from the other, and a third is watching "a dark-red crust" on the ocean; in Denise Levertov's "In Mind," one woman is "smelling of/apples or grass" and the other is a "turbulent moon-ridden girl"; in Naomi Replansky's "Two Women," one is "climbing a glass hill/Of clothes and dishes," while her double is a "bitch." While these images may now seem predictable, they remain haunting visions of women divided between "appropriate" womanly duties and the creative life of a poet. When the theme expands into narrative, as in Elinor Wylie's "Little Eclogue" or Denise Levertov's "An Embroidery (I)," the poems reveal a poignant longing for wholeness.

In Elinor Wylie's "Little Eclogue" (1932), twin sisters named Solitude and Loneliness live "like birds" in a wood. Much of the poem describes their differences as they serve "their appointed tasks": Loneliness, "freckle-faced, and full of sighs," really does not like the life they lead together, though she cannot say why. "Lovely" Solitude, "wild and holy," on the other hand, "Preferred the forest, and her private mind."

One day, the "wild and holy" twin "escaped into the dawn," leaving her sister more lonely than before. Wandering presumably in search of Solitude, Loneliness

> . . . found a sleeping demigod or man;
> And gazed entranced upon the creature's face,
> Which was adorable and commonplace.

Despite a witty reversal, the young man's presence/power turns Loneliness into a beauty. Wylie ends her poem sardonically:

> . . . Let you believe, let me unsurely guess
> This wonder wrought upon poor Loneliness;
> But what was done, to what intrinsic end,

And whether by a brother or a friend,
And whether by a lover or a foe,
Let men inquire, and gods obscurely know.

Wylie's point is that allegedly happy endings are not necessarily what they may seem. Who knows how Loneliness will feel about the "adorable" young man several years hence? But more interesting is the utter disappearance of the "wild and holy" twin—the sister who might have been a poet. Apparently these two, at least in Wylie's day, cannot coexist, and certainly not in the same individual.

Nearly forty years later, in a narrative poem called "An Embroidery (I)," Denise Levertov draws a pair reminiscent of Wylie's. Again, two sisters keep house in the woods, though this time they also prepare dinner for a "bear" that one of them will marry. After dinner, the bear falls asleep before the fire and the two sisters go to bed. Rose Red "dreams she is combing the fur of her cubs/with a golden comb," while "Rose White is lying awake" thinking about the dark forest. The poem concludes, however, not with Rose White's escape to the forest but with a prediction about her:

Rose White shall marry the bear's brother.
Shall he too
when the time is ripe,
step from the bear's hide?
Is that other, her bridegroom,
here in the room?

Do the questions (as well as the strong declarative sentence of prediction) tell us that the bear also contains a double? Young students have assumed that Rose White *will* marry someone as much like her as Rose Red is like the bear in the poem. Is that not, after all, what happens in fairy tales? Read differently, the two sisters are one woman with two desires—one for the bear and one for the scent (poetry) of the forest. Still, the outcome holds: She shall have them both.

The newer poems about split women are quite different, and for several reasons. In two of them, for example, the speakers have already had the "bears," the "house," even the "children." But the doubles are still there. Some of these are poems of the 1970s, in which marriage has not proved the answer to the search for wholeness. Tess Gallagher's "Instructions to the Double," for example, envisions a life away from

... an ornate piano
in a house on the other side
of the country.

The "double" is instructed to "Go/to the temple of the poets," a dangerous mission for many reasons, including the fact that the particular temple the double must find is "on fire/with so much it wants/to be done with." The final stanzas of the poem urge this double to be Lizzie Borden, if she needs to, and finally even a "witch":

... If anyone calls you a witch,
burn for him; if anyone calls you
less or more than you are
let him burn for you.

It's a dangerous mission. You
could die out there. You
could live forever.

In some ways, this is the ultimate seventies poem. Very early in that decade, Barbara Ehrenreich and Deirdre English wrote a pamphlet called "Witches, Midwives, and Nurses," restoring witches to their rightful place as healers and visionaries. A women's liberation movement group named themselves W.I.T.C.H., and the first edition of *No More Masks!* named Part Three for witches—"We are screaming,/we are flying,/laughing, and won't stop"— from a poem by Jean Tepperman. Gallagher's imagery connects the double's mission as poet with women's liberation: What was thought (by male standards) to be bad—including women's poetry—may indeed be good. Moreover, the poem insists that the (woman) poet cannot be domestic.

Alicia Ostriker's "The Exchange," written a decade later, is more chilling. Beneath the surface is anger sufficient, at least metaphorically, to murder. In a boat with her children, the poem's speaker sees the double, a beautiful mermaid swimming "below the surface." The rest of the poem hangs on an "if": *If* the speaker changes places, the double will "strangle my children" and then return to the husband, and here the poem is also ominous:

... When my husband answers the doorbell and sees
This magnificent naked woman, bits of sunlight
Glittering on her pubic fur, her muscular
Arm will surround his neck, once for each insult

Endured. He will see the blackbird in her eye,
Her drying mouth incapable of speech. . . .

And the speaker?

. . . And I, having exchanged with her, will swim
Away, in the cool water, out of reach.

At least metaphorically the poem returns to the irreconcilable split of
Wylie's "Little Eclogue." Such divisions continue to haunt at least the
poems of white women.

For women of color, a biracial heritage provides the text for another
kind of split woman. Linda Hogan, in "The Truth Is," graces the pain
of reality with humor:

In my left pocket a Chicksaw hand
rests on the bone of the pelvis.
In my right pocket
a white hand. Don't worry. It's mine
and not some thief's. . . .

This split offers little comfort: the doubles are "crowded together/and
knock against each other at night." "We want amnesty," the speaker
declares. Ultimately, she concludes, again with humor and a suggestion
of the strategy that might lead to wholeness:

. . . Girl, I say,
it is dangerous to be a woman of two countries.
You've got your hands in the dark
of two empty pockets. Even though
you walk and whistle like you aren't afraid
you know which pocket the enemy lives in

and you remember how to fight
so you better keep right on walking.

In another new turn, two poems by African-American poets Lucille
Clifton and Colleen McElroy, both a decade older than Linda Hogan,
speak to or for women aging. "There is a girl inside," Clifton tells us,
"randy as a wolf":

. . . she is a green girl
in a used poet.

In the end, she will "break through gray hairs/into blossom."

. . . and the woods will be wild
with the damn wonder of it.

Colleen McElroy's "Queen of the Ebony Isles" reverses the split, imagining the double as a cantankerous, difficult, screaming, raging "old woman": "without me who are you she asks." "Without her all sounds are hollow," the poet tells us.

when I complain she says I'm hearing voices
she's hacked my rocking chair into firewood
I am the clown in all her dreams

In both poems the woman, energized by the split, continues to write poetry. Both poems capture a powerful feeling of aging women (and men): that while their bodies may be aging, their inner selves remain unchanged. Such feelings may either sadden or encourage.

*The Search for Justice Through the Elimination of Violence*
In two poems of the 1980s, two poets, themselves nearly a generation apart, interested in the theme of the dutiful wife, turn to the biblical Sarah, the aged woman who miraculously gave birth to a child (the "gift" of God) and who suffered her husband's willingness to sacrifice that child at the command of God. In Elinor Wilner's "Sarah's Choice," the poet narrates an admittedly apochryphal biblical story in which God first approaches Sarah, asking her to sacrifice her son as a "gift" but without offering a reason. Sarah, however, is a reasonable "old woman," who remembers that God

. . . promised Abraham,
through this boy, a great nation. So either
this sacrifice is a sham, or else it is a sin.
"Shame," she said, for such is the presumption
of mothers, "for thinking me a fool,
for asking such a thing. You must have known

I would choose Isaac. What use have I
for History—an arrow already bent
when it is fired from the bow?"

The last third of the poem is the "History" that was not. Sarah finds
her son awake in the tent and, motherlike, extends the choice to
him: "You can be chosen/or you can choose." She tells him about
her rational reading of God's demand, a reading not of simple obe-
dience to "Authority" but, rather, of justice. If I were to follow this
voice, she reasons, "how shall we tell/the victims from the saints,/the
torturers from the agents of God?" And she tells the child also that
this experience has caused her to remember "Hagar the Egyptian
and her son/whom I cast out, drunk on pride" because of her mirac-
ulous late pregnancy. She urges the child to choose to come with
her, and childlike, he focuses on the question of how to greet this
lost brother. Sarah predicts: "You must know your brother/now."
Else,

"you will see your own face looking back
the day you're at each other's throats."

The poem ends with Sarah's rapid preparation for departure before
Abraham awakens, and with her response to the child's final question,
"But what will happen if we go?"

"I don't know," Sarah said.
"But it is written    what will happen    if you stay."

As if a coda on Wilner's narrative, Shirley Kaufman's "Déjà Vu"
describes an accidental *contemporary* meeting between Sarah and Hagar,
"at the rock/where Isaac was cut free." Sarah is a tour-guide; Hagar is
praying "in the women's section."

They bump into each other at the door. . . .
Sarah wants to find out what happened
to Ishmael but is afraid to ask.
Hagar's lips make a crooked seam
over her accusations.

They "walk out of each other's lives,"

> . . . not mentioning
> the angels of god and the bright
> miracles of birth and water. Not telling
> that the boys are gone. . . .

The final stanzas of the poem detail the two women's lives, Sarah's in service to the man "already seated/reading the afternoon paper/or listening to the news"; Hagar's alone, shopping in the market for "warm bread" and "ripe figs." The humdrum separateness of their (childless) lives both masks their enmity and emphasizes its futility. The bright "what if?" of Wilner's poem has fled. Where then is justice?

Another stream of visionary poems is haunted by the Holocaust. These are not poems like Sylvia Plath's "Daddy," in which the speaker identifies her father metaphorically as a Nazi, herself his victim as a Jew. These are poems about events and their meanings for Jews and others who live aware of a dangerous world. In a late poem, Muriel Rukeyser opens the word "Jew" beyond ethnicity. "If you refuse" the "gift" of being "a Jew in the twentieth century"—thus suggesting paradoxically that one has *a choice*—

> . . . you choose
> Death of the spirit, the stone insanity.
> Accepting, take full life, full agonies. . . .

"The gift is torment," and yet Rukeyser continues the paradox, "suffering to be free,/Daring to live for the impossible."

In the seventies, Irena Klepfisz, herself a camp survivor, published a series of poems that recapture brutal, fragmented scenes reminiscent of the black-and-white clips of newsreels or of recent films:

> . . . wiping the child's nose with her fingers
> she says      blow      his eyes shine      as she
> feels the pressure of the doorknob      palms
> wet slipping out of her grasp      she whispers
> not now      not yet      we've been so careful
> he's a good child      just a little more time
> she pleads with them      we will not be
> careless anymore      this time the knob falls
> into the glare of lights      voices scream

orders she does not understand      but obeys
blow       she tells him pulling down her skirt . . .

More recent poems, by poets thirty years apart and removed from the Holocaust experience by birth or by age, remind us of the persistence of these images. Amy Clampitt's vision emerges from a dream she calls "The Burning Child":

> . . . The people herded from the cattle cars
> first into barracks, then to killing chambers,
> stripped of clothes, of names, of chattels—all those
> of whom there would remain so few particulars:
> I think of them, I think of how your mother's
> people made the journey, and of how. . . .
>                     not one
> outlived the trip whose terminus was burning. . . .

Jorie Graham's poem "The New World" is nightmare partly in the form of writing a film script about the trial of "Ivan" in 1987:

> Has to do with the story about the girl who didn't die
>    in the gas chamber, who came back out asking
> for her mother. Then the moment—the next coil—where the guard,
>    Ivan, since the 50's an autoworker in Cleveland,
> orders a man on his way in to rape her.
>    Then the narrowing, the tightening. . . .

Graham's poem concludes with the young girl herself, "coming back out/alive," "whispering please." Like Clampitt, Klepfisz, and Rukeyser, Graham's "whisper" shouts the need: To be fully human, especially in an age of gratuitous, almost mechanical violence, one needs to feel the pain of those who have suffered beyond the ordinary limits of even the most acute imagination. For such poets the idea of justice seems impossible without a comprehension of the pain of unthinkable violence against millions, made palpable in poems focused on individual humans, often a woman, her children, or a young girl.

Among these poems, two offer relief: Jean Valentine's "The Forgiveness Dream" comes in the form of a confession of guilt, in a dream about a small child "speaking in Polish" to whom the poet speaks in English:

                    "I've lived the whole time
here in peace. A private life." "In shame,"
I said. He nodded. He was old now, kind,
my teacher's age; my mother's age. He nodded,
and wrote in my notebook—"Let it be good."

Mary Oliver's long poem, regretfully not in this volume, "1945–1985:
Poem for the Anniversary," frames brief glimpses of "films of Dachau
and Auschwitz and Bergen-Belsen" and "the face of Mengele" within
the embrace of an idyllic "good leafy place" in which the poet observes
a lost fawn. At the close of the poem, the doe finds her fawn, smells the
previous danger, and "nuzzle[s] her child wildly."

Why these poems now? I asked myself as I read enough of them to
fill a book by themselves. A long poem by Adrienne Rich, written at
the beginning of the eighties, provides one answer: "the immense
silence/of the Holocaust" itself. Mary Oliver's poem suggests another
reason: the silence of the planet.

This series of poems on the Holocaust is not an accident, a coinci-
dence of the moment. "There Will Be Animals," a recent poem by the
young African-American Thylias Moss, offers a view of a world after
destruction, in which animals "teach us/what we can't teach ourselves."
Surreal images—comic, morbid, and shocking—inform the poem,
including two allusions to the Holocaust:

    The coast horned lizard still won't be found
  without a bag of tricks; it will inflate and the first
  of six million Jewfish will emerge from its mouth.
  We will all be richer.


  . . . Then once and for all we will know it is no illusion:
  the lion lying with the lamb, the grandmother and Little
    Red Riding Hood
  walking out of a wolf named Dachau.

Such poems as Oliver's and Moss's are not only about saving the planet.
In them, as in the other Holocaust poems, that historical event
becomes a trope signaling danger, insisting on the power of memory
and feeling to wage war on violence and injustice.

Similarly, though with respect to classical myth, not European
history, a stream of poems revisions the stories of Leda and Medusa.

William Butler Yeats's "Leda and the Swan," a poem that many poet-minded women of my generation learned to recite, never *seemed* to be a poem about rape. Yeats, writing from his male perspective, not only beautifies the rape of Leda by Jupiter disguised as swan; he dignifies it with a seemingly significant philosophical question: Would the mortal woman, thus "mastered," "put on his knowledge with his power?" Whether one assumes that Yeats is thinking of the birth of Leda's twins that will follow this rape or is rhetorically alluding to the convention that male sexuality turns girls into women, one idea is clear in Yeats's mind: The male act controls; the female act responds (even willingly).

In "Leda Reconsidered," Mona Van Duyn portrays the sexual encounter itself from the point of view of Leda, watching the awkward swan step "out of water." She is a Leda imaginative enough to put herself into the swan's head, and she tries to understand his god/maleness sympathetically, "the pain of his transformations." She does not glorify herself at his expense:

> To love with the whole imagination—
> she had never tried.
> Was there a form for that?
> Deep, in her inmost, grubby
> female center
> (how could he know that,
> in his airiness?)
> lay the joy of being used,
> and its heavy peace, perhaps,
> would keep her down.

And then, still before the encounter, she wonders about the aftermath (remember Yeats's question about "knowledge"?):

> And now, how much would she try
> to see, to take,
> of what was not hers, of what
> was not going to be offered?

As Van Duyn concludes the poem, she envisions Leda's reflective mood controlling the violence, so that the sexual encounter is not the savage "brute force" of Yeats's version. She describes the swan moving "almost with tenderness," as she touches "the utter stranger."

Van Duyn's mid-sixties poem presages one central intellectual perspective of the next three decades: Leda does not want his knowledge, or the stories of his knowledge; they don't suit her. But Van Duyn is also not interested in sexual warfare—she would control the violence with "tenderness."

Given recent social history, perhaps it was inevitable that we should have still another and very different poem about Leda. In June Jordan's "The Female and the Silence of a Man," Leda "knows" male brutality firsthand, "The big fist shattering her face." The violated Leda disappears, first sinking into water, then floating in air, vanishing "like blood that people walk upon," a phrase reminiscent of Holocaust poems. When she reappears, centuries later perhaps, she is a "mad *bitch* dog"; she is "A fever withering the river and the crops"; she is "A lovely girl protected by her cruel/incandescent energies."

Another treatment of a rape victim out of classical mythology appears in Amy Clampitt's "Medusa." Within the past decade, Medusa's story has been revisioned not only by poets but by such artists as the sculptor Audrey Flack. Clampitt tells the story of the beautiful Medusa raped by Poseidon "on Athena's temple floor" and reveals how the victim rather than the violator is punished. With exquisite irony, Clampitt names Athena's act as:

A virginal revenge at one remove—there's none more
sordid or more apt to ramify, as this one did:
the fulgent tresses roiled to water-snake-
like writhe, and for long lashes'
come-hither flutterings, the stare
that hardens the psyche's soft parts to rock. . . .

Clampitt envisions the rape victim punished by a virgin goddess in a manner aimed also at punishing those (men?) who might look on her. For Clampitt, from such (in)justice follows ramification upon ramification, in literature and in life. Medusa becomes for "Puritan/revisionists" a "female ogre": in Milton's *Paradise Lost,* for example, "Sin." Clampitt identifies Medusa with creatures of the ocean, "The stinging jellyfish . . . the sea anemone's/whorled comb," and ultimately with the ocean itself, "the cold mother/of us all." While she does not diminish the rape, Clampitt demystifies the idea of Medusa as monster and moves the story on to consider the "Terror of origins," questioning what surgical (and metaphysically compassionate) complexity of knowledge and understanding might be needed to

. . . unthread those multiplicities of cause
of hurt from its effect; dislodge, spicule by spicule,
the fearful armories within; unclench the airless
petrifaction toward the core, the geode's rigor?

### The Question of Muse

Amy Clampitt's poem helps me understand why, more than twenty
years ago, I saw the muse in Louise Bogan's "Medusa," a fearful figure
captured in the moment of her poem. At the time I didn't know the
story of Medusa's rape. But I knew, reading that poem, that Bogan
knew something about Medusa I did not. The poem's speaker, as
though in a dream, arrives at "the house, in a cave of trees/Facing a
sheer sky." The key to the opening is motion: "Sun and reflection
wheeled by." But then there is the vision—Medusa—whose serpent
hair turns men (and not women?) to stone:

. . . When the bare eyes were before me
And the hissing hair,
Held up at a window, seen through a door.
The stiff bald eyes, the serpents on the forehead
formed in the air. . . .

The poet sees Medusa and survives: The scene becomes the poem—
"The water will always fall, and will not fall." And the poet herself is
caught forever in the act of vision:

. . . And I shall stand here like a shadow
Under the great balanced day,
My eyes on the yellow dust, that was lifting in the wind,
And does not drift away.

Considered in this context, it makes perfect sense that Medusa,
transformed from a victim to a potent creature deadly to men, should
become the woman poet's muse. It also makes sense that in Bogan's
poem and in several poems of the 1960s (see Sylvia Plath's "The Dis-
quieting Muses," for example, or Marilyn Hacker's "The Muses") the
poet's source of creative energy seems to be an opposing, unkindly, if
not terrifying force. Even two decades ago, I saw a connection between
the terrifying "muses" of the past and the "witches" of the present, now
transformed into healing, energizing creatures, in part validated by

new historical knowledge, in part serving the real need to see women-
—including poets—as capable of fighting back, as creative, as
prophetic.

Today the question of muse may be answered directly: The muse for
women poets certainly is a woman. Carolyn Kizer tells us in a frank
autobiographical note that her muse was always her mother; Vassar
Miller, motherless at birth, tells us the muse is her "stepmother." And
among the youngest poets in the volume, Marilyn Waniek writes a
deliciously amusing poem called "Levitation with Baby":

> The Muse bumped
> against my window this morning.
> No one was at home but me
> and the baby. The Muse said
> there was room on her back for two.
> *Okay,* I said, *but first I've got to. . . .*

Therein follows a tour de force of child care: collecting toys and books,
changing diapers and packing some, making lunch, feeding the baby,
cleaning up the mess around the high chair afterward, changing him
again, and washing him. Finally, mother/poet, having washed her own
hands, sits down at her desk and says, *"Now/I'm ready for takeoff"*:

> As he cried for a bottle
> I saw my next-door neighbor,
> shirtless, in the pants he wears
> to work in his garden,
> scribbling furiously on the back of a paper bag
> as he ascended over the roof of his house
> on the Muse's huge, sun-spangled wings.

What is feisty Marilyn Waniek telling us? That motherhood continues,
as in Amy Lowell's day, to narrow the field for women who would be
poets? Clearly not—ultimately, she reminds us of the body of poetry
produced with babies as subjects. Perhaps she is suggesting that the
living world about us is muse enough.

## A BRIEF CODA: THE POET AS TEACHER

We are at the beginning, not the conclusion, of a renaissance for
women writers and readers. The poetic wit sparkles as surely as the

energy and music of the line. The emotional range has opened beyond Muriel Rukeyser's profound dreams, and no subject is off limits. I tried to list all subjects of poems in this volume and ran beyond a page of type. Poets know they have an audience that will hear them, that needs to hear them. "I know you are reading this poem," Adrienne Rich writes in a section of the title poem in *An Atlas of the Difficult World.* She says this twelve times in less than forty lines, as she describes the ordinary world of readers in offices, bookstores, bedrooms, living rooms, a world of the very young and the very old, a world of mothers, a world beyond the borders of this country, a world "torn between bitterness and hope."

Perhaps at no time since the early nineteenth century have poets so consciously spoken to help change the world. And perhaps at no time have young women poets been able to read and hear and learn from multiple generations of older women poets still writing and often revered. If consciousness can make a difference in a world that often seems bent on destruction, these poets may be our best hope. They mirror the joys and torments of daily life in a fragile universe. Joy Harjo, through a story of almost unmitigated pain, rejoices in the "impossibility" but also "the truth" about the survival of "those who were never meant/to survive." Mary Jo Salter writes a poem about Hiroshima, "as if to make it plain/hope's only as renewable as pain." In "The Way Things Work," Jorie Graham writes:

I believe
forever in the hooks.
　　The way things work
　　is that eventually
　　something catches.

And Carolyn Forché, writing about El Salvador and a sister poet of that country, Claribel Alegría, asks, "Carolina, do you know how long it takes/any one voice to reach another?"

If there are shortcuts to the process of humanizing a world, surely they include this rich body of poetry that teaches, the poets themselves in the classroom, on the lecture circuit, and, many of them, in political action. They certainly include the audience of readers whose own lives are mirrored in these pages.

# PART I

*. . . we're a queer lot*
*We women who write poetry.*
—AMY LOWELL

# LOLA RIDGE, 1873–1941

from *The Ghetto*

## II

I room at Sodos'—in the little green room
    that was Bennie's—
With Sadie
And her old father and her mother,
Who is not so old and wears her own hair.

Old Sodos no longer makes saddles.
He has forgotten how.
He has forgotten most things—even Bennie who stays
    away and sends wine on holidays—
And he does not like Sadie's mother
Who hides God's candles,
Nor Sadie
Whose young pagan breath puts out the light—
That should burn always,
Like Aaron's before the Lord.

Time spins like a crazy dial in his brain,
And night by night
I see the love-gesture of his arm
In its green-greasy coat-sleeve
Circling the Book,
And the candles gleaming starkly
On the blotched-paper whiteness of his face,
Like a miswritten psalm . . .
Night by night
I hear his lifted praise,

Like a broken whinnying
Before the Lord's shut gate.

Sadie dresses in black.
She has black-wet hair full of cold lights
And a fine-drawn face, too white.
All day the power machines
Drone in her ears . . .
All day the fine dust flies
Till throats are parched and itch
And the heat—like a kept corpse—
Fouls to the last corner.

Then—when needles move more slowly on the cloth
And sweaty fingers slacken
And hair falls in damp wisps over the eyes—
Sped by some power within,
Sadie quivers like a rod . . .
A thin black piston flying,
One with her machine.

She—who stabs the piece-work with her bitter eye
And bids the girls: "Slow down—
You'll have him cutting us again!"
She—fiery static atom,
Held in place by the fierce pressure all about—
Speeds up the driven wheels
And biting steel—that twice
Has nipped her to the bone.

Nights, she reads
Those books that have most unset thought,
New-poured and malleable,
To which her thought
Leaps fusing at white heat,
Or spits her fire out in some dim manger of a hall,
Or at a protest meeting on the Square,
Her lit eyes kindling the mob . . .
Or dances madly at a festival.
Each dawn finds her a little whiter,
Though up and keyed to the long day,

Alert, yet weary . . . like a bird
That all night long has beat about a light.

The Gentile lover, that she charms and shrews,
Is one more pebble in the pack
For Sadie's mother,
Who greets him with her narrowed eyes
That hold some welcome back.
"What's to be done?" she'll say,
"When Sadie wants she takes . . .
Better than Bennie with his Christian woman . . .
A man is not so like,
If they should fight,
To call her Jew . . ."

Yet when she lies in bed
And the soft babble of their talk comes to her
And the silences . . .
I know she never sleeps
Till the keen draught blowing up the empty hall
edges through her transom
And she hears his foot on the first stairs . . .

[1918]

THE DREAM

I have a dream
to fill the golden sheath
of a remembered day. . . .
(Air
heavy and massed and blue
as the vapor of opium . . .
domes
fired in sulphurous mist . . .
sea
quiescent as a gray seal . . .
and the emerging sun
spurting up gold
over Sydney, smoke-pale, rising out of the bay. . . .)
But the day is an up-turned cup
and its sun a junk of red iron

guttering in sluggish-green water—
where shall I pour my dream?

[1920]


AMY LOWELL

Your words are frost on speargrass,
Your words are glancing light
On foils at play,
Your words are shapely . . . buoyant as balloons,
They make brave sallies at the stars.
When your words fall and grow cold
Little greedy hands
Will gather them for necklets.

[1927]


# AMY LOWELL, 1874–1925


## THE GARDEN BY MOONLIGHT

A black cat among roses,
Phlox, lilac-misted under a first-quarter moon,
The sweet smells of heliotrope and night-scented stock.
The garden is very still,
It is dazed with moonlight,
Contented with perfume,
Dreaming the opium dreams of its folded poppies.
Firefly lights open and vanish
High as the tip buds of the golden glow
Low as the sweet alyssum flowers at my feet.
Moon-shimmer on leaves and trellises,
Moon-spikes shafting through the snowball bush.
Only the little faces of the ladies' delight are alert and staring,
Only the cat, padding between the roses,
Shakes a branch and breaks the chequered pattern
As water is broken by the falling of a leaf.
Then you come,
And you are quiet like the garden,

And white like the alyssum flowers,
And beautiful as the silent sparks of the fireflies.
Ah, Beloved, do you see those orange lilies?
They knew my mother,
But who belonging to me will they know
When I am gone.

[1919]

## INTERLUDE

When I have baked white cakes
And grated green almonds to spread upon them;
When I have picked the green crowns from the strawberries
And piled them, cone-pointed, in a blue and yellow platter;
When I have smoothed the seam of the linen I have been working;
What then?
To-morrow it will be the same:
Cakes and strawberries,
And needles in and out of cloth.
If the sun is beautiful on bricks and pewter,
How much more beautiful is the moon,
Slanting down the gauffered branches of a plum-tree;
The moon
Wavering across a bed of tulips;
The moon,
Still,
Upon your face.
You shine, Beloved,
You and the moon.
But which is the reflection?
The clock is striking eleven.
I think, when we have shut and barred the door,
The night will be dark
Outside.

[1919]

## AUTUMN

They brought me a quilled, yellow dahlia,
Opulent, flaunting.
Round gold

Flung out of a pale green stalk.
Round, ripe gold
Of maturity,
Meticulously frilled and flaming,
A fire-ball of proclamation:
Fecundity decked in staring yellow
For all the world to see.
They brought a quilled, yellow dahlia,
To me who am barren.
Shall I send it to you,
You who have taken with you
All I once possessed?

[1919]

## THE SISTERS

Taking us by and large, we're a queer lot
We women who write poetry. And when you think
How few of us there've been, it's queerer still.
I wonder what it is that makes us do it,
Singles us out to scribble down, man-wise,
The fragments of ourselves. Why are we
Already mother-creatures, double-bearing,
With matrices in body and in brain?
I rather think that there is just the reason
We are so sparse a kind of human being;
The strength of forty thousand Atlases
Is needed for our every-day concerns.
There's Sapho, now I wonder what was Sapho.
I know a single slender thing about her:
That, loving, she was like a burning birch-tree
All tall and glittering fire, and that she wrote
Like the same fire caught up to Heaven and held there,
A frozen blaze before it broke and fell.
Ah, me! I wish I could have talked to Sapho,
Surprised her reticences by flinging mine
Into the wind. This tossing off of garments
Which cloud the soul is none too easy doing
With us to-day. But still I think with Sapho
One might accomplish it, were she in the mood
To bare her loveliness of words and tell

The reasons, as she possibly conceived them,
Of why they are so lovely. Just to know
How she came at them, just to watch
The crisp sea sunshine playing on her hair,
And listen, thinking all the while 'twas she
Who spoke and that we two were sisters
Of a strange, isolated little family.
And she is Sapho—Sapho—not Miss or Mrs.,
A leaping fire we call so for convenience;
But Mrs. Browning—who would ever think
Of such presumption as to call her "Ba."
Which draws the perfect line between sea-cliffs
And a close-shuttered room in Wimpole Street.
Sapho could fly her impulses like bright
Balloons tip-tilting to a morning air
And write about it. Mrs. Browning's heart
Was squeezed in stiff conventions. So she lay
Stretched out upon a sofa, reading Greek
And speculating, as I must suppose,
In just this way on Sapho; all the need,
The huge, imperious need of loving, crushed
Within the body she believed so sick.
And it was sick, poor lady, because words
Are merely simulacra after deeds
Have wrought a pattern; when they take the place
Of actions they breed a poisonous miasma
Which, though it leave the brain, eats up the body.
So Mrs. Browning, aloof and delicate,
Lay still upon her sofa, all her strength
Going to uphold her over-topping brain.
It seems miraculous, but she escaped
To freedom and another motherhood
Than that of poems. She was a very woman
And needed both.
                              If I had gone to call,
Would Wimpole Street have been the kindlier place,
Or Casa Guidi, in which to have met her?
I am a little doubtful of that meeting,
For Queen Victoria was very young and strong
And all-pervading in her apogee
At just that time. If we had stuck to poetry,

Sternly refusing to be drawn off by mesmerism
Or Roman revolutions, it might have done.
For, after all, she is another sister,
But always, I rather think, an older sister
And not herself so curious a technician
As to admit newfangled modes of writing—
"Except, of course, in Robert, and that is neither
Here nor there for Robert is a genius."
I do not like the turn this dream is taking,
Since I am very fond of Mrs. Browning
And very much indeed should like to hear her
Graciously asking me to call her "Ba."
But then the Devil of Verisimilitude
Creeps in and forces me to know she wouldn't.
Convention again, and how it chafes my nerves,
For we are such a little family
Of singing sisters, and as if I didn't know
What those years felt like tied down to the sofa.
Confound Victoria, and the slimy inhibitions
She loosed on all us Anglo-Saxon creatures!
Suppose there hadn't been a Robert Browning,
No "Sonnets from the Portuguese" would have been written.
They are the first of all her poems to be,
One might say, fertilized. For, after all,
A poet is flesh and blood as well as brain
And Mrs. Browning, as I said before,
Was very, very woman. Well, there are two
Of us, and vastly unlike that's for certain.
Unlike at least until we tear the veils
Away which commonly gird souls. I scarcely think
Mrs. Browning would have approved the process
In spite of what had surely been relief;
For speaking souls must always want to speak
Even when bat-eyed, narrow-minded Queens
Set prudishness to keep the keys of impulse.
Then do the frowning Gods invent new banes
And make the need of sofas. But Sapho was dead
And I, and others, not yet peeped above
The edge of possibility. So that's an end
To speculating over tea-time talks
Beyond the movement of pentameters

With Mrs. Browning.
                              But I go dreaming on,
In love with these my spiritual relations.
I rather think I see myself walk up
A flight of wooden steps and ring a bell
And send a card in to Miss Dickinson.
Yet that's a very silly way to do.
I should have taken the dream twist-ends about
And climbed over the fence and found her deep
Engrossed in the doings of a humming-bird
Among nasturtiums. Not having expected strangers,
She might forget to think me one, and holding up
A finger say quite casually: "Take care.
Don't frighten him, he's only just begun."
"Now this," I well believe I should have thought,
"Is even better than Sapho. With Emily
You're really here, or never anywhere at all
In range of mind." Wherefore, having begun
In the strict centre, we could slowly progress
To various circumferences, as we pleased.
We could, but should we? That would quite depend
On Emily. I think she'd be exacting,
Without intention possibly, and ask
A thousand tight-rope tricks of understanding.
But, bless you, I would somersault all day
If by so doing I might stay with her.
I hardly think that we should mention souls
Although they might just round the corner from us
In some half-quizzical, half-wistful metaphor.
I'm very sure that I should never seek
To turn her parables to stated fact.
Sapho would speak, I think, quite openly,
And Mrs. Browning guard a careful silence,
But Emily would set doors ajar and slam them
And love you for your speed of observation.

Strange trio of my sisters, most diverse,
And how extraordinarily unlike
Each is to me, and which way shall I go?
Sapho spent and gained; and Mrs. Browning,
After a miser girlhood, cut the strings

Which tied her money-bags and let them run;
But Emily hoarded—hoarded—only giving
Herself to cold, white paper. Starved and tortured,
She cheated her despair with games of patience
And fooled herself by winning. Frail little elf,
The lonely brain-child of a gaunt maturity,
She hung her womanhood upon a bough
And played ball with the stars—too long—too long—
The garment of herself hung on a tree
Until at last she lost even the desire
To take it down. Whose fault? Why let us say,
To be consistent, Queen Victoria's.
But really, not to over-rate the queen,
I feel obliged to mention Martin Luther,
And behind him the long line of Church Fathers
Who draped their prurience like a dirty cloth
About the naked majesty of God.
Good-bye, my sisters, all of you are great,
And all of you are marvellously strange,
And none of you has any word for me.
I cannot write like you, I cannot think
In terms of Pagan or of Christian now.
I only hope that possibly some day
Some other woman with an itch for writing
May turn to me as I have turned to you
And chat with me a brief few minutes. How
We lie, we poets! It is three good hours
I have been dreaming. Has it seemed so long
To you? And yet I thank you for the time
Although you leave me sad and self-distrustful,
For older sisters are very sobering things.
Put on your cloaks, my dears, the motor's waiting.
No, you have not seemed strange to me, but near,
Frightfully near, and rather terrifying.
I understand you all, for in myself—
Is that presumption? Yet indeed it's true—
We are one family. And still my answer
Will not be any one of yours, I see.
Well, never mind that now. Good night! Good night!

[1925]

# GERTRUDE STEIN, 1874–1946

## from *Patriarchal Poetry*

. . . Patriarchal poetry their origin their history their origin.
Patriarchal poetry their history their origin . . . She knew that is to
say she had really informed herself. Patriarchal poetry makes no
mistake . . .

Elegant replaced by delicate and tender, delicate and tender
replaced by one from there instead of five from there, there is not
there this is what has happened evidently.

Why while while why while why why identity identity why while
while why. Why while while while while identity.

Patriarchal poetry is the same as Patriotic poetry is the same
as patriarchal poetry is the same as Patriotic poetry is the same
as patriarchal poetry is the same.

Patriarchal poetry is the same. . . .


Let her be to be to be to be let her be to be to be to be let her to
be let her to be let her be to be when is it that they are shy.

Very well to try.

Let her be that is to be let her be that is to be let her be let
her try.

Let her be let her be let her be to be to be shy let her be to
be let her be to be let her try.

Let her try. . . .

To be shy.

Let her be.

Let her try. . . .

Let her be shy.

Let her

Let her

Let her be.

Let her be shy.

Let her be let her try. . . .

Let her try

Let her let her try to be let her try.

Let her try.

Just let her try.

Let her try.

Never to be what he said. . . .

Not to let her to be what he said not to let her to be what he said.

Never to be let her to be never let her to be what he said. Never let her to be what he said. . . .

Patriarchal she said what is it I know what it is I know I know so that I know what it is I know so I know. . . . at first it was the grandfather then it was not that in that the father not of that grandfather and then she to be to be sure to be sure to be I know to be sure to be I know to be sure to be not as good as that. To be sure not to be sure to be sure correctly saying to be sure to be that. It was that. She was right. It was that.

Patriarchal poetry.

### A Sonnet

To the wife of my bosom
All happiness from everything
And her husband.
May he be as good and considerate
Gay and cheerful and restful.
And make her the best wife
In the world
The happiest and the most content
With reason.
To the wife of my bosom
Whose transcendent virtues
Are those to be most admired
Loved and adored and indeed
Her virtues are all inclusive
Her virtues her beauty and her beauties
Her charms her qualities her joyous nature
All of it makes of her husband
A proud and happy man.

Patriarchal poetry makes no mistake makes no mistake in estimating the value to be placed upon the best and most arranged of considerations. . . .

\*   \*   \*

Patriarchal Poetry does not make it never made it will not have been making it be that way in their behalf.

Patriarchal Poetry insistance.

Insist. . . .

Patriarchal poetry they do their best at once more once more once more once more to do to do would it be left to advise advise realise realise dismay dismay delighted with her pleasure.

Patriarchal poetry left to inundate them.

Patriarchal Poetry in pieces. Pieces which have left it as names which have left it as names to to all said all said as delight.

Patriarchal poetry the difference.

Patriarchal poetry needed with weeded with seeded with payed it with left it without it with me. When this you see give it to me.

Patriarchal poetry makes it be have you it here.

Patriarchal Poetry twice.

Patriarchal Poetry in time.

It should be left. . . .

Patriarchal poetry might be finished to-morrow. . . .

[1927]

# ALICE RUTH MOORE DUNBAR-NELSON, 1875–1935

## I SIT AND SEW

I sit and sew—a useless task it seems,
My hands grown tired, my head weighed down with dreams—
The panoply of war, the martial tread of men,
Grim-faced, stern-eyed, gazing beyond the ken
Of lesser souls, whose eyes have not seen Death,
Nor learned to hold their lives but as a breath—
But—I must sit and sew.

I sit and sew—my heart aches with desire—
That pageant terrible, that fiercely pouring fire

On wasted fields, and writhing grotesque things
Once men. My soul in pity flings
Appealing cries, yearning only to go
There in that holocaust of hell, those fields of woe—
But—I must sit and sew.

The little useless seam, the idle patch;
Why dream I here beneath my homely thatch,
When there they lie in sodden mud and rain,
Pitifully calling me, the quick ones and the slain?
You need me, Christ! It is no roseate dream
That beckons me—this pretty futile seam,
It stifles me—God, must I sit and sew?

[1920]


## TO MADAME CURIE

Oft have I thrilled at deeds of high emprise,
And yearned to venture into realms unknown,
Thrice blessèd she, I deemed, whom God had shown
How to achieve great deeds in woman's guise.
Yet what discov'ry by expectant eyes
Of foreign shores, could vision half the throne
Full gained by her, whose power fully grown
Exceeds the conquerors of th' uncharted skies?
So would I be this woman whom the world
Avows its benefactor; nobler far,
Than Sybil, Joan, Sappho, or Egypt's queen.
In the alembic forged her shafts and hurled
At pain, diseases, waging a humane war;
Greater than this achievement, none, I ween.

[1921]


## THE PROLETARIAT SPEAKS

I love beautiful things:
Great trees, bending green winged branches to a velvet lawn,
Fountains sparkling in white marble basins,
Cool fragrance of lilacs and roses and honeysuckle.
Or exotic blooms, filling the air with heart-contracting odors;
Spacious rooms, cool and gracious with statues and books,

Carven seats and tapestries, and old masters
Whose patina shows the wealth of centuries.

And so I work
In a dusty office, whose grimèd windows
Look out in an alley of unbelievable squalor,
Where mangy cats, in their degradation, spurn
Swarming bits of meat and bread;
Where odors, vile and breathtaking, rise in fetid waves
Filling my nostrils, scorching my humid, bitter cheeks.

I love beautiful things:
Carven tables laid with lily-hued linen
And fragile china and sparkling irridescent glass;
Pale silver, etched with heraldries,
Where tender bits of regal dainties tempt,
And soft-stepped service anticipates the unspoken wish.

And so I eat
In the food-laden air of a greasy kitchen,
At an oil-clothed table:
Plate piled high with food that turns my head away,
Lest a squeamish stomach reject too soon
The lumpy gobs it never needed.
Or in a smoky cafeteria, balancing a slippery tray
To a table crowded with elbows
Which lately the bus boy wiped with a grimy rag.

I love beautiful things:
Soft linen sheets and silken coverlet,
Sweet coolth of chamber opened wide to fragrant breeze;
Rose-shaded lamps and golden atomizers,
Spraying Parisian fragrance over my relaxed limbs,
Fresh from a white marble bath, and sweet cool spray.

And so I sleep
In a hot hall-room whose half opened window,
Unscreened, refuses to budge another inch;
Admits no air, only insects, and hot choking gasps,
That make me writhe, nun-like, in sack-cloth sheets and lumps of
    straw.

And then I rise
To fight my way to a dubious tub,
Whose tiny, tepid stream threatens to make me late;
And hurrying out, dab my unrefreshed face
With bits of toiletry from the ten cent store.

[1929]


# ANGELINA WELD GRIMKÉ, 1880–1958

## CAPRICHOSA

### I

Little lady coyly shy
With deep shadows in each eye
Cast by lashes soft and long,
Tender lips just bowed for song,
And I oft have dreamed the bliss
Of the nectar in one kiss
      But 'tis clear
      That I fear
The white anger that can lie
In the depths of her veiled eye,
Little nose so bold and pert,
That I fear me she's a flirt
And her eyes and smile demure
Are intended for a lure,
Cruel, dainty, little lady.

### II

Dimples too in cheek and chin
Deep'ning when the smiles begin
Dancing o'er her mystic face;
Tiny hands of fragile grace
Yet for me their mighty sway
May crush out the light of day.
      And her feet

So discreet
Only dare to coyly flirt
From beneath her filmy skirt.
Soft her curls and dusky deep
Hoarding all the shades for sleep,
And in drinking their perfume
I sink down mid lotus-bloom,
Cruel, dainty, little lady.


## III

On some days she's shy and sweet
Gentler maid 'twere hard to meet:
Other days a lady grand
Cold and hard to understand
Greets me with a haughty stare—
Seeing naught but empty air;
           If I fume
           At my doom
Bows her dusky head to weep
Till I humbly to her creep
Groveling in the very dirt—
But she's laughing! Little flirt!
Then, when I am most forlorn,
Wishing I had ne'er been born,
Woos me with alluring eyes,
Cooing words, and monstrous sighs,
But, if my foot one step advances
Lightly, swiftly, from me dances,
Darting at me mocking glances,
Cruel, dainty, little lady.

[1901]


## THE GARDEN SEAT

I stood again within the garden old
Around whose edges grew the tall green box;
I saw again the winding, narrow, paths
So gay along their sides with pink sea shells;
I saw the holly-hocks so tall and prim
The humble sun-flower bowing 'neath the sun,

The mignonette and gay geranium,
The heliotrope and baby's breath so pure;
I saw the summer house with roses overgrown,
The quaint, old, bench whereon we used to sit
Day-dreaming hand in hand of times to come,
And on the bench I saw thee idly sit
The distaff at thy side all silent stood
(Thy listless hands forgetful of their stint)
Thy fair, dear, head was tilted slightly back
Against the bench's quaint and agèd side,
Thine eyes half-closed, and sweet lips gravely set,
And then I stole up all noiseless and unseen,
And kissed those eyes so dreamy and so sad—I
Ah God! if I might once again see all
Thy soul leap in their depths as then
So hungry with long waiting and so true,
I clasp thee close within my yearning arms
I kiss thine eyes, thy lips, thy silky hair,
I felt thy soft arms twining round my neck
Thy bashful, maiden, kisses on my cheek,
My whole heart leaping 'neath such wondrous joy—

And then the vision faded and was gone
And I was in my lonely, darkened, room
The old-time longing surging in my breast,
The old-time agony within my soul
As fresh, as new, as when I kissed thy lips
So cold, with frenzy begging thee to speak,
Believing not that thou wert lying dead.

Yes, lying dead these many, weary, years;
And when I push my darkened casement wide,
And gaze beyond the sleeping town of Life
Unto that town of Death upon the hill,
I see with streaming tears that vainly fall,
The plain, white, stone that marks the spot she sleeps.

[N.D.]

Toss your gay heads,
    Brown girl trees;
Toss your gay lovely heads;
Shake your downy russet curls
All about your brown faces;
Stretch your brown slim bodies;
Stretch your brown slim arms;
Stretch your brown slim toes.
Who knows better than we,
With the dark, dark bodies,
What it means
When April comes alaughing and aweeping
Once again
At our hearts?

[N.D.]


# ANNE SPENCER, 1882–1975


## LADY, LADY

Lady, Lady, I saw your face,
Dark as night withholding a star . . .
The chisel fell, or it might have been
You had borne so long the yoke of men.

Lady, Lady, I saw your hands,
Twisted, awry, like crumpled roots,
Bleached poor white in a sudsy tub,
Wrinkled and drawn from your rub-a-dub.

Lady, Lady, I saw your heart,
And altared there in its darksome place
Were the tongues of flame the ancients knew,
Where the good God sits to spangle through.

[1925]

## CREED

If my garden oak spares one bare ledge
For a boughed mistletoe to grow and wedge;
And all the wild birds this year should know
I cherish their freedom to come and go;
If a battered worthless dog, masterless, alone,
Slinks to my heels, sure of bed and bone;
And the boy just moved in, deigns a glance-assay,
Turns his pockets inside out, calls, "Come and play!"
If I should surprise in the eyes of my friend
That the deed was *my* favor he'd let me lend;
Or hear it repeated from a foe I despise,
That I whom he hated was chary of lies;
If a pilgrim stranger, fainting and poor,
Followed an urge and rapped at my door,
And my husband loves me till death puts apart,
Less as flesh unto flesh, more as heart unto heart:
I may challenge God when we meet That Day,
And He dare not be silent or send me away.

[1927]


## LETTER TO MY SISTER

It is dangerous for a woman to defy the gods;
To taunt them with the tongue's thin tip,
Or strut in the weakness of mere humanity,
Or draw a line daring them to cross;
The gods own the searing lightning,
The drowning waters, tormenting fears
And anger of red sins.

Oh, but worse still if you mince timidly—
Dodge this way or that, or kneel or pray,
Be kind, or sweat agony drops
Or lay your quick body over your feeble young;
If you have beauty or none, if celibate
Or vowed—the gods are Juggernaut,
Passing over . . . over . . .
*    *    *

This you may do:
Lock your heart, then, quietly,
And lest they peer within,
Light no lamp when dark comes down
Raise no shade for sun;
Breathless must your breath come through
If you'd die and dare deny
The gods their god-like fun.

[1927]

1975

Turn an earth clod
Peel a shaley rock
In fondness molest a curly worm
Whose *familiar* is everywhere
Kneel
And the curly worm     sentient *now*
Will *light* the word that tells the poet what a poem is

[1974]

# SARA TEASDALE, 1884–1933

THE KISS

I hoped that he would love me,
    And he has kissed my mouth,
But I am like a stricken bird
    That cannot reach the south.

For though I know he loves me,
    Tonight my heart is sad;
His kiss was not so wonderful
    As all the dreams I had.

[1910]

## THE WIND

A tall tree talking with the wind
   Leans as he leaned to me—
But oh the wind waits where she will,
   The wind is free.

I am a woman, I am weak,
   And custom leads me as one blind,
Only my songs go where they will
   Free as the wind.

[1914]

## I MIGHT HAVE SUNG OF THE WORLD

I might have sung of the world
   And said what I heard them say
Of the vast and passing dream
   Of today and yesterday.

But I chose to tell of myself,
   For that was all I knew—
I have made a chart of a small sea,
   But the chart I made is true.

[1919]

## WATER LILIES

If you have forgotten water lilies floating
   On a dark lake among mountains in the afternoon shade,
If you have forgotten their wet, sleepy fragrance,
   Then you can return and not be afraid.

But if you remember, then turn away forever
   To the plains and the prairies where pools are far apart,
There you will not come at dusk on closing water lilies,
   And the shadow of mountains will not fall on your heart.

[1920]

## HIDE AND SEEK

When I was a child we played sometimes in the dark;
    Hide and seek in the dark is a terrible game,
With the nerves pulled tight in fear of the stealthy seeker,
    With the brief exultance, and the blood in the veins like flame.

Now I see that life is a game in the dark,
    A groping in shadows, a brief exultance, a dread
Of what may crouch beside us or lurk behind us,
    A leaving of what we want to say unsaid,
Sure of one thing only, a long sleep
When the game is over and we are put to bed.

[1922]


# ELINOR WYLIE, 1885–1928


## LET NO CHARITABLE HOPE

Now let no charitable hope
Confuse my mind with images
Of eagle and of antelope:
I am in nature none of these.

I was, being human, born alone;
I am, being woman, hard beset;
I live by squeezing from a stone
The little nourishment I get.

In masks outrageous and austere
The years go by in single file;
But none has merited my fear,
And none has quite escaped my smile.

[1928]

Poor Loneliness and lovely Solitude
Were sisters who inhabited a wood;
And one was fair as cressets in the skies,
The other freckle-faced, and full of sighs.
And Solitude had builded them a bower
Set round with bergamot and gillyflower;
Wide windows, and a door without a latch,
Below the brier and the woodbine thatch.
They lived like birds, on rustic crusts and crumbs,
Mushrooms, and blackberries, and honey-combs,
Cream in a bowl and butter in a crock;
The moon for lantern, and the sun for clock.
Decorum did simplicity enrich;
A Parian Diana in a niche
Over the windows, and a harp between
With strings like gilded rain against the green;
Trifles their parents, Austerity and Peace,
Had bought in Paris, or picked up in Greece.
An infant's skull, which Loneliness had found
Without the churchyard, in unhallowed ground,
Under a little cross of blackthorn sticks;
For Solitude an ivory crucifix
Carved in a dream perversely Byzantine;
A silver mirror of a chaste design,
And Plato in white vellum; in levant
Shelley and Donne, presented by her aunt
(Who might have been a Muse, had she been got
By Jupiter, but unluckily was not.)
And Solitude was grave and beautiful
As the evening star, but Loneliness was dull;
And one was wild and holy, one was tame;
About their appointed tasks they went and came
One like a moth, the other like a mouse.
Like a new pin the cool and ordered house;
For lightly its divided burden fell;
But one did worse, the other very well.
For whatsoever Solitude had touched
Was clean, and not a finger of her smutched;
But oft the milk had soured in the pan

To see poor Loneliness morose and wan;
And when she polished copper she became
Listless as smoke against the augmented flame;
And when she walked below the lucent sun
Her freckled face was dust, her hair was dun;
And still with meek affection she pursued
Her lovelier twin, her sister Solitude,
Who, while that she was pitiful and kind,
Preferred the forest, and her private mind.
One day this nymph escaped into the dawn
And fled away, contemptuous as a fawn;
And through the hours she ran like fire and steel;
Imagination followed her at heel;
And what delights she tasted as she roved
Are metaphysical, and remain unproved.
Then Loneliness fell to weeping like a fool;
And wandered forth, because the wind was cool,
To dry her tears beneath a bracken fan;
And found a sleeping demigod or man;
And gazed entranced upon the creature's face,
Which was adorable and commonplace.
And when she saw him laid upon the leaves
Her hair was silver-gold as barley sheaves;
And when she saw his eyelids folded thin
Her eyes were amber, and with stars therein;
And when she saw his eyelashes unclose
Her freckles were the dew upon a rose;
Yea, all her freckles melted with her heart
To sun and dew, which drew his lids apart
As though the sun were shining in his eyes;
And she was fair as cressets in the skies;
And when she left the shadow of the wood
She was far lovelier than Solitude.
Let you believe, let me unsurely guess
This wonder wrought upon poor Loneliness;
But what was done, to what intrinsic end,
And whether by a brother or a friend,
And whether by a lover or a foe,
Let men inquire, and gods obscurely know.

[1932]

# H.D. [Hilda Doolittle], 1886–1961

## SHELTERED GARDEN

I have had enough.
I gasp for breath.

Every way ends, every road,
every foot-path leads at last
to the hill-crest—
then you retrace your steps,
or find the same slope on the other side,
precipitate.

I have had enough—
border-pinks, clove-pinks, wax-lilies,
herbs, sweet-cress.

O for some sharp swish of a branch—
there is no scent of resin
in this place,
no taste of bark, or coarse weeds,
aromatic, astringent—
only border on border of scented pinks.

Have you seen fruit under cover
that wanted light—
pears wadded in cloth,
protected from the frost,
melons, almost ripe,
smothered in straw?

Why not let the pears cling
to the empty branch?
All your coaxing will only make
a bitter fruit—
let them cling, ripen of themselves,
test their own worth,
nipped, shriveled by the frost,

to fall at last but fair
with a russet coat.

Or the melon—
let it bleach yellow
in the winter light,
even tart to the taste—
it is better to taste of frost—
the exquisite frost—
than of wadding and of dead grass.

For this beauty,
beauty without strength,
chokes out life.
I want wind to break,
scatter these pink-stalks,
snap off their spiced heads,
fling them about with dead leaves—
spread the paths with twigs,
limbs broken off,
trail great pine branches,
hurled across the melon-patch,
break pear and quince—
leave half-trees, torn, twisted
but showing the fight was valiant.

O to blot out this garden
to forget, to find a new beauty
in some terrible
wind-tortured place.

                                        [1916]


## from *Eurydice*


### I

So you have swept me back,
I who could have walked with the live souls
above the earth,

I who could have slept among the live flowers
at last;

so for your arrogance
and your ruthlessness
I am swept back
where dead lichens drip
dead cinders upon moss of ash;

so for your arrogance
I am broken at last,
I who had lived unconscious,
who was almost forgot;

if you had let me wait
I had grown from listlessness
into peace,
if you had let me rest with the dead,
I had forgot you
and the past.

V

So for your arrogance
and your ruthlessness
I have lost the earth
and the flowers of the earth,
and the live souls above the earth,
and you who passed across the light
and reached
ruthless;

you who have your own light,
who are to yourself a presence,
who need no presence;

yet for all your arrogance
and your glance,
I tell you this:
*    *    *

such loss is not loss,
such terror, such coils and strands and pitfalls
of blackness,
such terror
is no loss;

hell is no worse than your earth
above the earth,
hell is no worse,
no, nor your flowers
nor your veins of light
nor your presence,
a loss;

my hell is no worse than yours
though you pass among the flowers and speak
with the spirits above earth.

## VII

At least I have the flowers of myself,
and my thoughts, no god
can take that;
I have the fervour of myself for a presence
and my own spirit for light;

and my spirit with its loss
knows this;
though small against the black,
small against the formless rocks,
hell must break before I am lost;

before I am lost,
hell must open like a red rose
for the dead to pass.

[1917; 1925]

HELEN

All Greece hates
the still eyes in the white face,
the lustre as of olives
where she stands,
and the white hands.

All Greece reviles
the wan face when she smiles,
hating it deeper still
when it grows wan and white,
remembering past enchantments
and past ills.

Greece sees unmoved,
God's daughter, born of love,
the beauty of cool feet
and slenderest knees,
could love indeed the maid,
only if she were laid,
white ash amid funereal cypresses.

[1924]


# HAZEL HALL, 1886–1924

## INSTRUCTION

My hands that guide a needle
In their turn are led
Relentless and deftly
As a needle leads a thread.

Other hands are teaching
My needle; when I sew
I feel the cool, thin fingers
Of hands I do not know.

\* \* \*

They urge my needle onward,
They smooth my seams, until
The worry of my stitches
Smothers in their skill.

All the tired women,
Who sewed their lives away,
Speak in my deft fingers
As I sew today.

[1921]

WALKERS AT DUSK

The street fills slowly with the thin
Night light, and fluid shadows pass
Over the roofs as dark pours in
Like dusky wine into a glass.

Out of the gloom I watch them come—
Linked by an invisible chain,
Reconciled to the yoke and dumb
After the heat of pride or pain.

Nothing of the concerns of noon
Remains for them, or serves for me.
But portent, like the unrisen moon,
Begins to weigh unbearably.

[1923]

FOR A BROKEN NEEDLE

Even fine steel thinly made
To hold a raging thread
Comes to lie with purple shade
In a dreaded bed.

All its chiseled length, its nice
Grip, its moving gleam
That was once like chips of ice
In a heated seam,
*   *   *

Are no more. It is fit
We should chant a strain
Of lament, then tumble it
Out into the rain.

[1928]


# GEORGIA DOUGLAS JOHNSON, 1886–1966


## THE HEART OF A WOMAN

The heart of a woman goes forth with the dawn,
As a lone bird, soft winging, so restlessly on,
Afar o'er life's turrets and vales does it roam
In the wake of those echoes the heart calls home.

The heart of a woman falls back with the night,
And enters some alien cage in its plight,
And tries to forget it has dreamed of the stars
While it breaks, breaks, breaks on the sheltering bars.

[1927]


## OLD BLACK MEN

They have dreamed as young men dream
    Of glory, love and power;
They have hoped as youth will hope
    Of life's sun-minted hour.

They have seen as others saw
    Their bubbles burst in air,
And they have learned to live it down
    As though they did not care.

[1927]

## WHEN I AM DEAD

When I am dead, withhold, I pray, your blooming legacy;
Beneath the willows did I bide, and they should cover me;
I longed for light and fragrance, and I sought them far and near,
O, it would grieve me utterly, to find them on my bier!

[1927]

# MARIANNE MOORE, 1887–1972

## MARRIAGE

This institution,
perhaps one should say enterprise
out of respect for which
one says one need not change one's mind
about a thing one has believed in,
requiring public promises
of one's intention
to fulfill a private obligation:
I wonder what Adam and Eve
think of it by this time,
this fire-gilt steel
alive with goldenness;
how bright it shows—
"of circular traditions and impostures,
committing many spoils,"
requiring all one's criminal ingenuity
to avoid!
Psychology which explains everything
explains nothing,
and we are still in doubt.
Eve: beautiful woman—
I have seen her
when she was so handsome
she gave me a start,
able to write simultaneously
in three languages—

English, German, and French—
and talk in the meantime;
equally positive in demanding a commotion
and in stipulating quiet:
"I should like to be alone";
to which the visitor replies,
"*I* should like to be alone;
why not be alone together?"
Below the incandescent stars
below the incandescent fruit,
the strange experience of beauty;
its existence is too much;
it tears one to pieces
and each fresh wave of consciousness
is poison.
"See her, see her in this common world,"
the central flaw
in that first crystal-fine experiment,
this amalgamation which can never be more
than an interesting impossibility,
describing it
as "that strange paradise
unlike flesh, stones,
gold or stately buildings,
the choicest piece of my life:
the heart rising
in its estate of peace
as a boat rises
with the rising of the water";
constrained in speaking of the serpent—
shed snakeskin in the history of politeness
not to be returned to again—
that invaluable accident
exonerating Adam.
And he has beauty also;
it's distressing—the O thou
to whom from whom,
without whom nothing—Adam;
"something feline,
something colubrine"—how true!
a crouching mythological monster

in that Persian miniature of emerald mines,
raw silk—ivory white, snow white,
oyster white and six others—
that paddock full of leopards and giraffes—
long lemon-yellow bodies
sown with trapezoids of blue.
Alive with words,
vibrating like a cymbal
touched before it has been struck,
he has prophesied correctly—
the industrious waterfall,
"the speedy stream
which violently bears all before it,
at one time silent as the air
and now as powerful as the wind."
"Treading chasms
on the uncertain footing of a spear,"
forgetting that there is in woman
a quality of mind
which as an instinctive manifestation
is unsafe,
he goes on speaking
in a formal customary strain,
of "past states, the present state,
seals, promises,
the evil one suffered,
the good one enjoys,
hell, heaven,
everything convenient
to promote one's joy."
In him a state of mind
perceives what it was not
intended that he should;
"he experiences a solemn joy
in seeing that he has become an idol."
Plagued by the nightingale
in the new leaves,
with its silence—
not its silence but its silences,
he says of it:
"It clothes me with a shirt of fire."

"He dares not clap his hands
to make it go on
lest it fly off;
if he does nothing, it will sleep;
if he cries out, it will not understand."
Unnerved by the nightingale
and dazzled by the apple,
impelled by "the illusion of a fire
effectual to extinguish fire,"
compared with which
the shining of the earth
is but deformity—a fire
"as high as deep
as bright as broad
as long as life itself,"
he stumbles over marriage,
"a very trivial object indeed"
to have destroyed the attitude
in which he stood—
the ease of the philosopher
unfathered by a woman.
Unhelpful Hymen!
a kind of overgrown cupid
reduced to insignificance
by the mechanical advertising
parading as involuntary comment,
by that experiment of Adam's
with ways out but no way in—
the ritual of marriage,
augmenting all its lavishness;
its fiddle-head ferns,
lotus flowers, opuntias, white dromedaries,
its hippopotamus—
nose and mouth combined
in one magnificent hopper—
its snake and the potent apple.
He tells us
that "for love that will
gaze an eagle blind,
that is with Hercules

climbing the trees
in the garden of the Hesperides,
from forty-five to seventy
is the best age,"
commending it
as a fine art, as an experiment,
a duty or as merely recreation.
One must not call him ruffian
nor friction a calamity—
the fight to be affectionate:
"no truth can be fully known
until it has been tried
by the tooth of disputation."
The blue panther with black eyes,
the basalt panther with blue eyes,
entirely graceful—
one must give them the path—
the black obsidian Diana
who "darkeneth her countenance
as a bear doth,"
the spiked hand
that has an affection for one
and proves it to the bone,
impatient to assure you
that impatience is the mark of independence,
not of bondage.
"Married people often look that way"—
"seldom and cold, up and down,
mixed and malarial
with a good day and a bad."
"When do we feed?"
We occidentals are so unemotional,
we quarrel as we feed;
self lost, the irony preserved
in "the Ahasuerus *tête-à-tête* banquet"
with its small orchids like snakes' tongues,
with its "good monster, lead the way,"
with little laughter
and munificence of humor
in that quixotic atmosphere of frankness

in which, "four o'clock does not exist,
but at five o'clock
the ladies in their imperious humility
are ready to receive you";
in which experience attests
that men have power
and sometimes one is made to feel it.
He says, "'What monarch would not blush
to have a wife
with hair like a shaving-brush?'
The fact of woman
is 'not the sound of the flute
but very poison.'"
She says, "Men are monopolists
of 'stars, garters, buttons
and other shining baubles'—
unfit to be the guardians
of another person's happiness."
He says, "These mummies
must be handled carefully—
'the crumbs from a lion's meal,
a couple of shins and the bit of an ear';
turn to the letter M
and you will find
that a 'wife is a coffin,'
that severe object
with the pleasing geometry
stipulating space not people,
refusing to be buried
and uniquely disappointing,
revengefully wrought in the attitude
of an adoring child
to a distinguished parent."
She says, "This butterfly,
this waterfly, this nomad
that has 'proposed
to settle on my hand for life'—
What can one do with it?
There must have been more time
in Shakespeare's day

to sit and watch a play.
You know so many artists who are fools."
He says, "You know so many fools
who are not artists."
The fact forgot
that 'some have merely rights
while some have obligations,'
he loves himself so much,
he can permit himself
no rival in that love.
She loves herself so much,
she cannot see herself enough—
a statuette of ivory on ivory,
the logical last touch
to an expansive splendor
earned as wages for work done:
one is not rich but poor
when one can always seem so right.
What can one do for them—
these savages
condemned to disaffect
all those who are not visionaries
alert to undertake the silly task
of making people noble?
This model of petrine fidelity
who "leaves her peaceful husband
only because she has seen enough of him"—
that orator reminding you,
"I am yours to command."
"Everything to do with love is mystery;
it is more than a day's work
to investigate this science."
One sees that it is rare—
that striking grasp of opposites
opposed each to the other, not to unity,
which in cycloid inclusiveness
has dwarfed the demonstration
of Columbus with the egg—
a triumph of simplicity—
that charitive Euroclydon

of frightening disinterestedness
which the world hates,
admitting:

  "I am such a cow,
  if I had a sorrow
  I should feel it a long time;
  I am not one of those
  who have a great sorrow
  in the morning
  and a great joy at noon";

which says: "I have encountered it
among those unpretentious
protégés of wisdom,
where seeming to parade
as the debater and the Roman,
the statesmanship
of an archaic Daniel Webster
persists to their simplicity of temper
as the essence of the matter:

  'Liberty and union
  now and forever';

the Book on the writing-table;
the hand in the breast-pocket."

[1923]

## O TO BE A DRAGON

  If I, like Solomon, . . .
  could have my wish—

 my wish . . . O to be a dragon,
a symbol of the power of Heaven—of silkworm
size or immense; at times invisible.
 Felicitous phenomenon!

[1959]

# Edna St. Vincent Millay, 1892–1950

## from *Sonnets from an Ungrafted Tree*

### Sonnet XVII

Gazing upon him now, severe and dead,
It seemed a curious thing that she had lain
Beside him many a night in that cold bed,
And that had been which would not be again.
From his desirous body the great heat
Was gone at last, it seemed, and the taut nerves
Loosened forever. Formally the sheet
Set forth for her today those heavy curves
And lengths familiar as the bedroom door.
She was as one who enters, sly, and proud,
To where her husband speaks before a crowd,
And sees a man she never saw before—
The man who eats his victuals at her side,
Small, and absurd, and hers: for once, not hers, unclassified.

[1923]

### MENSES

*(He speaks, but to himself, being aware how it is with her)*

Think not I have not heard.
Well-fanged the double word
And well-directed flew.

I felt it. Down my side
Innocent as oil I see the ugly venom slide:
Poison enough to stiffen us both, and all our friends;
But I am not pierced, so there the mischief ends.

There is more to be said; I see it coiling;
The impact will be pain.
Yet coil; yet strike again.
You cannot riddle the stout mail I wove
Long since, of wit and love.

\*    \*    \*

As for my answer . . . stupid in the sun
He lies, his fangs drawn:
I will not war with you.

You know how wild you are. You are willing to be turned
To other matters; you would be grateful, even.
You watch me shyly. I (for I have learned
More things than one in our few years together)
Chafe at the churlish wind, the unseasonable weather.

"Unseasonable?" you cry, with harsher scorn
Than the theme warrants; "Every year it is the same!
'Unseasonable!' they whine, these stupid peasants!—and never
      since they were born
Have they known a spring less wintry! Lord, the shame,
The crying shame of seeing a man no wiser than the beasts he feeds—
His skull as empty as a shell!"
        ("Go to. You are unwell.")

        Such is my thought, but such are not my words.

        "What is the name," I ask, "of those big birds
        With yellow breast and low and heavy flight,
        That make such mournful whistling?"

                        "Meadowlarks,"
You answer primly, not a little cheered.
"Some people shoot them." Suddenly your eyes are wet
And your chin trembles. On my breast you lean,
And sob most pitifully for all the lovely things that are not and
      have been.

"How silly I am!—and I *know* how silly I am!"
You say: "You are very patient. You are very kind.
I shall be better soon. Just Heaven consign and damn
To tedious Hell this body with its muddy feet in my mind!"
                          [1928; 1939]

RENDEZVOUS

Not for these lovely blooms that prank your chambers did I come.
    Indeed,
I could have loved you better in the dark;
That is to say, in rooms less bright with roses, rooms more casual, less
    aware
Of History in the wings about to enter with benevolent air
On ponderous tiptoe, at the cue "Proceed."
Not that I like the ash-trays over-crowded and the place in a mess,
Or the monastic cubicle too unctuously austere and stark,
But partly that these formal garlands for our Eighth Street Aphrodite
    are a bit too Greek,
And partly that to make the poor walls rich with our unaided
    loveliness
Would have been more *chic*.

Yet here I am, having told you of my quarrel with the taxi-driver over
    a line of Milton, and you laugh; and you are you, none other.
Your laughter pelts my skin with small delicious blows.

But I am perverse: I wish you had not scrubbed—with pumice, I
    suppose—
The tobacco stains from your beautiful fingers. And I wish I did not
    feel like your mother.

                                                            [1939]


AN ANCIENT GESTURE

I thought, as I wiped my eyes on the corner of my apron:
Penelope did this too.
And more than once: you can't keep weaving all day
And undoing it all through the night;
Your arms get tired, and the back of your neck gets tight;
And along towards morning, when you think it will never be light,
And your husband has been gone, and you don't know where, for
    years,
Suddenly you burst into tears;
There is simply nothing else to do.
*   *   *

And I thought, as I wiped my eyes on the corner of my apron:
This is an ancient gesture, authentic, antique,
In the very best tradition, classic, Greek;
Ulysses did this too.
But only as a gesture,—a gesture which implied
To the assembled throng that he was much too moved to speak.
He learned it from Penelope . . .
Penelope, who really cried.

[1949]


# GENEVIEVE TAGGARD, 1894–1948


## WITH CHILD

Now I am slow and placid, fond of sun,
Like a sleek beast, or a worn one,
No slim and languid girl—not glad
With the windy trip I once had,
But velvet-footed, musing of my own,
Torpid, mellow, stupid as a stone.

You cleft me with your beauty's pulse, and now
Your pulse has taken body. Care not how
The old grace goes, how heavy I am grown,
Big with this loneliness, how you alone
Ponder our love. Touch my feet and feel
How earth tingles, teeming at my heel!
Earth's urge, not mine,—my little death, not hers;
And the pure beauty yearns and stirs.

It does not heed our ecstasies, it turns
With secrets of its own, its own concerns,
Toward a windy world of its own, toward stark
And solitary places. In the dark
Defiant even now, it tugs and moans
To be untangled from these mother's bones.

[1921]

# AT LAST THE WOMEN ARE MOVING

Last, walking with stiff legs as if they carried bundles
Came mothers, housewives, old women who knew why they
    abhorred war.
Their clothes bunched about them, they hobbled with anxious steps
To keep with the stride of the marchers, erect, bearing wide
    banners.

Such women looked odd, marching on American asphalt.
Kitchens they knew, sinks, suds, stew-pots and pennies . . .
Dull hurry and worry, clatter, wet hands and backache.
Here they were out in the glare on the militant march.

How did these timid, the slaves of breakfast and supper
Get out in the line, drop for once dish-rag and broom?
Here they are as work-worn as stitchers and fitters.
*Mama have you got some grub,* now none of their business.

Oh, but these who know in their growing sons and their husbands
How the exhausted body needs sleep, how often needs food,
These, whose business is keeping the body alive,
These are ready, if you talk their language, to strike.

Kitchen is small, the family story is sad.
Out of the musty flats the women come thinking:
*Not for me and mine only. For my class I have come*
*To walk city miles with many, my will in our work.*

[1935]

# NO ABSTRACTION

My hair is old. The startle of it!
Slant over my eyes in a river of air.
And I see here, ah, this my hair.
Oh, fright this,—still blowing and growing, but old.

Never so clearly in mirror
Caught I this—age in the edges.
And so slowly see
All powers work inward now

To dying centre, cark of care,
Coarse and inert, corpse, carcass,
Outcast, cold.

Say it clearly: this is dying.
The hair is not living, electric as it was.
Heavy substance of body,
Still in order, in labor strong,
Body obedient, heavily able,
The old, the only body
Makes no cave in mirrors,
No monster shade.

In the fringes,
The edges
Is the fright of me.
In the timid, the hopeful wisps . . .
This shocking, this horror hair,
Colorless, lustreless, human, unscented
Old. Lost the childish tousle.
Lost the quick swirl,
Pellucid brush, comet-warm
Young hair. (The possible
All forever gone by
Sliding like a comet with fiery train.)

Never the rich coil,
The mop of sheen
The girl wraps
Round the high spirit.

Now the hair of my head is old.
Old women accept me in your company.
Make room for me
In your truthful, your unattractive councils.
And I—(can it be true, dear vanity?)
Who loved myself that I was young
And the earth with me and in me,
Must I hate myself that I am old
And the earth not with me, not in me?

[1941]

48

## TO THE VETERANS OF THE
## ABRAHAM LINCOLN BRIGADE

Say of them
They knew no Spanish
At first, and nothing of the arts of war
At first,
     how to shoot, how to attack, how to retreat
How to kill, how to meet killing
At first.
Say they kept the air blue
Grousing and griping,
Arid words and harsh faces. Say
They were young;
The haggard in a trench, the dead on the olive slope
All young. And the thin, the ill and the shattered,
Sightless, in hospitals, all young.

Say of them they were young, there was much they did not know,
They were human. Say it all; it is true. Now say
When the eminent, the great, the easy, the old,
And the men on the make
Were busy bickering and selling,
Betraying, conniving, transacting, splitting hairs,
Writing bad articles, signing bad papers,
Passing bad bills,
Bribing, blackmailing,

Whimpering, meaching, garroting,—they
Knew and acted
          understood and died.

Or if they did not die came home to peace
That is not peace.
        Say of them
They are no longer young, they never learned
The arts, the stealth of peace, this peace, the tricks of fear;
And what they knew, they know.
And what they dared, they dare.

                            [1941]

DEMETER

In your dream you met Demeter
Splendid and severe, who said: Endure.
Study the art of seeds,
The nativity of caves.
Dance your gay body to the poise of waves;
Die out of the world to bring forth the obscure
Into blisses, into needs.
In all resources
Belong to love. Bless,
Join, fashion the deep forces,
Asserting your nature, priceless and feminine.
Peace, daughter. Find your true kin.
                    —then you felt her kiss.

                                        [1945]


# LOUISE BOGAN, 1897–1970


## MEDUSA

I had come to the house, in a cave of trees,
Facing a sheer sky.
Everything moved,—a bell hung ready to strike,
Sun and reflection wheeled by.

When the bare eyes were before me
And the hissing hair,
Held up at a window, seen through a door.
The stiff bald eyes, the serpents on the forehead
Formed in the air.

This is a dead scene forever now.
Nothing will ever stir.
The end will never brighten it more than this,
Nor the rain blur.
*   *   *

The water will always fall, and will not fall,
And the tipped bell make no sound.
The grass will always be growing for hay
Deep on the ground.

And I shall stand here like a shadow
Under the great balanced day,
My eyes on the yellow dust, that was lifting in the wind,
And does not drift away.

[1923]

## THE CROWS

The woman who has grown old
And knows desire must die,
Yet turns to love again,
Hears the crows' cry.

She is a stem long hardened,
A weed that no scythe mows.
The heart's laughter will be to her
The crying of the crows,

Who slide in the air with the same voice
Over what yields not, and what yields,
Alike in spring, and when there is only bitter
Winter-burning in the fields.

[1923]

## WOMEN

Women have no wilderness in them,
They are provident instead,
Content in the tight hot cell of their hearts
To eat dusty bread.

They do not see cattle cropping red winter grass,
They do not hear
Snow water going down under culverts
Shallow and clear.
*   *   *

They wait, when they should turn to journeys,
They stiffen, when they should bend.
They use against themselves that benevolence
To which no man is friend.

They cannot think of so many crops to a field
Or of clean wood cleft by an axe.
Their love is an eager meaninglessness
Too tense, or too lax.

They hear in every whisper that speaks to them
A shout and a cry.
As like as not, when they take life over their door-sills
They should let it go by.

[1923]


BETROTHED

You have put your two hands upon me, and your mouth,
You have said my name as a prayer.
Here where trees are planted by the water
I have watched your eyes, cleansed from regret,
And your lips, closed over all that love cannot say.

    My mother remembers the agony of her womb
    And long years that seemed to promise more than this.
    She says, "You do not love me,
    You do not want me,
    You will go away."

    In the country whereto I go
    I shall not see the face of my friend
    Nor her hair the color of sunburnt grasses;
    Together we shall not find
    The land on whose hills bends the new moon
    In air traversed of birds.

What have I thought of love?
I have said, "It is beauty and sorrow."
I have thought that it would bring me lost delights, and splendor
As a wind out of old time. . . .

\* \* \*

But there is only the evening here,
And the sound of willows
Now and again dipping their long oval leaves in the water.

[1923]


## MASKED WOMAN'S SONG

Before I saw the tall man
Few women should see,
Beautiful and imposing
Was marble to me.

And virtue had its place
And evil its alarms,
But not for that worn face,
And not in those roped arms.

[1967]


# KAY BOYLE, 1903–1992


## A COMMUNICATION TO NANCY CUNARD

These are not words set down for the rejected
Nor for outcasts cast by the mind's pity
Beyond the aid of lip or hand or from the speech
Of fires lighted in the wilderness by lost men
Reaching in fright and passion to each other.
This is not for the abandoned to hear.

It begins in the dark on a boxcar floor, the groaning timber
Stretched from bolt to bolt above the freight-train wheels
That grind and cry aloud like hounds upon the trail, the breathing
weaving
Unseen within the dark from mouth to nostril, nostril to speaking
mouth.
This is the theme of it, stated by one girl in a boxcar saying:
"Christ, what they pay you don't keep body and soul together."

"Where was you working?" "Working in a mill town."
The other girl in the corner saying: "Working the men when we could
    get them."
"Christ, what they pay you," wove the sound of breathing, "don't keep
    shoes on your feet.
Don't feed you. That's why we're shoving on."

(This is not for Virginia Price or Ruby Bates, the white girls dressed
like boys to go; not for Ozie Powell, six years in a cell playing the little
harp he played tap-dancing on the boxcar boards; not for Olen Mont-
gomery, the blind boy traveling towards Memphis that night, hopping
a ride to find a doctor who could cure his eyes; not for Eugene
Williams or Charlie Weems, not for Willie Robertson nor for Leroy
and Andy Wright, thirteen years old the time in March they took him
off the train in Paint Rock, Alabama; this is not for Clarence Norris or
Haywood Patterson, sentenced three times to die.)

    This is for the sheriff with a gold lodge pin
    And for the jury venireman who said: "Now, mos' folk don't go on
    And think things out. The Bible never speaks
    Of sexual intercourses. It jus' says a man knows a woman.
    So after Cain killed Abel he went off and knew a woman
    In the land of Nod. But the Bible tells as how
    There couldn't be no human folk there then.
    Now, jus' put two and two together. Cain had offspring
    In the land of Nod so he musta had him a female baboon
    Or chimpanzee or somethin' like it.
    And that's how the nigger race begun."

This is for the Sunday-school teacher with the tobacco plug
Who addressed the jury, the juice splattering on the wall,
Pleading: "Whether in overalls or furs a woman is protected by the
    Alabama law
Against the vilest crime the human species knows. Now, even dogs
    choose their mates,
But these nine boys are lower than the birds of the air,
Lower than the fish in the sea, lower than the beasts of the fields.
There is a law reaching down from the mountaintops to the swamps
    and caves—
It's the wisdom of the ages, there to protect the sacred parts of
    the female species

Without them having to buckle around their middles
Six-shooters or some other method of defense."

This is set down for the others: people who go and come,
Open a door and pass through it, walk in the streets
With the shops lit, loitering, lingering, gazing.
This is for two men riding, Deputy Sheriff Sandlin,
    Deputy Sheriff Blacock,
With Ozie Powell, handcuffed. Twelve miles out of Cullman
They shot him through the head.

## THE TESTIMONY

*Haywood Patterson*                                              *Victoria Price*

"So here goes an I shell try
Faithfully an I possibly can
Reference to myself in                                           "I
    particularly                                         cain't
And concerning the other boys                     remember."
    personal pride
And life time up to now.
You must be patiene with me
    and remember
Most of my English is not of                                 "I
    much interest                                       cain't
And that I am continually                         remember."
Stopping and searching for the
    word."

So here goes and I shall try faithfully as possible to tell you as I understand if not mistaken that Olen Montgomery, who was part blind then, kept saying because of the dark there was inside the boxcar and outside it: "It sure don't seem to me we're getting anywheres. It sure don't seem like it to me." I and my three comrades whom were with me, namely Roy Wright and his brother Andy and Eugene Williams, and about my character I have always been a good natural sort of boy, but as far as I am personally concerned about those pictures of me in the papers, why they are more or less undoubtedly not having the full likeness of me for I am a sight better-looking than those pictures make me out. Why all my life I spent in and around working for Jews in their stores and so on and I have quite a few Jew friends whom can and always have gave me a good reputation as having regards for those whom have regards for me. The depression ran me away from home, I was off on my way to try my very best to find some work elsewhere but misfortune befalled me without a moving cause. For it is events and misfortune which happens to people and how some must whom are less fortunate have their lives taken from them and how people die in chair for what they do not do.

## THE SPIRITUAL FOR NINE VOICES

I went last night to a turkey feast (Oh, God, don't fail your children
    now!)
My people were sitting there the way they'll sit in heaven
With their wings spread out and their hearts all singing
Their mouths full of food and the table set with glass
(Oh, God, don't fail your children now!)
There were poor men sitting with their fingers dripping honey
All the ugly sisters were fair. I saw my brother who never had a penny
With a silk shirt on and a pair of golden braces
And gems strewn through his hair.

(Were you looking, Father, when the sheriffs came in?
Was your face turned towards us when they had their say?)

    There was baked sweet potato and fried corn pone
    There was eating galore, there was plenty in the horn.
(Were you there when Victoria Price took the stand?
Did you see the state attorney with her drawers in his hand?
Did you hear him asking for me to burn?)

    There were oysters cooked in amplitude
    There was sauce in every mouth.
    There was ham done slow in spice and clove
    And chicken enough for the young and the old.
(Was it you stilled the water on horse-swapping day
When the mob came to the jail? Was it you come out in a long tail
    coat
Come dancing high with the word in your mouth?)

    I saw my sister who never had a cent
    Come shaking and shuffling between the seats.

Her hair was straight and her nails were pointed
Her breasts were high and her legs double-jointed.

(Oh, God, don't fail your children now!)

## THE SENTENCE

Hear how it goes, the wheels of it traveling fast on the rails
  The boxcars, the gondolas running drunk through the night.
Hear the long high wail as it flashes through stations unlit
  Past signals ungiven, running wild through a country
A time when sleepers rouse in their beds and listen
  And cannot sleep again.
Hear it passing in no direction, to no destination
Carrying people caught in the boxcars, trapped on the coupled
      chert cars
(Hear the rattle of gravel as it rides whistling through the day
      and night.)
Not the old or the young on it, nor people with any difference in
      their color or shape,
Not girls or men. Negroes or white, but people with this in common:
People that no one had use for, had nothing to give to, no place
      to offer
But the cars of a freight train careening through Paint Rock,
      through Memphis,
        Through town after town without halting.
        The loose hands hang down, and swing with the swing
            of the train in the darkness,
        Holding nothing but poverty, syphilis white as a
            handful of dust, taking nothing as baggage
        But the sound of the harp Ozie Powell is playing or the voice of
            Montgomery
        Half-blind in oblivion saying: "It sure don't seem to me like
            we're getting anywheres.
        It don't seem to me like we're getting anywheres at all."

[1937]

57

Carson, turn your coat collar up, throw the cigarette from your hand
And dance with me. The mazurka of women is easy to learn.
It is danced by the young, the high-heeled, and the doll-faced
Who swing on the bar stools, their soft drinks before them.
The polka of war brides is easy to follow. They dance down the streets
With their legs bare, their coats hanging open. In their pockets
Are letters written from home to be opened
Not to be read, but ripped wide by the fingernail (varnished
The color of blood), to be shaken for the check or the money order,
The dollar bill folded. These are the honeymooners
In one-room shacks, in overnight cabins, in trailer camps, dancing
The *pas seul* in shoes that strap fast at the ankle, talking
G.I. talk as if they had learned it not this year,
Not here, but months at the breast, years learning to spell still.
"Sweating out three weeks of maneuvers, or sweating the weekend
        pass,
Or sweating him out night after night," they'll say, sweet-tongued as
        thrushes.
"Say, who's fighting this war, the M.P.'s or our husbands?" they'll ask
As they swing on the bar stools. Their voices may say:
"Up on Kiska last year, he lost eighty bucks in a crap game
And twelve playing cards, two weeks before Christmas,"
While the music plays on for the dancers; or say:
"This is my ring. How do you like it? We didn't have diamonds
Put in this year. We can get them cheaper back home.
We were going to have something engraved inside. We wanted
        'forever'
Engraved, but we didn't have time yet," or saying:
"The night I had fever he wanted to go over the hill,"
But where is the hill that is high enough, wild enough, lost enough
Leading away? (Carson, dance with me.) This is the waltz
Of the wives whose men are in khaki. Their faces are painted
As flawless as children's, their hearts each the flame of a candle
That his breath can extinguish at will.

[1944]

## FOR JAMES BALDWIN

Black cat, sweet brother,
Walk into the room
On cat's feet where I lie dying
And I'll start breathing regularly again.
Witch doctor for the dispossessed,
Saint tipping your halo to the evicted,
The world starts remembering its postponed loyalties
When I call out your name. I knew you hot nights
When you kept stepping
The light fantastic to music only the wretched
Of the earth could hear; blizzards
In New Hampshire when you wore
A foxskin cap, its tail red as autumn
On your shoulder. In the waters of the Sound
You jumped the ripples, knees knocking,
Flesh blue with brine, your fingers
Cold as a dead child's holding mine.

You said it all, everything
A long time ago before anyone else knew
How to say it. This country was about to be
Transformed, you said; not by an act of God,
Nothing like that, but by us,
You and me. Young blacks saw Africa emerging
And knew for the first time, you said,
That they were related to kings and
To princes. It could be seen
In the way they walked, tall as cypresses,
Strong as bridges across the thundering falls.

        In the question period once
A lady asked isn't integration a two-way
Street, Mr. Baldwin, and you said
You mean you'll go back to Scarsdale tonight
And I'll go back to Harlem, is that the two ways
You mean?

We are a race in ourselves, you and I,
Sweet preacher. I talked with our ancestors

One night in dreams about it
And they bade me wear trappings of gold
And speak of it everywhere; speak of it on
The exultant mountain by day, and at night
On river banks where the stars touch fingers.
They said it might just save the world.

[1970]


## FOR MARIANNE MOORE'S BIRTHDAY
### NOVEMBER 15, 1967

I wish you triumphs that are yours already,
And also wish to say whatever I have done
Has been in admiration (imitation even)
Of all you marvelously proliferate. Once someone
Turned to me and said in lowered voice (because you too were in
      the room)
That William Carlos Williams gave to you at sight that
Singular esteem known by no other name save love. These words
      were
Spoken perhaps a half century ago
(In Monroe Wheeler's Eastside flat) when you
Wore amber braids around your head. And now,
As then, I cannot write this book or that
Without you. You have always been
Nightingale, baseball fan, librarian of my visions,
Poised on a moving ladder in the sun.

[1970]


## A POEM FOR FEBRUARY FIRST 1975
*for Jessica Mitford*

Glance back four years (yes, nearly four years now,
No matter how close, how shuddering the grief). Glance back
To the bonfires, to the curve of the moon lighting the walkways, the
      catwalks,
Lighting the faces of those who stood, arms locked, black links of a chain
Twisting motionless through D-Yard, a barrier of men, alive still

But rigid as the dead. That September the white horns of the moon and the
  bonfires
Shone for a moment in the lonely caverns of their eyes.


Hear the far clang of the syllables: Attica. Do not let them
Slip through the crevices of history, geography, be effaced from
The miraculous ledger of the stars. Say that a civilization was lost here,
Near to a city named for a dying species, Buffalo, not in that other Attica
Leafed delicately with quivering olive trees, washed on two sides by the
    Aegean Sea,
A triangle of ancient Greece refreshed by small, blue, brimming harbors,
Touched gently by the south wind as it passed. The heights were
Violet-crowned, the fields sweet with jasmine, the townships
Of ancient Attica bore the names of various plants and trees.
Its people are said to have walked gracefully through the luminous
Ether of its dusks. (Why not, with no irons at their ankles, no shackles
At their wrists?) That Attica overlooked the plain of Marathon,
Descended rock by sunbleached rock to the bright pulsing sea.
*Do these things matter now?*


The men locked arm in arm in the Attica of our dust, our maggots, our
    dereliction, stand
Halted at the edge, high on their hushed precipice, men whose names we
    have since learned,
Who choked, who wept, who fell on their knees in D-Yard as the helicopter
    dipped
And let its cargo of gas drift, lazy as smoke, quiet as cloud formations,
Across the rainy dawn. It is said that in ancient Attica
Torch-light processions descended from Athens, rejoicing, and turned the
    coastline
Radiant, fanned the dark harbors into waltzing light. *What torches can we
    carry,*
*Lit by the dry kindling of our hearts?*


At the first burst of rifle fire, those whose stark names we have since learned
Were mowed down like grain, their blood darker than poppies lying, dying,
In the wheat, and the single curse, "Rockefeller," cut deep in the curve of
    each bullet
That scythed them down. Down, down the walkways the assault units
Advanced in their curtain of fire, their cloaks of flame, came in yellow rain-
    gear,

In beetle-eyed masks, elephant-nosed, without ears, so that the pounding
On doors was silence to them, the pounding of fists at humble doors where
The locks broke, the wood split wide to the knocking, the knuckles of lost
    men
Beating at Rockefeller's door, inmates, hostages, pounding all night,
Pounding into the dawn like taps sounding at the barrier of his grinning
    door.
'If he had come, showed that he cared,' whispered the ashes of the
    extinguished fires,
'Things would have been different. Men would have lived who had not
    asked to die.'


As one approached ancient Attica, it is said that a change of temperature
Could be perceived, a softening of the breath of the wind, of the wash of the
    sea.
That Attica was famed for its marble (not for its blood), marble
    astonishingly white,
Astonishingly blue; famed as well for the brittle charcoal of its fuel.
(Charcoal obtained from bones is called 'bone black' in the trade.
It lay on the pavings of D-Yard after the fires were done and the pounding
    ceased on the stone
Of one man's door.) 'If he had come it would have shown . . . ' whispered
    the blowing ash.
But does not stone hold echoes in the hollow of its hands, echoes
That call forever down the corridor of history, across the congregation of
    the years,
Calling that all we can know of our own lives is learned
Through the despair of men whose names are not our own?
Remember the word Attica. Remember its syllables clanging, clanging.
*Do not let them go.*

                                [1986; 1990]


A POEM ON GETTING UP EARLY
IN THE MORNING (OR EVEN LATE
IN THE MORNING), WHEN ONE IS OLD


Wake, yes, wake (the Irish have a grimmer meaning
For the word and—so like the Irish—magic the verb
Into a noun.) Yes, wake and cross the Bridge of Sighs
Into the menace of the day. The buckling knees

Betray the thighs and hammer toes reduce their size,
Outraged that they are called upon to stride. "Fall, fall,"
The ankles urge, eager to sprain or to be sprained while,
Whether it rains now or has just rained, Tom's voice
Across the wire decrees that one must walk at least
Two miles a day; also that this pill or another be ingested
(Furosemide, or Lasix) on "arising," seemingly unaware that
Rising in the morning is the final chapter of despair.

As the curtain of fog descends (instead of "rising"), bull-frogs
Take on the operatic roles of tenor and baritone, their voices
Hoarse and the libretto lost in the morass. Useless to care
Whether or not the willows cease their weeping
As they braid and unbraid their long green tangled hair.

[1990]


# LORINE NIEDECKER, 1903–1970


## IN THE GREAT SNOWFALL BEFORE THE BOMB

In the great snowfall before the bomb
colored yule tree lights
windows, the only glow for contemplation
along this road

I worked the print shop
right down among em
the folk from whom all poetry flows
and dreadfully much else.

I was Blondie
I carried my bundles of hog feeder price lists
down by Larry the Lug,
I'd never get anywhere
because I'd never had suction,
pull, you know, favor, drag,
well-oiled protection.

\* \* \*

I heard their rehashed radio barbs—
more barbarous among hirelings
as higher-ups grow more corrupt.
But what vitality! The women hold jobs—
clean house, cook, raise children, bowl
and go to church.

What would they say if they knew
I sit for two months on six lines
of poetry?

[1961]

## NURSERY RHYME

### AS I NURSE MY PUMP

The greatest plumber
      in all the town
from Montgomery Ward
rode a Cadillac carriage
      by marriage
and visited my pump

A sensitive pump
      said he
that has at times a proper
      balance
   of water, air
and poetry

[1962]

## GRANDFATHER

Grandfather
      advised me:
            Learn a trade.
I learned
      to sit at desk
            and condense.

No layoff
    from this
        condensery.

                         [1968]


## I MARRIED

I married
in the world's black night
for warmth
        if not repose.
        At the close—
someone.

I hid with him
from the long range guns.
        We lay leg
        in the cupboard, head
in closet.

A slit of light
at no bird dawn—
        Untaught
        I thought
he drank

too much.
I say
        I married
        and lived unburied.
I thought—

                         [1976]


## MARGARET FULLER

She carried books
and chrysanthemums
to Boston
into a cold storm

                         [1976]

So he said
on radio

I have to fly
wit Venus arms
I found fishing
to Greece
then back to Univers of Wis
where they got stront. 90
to determ if same marble
as my arms

[1976]

# PHYLLIS MCGINLEY, 1905–1978

## WHY, SOME OF MY BEST FRIENDS ARE WOMEN

I learned in my credulous youth
    That women are shallow as fountains.
Women make lies out of truth
    And out of a molehill their mountains.
Women are giddy and vain,
    Cold-hearted or tiresomely tender;
Yet, nevertheless, I maintain
    I dote on the feminine gender.

*For the female of the species may be deadlier than the male*
*But she can make herself a cup of coffee without reducing*
*The entire kitchen to a shambles.*

Perverse though their taste in cravats
    Is deemed by their lords and their betters,
They know the importance of hats
    And they write you the news in their letters.
Their minds may be lighter than foam,
    Or altered in haste and in hurry,

But they seldom bring company home
When you're warming up yesterday's curry.

*And when lovely woman stoops to folly,*
*She does not invariably come in at four A.M.*
*Singing "Sweet Adeline."*

Oh, women are frail and they weep.
They are recklessly given to scions.
But, wakened unduly from sleep,
They are milder than tigers or lions.
Women hang clothes on their pegs
Nor groan at the toil and the trouble.
Women have rather nice legs
And chins that are guiltless of stubble.
Women are restless, uneasy to handle,
But when they are burning both ends of the scandal,
They do not insist with a vow that is votive,
How high are their minds and how noble the motive.

As shopping companions they're heroes and saints;
They meet you in tearooms nor murmur complaints;
They listen, entranced, to a list of your vapors;
At breakfast they sometimes emerge from the papers;
A Brave Little Widow's not apt to sob-story 'em,
And they keep a cool head in a grocery emporium.
Yes, I rise to defend
The quite possible She.
For the feminine gend-
Er is O.K. by me.

*Besides, everybody admits it's a Man's World.*
*And just look what they've done to it!*

[1932]

## THE 5:32

She said, If tomorrow my world were torn in two,
Blacked out, dissolved, I think I would remember
(As if transfixed in unsurrendering amber)
This hour best of all the hours I knew:
When cars came backing into the shabby station,
Children scuffing the seats, and the women driving
With ribbons around their hair, and the trains arriving,
And the men getting off with tired but practiced motion.

Yes, I would remember my life like this, she said:
Autumn, the platform red with Virginia creeper,
And a man coming toward me, smiling, the evening paper
Under his arm, and his hat pushed back on his head;
And wood smoke lying like haze on the quiet town,
And dinner waiting, and the sun not yet gone down.

[1932]

# JOSEPHINE JACOBSEN, 1908–

## WHEN THE FIVE PROMINENT POETS

gathered in inter-admiration
in a small hotel room, to listen
to each other, like Mme. Verdurin
made ill by ecstasy,
they dropped the Muse's name.
Who came.

It was awful.
The door in shivers and a path
plowed like a twister through everything.
Eyeballs and fingers littered that room.
When the floor exploded the ceiling
parted
and the Muse went on and up; and not a sound
came from the savage carpet.

[1967]

# FOOD

A woman of the more primitive tribes
of Eskimo, concerned with nourishment,
cooked with heather clawed out from under snow;

mittens too precious, tore the heather loose
in that weather. The bare malformed hands,
nails curved, grew flesh like smoked wood.

Under an open sky, such fuel burned too fast;
in the snow-house, the walls would soften—
worse, smoke trouble the house's master.

She lay, low, to cook in a flat hut with a hole
in its roof. Blow! Blow! The ashes flew
into her mane, her red mongoose eyes.

To eat is good. To trap, to kill, to drive
the dogs' ferocity is heroic to tell:
full-bellied sagas' stuff.

The clawing for heather, the black curved nails,
cramped breath for smoke, smoke for breath,
the witch mask clamped on the bride face

bring nothing, but life for the nourished.
Poor cannibals; we eat what we can:
it is honorable to sustain life.

By her breath, flesh, her hands, no
reputation will be made, no
saga descend. It is only the

next day made possible.

[1981]

# THE SISTERS

Everyone notices they are inseparable.
Though this isn't quite so, it might well be.
Talk about depending on each other . . .
One can't say they are totally
congenial—irritation isn't unknown.

Yet it is, truly, touching, how they go on
year after year, not just pairing lives but
taking even holidays and vacations together,
sharing what happens to come along.
Here they are in the Caribbean.

Choose a day—the eighteenth of March for example:
they awake at almost but not quite
the same instant, disoriented:
where is the east? where anything else?
But they aren't going to dog each other all day.

B, anyone would have to admit,
is the better adjusted—easily pleased.
What marvelous lobster! she cries.
Smell the air! (The island is full of spices
and the air is soft as well as fragrant.)

A's energy always seems to be erratic:
first she's on and on about something,
then she wants a nap. She's a great sleeper
and has been known to cast away
hour after precious hour asleep without shame.

And she gets fixations—dashing off
to some spot they've already seen,
and talking about it when she gets back.
Take the little group of graves by the Old Men's Home
the station-wagon passes on its way to the beach.

Both of them noticed it—how could they help?
It's a little patch, unfenced, with four or five

graves. One apparently new and covered
with brightness. They even both waved
to the four old men on the porch who waved back.

But later, it turns out, A went back by herself,
sharp-eyed as ever, to examine the yellow
and violet cellophane, the rubber pond-lilies
floating on dust; the whole glittering heap
of rainbow mound; even asked questions.

That happened this morning; with the result
that when B swam in the sea—that sea
like a sapphire flawed with gold and green—
A went to sleep. The time she wastes
like that, slack as a weed in a wave!

This means that tonight she'll keep B awake
probably for hours, prowling about.
But they fight less than most sisters
and when the question of separation once arose
you should have seen them recoil—both, both.

At scrabble this afternoon they played partners:
tiles smooth to the fingertips, words appear-
ing, solid as objects—*salmon, cat;* or abstract,
as *who, why, go.* They did very well.
Then A wouldn't participate in the talk at dinner.

On the whole, this was a good day; hard rain
rattled the roof, then the real rainbow threw up its arch,
and amicably they watched the blood-orange dip
into water; then stars, larger and brighter than elsewhere.
Before bed, A looked at herself in the mirror, using B's eyes.

[1987]

THE MOTION
*for Nancy Sullivan*

The geranium in my studio window
with its blaze of faceted globe
has put up another bloom,
not open. Red loose buds on top;
the tight green buds below point down.

I know trick film can show me what
happened. But that is fake. The real motion
can't be seen. If I had come at three
in the morning, at six, would I
have caught it moving? No. No.

It's like that game of Steps. When you open
your eyes, everything stops. But I want,
very much, to see it happen;
it's actual. And it's a hint of what
goes on the whole time. Without a sound.

The withering, too. When does that begin?
What is the first motion of the turn? the with-
drawal? It's like that June 22nd
green-blue day that turns over
without stir or whisper, to face winter.

If I could see it happen, I could
know when all tides tip; how luck
shifts; and when loss is ready. When
you are saying goodbye to someone you think
you'll see next week. And don't. Ever.

[1987]

# JEAN GARRIGUE 1912–1972

## UPON THE INTIMATION OF LOVE'S MORTALITY

It is the effort of the lie
Exacts a wounding pulse.
I loved you much
When everything had excellence at once.
First was our freshness and the stun of that.
Your body raved with music. What was lost
Is just that element our time always takes
And always in love we venture off some height
That nothing else can equal after it.
The thought of that bedevils me for miles.
How can I save you from my own despair
To think I may not love you as before?
Spoiled, we become accustomed to our luck.
This is the devil of the heart.
We were the smiles of gods awhile
And now, it seems, our ghosts must eat us up
Or wail in temples till our tombs are bought.
Attended now by shades of that great while,
Disguise is the nature of my guile
And yet the lie benumbs the soul.
Get me the purity of first sight!
Or strength to bear the truth of after light!

[1964]

## ON THE LEGENDS OF A DANCER

I was a child in a small midwestern town,
It was a still summer afternoon
Yellow under the great maple trees.
Perfumes of the close-shorn grass and the entranced
Loose-hanging clusters of dark-laced boughs
Sealed me into the heat of a grape-enclosed
Urn of summer's drowse
Under the arbors of vine-weaving ease
When a beautiful woman, my mother's friend,
Famed for her girlhood of violets and beau-taking
Sashes, valances at dances, of supreme

Dew-drenched, liquid-kissing, cyclamen-haunted eyes,
Came to inform us that you were dead.
Into which with the speaking of faraway *death* was mixed
A coquettish condemnation of ardors so fierce
It seemed leopards might spring from the dots and cirques
Of a heat-ringed shade stippled by sun on the wands of the boughs.
And a vast sadness commingled with a vast sense
Of a mystery so obscurely profound
Seemed to wring from the antiphonies
Of an everywhere that the trees described
A music flowing up from their roots
And down through the whole shivering sap of their lives
Whereupon it seemed that I understood
Love, womanhood, and dancing.

[1964]


## WRITTEN IN LONDON AFTER A PROTEST PARADE

Any messages, messages, any word?
Has the woman with her child gone home?
Has the Pole Anna, whose mother died,
Received good news? Is there a god?
And what of the gasman. Did he come?
The wind is high on this sea-blown isle
And it is tall in my room and dim.
At the shut window the curtains blow.
I don't want all that air. Don't let it in.
And the bulldog pup wrapped in a sweater
Whose obscene old grandmother barked at him,
Is he going to Brussels on the weekend?
His former father is a stud in Rome,
A most respectable pink-nosed pug,
And if he saw a bull would he bait him?

I walked with the women today, several abreast,
Escorted by policemen—"What a travesty!"
We set a fast pace and we had balloons
And black pennants on shepherd crooks
And ten or more trundled go-carts.
How the babies slept over their wheels
Up Kingsway through Ludgate Circus!

And at St. Paul's we waited an hour
To see a Masque and then it was over.

Any messages, messages, any word?
We were soluble in some concord,
For a while we were part of one
In an unproved, nearly abstract way.
Buttons were sold and *Peace News,*
We were "on the side of humanity"
Herded by policemen, shot
By photographers every which way.
A goodly company of good will
Not bound to win but bound to try said one
With a face from which intelligence shone.
There were ministers' wives and a cold sun
On grimy St. Paul's with its swollen domes.

And what of the woman in the small back room
Who looked as young as her daughter?
She has stolen her daughter, in the same lumpy bed
Too narrow for one they slept together.
A sad intensity set them apart,
They were pale and still when I saw them.
And the wind. Will her husband come?
Will he send a bailiff or procure a judge?
She would know *what* to do if she knew *where,* she said.

Any messages, messages, any word?
Up in arms, at sea, tossed resistlessly
Almost at times not right in the head,
Opposing by erratic decisions what the heart only knows
After choice has canceled too late, too late,
Nursing the murderer there
Whether it hunts by knives
Or the thought that denies . . .
I am elated, but should we try
As some of us said, to die
If it comes to that, for what we believe?
If it *must* come to that, that is. . . .

[1967]

75

# Muriel Rukeyser, 1913–1980

## More of a Corpse Than a Woman

Give them my regards when you go to the school reunion;
and at the marriage-supper, say that I'm thinking about them.
They'll remember my name; I went to the movies with that one;
feeling the weight of their death where she sat at my elbow;
           she never said a word
           but all of them were heard.

All of them alike, expensive girls, the leaden friends:
one used to play the piano, one of them once wrote a sonnet,
one even seemed awakened enough to photograph wheatfields—
the dull girls with the educated minds and technical passions—
           pure love was their employment,
           they tried it for enjoyment.

Meet them at the boat: they've brought the souvenirs of boredom,
a seashell from the faltering monarchy;
the nose of a marble saint; and from the battlefield,
an empty shell divulged from a flower-bed.
           The lady's wealthy breath
           perfumes the air with death.

The leaden lady faces the fine, voluptuous woman,
faces a rising world bearing its gifts in its hands.
Kisses her casual dreams upon the lips she kisses,
risen, she moves away; takes others; moves away.
           Inadequate to love,
           supposes she's enough.

Give my regards to the well-protected woman,
I knew the ice-cream girl, we went to school together.
There's something to bury, people, when you begin to bury.
When your women are ready and rich in their wish for the world,
           destroy the leaden heart,
           we've a new race to start.

[1935]

## NIGHT FEEDING

Deeper than sleep but not so deep as death
I lay there sleeping and my magic head
remembered and forgot.    On first cry I
remembered and forgot and did believe.
I knew love and I knew evil:
woke to the burning song and the tree burning blind,
despair of our days and the calm milk-giver who
knows sleep, knows growth, the sex of fire and grass,
and the black snake with gold bones.

Black sleeps, gold burns;    on second cry I woke
fully and gave to feed and fed on feeding.
Gold seed, green pain, my wizards in the earth
walked through the house, black in the morning dark.
Shadows grew in my veins, my bright belief,
my head of dreams deeper than night and sleep.
Voices of all black animals crying to drink,
cries of all birth arise, simple as we,
found in the leaves, in clouds and dark, in dream,
deep as this hour, ready again to sleep.

[1935]

## POEM OUT OF CHILDHOOD

### I

Breathe in experience, breathe out poetry—
Not Angels, angels—and the magnificent past
shot deep illuminations into high-school.
I opened the door into the concert-hall
and a rush of triumphant violins answered me
while the syphilitic woman turned her mouldered face
intruding upon Brahms. Suddenly, in an accident
the girl's brother was killed, but her father had just died:
she stood against the wall, leaning her cheek,
dumbly her arms fell, "What will become of me?" and
I went into the corridor for a drink of water.
These bandages of image wrap my head,
when I put my hand up I hardly feel the wounds.

77

We sat on the steps of the unrented house
raining blood down on Loeb and Leopold
creating again how they removed his glasses
and philosophically slit his throat.

They who manipulated and misused our youth
smearing those centuries upon our hands,
trapping us in a welter of dead names,
snuffing and shaking heads at patent truth . . .

We were ready to go the long descent with Virgil
the bough's gold shade advancing forever with us,
entering the populated cold of drawing-rooms;
Sappho, with her drowned hair trailing along Greek waters,
weed binding it, a fillet of kelp enclosing
the temples' ardent fruit—

　　　　　　　　　　　　　　Not Sappho, Sacco.
Rebellion, pioneered among our lives,
viewing from far-off many-branching deltas,
innumerable seas.


## I I

In adolescence I knew travellers
speakers digressing from the ink-pocked rooms,
bearing the unequivocal sunny word.

Prinzip's year bore us: see us turning at breast
quietly while the air throbs over Sarajevo
after the mechanic laugh of that bullet.
How could they know what sinister knowledge finds
its way among the brain's wet palpitance,
what words would nudge and giggle at our spine,
what murders dance?
These horrors have approached the growing child;
now that the factory is sealed-up brick
the kids throw stones, smashing the windows
membranes of uselessness in desolation.

We grew older quickly, watching the father shave
and the splatter of lather harden on the glass,

playing in sand-boxes to escape paralysis,
being victimized by fataller sly things.
"Oh, and you," he said, scraping his jaw, "What will you be?"
"Maybe—something—like—Joan—of—Arc. . . . "
Allies Advance, we see,
Six Miles South to Soissons. And we beat the drums,
Watchsprings snap in the mind, uncoil, relax,
the leafy years all somber with foreign war.
How could we know what exposed guts resembled?

A wave, shocked to motion, babbles margins
from Asia to Far Rockaway, spiralling
among clocks in its four-dimensional circles.
Disturbed by war, we pedalled bicycles
breakneck down the decline, until the treads
conquered our speed, and pulled our feet behind them,
and pulled our heads.
We never knew the war, standing so small
looking at eye-level toward the puttees, searching
the picture-books for sceptres, pennants for truth;
see Galahad unaided by puberty.

Rat-tat a drum upon the armistice,
Kodak As You Go—photo: they danced late,
and we were a generation of grim children
leaning over the bedroom sills, watching
the music and the shoulders and how the war was over,
laughing until the blow on the mouth broke night
wide out from cover.
The child's curls blow in a forgotten wind,
immortal ivy trembles on the wall:
the sun has crystallized these scenes, and tall
shadows remember time cannot rescind.

### III

Organize the full results of that rich past,
open the windows—potent catalyst,
harsh theory of knowledge, running down the aisles,
crying out in the classrooms, March ravening on the plain,
inexorable sun and wind and natural thought.

\* \* \*

Dialectically our youth unfolds:
the pale child walking to the river, passional
in ignorance, in loneliness, demanding
its habitations for the leaping dream, kissing
quick air, the vibrations of transient light,
not knowing substance or reverse, walking
in valvular air, each person in the street
conceived surrounded by his life and pain,
fixed against time, subtly by these impaled:
death and that shapeless war. Listening at dead doors,
our youth assumes a thousand differing fleshes
summoning fact from abandoned machines of trade,
knocking on the wall of the nailed-up power-plant,
telephoning hello, the deserted factory, ready
for the affirmative clap of truth
ricochetting from thought to thought among
the childhood, the gestures, the rigid travellers.

[1936]

## THE CONJUGATION OF THE PARAMECIUM

This has nothing
to do with
propagating

The species
is continued
as so many are
(among the smaller creatures)
by fission

(and this species
is very small
next in order to
the amoeba, the beginning one)

The paramecium
achieves, then,
immortality
by dividing

But when
the paramecium
desires renewal
strength    another joy
this is what
the paramecium does:

The paramecium
lies down beside
another
paramecium

Slowly    inexplicably
the exchange
takes place
in which
some bits
of the nucleus of each
are exchanged

for some bits
of the nucleus
of the other

This called
the conjugation of the paramecium.

[1968]


KÄTHE KOLLWITZ

I

Held between wars
my lifetime
                among wars, the big hands of the world of death
my lifetime
listens to yours.

The faces of the sufferers
in the street, in dailiness,

their lives showing
through their bodies
a look as of music
the revolutionary look
that says    I am in the world
to change the world
my lifetime
is to love to endure to suffer the music
to set its portrait
up as a sheet of the world
the most moving the most alive
Easter and bone
and Faust walking among the flowers of the world
and the child alive within the living woman, music of man,
and death holding my lifetime between great hands
the hands of enduring life
that suffers the gifts and madness of full life, on earth, in our time,
and through my life, through my eyes, through my arms and hands
may give the face of this music in portrait waiting for
the unknown person
held in the two hands, you.


## II

Woman as gates, saying:
"The process is after all like music,
like the development of a piece of music.
The fugues come back and
                                        again and again
interweave.
A theme may seem to have been put aside,
but it keeps returning—
the same thing modulated,
somewhat changed in form.
Usually richer.
And it is very good that this is so."

A woman pouring her opposites.
"After all there are happy things in life too.
Why do you show only the dark side?"
"I could not answer this. But I know—

in the beginning my impulse to know
the working life
                    had little to do with
pity or sympathy.
                    I simply felt
that the life of the workers was beautiful."

She said, "I am groping in the dark."

She said, "When the door opens, of sensuality,
then you will understand it too. The struggle begins.
Never again to be free of it,
often you will feel it to be your enemy.
Sometimes
you will almost suffocate,
such joy it brings."

Saying of her husband: "My wish
is to die after Karl.
I know no person who can love as he can,
with his whole soul.
Often this love has oppressed me;
I wanted to be free.
But often too it has made me
so terribly happy."

She said: "We rowed over to Carrara at dawn,
climbed up to the marble quarries
and rowed back at night. The drops of water
fell like glittering stars
from our oars."

She said: "As a matter of fact,
I believe
            that bisexuality
is almost a necessary factor
in artistic production; at any rate,
the tinge of masculinity within me
helped me
            in my work."
*    *    *

She said: "The only technique I can still manage.
It's hardly a technique at all, lithography.
In it
        only the essentials count."

A tight-lipped man in a restaurant last night
        saying to me:
"Kollwitz? She's too black-and-white."


## III

Held among wars, watching
    all of them
    all these people
    weavers,
    Carmagnole

Looking at
    all of them
    death, the children
    patients in waiting-rooms
    famine
    the street
    the corpse with the baby
    floating, on the dark river

A woman seeing
    the violent, inexorable
    movement of nakedness
    and the confession of No
    the confession of great weakness, war,
    all streaming to one son killed, Peter;
    even the son left living; repeated,
    the father, the mother; the grandson
    another Peter killed in another war; firestorm;
    dark, light, as two hands,
    this pole and that pole as the gates.

What would happen if one woman told the truth about her life?
The world would split open

IV SONG: THE CALLING-UP

Rumor, stir of ripeness
rising within this girl
sensual blossoming
of meaning, its light and form.

The birth-cry summoning
out of the male, the father
from the warm woman
a mother in response.

The word of death
calls up the fight with stone
wrestle with grief with time
from the material make
an art harder than bronze.

V SELF-PORTRAIT

Mouth looking directly at you
eyes in their inwardness looking
directly at you
half light    half darkness
woman, strong, German, young artist
flows into
wide sensual mouth meditating
looking right at you
eyes shadowed with brave hand
looking deep at you
flows into
wounded brave mouth
grieving and hooded eyes
alive, German, in her first War
flows into
strength of the worn face
a skein of lines
broods, flows into
mothers among the war graves
bent over death
facing the father

stubborn upon the field
flows into
the marks of her knowing—
*Nie Wieder Krieg*
repeated in the eyes
flows into
"Seedcorn must not be ground"
and the grooved cheek
lips drawn fine
the down-drawn grief
face of our age
flows into
*Pietà,* mother and
between her knees
life as her son in death
pouring from the sky of
one more war
flows into
face almost obliterated
hand over the mouth forever
hand over one eye now
the other great eye
closed

                                                    [1971]


## DESPISALS

In the human cities, never again to
despise the backside of the city, the ghetto,
or build it again as we build the despised
backsides of houses.      Look at your own building.
You are the city.

Among our secrecies, not to despise our Jews
(that is, ourselves) or our darkness, our blacks,
or in our sexuality    wherever it takes us
and we now know we are productive
too productive, too reproductive
for our present invention—never to despise
the homosexual who goes building another

*  *  *

with touch    with touch    (not to despise any touch)
each like himself, like herself each.
You are this.
                    In the body's ghetto
never to go despising the asshole
nor the useful shit that is our clean clue
to what we need.     Never to despise
the clitoris in her least speech.

Never to despise in myself what I have been taught
to despise.     Not to despise the other.
Not to despise the *it*.        To make this relation
with the it: to know that I am it.

[1973]

## TO BE A JEW IN THE TWENTIETH CENTURY

To be a Jew in the twentieth century
Is to be offered a gift.     If you refuse,
Wishing to be invisible, you choose
Death of the spirit, the stone insanity.
Accepting, take full life, full agonies:
Your evening deep in labyrinthine blood
Of those who resist, fail and resist; and God
Reduced to a hostage among hostages.

The gift is torment.     Not alone the still
Torture, isolation; or torture of the flesh.
That may come also.     But the accepting wish,
The whole and fertile spirit as guarantee
For every human freedom, suffering to be free,
Daring to live for the impossible.

[1973]

## FOR KAY BOYLE

What is the skill of this waking? Heard the singing
of that man rambling up Frederick Street in music
and his repeated ecstasy, in a long shaken line.

\*   \*   \*

After many and many a February storm, cyclamen
and many a curtain of rain, the tearing of all curtains
and, as you said, making love and facing the police

in one afternoon. A few bright colors in permanent ink:
black sea, light like streetlight green, blue sees in you
the sun and the moon that stand as your guardians.

And the young bearded rebels and students tearing it all away,
all of it, down to the truth that barefaced naked act of
light, streamings of the courage of the sources,
the sun and the moon that stand at your ears.

[1974]


RESURRECTION OF THE RIGHT SIDE

When the half-body dies its frightful death
forked pain, infection of snakes, lightning, pull down the
    voice. Waking
and I begin to climb the mountain on my mouth,
word by stammer, walk stammered, the lurching deck of
    earth.
Left-right with none of my own rhythms
the long-established sex and poetry.
                                         I go running in sleep,
but waking stumble down corridors of self, all rhythms
    gone.

The broken movement of love    sex out of rhythm
one halted name    in a shattered language
ruin of French-blue lights behind the eyes
slowly the left hand extends a hundred feet
and the right hand follows follows
but still the power of sight is very weak
but I go rolling this ball of life, it rolls
and I follow it whole up the slowly-brightening slope

A whisper attempts me, I whisper without stammer
I walk the long hall to the time of a metronome
set by a child's gun-target    left-right

* * *

the power of eyesight is very slowly arriving
       in this late impossible daybreak
       all the blue flowers open

[1974]


# RUTH STONE, 1915–


## IN AN IRIDESCENT TIME

My mother, when young, scrubbed laundry in a tub,
She and her sisters on an old brick walk
Under the apple trees, sweet rub-a-dub.
The bees came round their heads, the wrens made talk.
Four young ladies each with a rainbow board
Honed their knuckles, wrung their wrists to red,
Tossed back their braids and wiped their aprons wet.
The Jersey calf beyond the back fence roared;
And all the soft day, swarms about their pet
Buzzed at his big brown eyes and bullish head.
Four times they rinsed, they said. Some things they starched,
Then shook them from the baskets two by two,
And pinned the fluttering intimacies of life
Between the lilac bushes and the yew:
Brown gingham, pink, and skirts of Alice blue.

[1959]


## ADVICE

My hazard wouldn't be yours, not ever;
But every doom, like a hazelnut, comes down
To its own worm. So I am rocking here
Like any granny with her apron over her head
Saying, lordy me. It's my trouble.
There's nothing to be learned this way.
If I heard a girl crying help
I would go to save her;
But you hardly ever hear those words.

Dear children, you must try to say
Something when you are in need.
Don't confuse hunger with greed;
And don't wait until you are dead.

[1970]


## HOW TO CATCH AUNT HARRIETTE

Mary Cassatt has her in a striped dress with a
child on her lap, the child's foot in a wash basin.
Or Charlotte Mew speaks in her voice of the feeling
that comes at evening with home-cawing rooks.
Or Aunt Harriette sometimes makes an ineffable
gesture between the lines of Trollope.
In Indianapolis, together we rode the belching city bus to
high school. It was my first year, she was a senior. We were
nauseated every day by the fumes, by the unbearable
streets. Aunt Harriette was the last issue of my
Victorian grandparents. Once after school she
invited me to go with her to Verner's.
What was *Verner's?* I didn't ask and Aunt Harriette didn't say.
We walked three miles down manicured Meridian.
My heels rubbed to soft blisters. Entering an empty
wood-echoing room fronting the sidewalk,
we sat at a plain plank table and Aunt Harriette
ordered two glasses of iced ginger ale.
The varnish of light on Aunt Harriette
had the quality of a small eighteenth-century
Dutch painting. My tongue with all its buds intact
slipped in the amber sting. It was my first hint
of the connoisseur, an induction rarely repeated;
yet so bizarre, so beyond me,
that I planned my entire life from its indications.

[1987]


## POKEBERRIES

I started out in the Virginia mountains
with my grandma's pansy bed
and my Aunt Maud's dandelion wine.
We lived on greens and back-fat and biscuits.

My Aunt Maud scrubbed right through the linoleum.
My daddy was a northerner who played drums
and chewed tobacco and gambled.
He married my mama on the rebound.
Who would want an ignorant hill girl with red hair?
They took a Pullman up to Indianapolis
and someone stole my daddy's wallet.
My whole life has been stained with pokeberries.
No man seemed right for me. I was awkward
until I found a good wood-burning stove.
There is no use asking what it means.
With my first piece of ready cash I bought my own
place in Vermont; kerosene lamps, dirt road.
I'm sticking here like a porcupine up a tree.
Like the one our neighbor shot. Its bones and skin
hung there for three years in the orchard.
No amount of knowledge can shake my grandma out of me;
or my Aunt Maud; or my mama, who didn't just bite an apple
with her big white teeth. She split it in two.

[1987]


## FATHER'S DAY

When I was eight you put me
on the Sky-Line roller coaster at Riverside
where I screamed all day
holding to a steel bar
unable to get off.
While you were shaking dice behind a tent,
I was rising and falling,
a strip of tickets crumpled in my hand.
In 1950 you were reading Epictetus late at night
falling asleep in your chair.
Years earlier you wrote in your diary,
"New girl in town. Quinn and I
had a shot at her."
Sitting in the orchestra pit
drumming the pratfalls,
the vaudeville timed to your wrist rolls.
My first groom. Mother was shy.
She said I could not marry you.

She kept me for myself.
She did not know the wet lips
you kissed me with one morning.
What an irritable man you were.
Rising and falling,
I could not remember who I was.
Whole summers consumed
in the sound of glass wind-chimes.
When you died they scattered your ashes in a field.
At any moment I can breathe in the burned powder of
    your body,
the bitter taste, the residue.

[1991]


# MARGARET WALKER, 1915–


## MOLLY MEANS

Old Molly Means was a hag and a witch;
Chile of the devil, the dark, and sitch.
Her heavy hair hung thick in ropes
And her blazing eyes was black as pitch.
Imp at three and wench at 'leben
She counted her husbands to the number seben.
    O Molly, Molly, Molly Means
    There goes the ghost of Molly Means.

Some say she was born with a veil on her face
So she could look through unnatchal space
Through the future and through the past
And charm a body or an evil place
And every man could well despise
The evil look in her coal black eyes.
    Old Molly, Molly, Molly Means
    Dark is the ghost of Molly Means.
*   *   *

And when the tale begun to spread
Of evil and of holy dread:
Her black-hand arts and her evil powers
How she cast her spells and called the dead,
The younguns was afraid at night
And the farmers feared their crops would blight.
    Old Molly, Molly, Molly Means
    Cold is the ghost of Molly Means.

Then one dark day she put a spell
On a young gal-bride just come to dwell
In the lane just down from Molly's shack
And when her husband come riding back
His wife was barking like a dog
And on all fours like a common hog.
    O Molly, Molly, Molly Means
    Where is the ghost of Molly Means?

The neighbors come and they went away
And said she'd die before break of day
But her husband held her in his arms
And swore he'd break the wicked charms,
He'd search all up and down the land
And turn the spell on Molly's hand.
    O Molly, Molly, Molly Means
    Sharp is the ghost of Molly Means.

So he rode all day and he rode all night
And at the dawn he come in sight
Of a man who said he could move the spell
And cause the awful thing to dwell
On Molly Means, to bark and bleed
Till she died at the hands of her evil deed.
    Old Molly, Molly, Molly Means
    This is the ghost of Molly Means.

Sometimes at night through the shadowy trees
She rides along on a winter breeze.
You can hear her holler and whine and cry.
Her voice is thin and her moan is high,

And her cackling laugh or her barking cold
Bring terror to the young and old.
    O Molly, Molly, Molly Means
    Lean is the ghost of Molly Means.

[1942]


## LINEAGE

My grandmothers were strong.
They followed plows and bent to toil.
They moved through fields sowing seed.
They touched earth and grain grew.
They were full of sturdiness and singing.
My grandmothers were strong.

My grandmothers are full of memories
Smelling of soap and onions and wet clay
With veins rolling roughly over quick hands
They have many clean words to say.
My grandmothers were strong.
Why am I not as they?

[1942]


## FOR GWEN, 1969
### Gwendolyn Brooks

The slender, shy, and sensitive young girl
is woman now,
her words a power in the Ebon land.
Outside her window on the street
a mass of life moves by.
Chicago is her city.
Her heart flowers with its flame—
old stockyards, new beaches
all the little storefront churches
and the bar on the corner.
Dreamer and seer of tales
She witnesses rebellion,

struggle and sweat.
The people are her heartbeat—
In their footsteps pulsate daily
all her black words of fire and blood.

[1969]


# GWENDOLYN BROOKS, 1917–


## THE MOTHER

Abortions will not let you forget.
You remember the children you got that you did not get,
The damp small pulps with a little or with no hair,
The singers and workers that never handled the air.
You will never neglect or beat
Them, or silence or buy with a sweet.
You will never wind up the sucking-thumb
Or scuttle off ghosts that come.
You will never leave them, controlling your luscious sigh,
Return for a snack of them, with gobbling mother-eye.

I have heard in the voices of the wind the voices of my dim killed
        children.
I have contracted. I have eased
My dim dears at the breasts they could never suck.
I have said, Sweets, if I sinned, if I seized
Your luck
And your lives from your unfinished reach,
If I stole your births and your names,
Your straight baby tears and your games,
Your stilted or lovely loves, your tumults, your marriages, aches, and
        your deaths,
If I poisoned the beginnings of your breaths,
Believe that even in my deliberateness I was not deliberate.
Though why should I whine,
Whine that the crime was other than mine?—
Since anyhow you are dead.

Or rather, or instead,
You were never made.
But that too, I am afraid,
Is faulty: oh, what shall I say, how is the truth to be said?
You were born, you had body, you died.
It is just that you never giggled or planned or cried.

Believe me, I loved you all.
Believe me, I knew you, though faintly, and I loved, I loved you
All.

[1944]


## JESSIE MITCHELL'S MOTHER

Into her mother's bedroom to wash the ballooning body.
"My mother is jelly-hearted and she has a brain of jelly:
Sweet, quiver-soft, irrelevant. Not essential.
Only a habit would cry if she should die.
A pleasant sort of fool without the least iron. . . .
Are you better, mother, do you think it will come today?"
The stretched yellow rag that was Jessie Mitchell's mother
Reviewed her. Young, and so thin, and so straight.
So straight! as if nothing could ever bend her.
But poor men would bend her, and doing things with poor men,
Being much in bed, and babies would bend her over,
And the rest of things in life that were for poor women,
Coming to them grinning and pretty with intent to bend and to kill.
Comparisons shattered her heart, ate at her bulwarks:
The shabby and the bright: she, almost hating her daughter,
Crept into an old sly refuge: "Jessie's black
And her way will be black, and jerkier even than mine.
Mine, in fact, because I was lovely, had flowers
Tucked in the jerks, flowers were here and there. . . ."
She revived for the moment settled and dried-up triumphs,
Forced perfume into old petals, pulled up the droop,
Refueled
Triumphant long-exhaled breaths.
Her exquisite yellow youth. . . .

[1950]

96

## TO THOSE OF MY SISTERS
## WHO KEPT THEIR NATURALS

*Never to look*
*a hot comb in the teeth*

Sisters!
I love you.
Because you love you.
Because you are erect.
Because you are also bent.
In season, stern, kind.
Crisp, soft—in season.
And you withhold.
And you extend.
And you Step out.
And you go back.
And you extend again.
Your eyes, loud-soft, with crying and
    with smiles,
are older than a million years.
And they are young.
You reach, in season.
You subside, in season.
And All
below the richrough righttime of your hair.
You have not bought Blondine.
You have not hailed the hot-comb recently.
You never worshiped Marilyn Monroe.
You say: Farrah's hair is hers.
You have not wanted to be white.
Nor have you testified to adoration of that
    state
with the advertisement of imitation
(*never* successful because the hot-comb is
    laughing too.)

But oh the rough dark Other music!
the Real,
the Right.
The natural Respect of Self and Seal!
    Sisters!
Your hair is Celebration in the world!

[1987]

# Naomi Replansky, 1918–

## HOUSING SHORTAGE

I tried to live small.
I took a narrow bed.
I held my elbows to my sides.
I tried to step carefully
And to think softly
And to breathe shallowly
In my portion of air
And to disturb no one.

Yet see how I spread out and I cannot help it.
I take to myself more and more, and I take nothing
That I do not need, but my needs grow like weeds,
All over and invading; I clutter this place
With all the apparatus of living.
You stumble over it daily.

And then my lungs take their fill.
And then you gasp for air.

Excuse me for living,
But, since I am living,
Given inches, I take yards,
Taking yards, dream of miles,
And a landscape, unbounded
And vast in abandon.

You too dreaming the same.

[1952]

## TWO WOMEN

There is a woman climbing a glass hill
Of clothes and dishes on a dusty floor;
Today surmounted, tomorrow towers still.

There is a woman opening like a door.
Many come in, but only she is bitch.
Empty, is filled, then empty as before.

There are two women, standing, and on each
Is smiled salvation or is howled damnation,
And, saved or damned, must still stay within reach.

Until the end,
When all are served, the sermons and the omens,
The preachers served, the children and the elders,
And still they come,
And still demand,
And still stand on her floor and ask for more.

And still the clipped wing leans against
Her eagle of experience.

[1952]


## I MET MY SOLITUDE

I met my Solitude. We two stood glaring.
I had to tremble, meeting him face to face.
Then he saying, and I with bent head hearing:
"You sent me forth to exile and disgrace,

"Most faithful of your friends, then most forsaken,
Forgotten in breast, in bath, in books, in bed.
To someone else you gave the gifts I gave you,
And you embraced another in my stead.

"Though we meet now, it is not of your choosing.
I am not fooled. And I do not forgive.
I am less kind, but did you treat me kindly?
In armored peace from now on let us live."

*  *  *

So did my poor hurt Solitude accuse me.
Little was left of good between us two.
And I drew back: "How can we stay together,
You jealous of me, and I laid waste by you?

"By you, who used to be my good provider,
My secret nourisher, and mine alone.
The strength you taught me I must use against you,
And now with all my strength I wish you gone."

Then he, my enemy, and still my angel,
Said in that harsh voice that once was sweet:
"I will come back, and every time less handsome,
And I will look like Death when last we meet."

[1988]


# MAY SWENSON, 1919–1989


## A DREAM

I was a god and self-enchanted
I stood in a cabinet in the living wood
The doors were carved with the sign of the lizard
whose eye unblinks on emptiness
whose head turns slower than a tooth grows

I wore a mask of skin-thin silver
My hair was frenzied foam stiffened to ice
My feet gloved in petals of imperishable flowers
were hoofs and colder than hammers

I lived by magic
A little bag in my chest held a whirling stone
so hot it was past burning
so radiant it was blinding
*  *  *

When the moon rose worn and broken
her face like a coin endlessly exchanged
in the hands of the sea
her ray fell upon the doors which opened
and I walked in the living wood
The leaves turned bronze and the moss to marble

At morning I came back to my cabinet
It was a tree in the daylight
the lizard a scroll of its bark

[1954]

## THE CENTAUR

The summer that I was ten—
Can it be there was only one
summer that I was ten? It must

have been a long one then—
each day I'd go out to choose
a fresh horse from my stable

which was a willow grove
down by the old canal.
I'd go on my two bare feet.

But when, with my brother's jackknife,
I had cut me a long limber horse
with a good thick knob for a head,

and peeled him slick and clean
except a few leaves for the tail,
and cinched my brother's belt

around his head for a rein,
I'd straddle and canter him fast
up the grass bank to the path,

trot along in the lovely dust
that talcumed over his hoofs,
hiding my toes, and turning

*  *  *
his feet to swift half-moons.
The willow knob with the strap
jouncing between my thighs

was the pommel and yet the poll
of my nickering pony's head.
My head and my neck were mine,

yet they were shaped like a horse.
My hair flopped to the side
like the mane of a horse in the wind.

My forelock swung in my eyes,
my neck arched and I snorted.
I shied and skittered and reared,

stopped and raised my knees,
pawed at the ground and quivered.
My teeth bared as we wheeled

and swished through the dust again.
I was the horse and the rider,
and the leather I slapped to his rump

spanked my own behind.
Doubled, my two hoofs beat
a gallop along the bank,

the wind twanged in my mane,
my mouth squared to the bit.
And yet I sat on my steed

quiet, negligent riding,
my toes standing the stirrups,
my thighs hugging his ribs.

At a walk we drew up to the porch.
I tethered him to a paling.
Dismounting, I smoothed my skirt
*  *  *

and entered the dusky hall.
My feet on the clean linoleum
left ghostly toes in the hall.

*Where have you been?* said my mother.
*Been riding,* I said from the sink,
and filled me a glass of water.

*What's that in your pocket?* she said.
*Just my knife.* It weighted my pocket
and stretched my dress awry.

*Go tie back your hair,* said my mother,
and *Why is your mouth all green?*
*Rob Roy, he pulled some clover
as we crossed the field*, I told her.

[1956]

Or they
should be
little horses
those wooden
sweet
old-fashioned
painted
rocking
horses

s
ng
the
motions
of men

the gladdest things in the toyroom

The
pegs
of their
ears
so familiar
and dear
to the trusting
fists
To be chafed

feelingly
and then
unfeelingly
To be
joyfully
ridden
rockingly
ridden until
the restored

egos dismount and the legs stride away

Immobile
sweetlipped
sturdy
and smiling
women
should always
be waiting

willing
to be set
into motion
Women
should be
pedestals
to men

[1968]

# FEEL ME

"Feel me to do right," our father said on his deathbed.
We did not quite know—in fact, not at all—what he meant.
His last whisper was spent as through a slot in a wall.
He left us a key, but how did it fit? "Feel me
to do right." Did it mean that, though he died, he would be felt
through some aperture, or by some unseen instrument
our dad just then had come to know? So, to do right always,
we need but feel his spirit? Or was it merely his apology
for dying? "Feel that I do right in not trying,
as you insist, to stay on your side. There is the wide
gateway and the splendid tower, and you implore me
to wait here, with the worms!"

Had he defined his terms, and could we discriminate
among his motives, we might have found out how to "do right"
before *we* died—supposing he felt he suddenly knew
what dying was. "You do wrong because you do not feel
as I do now," was maybe the sense. "Feel me, and emulate
my state, for I am becoming less dense—I am feeling right
for the first time." And then the vessel burst,
and we were kneeling around an emptiness.

We cannot feel our father now. His power courses through us,
yes, but *he*—the chest and cheek, the foot and palm,
the mouth of oracle—is calm. And we still seek
his meaning. "Feel me," he said, and emphasized that word.
Should we have heard it as a plea for a caress—
a constant caress, since flesh to flesh was all that we
could do right if we would bless him?
The dying must feel the pressure of that question—
lying flat, turning cold from brow to heel—the hot
cowards there above protesting their love, and saying,
"What can we do? Are you all right?" While the wall opens
and the blue night pours through. "What can we do?
We want to do what's right."

"Lie down with me, and hold me, tight. Touch me. Be
with me. Feel with me. *Feel* me to do right."

[1968]

# IN THE BODIES OF WORDS

*for Elizabeth Bishop (1911–1979)*

Tips of the reeds silver in sunlight. A cold wind
sways them, it hisses through quills of the pines.
Sky is clearest blue because so cold. Birds drop down
in the dappled yard: white breast of nuthatch, slate
catbird, cardinal the color of blood.

Until today in Delaware, Elizabeth, I didn't know
you died in Boston a week ago. How can it be
you went from the world without my knowing?
Your body turned to ash before I knew. Why was there
no tremor of the ground or air? No lightning flick
between our nerves? How can I believe? How grieve?

I walk the shore. Scraped hard as a floor by wind.
Screams of terns. Smash of heavy waves. Wind rips
the corners of my eyes. Salty streams freeze on my face.
A life is little as a dropped feather. Or split shell
tossed ashore, lost under sand. . . . But vision lives!
Vision, potent, regenerative, lives in bodies of words.
Your vision lives, Elizabeth, your words
from lip to lip perpetuated.

Two days have passed. Enough time, I think, for death
to be over. As if your death were not *before* my knowing.
For a moment I jump back to when all was well and ordinary.
Today I could phone to Boston, say Hello. . . . Oh, no!
Time's tape runs forward only. There is no replay.

Light hurts. Yet the sky is dull today. I walk the shore.
I meet a red retriever, young, eager, galloping
out of the surf. At first I do not notice his impairment.
His right hind leg is missing. Omens. . . .
I thought I saw a rabbit in the yard this morning.
It was a squirrel, its tail torn off. Distortions. . . .

Ocean is gray again today, old and creased aluminum
without sheen. Nothing to see on that expanse.
Except, far out, low over sluggish waves, a long

clotted black string of cormorants trails south.
Fog-gray rags of foam swell in scallops up the beach,
their outlines traced by a troupe of pipers—
your pipers, Elizabeth!—their racing legs like spokes
of tiny wire wheels.

Faintly the flying string can still be seen.
It swerves, lowers, touching the farthest tips of waves.
Now it veers, appears to shorten, points straight out.
It slips behind the horizon. Vanished.

But vision lives, Elizabeth. Your vision multiplies,
is magnified in the bodies of words.
Not vanished, your vision lives from eye to eye,
your words from lip to lip perpetuated.

[1979; 1987]

## IN LOVE MADE VISIBLE

In love are we made visible
As in a magic bath
are unpeeled
to the sharp pit
so long concealed

With love's alertness
we recognize
the soundless whimper
of the soul
behind the eyes
A shaft opens
and the timid thing
at last leaps to surface
with full-spread wing

The fingertips of love discover
more than the body's smoothness
They uncover a hidden conduit
for the transfusion
of empathies that circumvent
the mind's intrusion

*   *   *

In love are we set free
Objective bone
and flesh no longer insulate us
to ourselves alone
We are released
and flow into each other's cup
Our two frail vials pierced
drink each other up

[1991]

# PART II

*The Will to Change*

—ADRIENNE RICH

# AMY CLAMPITT, 1920–

## THE BURNING CHILD

> After a few hours' sleep, the father had a dream
> that his child was standing beside his bed,
> caught him by the arm and whispered reproachfully:
> "Father, don't you see I'm burning?"
> —FREUD, *The Interpretation of Dreams*

Dreamwork, the mnemonic flicker
of the wave of lost particulars—
whose dream, whose child, where, when, all lost
except the singed reprieve, its fossil ardor
burnished to a paradigm of grief,
half a century before the cattle cars,
the shunted parceling—*links, rechts*—
in a blaspheming parody of judgment
by the Lord of burning: the bush, the lava flow,
the chariot, the pillar. What is, even so,
whatever breathes but a reprieve, a risk,
a catwalk stroll between the tinder
and the nurture whose embrace is drowning?

The dream redacted cannot sleep; it whimpers
so relentlessly of lost particulars, I can't
help thinking of the dreamer as your father,
sent for by the doctors the night he said the *Sh'ma*
over the dim phoenix-nest of scars
you were, survivor
pulled from behind a blazing gas tank
that summer on the Cape, those many years
before we two, by a shuttlecock-and-battle-

dore, a dreamworklike accretion of nitwit
trouvées, were cozened into finding how
minute particulars might build themselves
into a house that almost looks substantial:
just as I think of how, years earlier,
the waves at Surfside on Nantucket, curveting
like herded colts, subsiding, turned
against my staggering thighs, a manacle
of iron cold I had to be pulled out of. Drowning,
since, has seemed a native region's ocean,
that anxiety whose further shores are lurid
with recurrences of burning.

The people herded from the cattle cars
first into barracks, then to killing chambers,
stripped of clothes, of names, of chattels—all those
of whom there would remain so few particulars:
I think of them, I think of how your mother's
people made the journey, and of how

                                    unlike
   my own forebears who made the journey,
   when the rush was on, aboard a crowded
   train from Iowa to California, where,
   hedged by the Pacific's lunging barricades,
   they brought into the world the infant
   who would one day be my father, and
   (or the entire astonishment, for me, of
   having lived until this moment would
   have drowned unborn, unburied without
   ever having heard of Surfside) chose
   to return, were free to stay or go
   back home, go anywhere at all—
                             not one
outlived the trip whose terminus was burning.

The catwalk shadows of the cave, the whimper
of the burning child, the trapped
reprieve of nightmare between the
tinder and the nurture whose
embrace is drowning.

                                                  [1985]

WRITTEN IN WATER

From a woman's dream of being,
at her age, still deemed desirable,
preserved—the quivering reliquary
of the dew of decades snared
among the fernery—till morning,

to wake in winter to this antic
glare—the Snow Queen's frore
boudoir, the numbed orthography
of being seen, its milkweed
smithereens turned every which way—

is still to listen for the seep
within the crypt, the mirror-
drip of stalactites, blind milk
of perpetuity whose only witness
is the viewless salamander.

[1986]


MEDUSA

The tentacles, the brazen phiz whose glare
stands every fibril of the mind on end—
lust looked at backward as it were,
an antique scare tactic, either self-protection
or a libel on the sex whose periodic
blossom hangs its ungathered garland
from the horned clockwork of the moon:
as cause or consequence, or both, hysteric
symptoms no doubt figure here. She'd been
a beauty till Poseidon, in a flagrant
trespass, closed with her on Athena's temple floor.

The tide-rip torrents in the blood, the dark
gods not to be denied—or a mere indiscretion?
Athena had no time at all for talk like this.
The sea-god might be her old rival, but the woman
he'd gone to bed with was the one who paid.

A virginal revenge at one remove—there's none more
sordid or more apt to ramify, as this one did:
the fulgent tresses roiled to water-snake-
like writhe, and for long lashes'
come-hither flutterings, the stare
that hardens the psyche's soft parts to rock.

The female ogre, for the Puritan
revisionists who took her over had a new
and siren sliminess. John Milton
put her at the gate of hell, *a woman to*
*the waist, and fair; but ended foul, in*
*many a scaly fold, voluminous and vast—*
whose name indeed was Sin. And in the den
of doctrine run amok, the armored glister
of a plodding Holiness revealed her
as likewise divided but, all told, *most*
*loathsome, filthy, foul, and full of vile disdain.*

The Gorgon, though, is no such Manichean tease,
no mantrap caterer of forbidden dishes,
whose lewd stews keep transgression warm.
The stinging jellyfish, the tubeworm,
the tunicate, the sea anemone's
whorled comb are privier to her mysteries:
her salts are cold, her home-
land Hyperborean (the realm that gave us
the Snow Queen and the English gentleman),
her mask the ravening aspect of the moon,
her theater a threshing floor that terror froze.

Terror of origins: the sea's heave, the cold mother
of us all; disdain of the allure that draws us in,
that stifles as it nurtures, that feeds on
what it feeds, on what it comforts, whether male
or female: ay, in the very tissue of desire
lodge viscid barbs that turn the blood to coral,
the heartbeat to a bed of silicates. What surgeon
can unthread those multiplicities of cause
of hurt from its effect; dislodge, spicule by spicule,

the fearful armories within; unclench the airless
petrifaction toward the core, the geode's rigor?

[1987]

AMHERST
     *May 15, 1987*

The oriole, a charred and singing coal,
still burns aloud among the monuments,
its bugle call to singularity the same
unheard (she wrote) as to the crowd,
this graveyard gathering, the audience
          she never had.

Fame has its own dynamic, its smolderings
and ignitions, its necessary distance:
Colonel Higginson, who'd braved the cannon,
admitted his relief not to live near such
breathless, hushed excess (you cannot
          fold a flood,

she wrote, and put it in a drawer), such
stoppered prodigies, compressions and
devastations within the atom—*all this*
*world contains: his face*—the civil
wars of just one stanza. A universe
          might still applaud,

the red at bases of the trees (she wrote)
like mighty footlights burn, God still
look on, his badge a raised hyperbole—
inspector general of all that carnage,
those gulfs, those fleets and crews
          of solid blood:

the battle fought between the soul and No
One There, no one at all, where cities
ooze away: unbroken prairies of air
without a settlement. On Main Street

the hemlock hedge grows up untrimmed,
        the light that poured

in once like judgment (whether it was noon
at night, or only heaven at noon, she wrote,
she could not tell) cut off, the wistful,
the merely curious, in her hanging dress discern
an ikon; her ambiguities are made a shrine,
        then violated;

we've drunk champagne above her grave, declaimed
the lines of one who dared not live aloud.
I thought of writing her (Dear Emily, though,
seems too intrusive, Dear Miss Dickinson too prim)
to ask, not without irony, what, wherever she
        is now, is made

of all the racket, whether she's of two minds
still; and tell her how on one cleared hillside,
an ample peace that looks toward Norwottuck's
unaltered purple has been shaken since
by bloodshed on Iwo Jima, in Leyte Gulf
        and Belleau Wood.

[1987; 1990]

## MAUDE MEEHAN, 1920 —

### IS THERE LIFE AFTER FEMINISM
*(or how to wear boots and still be politically incorrect)*

I like to wear boots.
I like the noise they make.
I walk real uppity in boots.
I walk strong.
If pressed
I can land a punch, a kick,
demolish a rapist,

and if I want to
I can go to bed in boots.

I cook without Tofu or eggplant
and I hate alfalfa sprouts. Call it heresy.
I hug my husband, my sons,
and send my daughter radical feminist literature.
I hug her too. I hug my gay friends,
and don't apologize for being straight.
I hug my friends of color
and won't apologize for being white.
How can we stand up together
if we're putting each other down?

I am a senior citizen.
There are advantages.
I get ten percent off on pancakes at Golden West
and a dollar off at the Nickelodeon.
Sometimes I wear lipstick, mascara
and don't ask anyone's pardon.
I wear a dress when I visit my mother.
She's ninety-six, I'm sixty-five.
Spare me your arguments. Where is it written
that any one of us has all the right answers
for anyone else?

I am a good citizen.
There are *dis*advantages.
I write to presidents and politicians
and they do what they want anyway.
I go to marches, to meetings, to jail,
and I have a file in Washington in my very own name
which I refuse to send for.
I know who I am.
Even when I do dishes, mind kids or wear high heels
I know who I am.
But what I like about wearing boots is,
there's no confusion.
*Everyone* knows who I am. Watch out!

[1985]

## GIFT FOR MY MOTHER'S 90TH BIRTHDAY

*Burcham Hospital*

We watched the rain sluice down
against the window of your sterile room
and listened as you told of childhood's
summer showers at the farm; how you ran out
a colt unpenned, into their sudden soaking bliss.

Now you, aged changeling mother,
emptied and clean as a cracked china cup
on the wrong shelf, whisper, "What I would give
to feel that rain pelt hard against my face."

But you had nothing left, so we
conspirators of love, locked the white door
and your granddaughter wheeled you to the bath
where we unclothed your little sack of bones
and lifted you beneath the shower.

She held you up, your legs pale stalks a-dangle
and clasped your wasted body, bracing her taut
young flesh to your slack folds.
And you clung laughing, joyous as a child
to feel the clear fresh rivulets
course down your upturned face.

[1991]


# MARIE PONSOT, 1921–

### AMONG WOMEN

What women wander?
Not many. All. A few.
Most would, now & then,
& no wonder.
Some, and I'm one,

118

Wander sitting still.
My small grandmother
Bought from every peddler
Less for the ribbons and lace
Than for their scent
Of sleep where you will,
Walk out when you want, choose
Your bread and your company.

She warned me, "Have nothing to lose."

She looked fragile but had
High blood, runner's ankles,
Could endure, endure.
She loved her rooted garden, her
Grand children, her once
Wild once young man.
Women wander
As best they can.

[1981]


## RESIDUAL PARALYSIS
### for June Jordan

I'm an unable woman who loves to dance
but my polio leg won't go, or will
awhile, until yanked by muscle cramps
that grip the ankle so it gives way
& locks twisted, perpendicular. And then
of course the damned thing's sprained, fat, blue, & wrong.

When I hear music I think nothing's wrong
that I can't manage, and I start to dance,
inside at first, smiling for the beat; then
the sound strides up my back & claims it will,
if I let it, float me safe all the way
on the long waves of high style nothing cramps.

So I'm a chump, surprised, betrayed by cramps,
ashamed to admit I have something wrong

until it's too late & rhythm drains away.
Let drop, I fall untuned outside the dance
insulted in the body of the will
to hold control, that cooled my fever then.

That I was sick, I kept half secret then.
Years of vanity, vain practice, vain cramps
got me walking even downstairs at will.
I valued that, my false claim, "Nothing's wrong!
(I can't press down a clutch and I can't dance
but) I'm not lame (not very, anyway)."

Lies have small voice where dancing has its way;
old true tales sweeten into the now of then
which is the breathing beat of every dance;
the wrecks & twists of history uncramp
into trust that present kindness can't go wrong
among warm partners of a common will.

I try. If I can stop lying, I will.
I'll claim my cramps & limit them that way,
trust & forget my history, right & wrong,
while others dance. I might, less vain than then,
forgive dead muscles & relax their cramps.
I can love dancing from outside the dance.

When trust uncramps the ordinary will
to laugh its way past accidental wrong,
those outside then step inside the dance.

[1981]

"LOVE IS NOT LOVE"
(for Elena Cornaro, first woman PhD, Padua, 1647;
and for those whose children are in pain here and now)

It is cold. I am
drawing my life around me to get warm.
Holes in the blanket can't be rewoven.
Some thorns caught in it still scratch. Some tear.
\* \* \*

I reach for comfort
to the left-out lives of women here and gone.
They lend them willingly. They know my need.
They do not hate me for crying. It beats despair.

Elena Cornaro
hands me her cinderella cap & gown.
I put them on. Stiff fur. But intact: she
(when eleven! just in time) saw

in a flash the mortal needles
their rain of cupidity
aimed at eyes across the looking air,

laughed and in singleness averted them
shielded by choice against the dart & steel.
She stopped herself in herself, refined
her will, and brought her mind virgin to bear

stretched across nine languages—nine sun-
keepers, their word-clusters grapes
of intellect, for wine
she pours me now.

It stings like speed:
PhD, TB, breath on fire, young,
she sported her doctoral vair
in vain. She too died of blood.
Yet the mind she trained
had warmed her in the storm
(all storms one storm) where
she'd left no hostage howling to be freed,
no captive mouths to feed;
in her sight, no punctual winter swarm
of guilt—pale bees whose attack breeds
paralysis, and dread of the snow
that masks the snare.
I am stuck in cold. It is deaf. It is eiron.

What has happened to my child
is worse than I can tell you

and I'm ashamed to say
is more than I can bear.

Elena, listen.
My body speaks nine languages but the greed
of me is stuck, my exposed eyes prickle,
I think blank, he's lost out there, I'm scared.

What I have borne, I bear.

Oh I praise your continence, kind life, pure form.
Your way's one way, not mine; you're summer-stopped;
my meadow's mud, turned stone in this icy air.

Whose fault is it? It's at the root my fault.
But in your cape, I come to?
and I'm in your care?
As he is mine, so I am yours to bear
alive. He is still alive. He has not died of it.
Wronged. Wrong.

Regardless love is hard to bear.
It has no hospital.
It is its own fireplace.
All it takes is care.

Well, when you grew intimate with pain,
what did you do. How did you do it. Where.
That, this? Thanks. Suppose I'm not in time,
is it worth a try. I'll try,

try to conceive of room to spare,
a surround of walls steady & steadying
an uncracked ceiling & a quiet floor,
a morning room, a still room
where we'd bring mind to bear upon
our consequences—we who make
no difference, who ignoring
absence of response have chosen
ways to love we can't go back on
and we won't,

regardless:
like your holy aura, Elena,
like your singleness, my fertility,
your tiny eminence, your early death;

like our Vassar Miller, her persistent listening;
like our Tillie Olsen, her persistent flowering;
like our Djuna and our Emily
their insolent beauty visored,
disguised as hermit crabs;
like our Sara Jewett's faithful gaze—
cast down—
like my long-drawn-out mistakes.

Elena maybe we
remember each other as room
for when to cry, what to cry for,
cry to whom.

[1988]

# MONA VAN DUYN, 1921–

## LEDA

> "Did she put on his knowledge with his power
> Before the indifferent beak could let her drop?"

Not even for a moment. He knew, for one thing, what he was.
When he saw the swan in her eyes he could let her drop.
In the first look of love men find their great disguise,
and collecting these rare pictures of himself was his life.

Her body became the consequence of his juice,
while her mind closed on a bird and went to sleep.
Later, with the children in school, she opened her eyes
and saw her own openness, and felt relief.

* * *

In men's stories her life ended with his loss.
She stiffened under the storm of his wings to a glassy shape,
stricken and mysterious and immortal. But the fact is,
she was not, for such an ending, abstract enough.

She tried for a while to understand what it was
that had happened, and then decided to let it drop.
She married a smaller man with a beaky nose,
and melted away in the storm of everyday life.

[1964]


LEDA RECONSIDERED

She had a little time to think
as he stepped out of water
that paled from the loss of his whiteness
and came toward her.
A certain wit in the way he
handled his webbed feet,
the modesty of the light that lay on him,
a perfectly clear, and unforgiveable,
irony in the cock of his head
told her more than he knew.
She sat there in the sunshine,
naked as a new-hatched bird,
watching him come,
trying to put herself
in the place of the cob, and see
what he saw:

flesh comfortable, used,
but still neatly following the bones,
a posture relaxed,
almost unseemly, expressing
(for the imagination,
unlike the poor body it strips and stirs,
is never assaulted)
openness, complicity even,
the look of a woman
with a context in which she can put

what comes next
(no chance of maiden's hysteria
if his beak pinched hold of her neck-skin,
yet the strangeness of the thing
could still startle her
into new gestures)
and something—a heaviness,
as if she could bear things,
or as if, when he fertilized her,
he were seeding the bank she sat on,
the earth in its aspect of
quiescence.

And now, how much would she try
to see, to take,
of what was not hers, of what
was not going to be offered?
There was that old story
of matching him change for change,
pursuing, and at the solstice
devouring him.
A man's story.
No, she was not that hungry
for experience. She had her loves.
To re-imagine her life—
as if the effort were muscular
she lifted herself a little
and felt the pull at neck
and shoulderblade, back
to the usual.
And suppose she reached with practiced arms
past the bird, short of the god,
for a vulnerable mid-point,
and held on,
just how short-sighted would that
be? Would the heavens in a flurry record
a major injustice to the world's
possibilities?

He took his time,
pausing to shake out a wing.

The arrogance of that gesture!
And yet she saw him
as the true god.
She saw, with mortal eyes
that stung at the sight,
the pain of his transformations,
which, beautiful or comic,
came to the world
with the risk of the whole self.
She saw what he had to work through
as he took, over and over,
the risk of love,
the risk of being held,
and saw to the bare heart
of his soaring, his journeying,
his wish for the world
whose arms he could enter in the image
of what is brave or golden.

To love with the whole imagination—
she had never tried.
Was there a form for that?
Deep, in her inmost, grubby
female center
(how could he know that,
in his airiness?)
lay the joy of being used,
and its heavy peace, perhaps,
would keep her down.
To give: women and gods
are alike in enjoying that ceremony,
find its smoke filling and sweet.
But to give up was an offering
only she could savor,
simply by covering
her eyes.

He was close to some uncommitted
part of her.
Her thoughts dissolved and
fell out of her body like dew

onto the grass of the bank,
the small wild flowers,
as his shadow,
the first chill of his ghostliness,
fell on her skin.
She waited for him so quietly that
he came on her quietly,
almost with tenderness,
not treading her.
Her hand moved into the dense plumes
on his breast to touch
the utter stranger.

[1964]


## THE STREAM

*for my mother*

Four days with you, my father three months dead.
You can't tell months from years, but you feel sad,

and you hate the nursing home. I've arranged a lunch
for the two of us, and somehow you manage to pinch

the pin from Madrid I bought you closed at the neck
of your best red blouse, put on new slacks, and take

off your crocheted slippers to put on shiny shoes,
all by yourself. "I don't see how you could close

that pin. You look so nice!" "Well, I tried and tried,
and worked till I got it. They didn't come," you said.

"Mother, I'm sorry, this is the wrong day,
our lunch is tomorrow. Here's a big kiss anyway

for dressing up for me. The nurse will come in
tomorrow and help you put on your clothes and pin."

"These last few days her mind has certainly cleared.
Of course the memory's gone," your doctor said.
\* \* \*

Next day they bathed you, fixed your hair and dressed
you up again, got a wheelchair and wheeled you past

the fat happy babbler of nonsense who rolled her chair
all day in the hall, the silent stroller who wore

a farmer's cap and bib overalls with rows
of safety pins on the bib, rooms of old babies

in cribs, past the dining hall, on down to a sunny
lounge in the other wing. "Where can I pee,

if I have to pee? I don't like it here, I'm afraid.
Where's my room? I'm going to faint," you said.

But they came with the lunch and card table and chairs
and bustled and soothed you and you forgot the fears

and began to eat. The white tablecloth, the separate
plate for salad, the silvery little coffee pot,

the covers for dishes must have made you feel
you were in a restaurant again after all

those shut-in years. (Dad would never spend the money,
but long ago you loved to eat out with me.)

You cleaned your soup bowl and dishes, one by one,
and kept saying, "This is fun! This is *fun!*"

The cake fell from your trembly fork, so I fed
it to you. "Do you want mine, too?" "Yes," you said,

"and I'll drink your milk if you don't want it." (You'd
lost twelve pounds already by refusing your food.)

I wheeled you back. "Well, I never did *that* before!
Thank you, Jane." "We'll do it again." "Way down *there,*"
\* \* \*

you marveled. You thanked me twice more. My eyes were wet.
"You're welcome, Mother. You'll have a good nap now, I'll bet."

I arranged for your old companion, who came twice a day,
to bring you milkshakes, and reached the end of my stay.

On the last night I helped you undress. Flat dugs
like antimacassars lay on your chest, your legs

and arms beetle-thin swung from the swollen belly
(the body no more misshapen, no stranger to see,

after all, at the end than at the beloved beginning).
You chose your flowered nightgown as most becoming.

You stood at the dresser, put your teeth away,
washed your face, smoothed on Oil of Olay,

then Avon night cream, then put Vicks in your nose,
then lay on the bed. I sat beside your knees

to say goodbye for a month. "You know I'll call
every Sunday and write a lot. Try to eat well—"

Tears stopped my voice. With a girl's grace you sat up
and, as if you'd done it lifelong, reached out to cup

my face in both your hands, and, as easily
as if you'd said it lifelong, you said, "Don't cry,

don't cry. You'll never know how much I love you."
I kissed you and left, crying. It felt true.

I forgot to tell them that you always sneaked your meat,
you'd bragged, to the man who ate beside you. One night

at home, my heart ringing with what you'd said,
then morning, when the phone rang to say you were dead.

I see your loving look wherever I go.
What is love? Truly I do not know.

* * *
Sometimes, perhaps, instead of a great sea,
it is a narrow stream running urgently

far below ground, held down by rocky layers,
the deeds of mother and father, helpless sooth-sayers

of how our life is to be, weighted by clay,
the dense pressure of thwarted needs, the replay

of old misreadings, by hundreds of feet of soil,
the gifts and wounds of the genes, the short or tall

shape of our possibilities, seeking
and seeking a way to the top, while above, running

and stumbling this way and that on the clueless ground,
another seeker clutches a dowsing-wand

which bends, then lifts, dips, then straightens, everywhere,
saying to the dowser, it is there, it is not there,

and the untaught dowser believes, does not believe,
and finally simply stands on the ground above,

till a sliver of stream finds a crack and makes its way,
slowly, too slowly, through rock and earth and clay.

Here at my feet I see, after sixty years,
the welling water—to which I add these tears.

[1982]

# LATE LOVING

*"What Christ was saying, what he meant {in the story of Mary and Martha} was that the pleasures of that hair, that ointment, must be taken. Because the accidents of death would deprive us soon enough. We must not deprive ourselves, our loved ones, of the luxury of our extravagant affections. We must not try to second-guess death by refusing to love the ones we loved. . . . "* —MARY GORDON, *Final Payments*

If in my mind I marry you every year
it is to calm an extravagance of love
with dousing custom, for it flames up fierce
and wild whenever I forget that we live
in double rooms whose temperature's controlled
by matrimony's turned-down thermostat.
I need the mnemonics, now that we are old,
of oath and law in re-memorizing that.
Our dogs are dead, our child never came true.
I might use up, in my weak-mindedness,
the whole human supply of warmth on you
before I could think of others and digress.
"Love" is finding the familiar dear.
"In love" is to be taken by surprise.
Over, in the shifty face you wear,
and over, in the assessments of your eyes,
you change, and with new sweet or barbed word
find out new entrances to my inmost nerve.
When you stand at the stove it's I who am most stirred.
When you finish work I rest without reserve.
Daytimes, sometimes, our three-legged race seems slow.
Squabbling onward, we chafe from being so near.
But all night long we lie like crescents of Velcro,
turning together till we re-adhere.
Since you, with longer stride and better vision,
more clearly see the finish line, I stoke
my hurrying self, to keep it in condition,
with light and life-renouncing meals of smoke.
As when a collector scoops two Monarchs in
at once, whose fresh flights to and from each other
are netted down, so in vows I re-imagine
I re-invoke what keeps us stale together.
What you try to give is more than I want to receive,
yet each month when you pick up scissors for our appointment
and my cut hair falls and covers your feet I believe
that the house is filled again with the odor of ointment.     [1992]

# GRACE PALEY, 1922–

## THE WOMEN IN VIETNAM

This is about the women of that country
sometimes they spoke in slogans
They said
   We patch the roads as we patch our sweetheart's trousers
   The heart will stop but not the transport
They said
   We have ensured production even near bomb craters
   Children let your voices sing higher than the explosions of the bombs
They said
   We have important tasks to teach the children
   that the people are the collective masters
   to bear hardship
   to instill love in the family
   to guide for good health of the children (they must
   wear clothing according to climate)
They said
   once men beat their wives
   now they may not
   once a poor family sold its daughter to a rich old man
   now the young may love one another
They said
   once we planted our rice any old way
   now we plant the young shoots in straight rows
   so the imperialist pilot can see how steady our
   hands are

In the evening we walked along the shores of the Lake of the Restored
   Sword
I said is it true? we are sisters?
They said, Yes, we are of one family

                                                [1973]

## THE SAD CHILDREN'S SONG

This house is a wreck said the children
when they came home with their children

Your papers are all over the place
The chairs are covered with books
and look brown leaves are piled on the floor
under the wandering Jews

Your face is a wreck said the children
when they came home with their children
There are lines all over your face
your necks like curious turtles
Why did you let yourself go?
Where are you going without us?

This world is a wreck said the children
When they came home with their children
There are bombs all over the place
There's no water    the fields are all poisoned
Why did you leave things like this
Where can we go said the children
what can we say to our children?

[1985]

ON MOTHER'S DAY

I went out walking
in the old neighborhood

Look! more trees on the block
forget-me-nots all around them
ivy    lantana shining
and geraniums in the window

Twenty years ago
it was believed that the roots of trees
would insert themselves into gas lines
then fall    poisoned on houses and children

or tap the city's water pipes
or starved for nitrogen    obstruct the sewers

In those days in the afternoon I floated
by ferry to Hoboken or Staten Island

then pushed the babies in their carriages
along the river wall    observing Manhattan
See Manhattan I cried    New York!
even at sunset it doesn't shine
but stands in fire    charcoal to the waist

But this Sunday afternoon on Mother's Day
I walked west    and came to Hudson Street    tri-colored flags
were flying over old oak furniture for sale
brass bedspreads    copper pots and vases
by the pound from India

Suddenly before my eyes    twenty-two transvestites
in joyous parade stuffed pillows
under their lovely gowns
and entered a restaurant
under a sign which said    All Pregnant Mothers Free

I watched them place napkins over their bellies
and accept coffee and zabaglione

I am especially open to sadness and hilarity
since my father died as a child
one week ago in this his ninetieth year

[1985]

IN AIX

The doves    the speckled doves
are cooing in French    in high
female French    the shutters
clatter against their latches

The rain is the rain of Aix a-
wash in old paintings of
marsh and mist by Granet the rain
splashes the shutters the rain is

bathed in the clouds of Chernobyl
last night on the evening
news we heard how nightingales

blowing north from Poland
folded their wings    fell over
the border and died in Germany

[1989]


# SHIRLEY KAUFMAN, 1923–

## MOTHERS, DAUGHTERS

Through every night we hate,
preparing the next day's
war. She bangs the door.
Her face laps up my own
despair, the sour, brown eyes,
the heavy hair she won't
tie back. She's cruel,
as if my private meanness
found a way to punish us.
We gnaw at each other's
skulls. Give me what's mine.
I'd haul her back, choking
myself in her, herself
in me. There is a book
called *Poisons* on her shelf.
Her room stinks with incense,
animal turds, hamsters
she strokes like silk. They
exercise on the bathroom
floor, and two drop through
the furnace vent. The whole
house smells of the accident,
the hot skins, the small
flesh rotting. Six days
we turn the gas up then
to fry the dead. I'd fry
her head if I could until
she cried love, love me!
*   *   *

All she won't let me do.
Her stringy figure in
the windowed room shares
its thin bones with no one.
Only her shadow on the glass
waits like an older sister.
Now she stalks, leans forward,
concentrates merely on getting
from here to there. Her feet
are bare. I hear her breathe
where I can't get in. If I
break through to her, she will
drive nails into my tongue.

[1969]


APPLES

No use waiting for it to stop
raining in my face like a wet towel,
having to catch a plane,
to pick the apples from her tree
and bring them home.

The safest place to be
is under the branches. She
in her bed and her mouth
dry in the dry room.
Don't go out in the rain.

I stretch my arms for apples
anyway, feel how the ripe ones
slide in my hands like cups
that want to be perfect. Juices
locked up in the skin.

She used to slice them in quarters,
cut through the core,
open the inside out. Fingers
steady on the knife, expert
at stripping things.
*   *   *

Sometimes she split them sideways
into halves to let a star break
from the center with tight seeds,
because I wanted that,
six petals in the flesh.

Flavor of apples inhaled as flowers,
not even biting them.
Apples at lunch or after school
like soup, a fragrance rising
in the steam, eat and be well.

I bring the peeled fruit to her
where she lies, carve it
in narrow sections, celery white,
place them between her fingers,
Mother, eat. And be well.

Sit where her brown eyes
empty out the light, watching
her mind slip backwards
on the pillow, swallowing
apples, swallowing her life.

[1970]

DÉJÀ VU

Whatever they wanted for their sons
will be wanted forever, success,
the right wife, they should be
good to their mothers.

One day they meet at the rock
where Isaac was cut free
at the last minute. Sarah stands
with her shoes off under the dome
showing the tourists with their Minoltas
around their necks the place
where Mohammed flew up to heaven.
Hagar is on her knees
in the women's section praying.

*  *  *

They bump into each other at the door,
the dark still heavy on their backs
like the future always coming after them.
Sarah wants to find out what happened
to Ishmael but is afraid to ask.
Hagar's lips make a crooked seam
over her accusations.

They know that the world is flat,
and if they move to the edge
they're sure to fall over. They know
they can only follow their own feet
the way they came.
Jet planes fly over their heads
as they walk out of each other's lives
like the last time, silent, not mentioning
the angels of god and the bright
miracles of birth and water. Not telling
that the boys are gone.

The air ticks slowly. It's August
and the heat is sick of itself
waiting all summer for rain.

Sarah is in her cool villa.
She keeps her eyes on the pot
so it won't boil over.
She brings the food to the table
where he's already seated
reading the afternoon paper
or listening to the news,
the common corruptions they don't
even speak about now.
Guess who I met she says talking
across the dessert.

Hagar shops in the market.
There's a run on chickens, the grapes
are finished and the plums are soft.
She fills her bag with warm bread

fresh from the oven thinking
there's nothing to forgive,
I got what I wanted
from the old man.
The flight in the wilderness
is a morning stroll.
She buys a kilo of ripe figs. She
climbs the dusty path home.

[1984]


## NOTES TO MY DAUGHTERS

You were the reason for staying.
It's always the children who leave,
not the mother. It was the end
of winter, isn't that always
the best time. Freesias suddenly
out of the mud, little milk teeth,
plum trees unbuttoned and the sky
on the Bayshore freeway to the airport
lined with blue tile.

Do you feel abandoned,
now you are women?


From the ridge of our mountain
we can see the Judean wilderness
slide to the bottom of the world.


Sometimes the parched air ripples
with dust as if everyone's beating
carpets and the shudder of wind
is like nervous laughter out of the caves.


It's all getting smaller and farther.
The earth wears a thin green fuzz
where the sheep graze
stubby in the distance as if
they were cut out and pasted there.

\*   \*   \*

I've learned what he knows,
how to tell sonic booms from the others.
To mean what we say.

First thing in the morning
in the Valley of the Cross
when the night is still drying
on the leaves and the red poppies
stand up straight
as if pulled by strings,

a man balances on his head
in the wet grass, we're behind
two Ethiopian joggers
and a woman walking her boxer.

The rest of it empty
like the future no one plans for.


There's an overwrought smell of jasmine,
tiny wax flowers, wiry stems
around the railing of our balcony.
Too tame to fly, the vines
catch on and keep climbing.

Scent of my old life, where the light
falls back of my shoulders
into your day.


If not for the three of you, if not
for the two of us,
if not for my cousin's strawberry jam
at breakfast and a woodpecker
attacking our jacaranda
outside the kitchen window, drilling
so loud we don't hear
the seven o'clock news, if not

for persimmons and the first
green oranges we wait for
and the small hard peaches
that arrive in the market in April,
if not for the ripening
when we expect it, bulbs
of new garlic spread out to dry
just when the old garlic's rotting,
if not for Mary's latest recipes,
meat loaf with carrots and cumin
and fennel soup, and Mussa's
bottles of green-gold oil
from his olive trees in Beit Safafa,
and the crested larks, little tan females
singing their hearts out on both sides
of the green line, if not for
the bulbul's five purple eggs,
and all the glad birds on Yom Kippur
praising the parked cars
in the empty streets and the prayers
of the ones who keep praying,
if not for the archaeologist unlocking
the safe in the museum to show us
the yellowed bone, the rusty nail
still hammered through the heel,
if not for the gilded dome and the silver dome
balloons and bells
and the muezzin calling, peace
marches around the Old City wall and me
on the ramparts following my body,
if not for the two of us, waves
of white surf breaking
over the hawthorne's arthritic limbs,
if not for what flickers as joy
in the middle of grieving,
what could I say when you ask me
whether I'm happy.


One day I'll look up at the hills
and they won't be there. Lately

I think about my death.
It keeps me connected to the world.

I wonder if you'll come
to put little stones on me
the way Jews do to keep the unliving
where they belong.


I wish I could learn how
to strike matches in the wind
so they won't go out in my cupped hand.
I wish I could peel an orange
in one long ribbon that doesn't break.
I wish you were with me
in this hard land waiting for the first rain
after a long dry season
when the sky tilts and spills over
making a fresh start,
stirring the dust into muddy trickles,
clearing everything but not
washing it away.

[1993]


# DENISE LEVERTOV, 1923–


## TO THE SNAKE

Green Snake, when I hung you round my neck
and stroked your cold, pulsing throat
            as you hissed to me, glinting
arrowy gold scales, and I felt
            the weight of you on my shoulders,
and the whispering silver of your dryness
            sounded close at my ears—

Green Snake—I swore to my companions that certainly
            you were harmless! But truly

I had no certainty, and no hope, only desiring
　　　　　to hold you, for that joy,
　　　　　　　　　　which left
a long wake of pleasure, as the leaves moved
and you faded into the pattern
of grass and shadows, and I returned
smiling and haunted, to a dark morning.

　　　　　　　　　　　　　　　　[1958]


HYPOCRITE WOMEN

Hypocrite women, how seldom we speak
of our own doubts, while dubiously
we mother man in his doubt!

And if at Mill Valley perched in the trees
the sweet rain drifting through western air
a white sweating bull of a poet told us

our cunts are ugly—why didn't we
admit we have thought so too? (And
what shame? They are not for the eye!)

No, they are dark and wrinkled and hairy,
caves of the Moon . . .　　　And when a
dark humming fills us, a

coldness towards life,
we are too much women to
own to such unwomanliness.

Whorishly with the psychopomp
we play and plead—and say
nothing of this later.　　　And our dreams,

with what frivolity we have pared them
like toenails, clipped them like ends of
split hair.

　　　　　　　　　　　　　　　　[1962]


143

# IN MIND

There's in my mind a woman
of innocence, unadorned but

fair-featured, and smelling of
apples or grass. She wears

a utopian smock or shift, her hair
is light brown and smooth, and she

is kind and very clean without
ostentation—
                    but she has
no imagination.
                    And there's a
turbulent moon-ridden girl

or old woman, or both,
dressed in opals and rags, feathers

and torn taffeta,
who knows strange songs—

but she is not kind.

                                                [1962]

# STEPPING WESTWARD

What is green in me
darkens, muscadine.

If woman is inconstant,
good, I am faithful to

ebb and flow, I fall
in season and now

is a time of ripening.
If her part

\* \* \*
is to be true,
a north star,

good, I hold steady
in the black sky

and vanish by day,
yet burn there

in blue or above
quilts of cloud.

There is no savor
more sweet, more salt

than to be glad to be
what, woman,

and who, myself,
I am, a shadow

that grows longer as the sun
moves, drawn out

on a thread of wonder.
If I bear burdens

they begin to be remembered
as gifts, goods, a basket

of bread that hurts
my shoulders but closes me

in fragrance. I can
eat as I go.

                                    [1966]

The disasters numb within us
caught in the chest, rolling
in the brain like pebbles. The feeling
resembles lumps of raw dough

weighing down a child's stomach on baking day.
Or Rilke said it, "My heart . . .
Could I say of it, it overflows
with bitterness . . . but no, as though

its contents were simply balled into
formless lumps, thus
do I carry it about."
The same war

continues.
We have breathed the grits of it in, all our lives,
our lungs are pocked with it,
the mucous membrane of our dreams
coated with it, the imagination
filmed over with the gray filth of it:

the knowledge that humankind,

delicate Man, whose flesh
responds to a caress, whose eyes
are flowers that perceive the stars,

whose music excels the music of birds,
whose laughter matches the laughter of dogs,
whose understanding manifests designs
fairer than the spider's most intricate web,

still turns without surprise, with mere regret
to the scheduled breaking open of breasts whose milk
runs out over the entrails of still-alive babies,
transformation of witnessing eyes to pulp-fragments,
implosion of skinned penises into carcass-gulleys.
*   *   *

We are the humans, men who can make;
whose language imagines *mercy,*
*lovingkindness;* we have believed one another
mirrored forms of a God we felt as good—

who do these acts, who convince ourselves
it is necessary; these acts are done
to our own flesh; burned human flesh
is smelling in Viet Nam as I write.

Yes, this is the knowledge that jostles for space
in our bodies along with all we
go on knowing of joy, of love;

our nerve filaments twitch with its presence
day and night,
nothing we say has not the husky phlegm of it in the saying,
nothing we do has the quickness, the sureness,
the deep intelligence living at peace would have.

[1968]

## AN EMBROIDERY (I)

Rose Red's hair is brown as fur
and shines in firelight as she prepares
supper of honey and apples, curds and whey,
for the bear, and leaves it ready
on the hearth-stone.

Rose White's gray eyes
look into the dark forest.

Rose Red's cheeks are burning,
sign of her ardent, joyful
compassionate heart.
Rose White is pale,
turning away when she hears
the bear's paw on the latch.

When he enters, there is
frost on his fur,

he draws near to the fire
giving off sparks.

Rose White catches the scent of the forest,
of mushrooms, of rosin.

Together Rose Red and Rose White
sing to the bear;
it is a cradle song, a loom song,
a song about marriage, about
a pilgrimage to the mountains
long ago.
        Raised on an elbow,
the bear stretched on the hearth
nods and hums; soon he sighs
and puts down his head.

He sleeps; the Roses
bank the fire.
Sunk in the clouds of their feather bed
they prepare to dream.

Rose Red in a cave that smells of honey
dreams she is combing the fur of her cubs
with a golden comb.
Rose White is lying awake.

Rose White shall marry the bear's brother.
Shall he too
when the time is ripe,
step from the bear's hide?
Is that other, her bridegroom,
here in the room?

[1971]


A WOMAN ALONE

When she cannot be sure
which of two lovers it was with whom she felt
this or that moment of pleasure, of something fiery
streaking from head to heels, the way the white

flame of a cascade streaks a mountainside
seen from a car across a valley, the car
changing gear, skirting a precipice,
climbing . . .
When she can sit or walk for hours after a movie
talking earnestly and with bursts of laughter
with friends, without worrying
that it's late, dinner at midnight, her time
spent without counting the change . . .
When half her bed is covered with books
and no one is kept awake by the reading light
and she disconnects the phone, to sleep till noon . . .
Then
selfpity dries up, a joy
untainted by guilt lifts her.
She has fears, but not about loneliness;
fears about how to deal with the aging
of her body—how to deal
with photographs and the mirror. She feels
so much younger and more beautiful
than she looks. At her happiest
—or even in the midst of
some less than joyful hour, sweating
patiently through a heatwave in the city
or hearing the sparrows at daybreak, dully gray,
toneless, the sound of fatigue—
a kind of sober euphoria makes her believe
in her future as an old woman, a wanderer,
seamed and brown,
little luxuries of the middle of life all gone,
watching cities and rivers, people and mountains,
without being watched; not grim nor sad,
an old winedrinking woman, who knows
the old roads, grass-grown, and laughs to herself . . .
She knows it can't be:
that's Mrs. Doasyouwouldbedoneby from

                                   *The Water Babies,*

no one can walk the world any more,
a world of fumes and decibels.
But she thinks maybe
she could get to be tough and wise, some way,

anyway. Now at least
she is past the time of mourning,
now she can say without shame or deceit,
O blessed Solitude.

[1978]


## THE LONG WAY ROUND
*for Alice Walker and Carolyn Taylor*


### I

"The solution," they said to my friend,
"lies in eventual total"—they said (or "final"?),
"assimilation. Miscegeny. No more trouble—"
                    *Disappear,* they said.

I in America,
            white, an
                        indistinguishable mixture
of Kelt and Semite, grown under glass
in a British greenhouse, a happy
old-fashioned artist, sassy and free,

had to lean in yearning towards
the far-away daughters and sons of
Vietnamese struggle
before I could learn,
                    begin to learn,
by Imagination's slow ferment,
what it is to awaken
each day Black in White America,
each day struggling
                    to affirm
a who-I-am my white skin never
has to pay heed to.
                    Who I am
slowly, slowly
            took lessons
from distant Asia; and only then
from near-as-my-hand persons, Black sisters.

150

Pushing open my mind's
door on its grating hinges
to let in the smell of
pain, of destroyed
flesh, to know

                for one instant's agony,
                insisted on for the sake of knowing
                anything, anything at all
                in truth,
that that flesh belonged
to one's own most dear,
child, or lover, or mother—

pushing open my door I began
to know who I was and
who I was not.
And slowly—for though
it's in a flash we
know we know,
yet before that flash there's a long
slow, dull, movement of fire
along the well-hidden
line of the fuse—

I came to know,
              in the alembic
of grief and will and love,
just barely to know, by knowing
it never
      ever
          would be what I could
know in the flesh,

what it must be to wake each day
to the sense of one's own beautiful
human skin, hair, eyes, one's
whole warm sleep-caressed body
as something that others

hated,
     hunted,
          haunted by its otherness,
something they wanted to see disappear.


### III

Swimming, we are, all of us, swimming
in the rectangular indoor claustrophobic pool
—echoing, sharply smelling of chlorine,
stinging our eyes—
that is
our life,

     where,
       scared and put off our stroke
       but righting ourselves with a gasp
          sometimes we touch
an Other,
       another
breathing and gasping body,
"yellow," but not yellow at all,
"black," but most often
brown; shaped like ourselves, bodies we could
embrace in relief, finding
ourselves not alone in the water.

           And someone,
            some fool of a coach,
strutting the pool's edge, wading
the shallow end, waves his arms at us,
shouting,
     "If you're White
     *you* have
     the right of way!"

           While we
swim for dear life, all of us—"not,"
as it has been said, "*not* waving,
but drowning."

[1978]

# JULIA RANDALL, 1923–

## TO WILLIAM WORDSWORTH FROM VIRGINIA

I think, old bone, the world's not with us much.
I think it is too difficult to see.
But easy to discuss. Behold the bush.
His seasons out-maneuver Proteus.
This year, because of the drought, the barberry
Is all goldflakes in August, but I'll still say
To the First Grade next month, "*Now* it is Fall.
You see the leaves go bright, and then go small.
You see October's greatcoat. It is gold.
It will lie on the earth to keep the seed's foot warm.
Then, Andrew Obenchain, what happens in June?"
And Andrew, being mountain-bred, will know
Catawba runs too deep for the bus to get
Across the ford—at least it did last May,
And school was out, and the laundry wouldn't dry,
And when the creek went down, the bluebells lay
In Hancock's pasture-border, thick as hay.

What do they tell the First Grade in Peru,
I wonder? All the story: God is good,
He counts the children, and the sparrow's wing.
God loved William Wordsworth in the spring.
William Wordsworth had enough to eat.
Wye was his broth, Helvellyn was his meat,
And English was his cookstove. And where did words
Come from, Carlyle Rucker? Words that slide
The world together. Words that split the tide
Apart for Moses (not for Mahon's bus),
Words that say, the bushes burn for us—
Lilac, forsythia, orange, Sharon rose—
For us the seasons wheel, the lovers wait,
All things become the flesh of our delight,
The evidence of our wishes.

                            Witch, so might
I stand beside the barberry and dream

Wisdom to babes, and health to beggar men,
And help to David hunting in the hills
The Appalachian fox. By words, I might.
But, sir, I am tired of living in a lake
Among the watery weeds and weedy blue
Shadows of flowers that Hancock never grew.
I am tired of my wet wishes, of running away
Like all the nymphs, from the droughty eye of day.
Run, Daphne. Run, Europa, Io, run!
There is not a god left underneath the sun
To balk, to ride, to suffer, to obey.
Here is the unseasonable barberry.
Here is the black face of a child in need.
Here is the bloody figure of a man.
Run, Great Excursioner. Run if you can.

[1961]


RECIPES

When, late from France, I introduced
quiches to the campus, they became so common
I felt compelled to change my specialty.
It couldn't be cassoulet; you couldn't get
The Toulouse sausages. It couldn't be langoustines.
How often I wish
Americans could learn to grow crawfish.

Of course I gave my recipes away.
Last night I gave Esterlee
the zucchini casserole, and she'll give it to Jessie,
and so it goes. No keeping a secret. I may revert
to Maryland chicken and angel cake. The fit survive,
and the raw materials
don't change much in a lifetime, but they change:
there was no tea at Stonehenge. It's hard to think back—
no beans, no wheat—
but somehow there was always something to eat.
So much is fixed, but how it's mixed
with foreign influence, like wars,
weather, and trade winds, genes
and genius, who's to tell?

I poach the flounder in my mother's dish.
The scholars say my mother was a fish.
The strict constructionists say man
strutted on two legs of his own
all around Eden. Maybe he did,
sharing his recipe with only God, and his spare rib
with woman.

She found apples
good eating. Naturally she shared.
She discovered blood,
guts, seasonings; how to make stock; how best to grow
salads and sesames; and how to raise
bread. One son discovered how to raise the dead
but he never told.

Now she grows old, beyond experiment.
The harvests shrivel; hands are obsolete
in the modern kitchen, simples in the sickroom.
Her traveling grandchildren have much to learn
in secret space, where the bright planets turn
ocean, perhaps, come shore, come kitchen garden.

[1987]

A VALEDICTION

In the great shade of August, under the sycamores,
if it is hard to imagine Piedmont without trees,
think of Sahara, or the Hebrides.

Yet they are coming down,
the German woods, and templed Oregon;
deep in the Gros Ventre, and the Amazon,
the chain saws buzz like locusts all day long.

Where did pollution enter: acid rain,
base power? Caryatids cannot keep;
the Law and Prophets smolder on the heap
like California. We are left
whatever tinder memory can heft.
The very stuff of cells

forgets the fire, the glacier, the sea-swells,
sweet-breathing air, and finally ripe earth.
Nature and Liberty uphold a weight
like chastity—too grave, too great.

So poets enter, and forbid to mourn,
since by division we grew
into ourselves, and growing die,
still wanting our reunion
with earth or sea or sky. What planetary dust
made Cain the first contender for our meat,
saw Babylon and Rome fall out,
saw Donatello and Mozart? saw trees?
I shy at purposes,
and shriveling, like the branch of Noah's dove,
praise passengers like leaves of love.

[1987]

## MITSUYE YAMADA, 1923–

### HOMECOMING
#### *from Tillie Olsen*

I widow
redo my life
scratch out lies
lie buried inside
the house all the time
sorrows my nights
cries still survive.

You child
chide me too
often look cross
eye not see me cry
alone widow after thirty-five
years have final right to live.

\*    \*    \*
My first born your brother
all the time in my arms
cry his scrotum swell
screech in my ears
I cry alone
no sleep for me.

My second born
a son too
sickly brothers
born so close
together we cry
there was no one
else.

I was sick with you
soon to come
Papa say go home
to your mother in Japan
you born there
but my boys need me at home
in America
I must leave you there
with wet nurse
we send for you
later nothing else to do.

You only a girl
do not know what I suffer
you blame me too
much sickness in you
when you come home to us
we take you to hospital
at home I have two sons
your father and no help
no night nurse I
stay up with you
whine after me
when I leave.
\*    \*    \*

Loving you
could not know
what pains to live
without love
my friend kill
herself hang
her family with eight children
don't know
how she could
do it for good reason
I think of her often
bring me comfort.

So little you run
home everyday after school
because there you hope
to find Mama
alive.

[1976]

## THE NIGHT BEFORE GOOD-BYE

Mama is mending
my underwear
while my brothers sleep.
Her husband taken away by the FBI
one son lured away by the Army
now another son and daughter
lusting for the free world outside.
She must let go.
The war goes on.
She will take one still small son
and join Papa in internment
to make a family.
Still sewing
squinting in the dim light
in room C barrack 4 block 4
she whispers
Remember
keep your underwear
in good repair

in case of accident
don't bring shame
on us.

[1976]

## THE CLUB

He beat me with the hem of a kimono
worn by a Japanese woman
this prized
painted
wooden statue
carved to perfection
in Japan or maybe Hong Kong.

She was usually on display
in our living room atop his bookshelf
among his other overseas treasures
I was never to touch.
She posed there most of the day
her head tilted
her chin resting lightly
on the white pointed fingertips
of her right hand
her black hair
piled high on her head
her long slim neck bared
to her shoulders.
An invisible hand
under the full sleeve
clasped her kimono
close to her body
its hem flared
gracefully around her feet.

That hem
made fluted red marks
on these freckled arms
my shoulders
my back.
That head

inside his fist
made camel
bumps
on his knuckles.
I prayed for her
that her pencil thin neck
would not snap
or his rage would be unendurable.
She held fast for me
didn't even chip or crack.

One day, we were talking
as we often did the morning after.
Well, my sloe-eyed beauty, I said
have you served him enough?
I dared to pick her up with one hand
I held her gently by the flowing robe
around her slender legs.
She felt lighter than I had imagined.
I stroked her cold thighs
with the tips of my fingers
and felt a slight tremor.

I carried her into the kitchen and wrapped her
in two sheets of paper towels
We're leaving
I whispered
you and I
together.

I placed her
between my clothes in my packed suitcase.
That is how we left him
forever.

[1989]

# JANE COOPER, 1924–

## THE KNOWLEDGE THAT COMES
## THROUGH EXPERIENCE

I feel my face being bitten by the tides
Of knowledge as sea-tides bite at a beach;
Love leaves its implications, wars encroach
On the flat white square between my ear and jaw
Picking it as the sea hollows out sand. . . .
I might as well stick my head in the maw

Of the ocean as live this generously:
Feelings aside I never know my face.
I comb my hair and what I see is timeless,
Not a face at all but (besides the hair)
Lips and a pair of eyes, two hands, a body
Pale as a fish imprisoned in the mirror.

When shall I rest, when shall I find myself
The way I'll be, iced in a shop window?
Maybe I'll wake tonight in the undertow
Of sleep and lie adrift, gutted helpless
By the salt at my blue eyes—then the gulfs
Of looks and desire will shine clean at last.

Meanwhile I use myself. I am useful
Rather foolishly, like a fish who yearns
Dimly towards daylight. There is much to learn
And curiosity riddles our rewards.
It seems to me I may be capable
Once I'm a skeleton, of love and wars.

[1950; 1973]

## WAITING

My body knows it will never bear children.
What can I say to my body now,
this used violin?

Every night it cries out strenuously
from its secret cave.

Old body, old friend,
why are you so unforgiving?

Why are you so stiff and resistant,
clenched around empty space?
An instrument is not a box.

But suppose you are an empty box?
Suppose you are like that famous wooden music hall in Troy,
                    New York,
waiting to be torn down,
where the orchestras love to play?

Let compassion breathe in and out of you,
filling you and
singing

                                        [1971]


HOTEL DE DREAM

                    *Justice-keepers! justice-keepers!*
                    *for Muriel Rukeyser and James Wright*

Suppose we could telephone the dead.
Muriel, I'd say, can you hear me?
Jim, can you talk again?

And I'd begin to tell them the stories they loved to hear:
how my father, as a young boy, watched Cora Crane
parade through the streets of Jacksonville with her girls
in an open barouche with silver fittings;
how the bay haunches gleamed as they twitched off flies,
polished hooves fetched down smartly into the dust,
ostrich feathers tickled the palates of passers-by.

Muriel, I'd say, shall we swing along Hudson Street
underneath the highway and walk out together on the docks?
* * *

. . . the river would be glittering, my grandmother
would be bargaining
with a black man on a dock in Jacksonville;
grapefruit and oranges would be piled up like cannonballs
at the fort in Old St. Augustine . . .

I'll never put you in a nursing home, you said early that year,
I promise, Jane, I'll never put you in a nursing home.

Later Cora Crane showed her dogs right next to my aunt's.
They had a good conversation about bloodlines
amidst the clean smells of kennel shavings and well-brushed dog
but never, of course, met socially
although she had dined with Henry James.

Jim, I'd say, remember that old poem "The Faithful"
you helped me by caring for? how what we owe to the dead
is to go on living? More than ever
I want to go on living.

But now you have become part of it, friends of my choosing years,
friends whose magnificent voices
will reverberate always, if only through machines,
tell me how to redress the past,
how to relish yet redress
my sensuous, precious, upper-class,
unjust white child's past.

[1990]

Note: Cora Crane, the common-law wife of Stephen Crane, both before and after their liter-
ary life together in England, ran a bawdy house in Jacksonville, Florida, called Hotel de
Dream.

# VASSAR MILLER, 1924–

## SPINSTER'S LULLABY
### *For Jeff*

Clinging to my breast, no stronger
Than a small snail snugly curled,
Safe a moment from the world,
Lullaby a little longer.

Wondering how one tiny human
Resting so, on toothpick knees
In my scraggly lap, gets ease,
I rejoice, no less a woman

With my nipples pinched and dumb
To your need whose one word's sucking.
Never mind, though. To my rocking
Nap a minute, find your thumb

While I gnaw a dream and nod
To the gracious sway that settles
Both our hearts, imperiled petals
Trembling on the pulse of God.

[1960]

## TRIMMING THE SAILS

I move among my pots and pans
That have no life except my own,
Nor warmth save from my flesh and bone,
That serve my tastes and not a man's.

I'm jealous of each plate and cup,
Frail symbol of my womanhood.
Creator-like, I call it good
And vow I will not give it up.

I move among my things and think
Of Woolman, who, for loving care

He had for slaves, used wooden ware,
And wash my silver in the sink,

Wishing my knives and forks were finer.
Though Lady Poverty won heart
Of Francis, her male counterpart
Would find in me a sad decliner.

Sometimes regret's old dogs will hound me
With feeble barks, yet my true love
Is Brother Fire and Sister Stove
And walls and friends and books around me.

Yet to renounce your high romances
Being part pain—may so to do
Prove half humility that you
May bless, good Woolman and sweet Francis!

[1960]

## ON APPROACHING MY BIRTHDAY

My mother bore me in the heat of summer
when the grass blanched under sun's hammer stroke
and the birds sang off key, panting between notes,
and the pear trees once all winged with whiteness
sagged, breaking with fruit, and only the zinnias,
like harlots, bloomed out vulgar and audacious,
and when the cicadas played all day long
their hidden harpsichords accompanying
her grief, my mother bore me, as I say,
then died shortly thereafter, no doubt
of her disgust and left me her disease
when I grew up to wither into truth.

[1968]

## SUBTERFUGE

I remember my father, slight,
staggering in with his Underwood,
bearing it in his arms like an awkward bouquet

\* \* \*

for his spastic child who sits down
on the floor, one knee on the frame
of the typewriter, and holding her left wrist

with her right hand, in that precision known
to the crippled, pecks at the keys
with a sparrow's preoccupation.

Falling by chance on rhyme,    novel and curious bubble
blown with a magic pipe, she tries them over and over,
spellbound by life's clashing in accord or against itself,

pretending pretense and playing at playing,
she does her childhood backward as children do,
her fun a delaying action against what she knows.

My father must lose her, his runaway on her treadmill,
will lose the terrible favor that life has done him
as she toils at tomorrow, tensed at her makeshift toy.

[1981]

## PRAYER TO MY MUSE

The door is closing

where ghosts hide,
where gods hide,
where even I hide.

I'm none too sorry,
longing to be back
coiled in my wombworld,

too smug and small, I know,
no wider than my bed
where no one sleeps but me.

Still, crack the door a little,
stepmother muse to show
a night light burning.

[1981]

## A MOURNING

I could be eased easier than the apple Eve
took from the tree untugged only touched and the
tender places open up offering all to a whisper
of flesh to a murmur of skin against skin to
delicacies dancing together.

You could be held for the holding lighter than leaves
touching like fingertips taking the pick of you
yielding wherever one would wandering over these
smooth joys of eyelid, tissue surrounding mouth
hollow of breast down slipping down toward tongue's
softest bruising.

We could be pilfered picked each in clean sight of the
other, one naked as bellies kissing needing no bridge
of a breath every space between them this night
narrowed to nothing, how much leaner than hounds how
much hungrier for the bones of thin human love.

Yet now we sleep safe from the nag and nudge of desire
smug as two corpses laid out drained of their sundry
fluids their pallidness painted and prettied up by the
smirking proprieties rubbing their hands trained in how
to impress those bereaved.

[1991]

## CAROLYN KIZER, 1925–

### HERA, HUNG FROM THE SKY

I hang by my heels from the sky.
The sun, exploded at last,
Hammered his wrath to chains
Forged for my lightest bones.
Once I was warmed to my ears,
Kept close; now blind with fire!

What a child, taking heat for delight
So simply! Scorched within,
I still burn as I swing,
A pendulum kicking the night,
An alarum at dawn, I deflect
The passage of birds, ring down
The bannering rain. I indict
This body, its ruses, games,
Its plot to unseat the sun.
I pitted my feminine weight
Against God, his terrible throne.
From the great dome of despair,
I groan, I swing, I swing
In unconstellated air.

I had shared a sovereign cloud:
The lesser, the shadowy twin
To my lord. All woman and weight
Of connubial love that sings
Within the cabinet's close
And embracing intimacy.
I threw it all to the skies
In an instant of power, poise—
Arrogant, flushed with his love,
His condescending praise;
From envy of shine and blaze,
Mad, but beautifully mad,
Hypnotized by the gaze
Of self into self, the dream
That woman was great as man—
As humid, as blown with fame,
So great I seemed to be!
I threw myself to the skies
And the sky has cast me down.
I have lost the war of the air:
Half strangled in my hair,
I dangle, drowned in fire.

[1961]

# From *Pro Femina*

## ONE

From Sappho to myself, consider the fate of women.
How unwomanly to discuss it! Like a noose or an albatross necktie
The clinical sobriquet hangs us: cod-piece coveters.
Never mind these epithets; I myself have collected some honeys.
Juvenal set us apart in denouncing our vices
Which had grown, in part, from having been set apart:
Women abused their spouses, cuckolded them, even plotted
To poison them. Sensing, behind the violence of his manner—
"Think I'm crazy or drunk?"—his emotional stake in us,
As we forgive Strindberg and Nietzsche, we forgive all those
Who cannot forget us. We *are* hyenas. Yes, we admit it.

While men have politely debated free will, we have howled for it,
Howl still, pacing the centuries, tragedy heroines.
Some who sat quietly in the corner with their embroidery
Were Defarges, stabbing the wool with the names of their ancient
Oppressors, who ruled by the divine right of the male—
I'm impatient of interruptions! I'm aware there were millions
Of mutes for every Saint Joan or sainted Jane Austen,
Who, vague-eyed and acquiescent, worshiped God as a man.
I'm not concerned with those cabbageheads, not truly feminine
But neutered by labor. I mean real women, like *you* and like *me.*

Freed in fact, not in custom, lifted from furrow and scullery,
Not obliged, now, to be the pot for the annual chicken,
*Have we begun to arrive in time?* With our well-known
Respect for life because it hurts so much to come out with it;
Disdainful of "sovereignty," "national honor" and other abstractions;
We can say, like the ancient Chinese to successive waves of invaders,
"Relax, and let us absorb you. You can learn temperance
In a more temperate climate." Give us just a few decades
Of grace, to encourage the fine art of acquiescence
And we might save the race. Meanwhile, observe our creative chaos,
Flux, efflorescence—whatever you care to call it!
\*   \*   \*

## Two

I take as my theme "The Independent Woman,"
Independent but maimed: observe the exigent neckties
Choking violet writers; the sad slacks of stipple-faced matrons;
Indigo intellectuals, crop-haired and callous-toed,
Cute spectacles, chewed cuticles, aced out by full-time beauties
In the race for a male. Retreating to drabness, bad manners
And sleeping with manuscripts. Forgive our transgressions
Of old gallantries as we hitch in chairs, light our own cigarettes,
Not expecting your care, having forfeited it by trying to get even.

But we need dependency, cosseting and well-treatment.
So do men sometimes. Why don't they admit it?
We will be cows for a while, because babies howl for us,
Be kittens or bitches, who want to eat grass now and then
For the sake of our health. But the role of pastoral heroine
Is not permanent, Jack. We want to get back to the meeting.

Knitting booties and brows, tartars or termagants, ancient
Fertility symbols, chained to our cycle, released
Only in part by devices of hygiene and personal daintiness,
Strapped into our girdles, held down, yet uplifted by man's
Ingenious constructions, holding coiffures in a breeze,
Hobbled and swathed in whimsy, tripping on feminine
Shoes with fool heels, losing our lipsticks, you, me,
In ephemeral stockings, clutching our handbags and packages.

Our masks, always in peril of smearing or cracking,
In need of continuous check in the mirror or silverware,
Keep us in thrall to ourselves, concerned with our surfaces.
Look at man's uniform drabness, his impersonal envelope!
Over chicken wrists or meek shoulders, a formal, hard-fibered assurance.
The drape of the male is designed to achieve self-forgetfulness.

So, sister, forget yourself a few times and see where it gets you:
Up the creek, alone with your talent, sans everything else.
You can wait for the menopause, and catch up on your reading.
So primp, preen, prink, pluck and prize your flesh,
All posturings! All ravishment! All sensibility!
Meanwhile, have you used your mind today?

What pomegranate raised you from the dead,
Springing, full-grown, from your own head, Athena?


## THREE

I will speak about women of letters, for I'm in the racket.
Our biggest successes to date? Old maids to a woman.
And our saddest conspicuous failures? The married spinsters
On loan to the husbands they treated like surrogate fathers.
Think of that crew of self-pitiers, not-very-distant,
Who carried the torch for themselves and got first-degree burns.
Or the sad sonneteers, toast-and-teasdales we loved at thirteen;
Middle-aged virgins seducing the purile anthologists
Through lust-of-the-mind; barbiturate-drenched Camilles
With continuous periods, murmuring softly on sofas
When poetry wasn't a craft but a sickly effluvium,
The air thick with incense, musk, and emotional blackmail.

I suppose they reacted from an earlier womanly modesty
When too many girls were scabs to their stricken sisterhood,
Impugning our sex to stay in good with the men,
Commencing their insecure bluster. How they must have swaggered
When women themselves endorsed their own inferiority!
Vestals, vassals and vessels, rolled into several,
They took notes in rolling syllabics, in careful journals,
Aiming to please a posterity that despises them.
But we'll always have traitors who swear that a woman surrenders
Her Supreme Function, by equating Art with aggression
And failure with Femininity. Still, it's just as unfair
To equate Art with Femininity, like a prettily-packaged commodity
When we are the custodians of the world's best-kept secret:
Merely the private lives of one-half of humanity.

But even with masculine dominance, we mares and mistresses
Produced some sleek saboteuses, making their cracks
Which the porridge-brained males of the day were too thick to perceive,
Mistaking young hornets for perfectly harmless bumblebees.
Being thought innocuous rouses some women to frenzy;
They try to be ugly by aping the ways of the men
And succeed. Swearing, sucking cigars and scorching the bedspread,
*   *   *

Slopping straight shots, eyes blotted, vanity-blown
In the expectation of glory: *she writes like a man!*
This drives other women mad in a mist of chiffon.
(One poetess draped her gauze over red flannels, a practical feminist).

But we're emerging from all that, more or less,
Except for some lady-like laggards and Quarterly priestesses
Who flog men for fun, and kick women to maim competition.
Now, if we struggle abnormally, we may almost seem normal;
If we submerge our self-pity in disciplined industry;
If we stand up and be hated, and swear not to sleep with editors;
If we regard ourselves formally, respecting our true limitations
Without making an unseemly show of trying to unfreeze our assets;
Keeping our heads and our pride while remaining unmarried;
And if wedded, kill guilt in its tracks when we stack up the dishes
And defect to the typewriter. And if mothers, believe in the luck of
    our children,
Whom we forbid to devour us, whom we shall not devour,
And the luck of our husbands and lovers, who keep free women.

[1965]

## BITCH

Now, when he and I meet, after all these years,
I say to the bitch inside me, don't start growling.
He isn't a trespasser anymore,
Just an old acquaintance tipping his hat.
My voice says, "Nice to see you,"
As the bitch starts to bark hysterically.
He isn't an enemy now.
Where are your manners, I say, as I say,
"How are the children? They must be growing up."
At a kind word from him, a look like the old days,
The bitch changes her tone: she begins to whimper.
She wants to snuggle up to him, to cringe.
Down, girl! Keep your distance
Or I'll give you a taste of the choke-chain.
"Fine, I'm just fine," I tell him.
She slobbers and grovels.
After all, I am her mistress. She is basically loyal.

It's just that she remembers how she came running
Each evening, when she heard his step;
How she lay at his feet and looked up adoringly
Though he was absorbed in his paper;
Or, bored with her devotion, ordered her to the kitchen
Until he was ready to play.
But the small careless kindnesses
When he'd had a good day, or a couple of drinks,
Come back to her now, seem more important
Than the casual cruelties, the ultimate dismissal.
"It's nice to know you are doing so well," I say.
He couldn't have taken you with him;
You were too demonstrative, too clumsy,
Not like the well-groomed pets of his new friends.
"Give my regards to your wife," I say. You gag
As I drag you off by the scruff,
Saying, "Goodbye! Goodbye! Nice to have seen you again."

[1984]


## THE BLESSING
### *for Ashley*


### I

Daughter-my-mother
you have observed my worst.
Holding me together at your expense
has made you burn cool.

So did I in childhood:
nursed her old hurts and doubts
myself made cool to shallowness.
She grew out as I grew in.
At mid-point, our furies met.

My mother's dust has rested
for fifteen years
in the front hall closet
because we couldn't bear to bury it.
Her dust-lined, dust-coated urn

squats among the size-eleven overshoes.
My father, who never forgets
his overshoes,
has forgotten that.

Hysterical-tongued daughter
of a dead marriage
you shed hot tears in the bed
of that benign old woman
whose fierce joy you were:
tantrums in the closet
taking upon yourself the guilt
the split parents never felt.
Child and old woman
soothing each other
sharing the same face
in a span of seventy years
the same mother wit.

*I must go home,* says my father,
his mind straying;
*this is a hard time*
*for your mother*. But she's been dead
these fifteen years.
Daughter and daughter, we sit
on either side.
Whose? Which? He's not sure.
After long silence
*don't press me,* he says.

## II

Mother, hysterical-tongued,
age and grace burned away
your excesses, left
that lavender-sweet child
who turned up the thermostat
on her electric blanket, folded
her hands on her breast;
you had dreamed death

as a silver prince;
*like marrying Nehru,* you said.

Dearest, does your dust hum
in the front hall closet
*this is a hard time for me*
among the umbrella points
the canes and overshoes
of that cold climate?
Each week she denies it
my blithe mother
in that green, cloud-free landscape
where we whisper our dream-secrets
to each other.

### III

Daughter, you lived through
my difficult affairs
as I tried to console
your burnt-out childhood.
We coped with our fathers
compared notes
on the old one and the cold one,
learned to moderate our hates.
Risible in suffering
we grew up together.

Mother-my-daughter
I have been blessed
on both sides of my life.
Forgive me if sometimes
like my fading father
I see you as one.

Not that I confuse
your two identities
as he does, taking off
or putting on his overshoes,
but my own role:
\*    \*    \*

I lean on the bosom
of that double mother
the ghost by night, the girl by day.

# MAXINE KUMIN, 1925–


## A VOICE FROM THE ROSES
*After Arachne*

Having confused me
with the nearest of her nine
nimble sisters—
the beautiful one
she witched into seizures
of drools and tremors
for picking away at her needlepoint—
my mother directed the craft
of her vengeance against me.

I have lain
on this thorn thirty years,
spinning out of my
pear-shaped belly,
my puffball pearl-gray belly
always perfectly damp,
intricate maps of my brainpan,
lines and ligatures
that catch the morning light
and carve it into prisms;
you might say, messages.

The furious barb
that I fed with my body's juices,
this nib of my babyhood
has softened, as even saliva
will eat away porcelain.
Tugged this way and that

by the force of my spinning,
the old thorn
now clasps me lightly.

Nevertheless
it is rooted. It is
raising a tree inside me.
The buds of my mother's arbor
grow ripe in my sex.
Mother, Queen of the roses,
wearer of forks and petals,
when may I be free of you?
When will I be done
with the force of your magic?

                                          [1961]


AFTER LOVE

Afterwards, the compromise.
Bodies resume their boundaries.

These legs, for instance, mine.
Your arms take you back in.

Spoons of our fingers, lips
admit their ownership.

The bedding yawns, a door
blows aimlessly ajar

and overhead, a plane
singsongs coming down.

Nothing is changed, except
there was a moment when

the wolf, the mongering wolf
who stands outside the self

lay lightly down, and slept.

                                          [1970]

## LOUISE BOURGEOIS EXHIBIT

*Museum of Modern Art, 1983*

This is no place for Renoir's little girls
or their rapturous mothers. Interiors here
—however grotesque, they are perfectly tidy—
beckon or seize suggesting ways
we are held male and female, pinned inside
or beneath. And yet we assume she painted
her share of apples and pears highlighted
on velvet before taking up picket fences
stones and pillars, toothy vaginas
roomsful of phalluses.

In the photograph on the frontispiece
of the Museum's brochure we have
her likeness wrapped in something feathery:
kind face worked in little rivulets
old-fashioned hairdo pulled back with waves
at the temples. She looks like everyone's
oldest, wisest, happiest and most untrammeled
auntie going her own way crumbling
graham crackers in bed

getting up to paint, pace, sculpt, pour latex
at three in the morning, carving body parts
bubbles and blisters, pods, poles
bulges of life force, nests and lairs
to contain them. In marble or wood
plaster or rubber she makes sweet clusters
of penises wearing hats, fat clumps
of breasts pillowed like clouds
or torpedoes.

Wherever we look things stand up
register one another's width and breadth.
Bourgeois announces *I am not
particularly aware of the erotic
in my art*. She tells the world *This is
my statement of refusal to death*.

[1985]

# THE CHAIN

My mother's insomnia over at last,
at dawn I enter her bureau drawers.
Under the petticoats, bedjackets, corsets,
under the unfinished knitting that crossed
continents with her, an affable animal,
I come on a hatbox of type-O any-hair,
heavy braids that have lain fifty years in this oval.
Between them, my mother's mother's calling card
engraved on brittle ivory vellum:
Mrs. Abraham Simon, Star Route 3, Radford.

Radford, Virginia, three thousand souls.
Here my mother spent her girlhood, not
without complications, playing
the Methodist church organ for weddings,
funerals, and the Sunday choir.
Here her mother, holding a lily-shaped
ear trumpet, stepped down from the surrey
Grandfather drove forty miles to Roanoke
to witness the blowing of the shofar
on Rosh Hashonah and Yom Kippur.

Affirming my past, our past in
a nation losing its memory, turning
its battlegrounds into parking lots,
slicking its regional differences over
with video games, substituting outer
space for history, I mourn
the type-O any-deaths of Mecca,
Athens, Babylon, Rome,
Radford, country towns
of middle-class hopes and tall corn.

Every year a new itinerant
piano teacher. New exercises
in the key of most-flats. 1908,
the first indoor toilet. The first
running hot water. My mother
takes weekly elocution lessons.

The radio, the telephone,
the Model T arrive. One by one
her sisters are sent north to cousins
in search of kindly Jewish husbands.

Surely having lived this long confers
a kind of aristocracy on my mother,
who kept to the end these talismans,
two dry links in the chain of daughters.
In the land of burley tobacco,
of mules in the narrow furrows,
in the land of diphtheria and strangles,
of revival meetings and stillborn angels,
in the land of eleven living siblings
I make my mother a dowager queen.

I give her back the chipped ruby goblets.
I hand over the battered Sheffield tureen
and the child I was, whose once-auburn hair
she scooped up like gems from the beauty-shop floor.

                                                    [1985]


CREDO

I believe in magic. I believe in the rights
of animals to leap out of our skins
as recorded in the Kiowa legend:
*Directly there was a bear where the boy had been*

as I believe in the resurrected wake-robin,
first wet knob of trillium to knock
in April at the underside of earth's door
in central New Hampshire where bears are

though still denned up at that early greening.
I believe in living on grateful terms
with the earth, with the black crumbles
of ancient manure that sift through my fingers

when I topdress the garden for winter. I believe
in the wet strings of earthworms aroused out of season

and in the bear, asleep now in the rock cave
where my outermost pasture abuts the forest.

I cede him a swale of chokecherries in August.
I give the sow and her cub as much yardage
as they desire when our paths intersect
as does my horse shifting under me

respectful but not cowed by our encounter.
I believe in the gift of the horse, which is magic,
their deep fear-snorts in play when the wind comes up,
the ballet of nip and jostle, plunge and crow hop.

I trust them to run from me, necks arched in a full
swan's S, tails cocked up over their backs
like plumes on a Cavalier's hat. I trust them
to gallop back, skid to a stop, their nostrils

level with my mouth, asking for my human breath
that they may test its intent, taste the smell of it.
I believe in myself as their sanctuary
and the earth with its summer plumes of carrots,

its clamber of peas, beans, masses of tendrils
as mine. I believe in the acrobatics of boy
into bear, the grace of animals
in my keeping, the thrust to go on.

[1992]

## THE RENDEZVOUS

How narrow the bear trail
through the forest,
one paw print following
the other in the manner
of good King Wenceslas
tagged by his faithful serf.

How, according to the legend,
a bear is able to feel shame
and if a woman meets a male bear

she should take off all her clothes,
thereby causing him
to run away.

How I meet a male bear.
How I am careful not
to insult him. I unbutton
my blouse. He takes out
his teeth. I slip off
my skirt. He turns
his back and works his way
out of his pelt,
which he casts to the ground
for a rug.

[1992]

## ANNE HALLEY, 1928–

### HOUSEWIFE'S LETTER: TO MARY

      If I could, I'd write
how glad I live and cultivate:
to put tomatoes in and squash,
green salad on a yellow cloth,
how especially the white and blue
plates please me then. Also, I do
ironing mornings, make my list,
go squeeze fruit, open corn husks, watch
the butcher while he cuts our meat,
and tote up prices in my head.
Evenings, I shake the cloth and fold
clean sheets away, count socks, and read
desultorily, and then to bed.

All this, could I, I'd write to you
and—doctored—parts are almost true.
But this is so: some days I've seen
my neighbor in her curlers, frown-

ing intently, sweeping hard
her porch, her sidewalk, her paved yard.
Her serious eye, following broom,
penetrates to my scratchpad room
and so—on my good days—I sweep
the front porch hard, and hope to keep
a neighbor image in my eye,
good aproned neighbor, whom I'd try
to emulate, to mimic, be—
translate some certainties to me.

That mothers' meeting, visit, when
Elisabeth first felt her son
leap into life: Mother of God
and Prophet's Mother, forward bowed,
embracing secrets, each in each,
they celebrate each other's fruit—
cylindrical and gravid, plain,
I puzzle over what they mean;
what do they speak of, in what tone,
how calmly stand. If mortal men
could touch them thus—O sacred, grim
they look to me: this year, I'm thin
have cut my washerwoman hair—
yet they persist, so solid, there,
content to carry, bear this weight
and be as vines, initiate.

I have been fruitful, lucky, blessed
more ways than I can count, at rest—
or ought to be—and even thrive
efficiently: yet come alive
odd moments in surprise that I
should still expect, impossibly,
and at the same time wholly hate
my old expectancy. I wait
long past my time, like the old Saint,
but unlike her, I'll make complaint.

For when I stand here on the step
and sigh and nod my housewife's head

and wipe my hands and click my tongue
at dust, or rain, or noise, or sun,
though motion's right, I feel it wrong.
I can remember all my dolls'
tea-sets and washboards, cribs on wheels,
and the whole mess, the miniatures
of pie-tins, babies, plastic meals—
a dustblown attic full of wrapped-
up child's play. How begin, unpack,
through splintery crates and newsprint feel
the living child and make it real.

It's real enough. Inside my house,
uncustomed, unceremonious,
I seem to wade among the shards
proliferating, wrecked discards,
a whole decline of Western Man
in microcosm: who'd begin
to sort it out, make do, decide
to deal with this, to let that ride—
make love, patch plaster, choose your work,
your car, your party, and your church,
keep conscience, throw out sense of sin,
free impulse, but in discipline—
a ruptured rug, a beaten chair
stare at me, stupid as despair.

And I am full of anger, need
not words made flesh, nor wordless act,
nor cycles inarticulate,
have never felt a moral thrill
at choosing good against my will
and no orgasm, man or God's,
delivers long from my black thoughts—
Housewifely Guardians, sweeping yet,
sweep out their graves and ours: O let
those flourish surely on, who know
the laws in which they bear and grow,
let multiply, secure from ill,
vessels wellformed for grace to fill.

[1965]

## AGAINST DARK'S HARM

The baby at my breast
suckles me to rest.
Who lately rode my blood
finds me further flood,
pulls me to his dim
unimagined dream.

Amulet and charm
against dark's harm,
coiled in my side,
shelter me from fright
and the edged knife,
despair, distress
and all self-sickness.

[1965]


## I'D RATHER SEE THAN BE ONE, BUT

I went out to a festival
a parliament, a conference
with emphasis on assonance,
on prophecy, on utterance—

a jolly bardic picnic
polysyllabic and sylvan
in stereo in video
in a laurel-wreathed pavilion.

Well, I was naive.

All the boys had something. I felt a loss.
We were all amplified. It wasn't voice.
But more a stance, a posture, a poise
each keeping close to some odd kind of piece—
maybe a stash-sack or an attaché case.

And me wondering what could be its use?
\* \* \*

The director blanched, turned away his face.
Professionals, Madam.
And poets, Madam.
Every poet has his Muse.

I thought they kept them in Museums.
But he says, Now they're able
to make them portable, diaphanous, fully in-
and de-fla-table.
Some of our most progressive foundations
famed international bodies
newly interested in the modern procurement of Muses
financed preliminary studies—
that now our poets need no longer share her favors,
no more dry spells, solitary nights,
no more fruitless labors.
Each according to his need
you will know what I mean
sterile at point of entry, boilable if desired,
easy to clean.
Think of the putative children,
aging probable wives—
Ah Madam, dear Madam—reflect on poets' lives!

Sure, I understood
                              the old divine afflatus
and the certified connection for poetic apparatus.
But, I say, isn't the Muse free?
Doesn't she simply blow—
Madam, he says, MADAM PLEASE.   I beg you.   NO!
—in the poet's ear, I would have said—
as she lists, as she pleases?

Dear Lady, he mumbles. Processes, mysteries,
specifics of conception, details of creation,
I am not free to divulge.
Remember, initiation
involves, I fear, extremely high fees
and gruelling examination, the most rigid standards,
and every kind of test of manhood and mandates—

*   *   *
But couldn't I get one? Apply and be considered?
Won't there be another shipment? Couldn't I be fitted?
I'll take my chances—suffer, sweat, and swot,
pay any price, take whatever you've got:
one that can't spell, won't take shorthand, can't scan,
a left-over, say, too sharp-fanged for a man?

An early model, rubbery or wrinkled?
One returned, damaged goods, too freckled, bulky, pimpled?
Please won't you let me fill out an application?

And he:
the Republic, the health of the nation,
forces involved, quite beyond the immediate,
international ethics, reasons of church and state,
all require a Muse built to absolute scale.
To be blunt, Madam, as of this date
down to the last inspiring feature
every bit of classical detail
is, in accord with the law of nature,
calculated to arouse, limited to fit,
that normative modern poet
                              who is your opposite.

Oh I did feel low
trying to learn to live with the usual
evasive bureaucratic sympathetic
meaching NO

And naturally I wondered, was I perverse?

Yes, I was.


Our mistress whose changes
turn the Great Names' song

will not be contained
*   *   *

flows, a thin bitter wine
falls, a sweeping of shards

leaps, a triple-edged thorn, from the tongue.

[1979]


# Cynthia Macdonald, 1928–

## INSTRUCTION FROM BLY

The poet told me if I was serious
I must isolate myself for at least a year—
Not become a hermit, but leave
My family, job, friends—so I did. My sister
Agreed to take over as mother though not
As wife. I wonder if she will become that too;
I've always thought maybe she didn't marry
Because she wanted Howard herself. So I
Have moved here to North Dakota where
I work in a gas station, the only woman s.s.
Attendant in N.D. Nowhere could be more isolated
And no job could: whistles and "baby
Pump some of that to me" crack in the cold
Or melt in the summer.

      try         try         try
   crycry     crycry     crycry       cry

I have been here seven months. Poetry should
Be flowing from my navel by now, if . . .
Out of the solitude, I expected I would erect
Something magnificent, the feminine analogue
Of Jeffers' tower. Maybe it would have gone
Into the ground instead of up.

           s          k         y
              high

\*   \*   \*

I have discovered I drink when I am solitary. I
Have discovered I can read page ninety-two of
*Remembrance of Things Past* twenty times in solitary
Without ever reading it. If I don't die of alcoholism,
I will of cholesterol: solitary cooking.

    fryfryfry       fryfry       fryfryfryfry     frydie

Rhyme is important, my way of keeping
A grip on things. I wonder if the poet meant
It would all happen after I left, or if he is a sadist
Who wants to send all those stupid enough to sit
At his feet to N.D. or S.D. or West Va.,
Hazing before possible joining. I wonder if Jean
Is in the double bed.

                  tower

                  power

I cannot think about the children, but I
Do all the time. "Women artists fail
Because they have babies." The last thing I wrote
Was "The Children at the Beach" and that was over
A month ago. I am alone so I have to have company so
I turn on TV; at home
I only turned it off.

             thumbtacks       processionals
                     north
                      red

It is time to go to work. First I need a drink. I consider
The Smirnoff bottle on the coffee table; a fly
Lands on it. And then it all happens: the life
Of that bottle flashes before me. Little by little,
Or quickly, it is used up; empty, as clear as it was
Full, it journeys to the dump; it rests upon the mounds of
Beautiful excess where what we are—
Sunflowers, grass, sand—
Is joined to what we make—
Cans, tires and it itself in every form of bottle.

I put on my s.s. coveralls, a saffron robe, knowing I have found
What I was sent to find. The sky speaks to me; the sound
Of the cars on Highway 2 is a song. Soon I will see the pumps,
Those curved rectangles shaped like the U.S. and smell the gas,
Our incense. O country, O moon, O stars,
O american rhyme is yours is mine is ours.

[1973]


OBJETS D'ART

When I was seventeen, a man in the Dakar Station
Men's Room (I couldn't read the signs) said to me:
You're a real ball cutter. I thought about that
For months and finally decided
He was right. Once I knew that was my thing,
Or whatever we would have said in those days,
I began to perfect my methods. Until then
I had never thought of trophies. Preservation
Was at first a problem: pickling worked
But was a lot of trouble. Freezing
Proved to be the answer. I had to buy
A second freezer just last year; the first
Was filled with rows and rows of
Pink and purple lumps encased in Saran wrap.

I have more subjects than I can handle,
But only volunteers. It is an art like hypnosis
Which cannot be imposed on the unwilling victim.
If you desire further information about the process and
The benefits, please drop in any night from nine to twelve.
My place is east of Third on Fifty-sixth.
You'll know it by the three gold ones over the door.

[1973]


INHERITANCE

I see my mother's last breath
Which has not been drawn
In pen and ink, its jagged graph scrawled on my face,
Crossing out my features
With her lines.

Her lines come out of my mouth so that I discuss
The appearance of the neighbor's children,
The dirty streets of New York
And love, in the same tone of smooth disapproval.
Disapproval sours
My skin into hers,
Implants her congealed brown eyes, her long nose to
Look down, her lips
Like the edges of oysters.

Once a day I sandpaper my features. The swelling
Has obliterated both of us. The basin
On my lap catches our common blood.

[1976]


# ANNE SEXTON, 1928–1974


HOUSEWIFE

Some women marry houses.
It's another kind of skin; it has a heart,
a mouth, a liver and bowel movements.
The walls are permanent and pink.
See how she sits on her knees all day,
faithfully washing herself down.
Men enter by force, drawn back like Jonah
into their fleshy mothers.
A woman *is* her mother.
That's the main thing.

[1961]

# THE ABORTION

*Somebody who should have been born*
*is gone.*

Just as the earth puckered its mouth,
each bud puffing out from its knot,
I changed my shoes, and then drove south.

Up past the Blue Mountains, where
Pennsylvania humps on endlessly,
wearing, like a crayoned cat, its green hair,

its roads sunken in like a gray washboard;
where, in truth, the ground cracks evilly,
a dark socket from which the coal has poured,

*Somebody who should have been born*
*is gone.*

the grass as bristly and stout as chives,
and me wondering when the ground would break,
and me wondering how anything fragile survives;

up in Pennsylvania, I met a little man,
not Rumpelstiltskin, at all, at all . . .
he took the fullness that love began.

Returning north, even the sky grew thin
like a high window looking nowhere.
The road was as flat as a sheet of tin.

*Somebody who should have been born*
*is gone.*

Yes, woman, such logic will lead
to loss without death. Or say what you meant,
you coward . . . this baby that I bleed.

[1961]

# CONSORTING WITH ANGELS

I was tired of being a woman,
tired of the spoons and the pots,
tired of my mouth and my breasts,
tired of the cosmetics and the silks.
There were still men who sat at my table,
circled around the bowl I offered up.
The bowl was filled with purple grapes
and the flies hovered in for the scent
and even my father came with his white bone.
But I was tired of the gender of things.

Last night I had a dream
and I said to it . . .
"You are the answer.
You will outlive my husband and my father."
In that dream there was a city made of chains
where Joan was put to death in man's clothes
and the nature of the angels went unexplained,
no two made in the same species,
one with a nose, one with an ear in its hand,
one chewing a star and recording its orbit,
each one like a poem obeying itself,
performing God's functions,
a people apart.

"You are the answer,"
I said, and entered,
lying down on the gates of the city.
Then the chains were fastened around me
and I lost my common gender and my final aspect.
Adam was on the left of me
and Eve was on the right of me,
both thoroughly inconsistent with the world of reason.
We wove our arms together
and rode under the sun.
I was not a woman anymore,
not one thing or the other.
*  *  *

O daughters of Jerusalem,
the king has brought me into his chamber.
I am black and I am beautiful.
I've been opened and undressed.
I have no arms or legs.
I'm all one skin like a fish.
I'm no more a woman
than Christ was a man.

[1966]


FOR MY LOVER, RETURNING TO HIS WIFE

She is all there.
She was melted carefully down for you
and cast up from your childhood,
cast up from your one hundred favorite aggies.

She has always been there, my darling.
She is, in fact, exquisite.
Fireworks in the dull middle of February
and as real as a cast-iron pot.

Let's face it, I have been momentary.
A luxury. A bright red sloop in the harbor.
My hair rising like smoke from the car window.
Littleneck clams out of season.

She is more than that. She is your have to have,
has grown you your practical your tropical growth.
This is not an experiment. She is all harmony.
She sees to oars and oarlocks for the dinghy,

has placed wild flowers at the window at breakfast,
sat by the potter's wheel at midday,
set forth three children under the moon,
three cherubs drawn by Michelangelo,

done this with her legs spread out
in the terrible months in the chapel.
If you glance up, the children are there
like delicate balloons resting on the ceiling.

*   *   *

She has also carried each one down the hall
after supper, their heads privately bent,
two legs protesting, person to person,
her face flushed with a song and their little sleep.

I give you back your heart.
I give you permission—

for the fuse inside her, throbbing
angrily in the dirt, for the bitch in her
and the burying of her wound—
for the burying of her small red wound alive—

for the pale flickering flare under her ribs,
for the drunken sailor who waits in her left pulse,
for the mother's knee, for the stockings,
for the garter belt, for the call—

the curious call
when you will burrow in arms and breasts
and tug at the orange ribbon in her hair
and answer the call, the curious call.

She is so naked and singular.
She is the sum of yourself and your dream.
Climb her like a monument, step after step.
She is solid.

As for me, I am a watercolor.
I wash off.

[1967]

# ADRIENNE RICH, 1929–

## SNAPSHOTS OF A DAUGHTER-IN-LAW

1. You, once a belle in Shreveport,
   with henna-colored hair, skin like a peachbud,
   still have your dresses copied from that time,
   and play a Chopin prelude
   called by Cortot: *"Delicious recollections
   float like perfume through the memory."*

   Your mind now, moldering like wedding-cake,
   heavy with useless experience, rich
   with suspicion, rumor, fantasy,
   crumbling to pieces under the knife-edge
   of mere fact. In the prime of your life.

   Nervy, glowering, your daughter
   wipes the teaspoons, grows another way.

2. Banging the coffee-pot into the sink
   she hears the angels chiding, and looks out
   past the raked gardens to the sloppy sky.
   Only a week since They said: *Have no patience.*
   The next time it was: *Be insatiable.*
   Then: *Save yourself; others you cannot save.*
   Sometimes she's let the tapstream scald her arm,
   a match burn to her thumbnail,

   or held her hand above the kettle's snout
   right in the woolly steam. They are probably angels,
   since nothing hurts her any more, except
   each morning's grit blowing into her eyes.

3. A thinking woman sleeps with monsters.
   The beak that grips her, she becomes. And Nature,
   that sprung-lidded, still commodious
   steamer-trunk of *tempora* and *mores*

gets stuffed with it all:     the mildewed orange-flowers,
the female pills, the terrible breasts
of Boadicea beneath flat foxes' heads and orchids.

Two handsome women, gripped in argument,
each proud, acute, subtle, I hear scream
across the cut glass and majolica
like Furies cornered from their prey:
The argument *ad feminem,* all the old knives
that have rusted in my back, I drive in yours,
*ma semblable, ma soeur!*


4. Knowing themselves too well in one another;
   their gifts no pure fruition, but a thorn,
   the prick filed sharp against a hint of scorn . . .
   Reading while waiting
   for the iron to heat,
   writing, *This is the gnat that mangles men,*
   in that Amherst pantry while the jellies boil and scum,
   or, more often,
   iron-eyed and beaked and purposed as a bird,
   dusting everything on the whatnot every day of life.


5. *Dulce ridentem, dulce loquentem,*
   she shaves her legs until they gleam
   like petrified mammoth-tusk.


6. When to her lute Corinna sings
   neither words nor music are her own;
   only the long hair dipping
   over her cheek, only the song
   of silk against her knees
   and these
   adjusted in reflections of an eye.

   Poised, trembling and unsatisfied, before
   an unlocked door, that cage of cages,
   tell us, you bird, you tragical machine—

is this *fertilisante douleur?* Pinned down
by love, for you the only natural action,
are you edged more keen
to prise the secrets of the vault? has Nature shown
her household books to you, daughter-in-law,
that her sons never saw?


7. *"To have in this uncertain world some stay*
   *which cannot be undermined, is*
   *of the utmost consequence."*
                              Thus wrote
   a woman, partly brave and partly good,
   who fought with what she partly understood.
   Few men about her would or could do more,
   hence she was labeled harpy, shrew and whore.


8. "You all die at fifteen," said Diderot,
   and turn part legend, part convention.
   Still, eyes inaccurately dream
   behind closed windows blankening with steam.
   Deliciously, all that we might have been,
   all that we were—fire, tears,
   wit, taste, martyred ambition—
   stirs like the memory of refused adultery
   the drained and flagging bosom of our middle years.


9. *Not that it is done well, but*
   *that it is done at all?* Yes, think
   of the odds! or shrug them off forever.
   This luxury of the precocious child,
   Time's precious chronic invalid—
   would we, darlings, resign it if we could?
   Our blight has been our sinecure:
   mere talent was enough for us—
   glitter in fragments and rough drafts.

Sigh no more, ladies.
                         Time is male
and in his cups drinks to the fair.
Bemused by gallantry, we hear
our mediocrities over-praised,
indolence read as abnegation,
slattern thought styled intuition,
every lapse forgiven, our crime
only to cast too bold a shadow
or smash the mould straight off.

For that, solitary confinement,
tear gas, attrition shelling.
Few applicants for that honor.


10.                                  Well,
   she's long about her coming, who must be
more merciless to herself than history.
Her mind full to the wind, I see her plunge
breasted and glancing through the currents,
taking the light upon her
at least as beautiful as any boy
or helicopter,
                   poised, still coming,
her fine blades making the air wince
but her cargo
no promise then:
delivered
palpable
ours.

                                         [1963]


WOMEN
      *(for C.R.G.)*

My three sisters are sitting
on rocks of black obsidian.
For the first time, in this light, I can see who they are.
\*   \*   \*

My first sister is sewing her costume for the procession.
She is going as the Transparent Lady
and all her nerves will be visible.

My second sister is also sewing,
at the seam over her heart which has never healed entirely.
At last, she hopes, this tightness in her chest will ease.

My third sister is gazing
at a dark-red crust spreading westward far out on the sea.
Her stockings are torn but she is beautiful.

[1969]


HUNGER
      *(for Audre Lorde)*


1

A fogged hill-scene on an enormous continent,
intimacy rigged with terrors,
a sequence of blurs the Chinese painter's ink-stick planned,
a scene of desolation comforted
by two human figures recklessly exposed,
leaning together in a sticklike boat
in the foreground. Maybe we look like this,
I don't know. I'm wondering
whether we even have what we think we have—
lighted windows signifying shelter,
a film of domesticity
over fragile roofs. I know I'm partly somewhere else—
huts strung across a drought-stretched land
not mine, dried breasts, mine and not mine, a mother
watching my children shrink with hunger.
I live in my Western skin,
my Western vision, torn
and flung to what I can't control or even fathom.
Quantify suffering, you could rule the world.

**2**

They can rule the world while they can persuade us
our pain belongs in some order.
Is death by famine worse than death by suicide,
than a life of famine and suicide, if a black lesbian dies,
if a white prostitute dies, if a woman genius
starves herself to feed others,
self-hatred battening on her body?
Something that kills us or leaves us half alive
is raging under the name of an "act of god"
in Chad, in Niger, in the Upper Volta—
yes, that male god that acts on us and on our children,
that male State that acts on us and on our children
till our brains are blunted by malnutrition,
yet sharpened by the passion for survival,
our powers expended daily on the struggle
to hand a kind of life on to our children,
to change reality for our lovers
even in a single trembling drop of water.


**3**

We can look at each other through both our lifetimes
like those two figures in the sticklike boat
flung together in the Chinese ink-scene;
even our intimacies are rigged with terror.
Quantify suffering? My guilt at least is open,
I stand convicted by all my convictions—
you, too. We shrink from touching
our power, we shrink away, we starve ourselves
and each other, we're scared shitless
of what it could be to take and use our love,
hose it on a city, on a world,
to wield and guide its spray, destroying
poisons, parasites, rats, viruses—
like the terrible mothers we long and dread to be.

4

The decision to feed the world
is the real decision. No revolution
has chosen it. For that choice requires
that women shall be free.
I choke on the taste of bread in North America
but the taste of hunger in North America
is poisoning me. Yes, I'm alive to write these words,
to leaf through Kollwitz's women
huddling the stricken children into their stricken arms
the "mothers" drained of milk, the "survivors" driven
to self-abortion, self-starvation, to a vision
bitter, concrete, and wordless.
I'm alive to want more than life,
want it for others starving and unborn,
to name the deprivations boring
into my will, my affections, into the brains
of daughters, sisters, lovers caught in the crossfire
of terrorists of the mind.
In the black mirror of the subway window
hangs my own face, hollow with anger and desire.
Swathed in exhaustion, on the trampled newsprint,
a woman shields a dead child from the camera.
The passion to be inscribes her body.
Until we find each other, we are alone.

[1974–1975]


(THE FLOATING POEM)
from *Twenty-One Love Poems*


Whatever happens with us, your body
Will haunt mine—tender, delicate
your lovemaking, like the half-curled frond
of the fiddlehead fern in forests
just washed by sun. Your traveled, generous thighs
between which my whole face has come and come—
the innocence and wisdom of the place my tongue has found there—
the live, insatiate dance of your nipples in my mouth—
your touch on me, firm, protective, searching

me out, your strong tongue and slender fingers
reaching where I had been waiting years for you
in my rose-wet cave—whatever happens, this is.

[1974–1976]

FRAME

Winter twilight. She comes out of the lab-
oratory, last class of the day
a pile of notebooks slung in her knapsack, coat
zipped high against the already swirling
evening sleet. The wind is wicked and the
busses slower than usual. On her mind
is organic chemistry and the issue
of next month's rent and will it be possible to
bypass the professor with the coldest eyes
to get a reference for graduate school,
and whether any of them, even those who smile
can see, looking at her, a biochemist
or a marine biologist, which of the faces
can she trust to see her at all, either today
or in any future. The busses are worm-slow in the
quickly gathering dark. *I don't know her. I am
standing though somewhere just outside the frame
of all this, trying to see.* At her back
the newly finished building suddenly looks
like shelter, it has glass doors, lighted halls
presumably heat. The wind is wicked. She throws a
glance down the street, sees no bus coming and runs
up the newly constructed steps into the newly
constructed hallway. *I am standing all this time
just beyond the frame, trying to see.* She runs
her hand through the crystals of sleet about to melt
on her hair. She shifts the weight of the books
on her back. It isn't warm here exactly but it's
out of that wind. Through the glass
door panels she can watch for the bus through the thickening
weather. Watching so, she is not
watching for the white man who watches the building
who has been watching her. This is Boston 1979.

*I am standing somewhere at the edge of the frame*
*watching the man, we are both white, who watches the building*
*telling her to move on, get out of the hallway.*
*I can hear nothing because I am not supposed to be*
*present but I can see her gesturing*
*out toward the street at the wind-raked curb*
*I see her drawing her small body up*
*against the implied charges.* The man
goes away. Her body is different now.
It is holding together with more than a hint of fury
and more than a hint of fear. She is smaller, thinner
more fragile-looking than I am. *But I am not supposed to be*
*there. I am just outside the frame*
*of this action when the anonymous white man*
*returns with a white police officer.* Then she starts
to leave into the windraked night but already
the policeman is going to work, the handcuffs are on her
wrists he is throwing her down his knee has gone into
her breast he is dragging her down the stairs *I am unable*
*to hear a sound of all this all that I know is what*
*I can see from this position there is no soundtrack*
*to go with this and I understand at once*
*it is meant to be in silence that this happens*
in silence that he pushes her into the car
banging her head in silence that she cries out
in silence that she tries to explain she was only
waiting for a bus
in silence that he twists the flesh of her thigh
with his nails in silence that her tears begin to flow
that she pleads with the other policeman as if
he could be trusted to see her at all
in silence that in the precinct she refuses to give her name
in silence that they throw her into the cell
in silence that she stares him
straight in the face in silence that he sprays her
in her eyes with Mace in silence that she sinks her teeth
into his hand in silence that she is charged
with trespass assault and battery in
silence that at the sleet-swept corner her bus
passes without stopping and goes on

in silence. *What I am telling you*
*is told by a white woman who they will say*
*was never there. I say I am there.*

[1980]

## XIII (DEDICATIONS),
from *An Atlas of the Difficult World*

I know you are reading this poem
late, before leaving your office
of the one intense yellow lamp-spot and the darkening window
in the lassitude of a building faded to quiet
long after rush-hour.   I know you are reading this poem
standing up in a bookstore far from the ocean
on a gray day of early spring, faint flakes driven
across the plains' enormous spaces around you.
I know you are reading this poem
in a room where too much has happened for you to bear
where the bedclothes lie in stagnant coils on the bed
and the open valise speaks of flight
but you cannot leave yet.   I know you are reading this poem
as the underground train loses momentum and before running
                    up the stairs
toward a new kind of love
your life has never allowed.
I know you are reading this poem by the light
of the television screen where soundless images jerk and slide
while you wait for the newscast from the *intifada.*
I know you are reading this poem in a waiting-room
of eyes met and unmeeting, of identity with strangers.
I know you are reading this poem by fluorescent light
in the boredom and fatigue of the young who are counted out,
count themselves out, at too early an age.   I know
you are reading this poem through your failing sight, the thick
lens enlarging these letters beyond all meaning yet you read on
because even the alphabet is precious.
I know you are reading this poem as you pace beside the stove
warming milk, a crying child on your shoulder, a book in your
                    hand
because life is short and you too are thirsty.

I know you are reading this poem which is not in your language
guessing at some words while others keep you reading
and I want to know which words they are.
I know you are reading this poem listening for something, torn
                    between bitterness and hope
turning back once again to the task you cannot refuse.
I know you are reading this poem because there is nothing else
            left to read
there where you have landed, stripped as you are.

                                                [1990–1991]


# PATRICIA GOEDICKE, 1931–


## IN THE OCEAN

At first my mother would be shy
Leaving my lame father behind

But then she would tuck up her bathing cap
And fly into the water like a dolphin,

Slippery as bamboo she would bend
Everywhere, everywhere I remember

For though he would often be criticizing her,
Blaming her, finding fault

Behind her back he would talk about her
All through our childhood, to me and my sister,

She rarely spoke against him

Except to take us by the hand
In the ocean we would laugh together

As we never did, on dry land

\*   \*   \*

Because he was an invalid
Usually she was silent

But this once, on her deathbed

Hearing me tell it she remembered
Almost before I did, and she smiled

One more time to think of it,
How, with the waves crashing at our feet

Slithering all over her wet skin

We would rub against her like minnows
We would flow between her legs, in the surf

Smooth as spaghetti she would hold us
Close against her like small polliwogs climbing

All over her as if she were a hill,
A hill that moved, our element

But hers also, safe
In the oval of each other's arms

This once she would be weightless
As guiltless, utterly free

Of all but what she loved
Smoothly, with no hard edges,

My long beautiful mother
In her white bathing cap, crowned

Like an enormous lily

Over the brown arrow of her body,
The limber poles of her legs,
\*   \*   \*

The strong cheekbones, and the shadows
Like fluid lavender, everywhere

In a rainbow of breaking foam

Looping and sliding through the waves
We would swim together as one

Mother and sea calves gliding,
Floating as if all three of us were flying.

[1980]

## IN THE WAITING ROOM

But still, carrying my illness to the hospital
Every day, carefully
As if it were a rare gift

I think I am something special,
I want everyone to pity me, to exclaim . . .

But lost in the hubbub on the main floor
There is so much merriment I could cry:

Among all the expensive flower arrangements
Like small hedges to conceal the truth

Upstairs there is gossip, there is nervous laughter
But downstairs it is quiet.
Outside the radiotherapy room

The patients stick together, in the half-light
Awkwardly leaning themselves against the wall

Like barnacles on a dim raft,
Defenseless as marshmallows, hunched
Stuffed into their gray hospital sacks

And shivering a little, in the cold
Feeling their frayed bandages
*   *   *

They nod but they do not speak,
The thin man with the mustache,
The woman in dark glasses

Sitting on the edge of pain
They absolutely refuse to share my grief

And suddenly it occurs to me,
In all honesty they are only interested in their own,
There is nothing special about it,

Settling uneasily among them
I stop poking at myself, oddly
But finally relieved, at home.

[1980]


## LUCKY
### *(on June 21, 1976)*

By sheer accident having met him,
The man with harvest in his pockets,

With clean new irrigation ditches
And oranges and other fruit trees,

With harrow and fertilizer and honey
And pickaxes and pepper in his eyes

Outside the house I had locked
And barricaded against flood

The land all around it is mine
And rises up to me

Gently, on either side of the river
He has returned it to me

With a sense of balance,
With water under my arms like wings

*    *    *

And even though I capsize often,
Though rocks rake my cheeks,

Though fear rides the center current,
The shape of it shadowy, defined

By dim flashings, foghorns,
The noose tightening around my neck,

Though the life that pretends to float me
Is honeycombed with emptiness, great pits

The first hollowings of the disease
That is sucking everyone's strength away

Because he says so it is easy
Simply to go right on bailing,

Patching up the leaks but hardly noticing,
Sailing along with the wind

Power comes to the right hand
Skill tingles in the left

Relishing even the dangerous rapids
Everything seems brand new

And beautiful, even after forty-five years
All the doors of the house are wide open,
And the river running through it.

[1986]

# WITHOUT LOOKING

Either at my friend's daughter's
sixteen-year-old body dumped
on the morgue slab, T-shirt
stuck fast to one ripped
breast I identified
quick, and then
*got out of there*

or at the old gentleman
with tubes in the living room, spittle
stained in his wispy
beard, out of
the corner of my eye I hardly
notice it, how

could I, drink in hand
at five-thirty, at the least
sign of pain one of us always itches
to turn away, another turns
over in sleep, groans
*O, we who are so lucky*

just to be able to
ignore, go back
quick, to our books, to
*have* books, even, how
difficult it is to look
hard and head
on has not been said

often enough, if prayer
is an act of attention
even to dropped stitches, blood
dangling beneath the lines, the
poem? I said,
*what prepares us for what
will never save us?*

[1992]

# COLETTE INEZ, 1931–

## THE WOMAN WHO LOVED WORMS

*(From a Japanese Legend)*

Disdaining butterflies
as frivolous,
she puttered with caterpillars,
and wore a coarse kimono,
crinkled and loose at the neck.

Refused to tweeze her brows
to crescents,
and scowled beneath dark bands
of caterpillar fur.

Even the stationery
on which she scrawled
unkempt calligraphy,
startled the jade-inlaid
indolent ladies,
whom she despised
like the butterflies
wafting kimono sleeves
through senseless poems
about moonsets and peonies:
popular rot of the times.
No, she loved worms,
blackening the moon of her nails
with mud and slugs,
root-gnawing grubs,
and the wing case of beetles.

And crouched in the garden,
tugging at her unpinned hair,
weevils queuing across her bare
and unbound feet.

Swift as wasps, the years.
Midge tick and maggot words

crowded her haiku
and lines on her skin turned her old,
thin as a spinster cricket.

Noon in the snow pavilion,
gulping heated saki,
she recalled Lord Unamuro,
preposterous toad
squatting by the teatray,
proposing with conditions,
a suitable marriage.

Ha! She stoned imaginary butterflies,
and pinching dirt,
crawled to death's cocoon
dragging a moth to inspect
in the long afternoon.

[1969]

## WARRIOR DAUGHTERS

with speculums examining
that real estate men want,
a few moist inches
leading to miles
of complex ills and lies,

when I was ten
I saw it in a mirror,
a hideous Medusa,
half a face and oily lips.

I was one in a stream
of obedient V's; blind cave fish
probed my depth. "Who's the intruder?"
I asked. "I've sucked up his hand."
He was Herr Doktor of the ruling cures.

Warrior daughters, I belonged to that breed
of women as consolers. Consolers can't be
truthful. The fawning went on.

I sometimes lost count of the loss,
my body spoke from the mirror
in one stunned glance.

Years later, I want to see it
as an involute garden, the glyphs of a rose
but it's my vagina
no better that it ought to be
in the dark.

[1983]

## ABSOLVING YOU
### *for Nana*

I and my zero face
quivered in the mirror and sighed.
We were not about to dematerialize
although you'd said: "You're nothing
and won't amount to much."

How could nothing be much?
I learned to mull on paradox
and tried to tote up what my body
might fetch, the penny's worth
of chemicals.

"You'd better learn to sew,"
you stared past me when you spoke.
I stitched up your mouth
in my fantasy of bliss.

And later on, in a home-made dress,
I stood beside your corpse,
pulled the rings from your fingers;
for once, you kept a civil tongue,
my icy-eyed appraiser,
tough to the dingy, fly-specked end
in the charity ward of the hospital,

you, who are almost nothing now,
the puncture mark of a lost stitch

I trace in a dream
of altering a crooked seam,
of mending the past.

{1988}


# LINDA PASTAN, 1932–


## NOTES FROM THE DELIVERY ROOM

Strapped down,
victim in an old comic book,
I have been here before,
this place where pain winces
off the walls
like too bright light.
Bear down a doctor says,
foreman to sweating laborer,
but this work, this forcing
of one life from another
is something that I signed for
at a moment when I would have signed anything.
Babies should grow in fields;
common as beets or turnips
they should be picked and held
root end up, soil spilling
from between their toes—
and how much easier it would be later,
returning them to earth.
Bear up . . . bear down . . . the audience
grows restive, and I'm a new magician
who can't produce the rabbit
from my swollen hat.
She's crowning, someone says,
but there is no one royal here,
just me, quite barefoot,
greeting my barefoot child.

{1971}

## AFTER READING NELLY SACHS

Poetry has opened all my pores,
and pain as colorless as gas
moves in. I notice now the bones
that weld my child together
under her fragile skin; the crowds
of unassuming leaves that wait
on every corner for burning;
even your careless smile—bright teeth
that surely time will cut through
like a rough knife kerneling corn.

[1971]

## PASSOVER

### I

I set my table with metaphor:
the curling parsley—green sign nailed to the doors
of God's underground; salt of desert and eyes;
the roasted shank bone of a Pascal lamb,
relic of sacrifice and bleating spring.
Down the long table, past fresh shoots of a root
they have been hacking at for centuries,
you hold up the unleavened bread—a baked scroll
whose wavy lines are undecipherable.

### II

The wise son and the wicked, the simple son
and the son who doesn't ask, are all my son
leaning tonight as it is written,
slouching his father calls it. His hair is long;
hippie hair, hassid hair, how strangely alike
they seem tonight.
                    First Born, a live child cried
among the bullrushes, but the only root
you know stirs between your legs, ready
to spill its seed in gentile gardens.
And if the flowers be delicate and fair,
I only mind this one night of the year

when far beyond the lights of Jersey,
Jerusalem still beckons us, in tongues.


### III

What black-throated bird
in a warm country
sings spirituals,
sings spirituals
to Moses now?


### IV

One exodus prefigures the next.
The glaciers fled before hot whips of air.
Waves bowed at God's gesture
for fugitive Israel to pass;
while fish, caught then behind windows
of water, remembered how their brothers once
pulled themselves painfully from the sea,
willing legs to grow
from slanted fins.
Now the blossoms pass from April's tree,
refugee raindrops mar the glass,
borders are transitory.
And the changeling gene, still seeking
stone sanctuary, moves on.


### V

Far from Egypt, I have sighted blood,
have heard the throaty mating of frogs.
My city knows vermin, animals loose in hallways,
boils, sickness, hail.
In the suburban gardens
seventeen-year locusts rise
from their heavy beds
in small explosions of sod.
Darkness of newsprint.
My son, my son.

[1971]

## DUET FOR ONE VOICE

### 1

I sit at your side
watching the tides of consciousness
move in and out, watching
the nurses, their caps
like so many white gulls circling
the bed. The window
grows slowly dark,
and light again,
and dark. The clock
tells the same old stories.
Last week you said, now
you'll have to learn
to sew for yourself.
If the thread is boredom,
the needle is grief.
I sit here learning.

### 2

In place of spring
I offer this branch
of forsythia
whose yellow blossoms
I have forced.
Your tired mouth
forces a smile
in thanks. Outside
it is still cold;
who knows how long
the cold will last?
But underground,
their banners still furled,
whole armies of flowers wait.

### 3

I am waiting for you to die,
even as I try to coax you
back to life
with custards and soup

and colored pills I shake
from the bottle like dice,
though their magic
went out of the world
with my surgeon father,
the last magician.
I am waiting

for you to be again
what you always were,
for you to be there whole
for me to run to with this new grief—
your death—the hair grown back
on your skull the way it used to be,
your widow's peak the one sure landmark
on the map of my childhood,
those years when I believed
that medicine and love and being good
could save us all.


4
We escape from our mothers
again and again, young
Houdinis, playing the usual matinées.
First comes escape down
the birth canal, our newly carved faces
leading the way like figureheads
on ancient slaveships,
our small hands rowing for life.
Later escape into silence, escape
behind slammed doors,
the flight into marriage.
I thought I was finally old enough
to sit with you, sharing a book.
But when I look up
from the page, you
have escaped from me.

[1985]

# SYLVIA PLATH, 1932–1963

## THE DISQUIETING MUSES

Mother, mother, what illbred aunt
Or what disfigured and unsightly
Cousin did you so unwisely keep
Unasked to my christening, that she
Sent these ladies in her stead
With heads like darning-eggs to nod
And nod and nod at foot and head
And at the left side of my crib?

Mother, who made to order stories
Of Mixie Blackshort the heroic bear,
Mother, whose witches always, always
Got baked into gingerbread, I wonder
Whether you saw them, whether you said
Words to rid me of those three ladies
Nodding by night around my bed,
Mouthless, eyeless, with stitched bald head.

In the hurricane, when father's twelve
Study windows bellied in
Like bubbles about to break, you fed
My brother and me cookies and Ovaltine
And helped the two of us to choir:
"Thor is angry: boom boom boom!
Thor is angry: we don't care!"
But those ladies broke the panes.

When on tiptoe the schoolgirls danced,
Blinking flashlights like fireflies
And singing the glowworm song, I could
Not lift a foot in the twinkle-dress
But, heavy-footed, stood aside
In the shadow cast by my dismal-headed
Godmothers, and you cried and cried:
And the shadow stretched, the lights went out.

Mother, you sent me to piano lessons
And praised my arabesques and trills
Although each teacher found my touch
Oddly wooden in spite of scales
And the hours of practicing, my ear
Tone-deaf and yes, unteachable.
I learned, I learned, I learned elsewhere,
From muses unhired by you, dear mother,

I woke one day to see you, mother,
Floating above me in bluest air
On a green balloon bright with a million
Flowers and bluebirds that never were
Never, never, found anywhere.
But the little planet bobbed away
Like a soap-bubble as you called: Come here!
And I faced my traveling companions.

Day now, night now, at head, side, feet,
They stand their vigil in gowns of stone,
Faces blank as the day I was born,
Their shadows long in the setting sun
That never brightens or goes down.
And this is the kingdom you bore me to,
Mother, mother. But no frown of mine
Will betray the company I keep.

[1959]


CANDLES

They are the last romantics, these candles:
Upside-down hearts of light tipping wax fingers,
And the fingers, taken in by their own haloes,
Grown milky, almost clear, like the bodies of saints.
It is touching, the way they'll ignore

A whole family of prominent objects
Simply to plumb the deeps of an eye
In its hollow of shadows, its fringe of reeds,

And the owner past thirty, no beauty at all.
Daylight would be more judicious,

Giving everybody a fair hearing.
They should have gone out with balloon flights and the stereopticon.
This is no time for the private point of view.
When I light them, my nostrils prickle.
Their pale, tentative yellows

Drag up false, Edwardian sentiments,
And I remember my maternal grandmother from Vienna.
As a schoolgirl she gave roses to Franz Josef.
The burghers sweated and wept. The children wore white.
And my grandfather moped in the Tyrol,

Imagining himself a headwaiter in America,
Floating in a high-church hush
Among ice buckets, frosty napkins.
These little globes of light are sweet as pears.
Kindly with invalids and mawkish women,

They mollify the bald moon.
Nun-souled, they burn heavenward and never marry.
The eyes of the child I nurse are scarcely open.
In twenty years I shall be retrograde
As these drafty ephemerids.

I watch their split tears cloud and dull to pearls.
How shall I tell anything at all
To this infant still in a birth-drowse?
Tonight, like a shawl, the mild light enfolds her,
The shadows stoop over like guests at a christening.

[1960]

## DADDY

You do not do, you do not do
Any more, black shoe
In which I have lived like a foot
For thirty years, poor and white,
Barely daring to breathe or Achoo.

Daddy, I have had to kill you.
You died before I had time—
Marble-heavy, a bag full of God,
Ghastly statue with one gray toe
Big as a Frisco seal

And a head in the freakish Atlantic
Where it pours bean green over blue
In the waters off beautiful Nauset.
I used to pray to recover you.
Ach, du.

In the German tongue, in the Polish town
Scraped flat by the roller
Of wars, wars, wars.
But the name of the town is common.
My Polack friend

Says there are a dozen or two.
So I never could tell where you
Put your foot, your root,
I never could talk to you.
The tongue stuck in my jaw.

It stuck in a barb wire snare.
Ich, ich, ich, ich,
I could hardly speak.
I thought every German was you.
And the language obscene

An engine, an engine
Chuffing me off like a Jew.
A Jew to Dachau, Auschwitz, Belsen.

I began to talk like a Jew.
I think I may well be a Jew.

The snows of the Tyrol, the clear beer of Vienna
Are not very pure or true.
With my gypsy ancestress and my weird luck
And my Taroc pack and my Taroc pack
I may be a bit of a Jew.

I have always been scared of *you*,
With your Luftwaffe, your gobbledygoo.
And your neat mustache
And your Aryan eye, bright blue.
Panzer-man, panzer-man, O You—

Not God but a swastika
So black no sky could squeak through.
Every woman adores a Fascist,
The boot in the face, the brute
Brute heart of a brute like you.

You stand at the blackboard, daddy,
In the picture I have of you,
A cleft in your chin instead of your foot
But no less a devil for that, no not
Any less the black man who

Bit my pretty red heart in two.
I was ten when they buried you.
At twenty I tried to die.
And get back, back, back to you.
I thought even the bones would do.

But they pulled me out of the sack,
And they stuck me together with glue.
And then I knew what to do.
I made a model of you,
A man in black with a Meinkampf look

And a love of the rack and the screw.
And I said I do, I do.

So daddy, I'm finally through.
The black telephone's off at the root,
The voices just can't worm through.

If I've killed one man, I've killed two—
The vampire who said he was you
And drank my blood for a year,
Seven years, if you want to know.
Daddy, you can lie back now.

There's a stake in your fat black heart
And the villagers never liked you.
They are dancing and stamping on you.
They always *knew* it was you.
Daddy, daddy, you bastard, I'm through.

[1963]


## WINTERING

This is the easy time, there is nothing doing.
I have whirled the midwife's extractor,
I have my honey,
Six jars of it,
Six cat's eyes in the wine cellar,

Wintering in a dark without window
At the heart of the house
Next to the last tenant's rancid jam
And the bottles of empty glitters—
Sir So-and-so's gin.

This is the room I have never been in.
This is the room I could never breathe in.
The black bunched in there like a bat,
No light
But the torch and its faint

Chinese yellow on appalling objects—
Black asininity. Decay.
Possession.

It is they who own me.
Neither cruel nor indifferent,

Only ignorant.
This is the time of hanging on for the bees—the bees
So slow I hardly know them,
Filing like soldiers
To the syrup tin

To make up for the honey I've taken.
Tate and Lyle keeps them going,
The refined snow.
It is Tate and Lyle they live on, instead of flowers.
They take it. The cold sets in.

Now they ball in a mass,
Black
Mind against all that white.
The smile of the snow is white.
It spreads itself out, a mile-long body of Meissen,

Into which, on warm days,
They can only carry their dead.
The bees are all women,
Maids and the long royal lady.
They have got rid of the men,

The blunt, clumsy stumblers, the boors.
Winter is for women—
The woman, still at her knitting,
At the cradle of Spanish walnut,
Her body a bulb in the cold and too dumb to think.

Will the hive survive, will the gladiolas
Succeed in banking their fires
To enter another year?
What will they taste of, the Christmas roses?
The bees are flying. They taste the spring.

[1963]

# ANNE STEVENSON, 1933–

## THE SUBURB

No time, no time,
and with so many in line to be
born or fed or made love to, there is no
excuse for staring at it, though it's spring again
and the leaves have come out looking
limp and wet like little green newborn babies.

The girls have come out in their new bought dresses,
carefully, carefully. They know they're in danger.
Already there are couples crumpled under the chestnuts.
The houses crowd closer, listening to each other's radios.
Weeds have got into the window boxes. The washing hangs,
helpless. Children are lusting for ice cream.

It is my lot each May to be hot and pregnant,
a long way away from the years when I slept by myself—
the white bed by the dressing table, pious with cherry blossoms,
the flatteries and punishments of photographs and mirrors.
We walked home by starlight and he touched my breasts.
"Please, please!" Then I let him anyway. Cars
droned and flashed, sucking at the cow parsley. Later
there were teas and the engagement party. The wedding
in the rain. The hotel where I slept in the bathroom.
The night when he slept on the floor.

The ache of remembering, bitterer than a birth. Better
to lie still and let the babies run through me.
To let them possess me. They will spare me
spring after spring. Their hungers deliver me.
I grow fat as they devour me. I give them my sleep
and they absolve me from waking. Who can accuse me?
I am beyond blame.

[1964]

# POEM TO MY DAUGHTER

"I think I'm going to have it,"
I said, joking between pains.
The midwife rolled competent
sleeves over corpulent milky arms.
"Dear, you never have it,
we deliver it."
A judgment years proved true.
Certainly I've never had you

as you still have me, Caroline.
Why does a mother need a daughter?
Heart's needle—hostage to fortune—
freedom's end. Yet nothing's more perfect
than that bleating, razor-shaped cry
that delivers a mother to her baby.
The bloodcord snaps that held
their sphere together. The child,
tiny and alone, creates the mother.

A woman's life is her own
until it is taken away
by a first particular cry.
Then she is not alone
but a part of the premises
of everything there is.
A branch, a tide . . . a war.
When we belong to the world
we become what we are.

[1982]

# DIANE DI PRIMA, 1934–

## THE QUARREL

You know I said to Mark that I'm furious at you.

No he said are you bugged. He was drawing Brad who was asleep on
the bed.

Yes I said I'm pretty god-damned bugged. I sat down by the fire and
stuck my feet out to warm them up.

Jesus I thought you think it's so easy. There you sit innocence
personified. I didn't say anything else to him.

You know I thought I've got work to do too sometimes. In fact I
probably have just as fucking much work to do as you do. A piece of
wood fell out of the fire and I poked it back in with my toe.

I am sick I said to the woodpile of doing dishes. I am just as lazy as
you. Maybe lazier. The toe of my shoe was scorched from the fire and
I rubbed it where the suede was gone.

Just because I happen to be a chick I thought.

Mark finished one drawing and looked at it. Then he put it down
and started another one.

It's damned arrogant of you I thought to assume that only you have
things to do. Especially tonight.

And what a god-damned concession it was for me to bother to tell
you that I was bugged at all I said to the back of his neck. I didn't
say it out loud.

I got up and went into the kitchen to do the dishes. And shit I thought
I probably won't bother again. But I'll get bugged and not bother to
tell you and after a while everything will be awful and I'll never say
anything because it's so fucking uncool to talk about it. And that I
thought will be that and what a shame.

Hey hon Mark yelled at me from the living room. It says here
Picasso produces fourteen hours a day.

[1961]

## APRIL FOOL BIRTHDAY POEM FOR GRANDPA

Today is your
birthday and I have tried
writing these things before,
but now
in the gathering madness, I want to
thank you
for telling me what to expect
for pulling
no punches, back there in that scrubbed Bronx parlor
thank you
for honestly weeping in time to
innumerable heartbreaking
Italian operas for
pulling my hair when I
pulled the leaves off the trees so I'd
know how it feels, we are
involved in it now, revolution, up to our
knees and the tide is rising, I embrace
strangers on the street, filled with their love and
mine, the love you told us had to come or we
die, told them all in that Bronx park, me listening in
spring Bronx dusk, breathing stars, so glorious
to me your white hair, your height your fierce
blue eyes, rare among Italians, I stood
a ways off, looking up at you, my grandpa
people listened to, I stand
a ways off listening as I pour out soup
young men with light in their faces
at my table, talking love, talking revolution
which is love, spelled backwards, how
you would love us all, would thunder your anarchist wisdom
at us, would thunder Dante, and Giordano Bruno, orderly men
bent to your ends, well I want you to know
we do it for you, and your ilk, for Carlo Tresca,

for Sacco and Vanzetti, without knowing
it, or thinking about it, as we do it for Aubrey Beardsley
Oscar Wilde (all street lights
shall be purple), do it
for Trotsky and Shelley and big dumb
Kropotkin
Eisenstein's Strike people, Jean Cocteau's ennui, we do it for
the stars over the Bronx
that they may look on earth
and not be ashamed.

[1975]


NARROW PATH INTO THE BACK COUNTRY
*For Audre Lorde*


I

You are flying to Dahomey, going back
to some dream, or never-never land
more forbidding & perfect
than Oz. Will land in Western airport
noisy, small & tacky, will look around
for Oshun, as she stands
waiting for baggage. Well, we carry
pure-land paradise within, you carry
it to Dahomey, from Staten Island,


2

we endure, this we are certain of, no more,
we endure: famine, depression, earthquake,
        pestilence, war, flood, police state,
        inflation
ersatz food, burning cities, you endure,
        I endure. It is written
on the faces of our children. Pliant, persistent
        joy: Will like mountains, hope
that batters yr heart & mine. (Hear them shout)
And I will not bow out, cannot see
your war as different. Turf stolen from
        yours & mine; clandestine magics

we practice, all of us, for their protection.
That they have fruit to eat & rice & fish
till they grow strong.

(Remember the octopus we did not cook
Sicilian style/West African style—it fills
your daughter's dream)    I refuse
to leave you to yr battles, me to mine

my girl
chased white coyote, sister to my wolf
& not thru mesas.

3

How to get the food on the table
how to heal
what survives this whirlwind:
people and land. The sea
tosses feverish; screams in delirium.
To have the right herb drying in the kitchen:
your world & mine/ all others: not the Third
this is Fourth World going down, the Hopi say.
Yet we endure.

4

And more, we fly to light, fly into
pure-land paradise, New York
Dahomey, Mars, Djakarta, Wales
The willful, stubborn children carrying seed
all races; hurtling time & space & stars
to find container large & fine enough
fine-wrought enough for our joy.
For all our joy.

[1975]

## POEM IN PRAISE OF MY HUSBAND

*Taos*

I suppose it hasn't been easy living with me either,
with my piques, and ups and downs, my need for privacy
leo pride and weeping in bed when you're trying to sleep
and you, interrupting me in the middle of a thousand poems
did I call the insurance people? the time you stopped a poem
in the middle of our drive over the nebraska hills and
into colorado, odetta singing, the whole world singing in me
the triumph of our revolution in the air
me about to get that down, and you
you saying something about the carburetor
so that it all went away

but we cling to each other
as if each thought the other was the raft
and he adrift alone, as in this mud house
not big enough, the walls dusting down around us, a fine dust rain
counteracting the good, high air, and stuffing our nostrils
we hang our pictures of the several worlds:
new york collage, and san francisco posters,
set out our japanese dishes, chinese knives
hammer small indian marriage cloths into the adobe
we stumble thru silence into each other's gut

blundering thru from one wrong place to the next
like kids who snuck out to play on a boat at night
and the boat slipped from its moorings, and they look at the stars
about which they know nothing, to find out
where they are going

[1990]

# Audre Lorde, 1934–1992

## THE WOMAN THING

The hunters are back
from beating the winter's face
in search of a challenge or task
in search of food
making fresh tracks
for their children's hunger
they do not watch the sun
they cannot wear its heat
for a sign of triumph
or freedom.

The hunters are treading heavily
homeward through snow
marked by their own bloody footprints.
Emptyhanded     the hunters return
snow-maddened
sustained by their rages.

In the night after food they will seek
young girls for their amusement.
Now the hunters are coming
and the unbaked girls
flee from their angers.

All this day I have craved
food for my child's hunger
emptyhanded
the hunters come shouting
injustice drips from their mouths
like stale snow
melted in sunlight.

The woman thing
my mother taught me
bakes off its covering of snow
like a rising Blackening sun.

[1964]

# HANGING FIRE

I am fourteen
and my skin has betrayed me
the boy I cannot live without
still sucks his thumb
in secret
how come my knees are
always so ashy
what if I die
before morning
and momma's in the bedroom
with the door closed.

I have to learn how to dance
in time for the next party
my room is too small for me
suppose I die before graduation
they will sing sad melodies
but finally
tell the truth about me
there is nothing I want to do
and too much
that has to be done
and momma's in the bedroom
with the door closed.

Nobody even stops to think
about my side of it
I should have been on Math Team
my marks were better than his
why do I have to be
the one
wearing braces
I have nothing to wear tomorrow
will I live long enough
to grow up
and momma's in the bedroom
with the door closed.

[1978]

SISTERS IN ARMS

The edge of our bed was a wide grid
where your fifteen-year-old daughter was hanging
gut-sprung on police wheels
a cablegram nailed to the wood
next to a map of the Western Reserve
I could not return with you to bury the body
reconstruct your nightly cardboards
against the seeping Transvaal cold
I could not plant the other limpet mine
against a wall at the railroad station
nor carry either of your souls back from the river
in a calabash upon my head
so I bought you a ticket to Durban
on my American Express
and we lay together
in the first light of a new season.

Now clearing roughage from my autumn garden
cow sorrel    overgrown rocket gone to seed
I reach for the taste of today
the *New York Times* finally mentions your country
a half-page story
of the first white south african killed in the "unrest"
Not of Black children massacred at Sebokeng
six-year-olds imprisoned for threatening the state
not of Thabo Sibeko, first grader, in his own blood
on his grandmother's parlor floor
Joyce, nine, trying to crawl to him
shitting through her navel
not of a three-week-old infant, nameless
lost under the burned beds of Tembisa
my hand comes down like a brown vise over the marigolds
reckless through despair
we were two Black women touching our flame
and we left our dead behind us
I hovered    you rose    the last ritual of healing
"It is spring," you whispered
"I sold the ticket for guns and sulfa
I leave for home tomorrow"

and wherever I touch you
I lick cold from my fingers
taste rage
like salt from the lips of a woman
who has killed too often to forget
and carries each death in her eyes
your mouth a parting orchid
"Someday you will come to *my* country
and we will fight side by side?"

Keys jingle in the door ajar    threatening
whatever is coming belongs here
I reach for your sweetness
but silence explodes like a pregnant belly
into my face
a vomit of nevers.

Mmanthatisi turns away from the cloth
her daughters-in-law are dyeing
the baby drools milk from her breast
she hands him half-asleep to his sister
dresses again for war
knowing the men will follow.
In the intricate Maseru twilights
quick    sad    vital
she maps the next day's battle
dreams of Durban    sometimes
visions the deep wry song of beach pebbles
running after the sea.

Note: *M-mán-tha-tisi:* warrior queen and leader of the Tlokwa (Sotho) people during the
*mfecane* (crushing), one of the greatest crises in southern African history. The Sotho now live
in the Orange Free State, S.A.
  *Má-se-ru:* scene of a great Tlokwa battle and now the capital of Lesotho.
  *Durban:* Indian Ocean seaport and resort area in Natal Province, S.A.

[1986]

# SONIA SANCHEZ, 1934–

## POEM AT THIRTY

it is midnight
no magical bewitching
hour for me
i know only that
i am here waiting
remembering that
once as a child
i walked two
miles in my sleep.
did i know
then where i
was going?
traveling. i'm
always traveling.
i want to tell
you about me
about nights on a
brown couch when
i wrapped my
bones in lint and
refused to move.
no one touches
me anymore.
father do not
send me out
among strangers.
you you black man
stretching scraping
the mold from your body
here is my hand.
i am not afraid
of the night.

[1968]

## A POEM FOR MY MOST INTELLIGENT 10:30 AM CLASS/FALL 1985

it was autumn. the day insistent
as rust. the city standing
at the edge of confessionals.
i had come to this room from other
rooms. footsteps walking from
under my feet. and i saw
your faces eavesdropping on shadows
rinsing the assassins from your eyes.
and our legs genuflected
beyond pain. incest. rage. and
we turned corners where the scare
crow smiles of priapus would never
dominate. and we braided our
tongues with sequins gathered
up our mothers' veins in
skirts of incense. what we
know now is that the coming spring
will not satisfy this thirst.

[1987]


## A POEM FOR MY BROTHER
*(reflections on his death from AIDS:*
*June 8, 1981)*


### 1. death

The day you died
a fever starched my bones.
within the slurred
sheets, i hoarded my legs
while you rowed out among the boulevards
balancing your veins on sails.
easy the eye of hunger
as i peeled the sharp
sweat and swallowed wholesale molds.

## 2. recovery (a)

What comes after
is consciousness of the morning
of the licensed sun that subdues
immoderate elements.
there is a kindness in illness
the indulgence of discrepancies.


reduced to the ménage of houses
and green drapes that puff their seasons
toward the face.
i wonder what to do now.
i am afraid.
i remember a childhood that cried
after extinguished lights
when only the coated banners answered.


## 3. recovery (b)

There is a savior in these buds
look how the phallic stems distend
in welcome.
O copper flowerheads
confine my womb that i may dwell within.
i see these gardens, whom i love
i feel the sky's sweat on my face
now that these robes no longer bark
i praise abandonment.


## 4. wake

i have not come for summary.
must i renounce all babylons?
here, without psalms.
these leaves grow white
and burn the bones with dance.
here, without surfs.
young panicles bloom on the clouds and fly
while myths tick grey as thunder.

### 5. burial

you in the crow's rain
rusting amid ribs
my mouth spills your birth
i have named you prince of boards
stretching with the tides.

you in the toad's tongue
peeling on nerves
look. look. the earth is running palms.


### 6. (on) (the) (road) again

somewhere a flower walks in mass
purchasing wholesale christs
sealing white-willow sacraments.

naked on steeples
where trappist idioms sail
an atom peels the air.

O i will gather my pulse
muffled by sibilants
and follow disposable dreams.

[1987]


# JEAN VALENTINE, 1934–

## FIRST LOVE

How deep we met in the sea, my love,
My double, my Siamese heart, my whiskery,
Fish-belly, glue-eyed prince, my dearest black nudge,
How flat and reflective my eye reflecting you

Blue, gorgeous in the weaving grasses
I wound round for your crown, how I loved your touch
On my fair, speckled breast, or was it my own turning;
How nobly you spilled yourself across my trembling
Darlings: or was that the pull of the moon,
It was all so dark, and you were green in my eye,
Green above and green below, all dark,
And not a living soul in the parish
Saw you go, hélas!
Gone your feathery nuzzle, or was it mine,
Gone your serpentine
Smile wherein I saw my maidenhood smile,
Gone, gone all your brackish shine,
Your hidden curl, your abandoned kill,
Aping the man, liebchen! my angel, my own!
How deep we met, how dark,
How wet! before the world began.

[1965]


## THE FORGIVENESS DREAM:
## MAN FROM THE WARSAW GHETTO

He looked about six or seven, only much too thin.
It seemed right he would be there, but everything,
every lineation, was slow . . .    He was speaking in Polish,
I couldn't answer him.
He pointed at the window, the trees, the snow,
our silver auditorium.

I said to him in English, "I've lived the whole time
here, in peace. A private life."    "In shame,"
I said.    He nodded.    He was old now, kind,
my teacher's age; my mother's age.    He nodded,
and wrote in my notebook—"Let it be good."

He frowned, and stopped,
as if he'd forgotten something,
and wrote again,
"Let it."
*    *    *

I walk, and stop, and walk—
touch the birch bark    shining, powdery, cold:
taste the snow, hot on my tongue—
pure cold, licked from the salt of my hand:

This quiet, these still unvisitable stars
move with choices.
Our kin are here.
Were here.

[1979]

## SNOW LANDSCAPE, IN A GLASS GLOBE
*In memory of Elizabeth Bishop*

A thumb's-length landscape: Snow, on a hill
in China. I turn the glass ball over in my hand,
and watch the snow
blow around the Chinese woman,
calm at her work,
carrying her heavy yoke
uphill, towards the distant house.
Looking out through the thick glass ball
she would see the lines of my hand,
unearthly winter trees, unmoving, behind the snow . . .

No more elders.
The Boston snow grays and softens
the streets where you were . . .
Trees older than you, alive.

The snow is over and the sky is light.
Pale, pale blue distance . . .
Is there an east? A west? A river?
*There,* can we live right?

I look back in through the glass. You,
in China, I can talk to you.
The snow has settled; but it's cold
there, where you are.
\*   \*   \*

What are you carrying?
For the sake of what? through such hard wind
and light.
              —And you look out to me,
and you say, "Only the same as everyone; your breath,
your words, move with mine,
under and over this glass; we who were born
and lived on the living earth."

[1989]

## MY MOTHER'S BODY, MY PROFESSOR, MY BOWER

Who died? My mother's body,
my professor, my bower,
my giant clam.
Serene water, professor
of copious clay,
of spiraling finger-holes in the clay,
of blue breast-milk,
first pulse, all thought:
there is nothing to get. You can't eat money,
dear throat, dear longing,
dear belly, dear fatness,
dear silky fastness: ecstatic lungs' breath,
you can't protect yourself,
there is nothing to get.

[1992]

## X

> *I have decorated this banner to honor my brother. Our parents did not
> want his name used publicly.*
> —from an unnamed child's banner in the AIDS Memorial Quilt

The boatpond, broken off, looks back at the sky.
I remember looking at you, X, this way,
taking in your red hair, your eyes' light, and I miss you
so. I know,
you are you, and real, standing there in the doorway,
whether dead or whether living, real.—Then Y
said, "Who will remember me three years after I die?

What is there for my eye
to read then?"
The lamb should not have given
his wool.
He was so small. At the end, X, you were so small.
Playing with a stone
on your bedspread at the edge of the ocean.

[1992]


# NELLIE WONG, 1934–


## RELINING SHELVES

Can you imagine joy
in relining kitchen shelves?
In rows of tiny red tulips
splashed on yellow?
Ah, the grease, the grime
they play their part
nagging silently
each time you open
the doors for some oil,
a covered casserole.

And you wonder if the Chinese bowl
with pink peonies,
if the handthrown jar
with brown and gray waves,
if the yellow dish
with a crack in its belly
will meet with the Snowdrift,
collide with the peppercorns,
tackle the mustard,
ruminate with the rum abstract.

Do they creep out of the cupboards
at night, talk with the ants,

collaborate with the dust?
And instead of going to the beach,
I contemplate hours
at the Dime & Dollar
and reline the shelves.

Oh, kitchen of dreams,
you make the broom dance
the question of domesticity.
If I could eat
and sweep.

Meanwhile on the evening news
a girl testifies
she has been raped.
Did she resist?
Oh yes, she did,
she stood up
not even five feet tall
against her attackers
and her attorney admits
his client once had sex
with a woman
but in that case
she had been willing.

In a news article
a GI raps about Vietnam
how a prostitute was taken
like a sack of rice
from a GI's bed,
how the girl
had to be returned
to the first GI,
because the chick was his,
because the sergeant said so.

And I ask myself
what does relining shelves
have to do

with a girl who's been raped
who's had sex with a woman,
what does relining shelves
have to do
with a prostitute
who is called a "gook"?

[1977]

## TOWARD A 44TH BIRTHDAY

Mornings and eggshells crack, the eggshells scatter
to the wind. You carry them within you, the wind,
and lift your feet toward construction sites and know
that construction men eye women from the corners
of their eyes. Silence sniffs at you like a cat
and still you walk toward work, toward skyscrapers,
imagine the shattering of old plateglass. You forget
the Ko-Rec-Type, the carbon copies, the Xerox machines.
The timeclock ticks, a medallion on the wall. You dream
of grinding coffee beans, relaxing in the hot sun of Egypt,
forget that the pyramids are a wonder of the world.
Is it another vacation you need, apple trees to sit
under, the longings of a girl searching for arms,
hands to link to her tiny fingers? You sigh, reading
of diamonds in millionaires' teeth, of maids tidying
beds for other maids, of a Luckys strikebreaker being struck
by a car. No, not a car, but a driver, a human being.
What life will you find in your roamings toward China,
toward Asian America in its kitchens crowded with dreams,
on its streets teeming with cracks, toward young men
being tried for killings at the Golden Dragon, toward
pioneer women of the 19th century, the pioneer women
who live within your bones and the voice of Siu Sin Far
nudges you awake. How far, how near will sisters talk?
Will art atrophy, will it become the tools in our hands?

[1984]

# COLLEEN MCELROY, 1935–

## GRA'MA

Gra'ma was a little bit of a thing,
Full of spirits wandering
From an Alabama plantation to St. Louis.
Three on a match and a hat on the bed
Says the oldest will die.
She told me this at the age of five.
Her skin spoke of Chinese coolies
And overseers. Her face sang
Of Tanzania near Congolese waters,
Crocodiles running rapidly by
Gathering stones as a village screamed
Its death throes. That combination
Got her in the house when she was young;
Scrubbing, serving and suckling
Pink babies. Kept her there
Until 40 acres and a mule
Times a hundred kin freed her
With that long tall man
We came to love as Papa.
Set them near a Georgia swamp,
Pulling half a year's living
From the soil. He moved her north
Where she had a story for every day.
Told me: Listen close, child,
The world and the Lord are both profound.
When Papa died, her stories grew shorter;
She forgot which of those 40 acres
Could be mine or how many mules
You need to pull a plow.
When she finally saw my son,
She said: I guess the mules
Done long since gone.

[1972]

# IN MY MOTHER'S ROOM
*(for Vanessa)*

my mother lies spread-eagle upon the bed
I am in the next room with my daughter
slowly passing away the evening
in a late summer's drone of hours
muffled sounds of children's games
drift through the window
along with the odor of thick honeysuckle
and the flicker of yellow fireflies
the warp and weft of their flight
draws me to the edge of a time when I was
a child, this house my prison
and my mother sprawled naked on the bed
signaled hours to be spent alone
hiding in a book
or in my room under the clapboard eaves
now my father sits by himself in the garden

my mother snores
her mouth open in a sagging *oh*
her flowered bathrobe
slipping from the edge of the bed
in a cascade of roses
I am slumped in the overstuffed chair
watching the TV grind past endless hours
my daughter frowns
but will not look directly at us
fully clothed, I am as vulnerable
as my mother, whose childbearing scars
are slightly visible as she lies under
the humid blanket of another midwestern summer

cankered by antagonisms
we are shadows of black into black
one of the other
I can draw my own body into the damp out-
line she will leave when she awakens
one day, I will walk into this house
lift her flowered robe from my shoulders

then stumble and sink onto that bed
in perfect mimicry
my legs will flow into the age-old patterns
my pubic hairs will curl tightly
into the early evening heat
and I will breathe the labors
of a hundred midwestern summers

but tonight, I am fully clothed
and I smile at my daughter's frowns
she has wrapped herself in innocence
against this scene
I motion her to the door
toward the scent of flowers and children playing
knowing all too soon
she will finally
finger her breasts
and disappear into crowds
of us naked women

[1984]

## THIS IS THE POEM I NEVER MEANT TO WRITE

my grandmother
raised me Georgia style
a broken mirror
spilled salt
a tattered hemline
all add up to bad spirits
when she died, I learned to worship
stranger things
a faded textbook full of bad theories
has no spirit at all
now I've gone full circle
in a town some still call Bahia
the drumbeat of the alabés
echoes my grandmother's warnings
I watch the daughters of the candomblé
dance to the rhythms of ancient spirits
as the ceremony begins

my lungs expand
like gas-filled dirigibles
stretched latex-thin

my grandmother spoke
the language of this scene
the mystery and magic
of rich colors in a tapestry
of brown and black skin
white candles
a small reed boat
six bloody gamecocks
all bind this church to its African source
I follow my people past spirit houses
past tight Spanish streets
where houses are painted blue and white
like any Moorish town
when we reach the sea
water seems to flow uphill
tropical landscapes turn mustard yellow
and above us the moon swallows the night

this is the poem
I never meant to write
I am learning to worship
my grandmother's spirits
an old woman
splinters of wood embedded
in her black leathery cheeks
three crosses tattooed
on the fleshy black skin
of her upper arms
draws my picture upon her palm
in blue ink
then tells me we are all strangers
bound by the same spirit
I have gone home
in the dim light
my grandmother smiles

[1984]

QUEEN OF THE EBONY ISLES

this old woman follows me from room to room
screams like my mother    angers like my child
teases me    rolling her tattooed hips forward
and out    steals my food    my name    my smile
when you call her I come running

when we were young and perfect
we danced together and oh we loved well
all the husbands and lovers    children and books
the sunshine and long walks on lonely nights
now she sucks me thin with her affairs

weaves romantic shadows over the windows
and curses my sober moods    kisses everyone
and insists on wearing red shoes
she hums the same songs over and over
something about love and centuries turning upon us

each time she changes the verse
shifting the words like cards in a game
of solitaire    the hot patent-leather colors
her mercurial moods as she flies about
her red heels glittering and clicking out of tune

she has seen too many comic strips
believes she's as deadly lovely
as Dragon Lady and Leopard Girl    I resist
but her limbs are daring    oiled for movement

without me who are you she asks    I am heavy
with silence    my hands are maps of broken lines
without her all sounds are hollow    I am numbed
cold and cannot read the cycles of the moon
even the sun    the sun cannot warm me

aloneness is a bad fiddle I play against my own
burning    bet your kinky muff she cackles knowing
the symptoms    then draped in feather boas

she drags me toward yet another lover    beckoning
with her brash reds pulsing like haunting violins

on midnight-blue nights she screams
into the eyes of the moon    twirling her war machine
like some kamikaze pilot    her heat bakes my skin
even blacker    she's never happy unless we're falling
in love or hate    she grows younger while I

age and age    bandage wounds and tire too easily
she says    play the game    play the game she says
when I complain she says I'm hearing voices
she's hacked my rocking chair into firewood
I am the clown in all her dreams

when she looks into the mirror from my eyes
I want to float away unscathed
drift like patches of early morning fog
she thinks I stay because I love her
one day soon I'll move while she's sleeping

[1984]


## FOUL LINE — 1987

Her back in a line straight
As an ironing board
She serves my lunch
And never shows her face
            My companion is right
            For her menu—white and male
            She gives him all her attention
            Reading his every wish
            With careful eyes as she avoids
            My gaze
Nothing personal
But all she sees is color
Black, a shadow, something dark
Near her left hip, the one she rests
Her elbow against when she wrist-
Flicks the plate dead center

On my placemat like a back-
Handed pitcher
       Such a little
       Gesture with all the effort
       Of breeding behind it
       So dainty, the proper flaunt
       Of a Southern girl's hanky
       And all within legal
If not civil limits
And I wonder vaguely if I might
Have met her in Selma
Or later opposite some other picket
Lines—we're the right age
For such encounters
       And despite laws to the contrary
       Neither of us has ever lost
       Our sense of misplacement
       And can say politely
       We both know how far we've come

                                                    [1990]


# LUCILLE CLIFTON, 1936–


## MISS ROSIE

When I watch you
wrapped up like garbage
sitting, surrounded by the smell
of too old potato peels
or
when I watch you
in your old man's shoes
with the little toe cut out
sitting, waiting for your mind
like next week's grocery
I say
when I watch you
you wet brown bag of a woman

who used to be the best looking gal in Georgia
used to be called the Georgia Rose
I stand up
through your destruction
I stand up

[1969]


## ADMONITIONS

boys
i don't promise you nothing
but this
what you pawn
i will redeem
what you steal
i will conceal
my private silence to
your public guilt
is all i got

girls
first time a white man
opens his fly
like a good thing
we'll just laugh
laugh real loud my
black women

children
when they ask you
why is your mama so funny
say
she is a poet
she don't have no sense

[1969]


## THE WAY IT WAS

mornings
i got up early
greased my legs

straightened my hair and
walked quietly out
not touching

in the same place
the tree    the lot
the poolroom    deacon moore
everything was stayed

nothing changed
(nothing remained the same)
i walked out quietly
mornings
in the '40s
a nice girl
not touching
trying to be white                                    [1972]

## TURNING

turning into my own
turning on in
to my own self
at last
turning out of the
white cage, turning out of the
lady cage
turning at last
on a stem like a black fruit
in my own season
at last                                               [1974]

## THE THIRTY-EIGHTH YEAR

the thirty-eighth year
of my life,
plain as bread
round as a cake
an ordinary woman.

an ordinary woman.

\*   \*   \*

i had expected to be
smaller than this,
more beautiful,
wiser in afrikan ways,
more confident,
i had expected
more than this.

i will be forty soon.
my mother once was forty.

my mother died at forty-four,
a woman of sad countenance
leaving behind a girl
awkward as a stork.
my mother was thick,
her hair was a jungle and
she was very wise
and beautiful
and sad.

i have dreamed dreams
for you mama
more than once.
i have wrapped me
in your skin
and made you live again

more than once.
i have taken the bones you hardened
and built daughters
and they blossom and promise fruit
like afrikan trees.
i am a woman now.
an ordinary woman.

in the thirty-eighth
year of my life,
surrounded by life,
a perfect picture of

blackness blessed,
i had not expected this
loneliness.

if it is western,
if it is the final
europe in my mind,
if in the middle of my life
i am turning the final turn
into the shining dark
let me come to it whole
and holy
not afraid
not lonely
out of my mother's life
into my own.
into my own.

i had expected more than this.
i had not expected to be
an ordinary woman.                                      [1974]

## THE COMING OF KALI

it is the black God, Kali,
a woman God and terrible
with her skulls and breasts.
i am one side of your skin,
she sings, softness is the other,
you know you know me well, she sings,
you know you know me well.

running Kali off is hard.
she is persistent with her
black terrible self. she
knows places in my bones
i never sing about but
she knows i know them well.
she knows.
she knows.

                                                        [1974]

# THERE IS A GIRL INSIDE

there is a girl inside.
she is randy as a wolf.
she will not walk away
and leave these bones
to an old woman.

she is a green tree
in a forest of kindling.
she is a green girl
in a used poet.

she has waited
patient as a nun
for the second coming,
when she can break through gray hairs
into blossom

and her lovers will harvest
honey and thyme
and the woods will be wild
with the damn wonder of it.

[1980]

## TO MY FRIEND, JERINA

listen,
when i found there was no safety
in my father's house
i knew there was none anywhere.
you are right about this,
how i nurtured my work
not my self, how i left the girl
wallowing in her own shame
and took on the flesh of my mother.
but listen,
the girl is rising in me,
not willing to be left to
the silent fingers in the dark,
and you are right,

she is asking for more than
most men are able to give,
but she means to have what she
has earned,
sweet sighs, safe houses,
hands she can trust.

[1991]

## WISHES FOR SONS

i wish them cramps.
i wish them a strange town
and the last tampon.
i wish them no 7-11.

i wish them one week early
and wearing a white skirt.
i wish them one week late.

later i wish them hot flashes
and clots like you
wouldn't believe.   let the
flashes come when they
meet someone special.
let the clots come
when they want to.

let them think they have accepted
arrogance in the universe,
then bring them to gynecologists
not unlike themselves.

[1991]

# Jayne Cortez, 1936–

## RAPE

What was Inez supposed to do for
the man who declared war on her body
the man who carved a combat zone between her breasts
Was she supposed to lick crabs from his hairy ass
kiss every pimple on his butt
blow hot breath on his big toe
draw back the corners of her vagina and
hee haw like a Calif. burro

This being wartime for Inez
she stood facing the knife
the insults and
her own smell drying on the penis of
the man who raped her

She stood with a rifle in her hand
doing what a defense department will do in times of war
And when the man started grunting and panting and wobbling
    forward like
a giant hog
She pumped lead into his three hundred pounds of shaking flesh
Sent it flying to the virgin of Guadalupe
then celebrated day of the dead rapist punk
and just what the fuck else was she supposed to do?

And what was Joanne supposed to do for
the man who declared war on her life
Was she supposed to tongue his encrusted toilet stool lips
suck the numbers off of his tin badge
choke on his clap trap balls
squeeze on his nub of rotten maggots and
sing god bless america thank you for fucking my life away

This being wartime for Joanne
she did what a defense department will do in times of war

and when the piss drinking    shit sniffing guard said
I'm gonna make you wish you were dead black bitch come here
Joanne came down with an ice pick in
the swat freak mother fucker's chest
yes in the fat neck of that racist policeman
Joanne did the dance of the ice picks and once again
from coast to coast
house to house
we celebrated day of the dead rapist punk
and just what the fuck else were we supposed to do

[1982]


## STOCKPILING

The stockpiling of frozen trees
        in the deep freeze of the earth
The stockpiling of dead animals
        in the exhaust pipes of supersonic rockets
The stockpiling of desiccated plants
        on the death root of an abcessed tooth
The stockpiling of defoliants
        in the pine forest of the skull
The stockpiling of aerosols
        in the pink smoke of a human corpse
Stockpiles
        of agent orange agent blue agent white acids
        burning like the hot hoof of a race horse on
                                the tongue
Look at it
        through the anti-bodies in the body
        through the multiple vaccines belching in the
                                veins
        through the cross-infection of viruses
                        stockpiled
                        in the mouth
        through the benzine vapors shooting
                        into the muscles of the
                        stars
        through the gaseous bowels of military
                        fantasies

through the white radiation of delirious
dreams
Look
this stockpile marries that stockpile
to mix and release a double stockpile of
fissions
exploding
into the shadows of disappearing space
Global incapacitations
Zero
and boom
This is the nuclear bleach of reality
the inflated thigh of edema
the filthy dampness in the scientific pants
of a peace prize
the final stockpile of flesh dancing in
the terrible whooping cough of the wind
And even if you think you have a shelter
that can survive this stockpiling
of communal graves
tell me

Where are you going
with the sucked liver of mustard flint
the split breath of hydrogen fumes
the navel pit of invisible clams
the biological lung of human fleas
the carcinogenic bladder of sponges
lips made of keloid scars
poems in the numb section of the chromosomes
Just where do you think you're going
with that stockpile of
contaminated stink

Listen
When I think of the tactical missiles plunging
into the rancid goiters of the sun
The artillery shells of wiretapping snakes hissing and
vomiting
into the depths of a colorless sky

The accumulation of fried phosphoric pus graffittied
            on the fragile fierceness of the moon
The pestering warheads of death-wings stockpiling
                        feathers upon feathers
                        in the brain
And the mass media's larval of lies stockpiled
                        in the plasma of the ears
And the stockpiling of foreign sap in the fluxes
                        of the blood
And the stockpiling of shattered spines
                        in chromium suits
                                    under
                                    polyurethane
                                    sheets
        I look at this stockpiling
at this rotting vegetation
and I make myself understand the target
That's why I say I'm into life
        preservation of life now
        revolutionary change now
before the choking
        before the panic
            before the penetration
                    of apathy
                            rises up
        and spits fire
    into the toxic tears
        of this stockpile

                                            [1984]


# JUNE JORDAN, 1936–

## WHAT WOULD I DO WHITE?

What would I do white?
What would I do clearly full
of not exactly beans nor

pearls my nose a manicure
my eyes a picture of your wall?

I would disturb the streets by
passing by so pretty kids
on stolen petty cash would look
at me like foreign
writing in the sky
I would forget my furs on any chair.
I would ignore the doormen at the knob
the social sanskrit of my life
unwilling to disclose my cosmetology,
I would forget.

Over my wine I would acquire
I would inspire big returns to equity
the equity of capital I am
accustomed to accept

like wintertime.

I would do nothing.
That would be enough.

[1967]

## IF YOU SAW A NEGRO LADY

If you saw a Negro lady
sitting on a Tuesday
near the whirl-sludge doors of
Horn & Hardart on the main drag
of downtown Brooklyn

solitary and conspicuous as plain
and neat as walls impossible to
fresco and you watched her self-
conscious features shape about
a Horn & Hardart teaspoon
with a pucker from a cartoon
*   *   *

she would not understand
with spine as straight and solid
as her years of bending over floors
allowed

skin cleared of interest by a ruthless
soap    nails square and yellowclean
from metal files

sitting in a forty-year-old flush
of solitude and prickling
from the new white cotton blouse
concealing nothing she had ever noticed
even when she bathed and never
hummed a bathtub tune nor knew one

If you saw her square
above the dirty
mopped-on antiseptic floors
before the rag-wiped table tops

little finger    broad and stiff
in heavy emulation of a cockney

mannerism

would you turn her treat
into surprise observing
happy birthday

[1970]

## CASE IN POINT

A friend of mine who raised six daughters and
who never wrote what she regards as serious
until she
was fifty-three
tells me there is no silence peculiar
to the female
*   *   *

I have decided I have something to say
about female silence: so to speak
these are my 2¢ on the subject:
2 weeks ago I was raped for the second
time in my life the first occasion
being a whiteman and the most recent
situation being a blackman actually
head of the local NAACP

Today is 2 weeks after the fact
of that man straddling
his knees either side of my chest
his hairy arm and powerful left hand
forcing my arms and my hands over my head
flat to the pillow while he rammed
what he described as his quote big dick
unquote into my mouth
and shouted out: "D'ya want to swallow
my big dick; well, do ya?"

He was being rhetorical.
My silence was peculiar
to the female.

[1980]

POEM ABOUT MY RIGHTS

Even tonight and I need to take a walk and clear
my head about this poem about why I can't
go out without changing my clothes my shoes
my body posture my gender identity my age
my status as a woman alone in the evening/
alone on the streets/alone not being the point/
the point being that I can't do what I want
to do with my own body because I am the wrong
sex the wrong age the wrong skin and
suppose it was not here in the city but down on the beach/
or far into the woods and I wanted to go
there by myself thinking about God/or thinking
about children or thinking about the world/all of it

267

disclosed by the stars and the silence:
I could not go and I could not think and I could not
stay there
alone
as I need to be
alone because I can't do what I want to do with my own
body and
who in the hell set things up
like this
and in France they say if the guy penetrates
but does not ejaculate then he did not rape me
and if after stabbing him if after screams if
after begging the bastard and if even after smashing
a hammer to his head if even after that if he
and his buddies fuck me after that
then I consented and there was
no rape because finally you understand finally
they fucked me over because I was wrong I was
wrong again to be me being me where I was/wrong
to be who I am
which is exactly like South Africa
penetrating into Namibia penetrating into
Angola and does that mean I mean how do you know if
Pretoria ejaculates what will the evidence look like the
proof of the monster jackboot ejaculation on Blackland
and if
after Namibia and if after Angola and if after Zimbabwe
and if after all of my kinsmen and women resist even to
self-immolation of the villages and if after that
we lose nevertheless what will the big boys say will they
claim my consent:
Do You Follow Me: We are the wrong people of
the wrong skin on the wrong continent and what
in the hell is everybody being reasonable about
and according to the *Times* this week
back in 1966 the C.I.A. decided that they had this problem
and the problem was a man named Nkrumah so they
killed him and before that it was Patrice Lumumba
and before that it was my father on the campus
of my Ivy League school and my father afraid
to walk into the cafeteria because he said he

was wrong the wrong age the wrong skin the wrong
gender identity and he was paying my tuition and
before that
it was my father saying I was wrong saying that
I should have been a boy because he wanted one/a
boy and that I should have been lighter skinned and
that I should have had straighter hair and that
I should not be so boy crazy but instead I should
just be one/a boy and before that
it was my mother pleading plastic surgery for
my nose and braces for my teeth and telling me
to let the books loose to let them loose in other
words
I am very familiar with the problems of the C.I.A.
and the problems of South Africa and the problems
of Exxon Corporation and the problems of white
America in general and the problems of the teachers
and the preachers and the F.B.I. and the social
workers and my particular Mom and Dad/I am very
familiar with the problems because the problems
turn out to be
me
I am the history of rape
I am the history of the rejection of who I am
I am the history of the terrorized incarceration of
my self
I am the history of battery assault and limitless
armies against whatever I want to do with my mind
and my body and my soul and
whether it's about walking out at night
or whether it's about the love that I feel or
whether it's about the sanctity of my vagina or
the sanctity of my national boundaries
or the sanctity of my leaders or the sanctity
of each and every desire
that I know from my personal and idiosyncratic
and indisputably single and singular heart
I have been raped
be-
cause I have been wrong the wrong sex the wrong age
the wrong skin the wrong nose the wrong hair the

wrong need the wrong dream the wrong geographic
the wrong sartorial I
I have been the meaning of rape
I have been the problem everyone seeks to
eliminate by forced
penetration with or without the evidence of slime and/
but let this be unmistakable this poem
is not consent I do not consent
to my mother to my father to the teachers to
the F.B.I. to South Africa to Bedford-Stuy
to Park Avenue to American Airlines to the hardon
idlers on the corners to the sneaky creeps in
cars
*I am not wrong: Wrong is not my name*
My name is my own my own my own
and I can't tell you who the hell set things up like this
but I can tell you that from now on my resistance
my simple and daily and nightly self-determination
may very well cost you your life

[1980]


## 1977: POEM FOR MRS. FANNIE LOU HAMER

You used to say, "June?
Honey when you come down here you
supposed to stay with me. Where
else?"
Meanin home
against the beer the shotguns and the
point of view of whitemen don'
never see Black anybodies without
some violent itch start up.
                          The ones who
said, "No Nigga's Votin in This Town . . .
lessen it be feet first to the booth"
Then jailed you
beat you brutal
bloody/battered/beat
you blue beyond the feeling
of the terrible

\*    \*    \*

And failed to stop you.
Only God could but He
wouldn't stop
you
fortress from self-
pity

Humble as a woman anywhere
I remember finding you inside the laundromat
in Ruleville
           lion spine relaxed/hell
           what's the point to courage
           when you washin clothes?

But that took courage

           just to sit there/target
           to the killers lookin
           for your singin face
           perspirey through the rinse
           and spin

and later
you stood mighty in the door on James Street
loud callin:

           "BULLETS OR NO BULLETS!
           THE FOOD IS COOKED
           AN' GETTIN COLD!"

We ate
A family tremulous but fortified
by turnips/okra/handpicked
like the lilies

filled to the very living
full

one solid gospel
           (*sanctified*)

one gospel
          (*peace*)

one full Black lily
luminescent
in a homemade field

of love                                                    [1980]

## SOME PEOPLE

Some people despise me be-
cause I have a Venus mound
and not a penis

Does that *sound*
right
to you?                                                    [1989]

## THE FEMALE AND THE SILENCE OF A MAN
### (*cf. W. B. Yeats's "Leda and the Swan"*)

And now she knows: The big fist shattering her face.
Above, the sky conceals the sadness of the moon.
And windows light, doors close, against all trace
of her: She falls into the violence of a woman's ruin.

How should she rise against the plunging of his lust?
She vomits out her teeth. He tears the slender legs apart.
The hairy torso of his rage destroys the soft last bastion
                    of her trust.
He lacerates her breasts. He claws and squeezes out her heart.

She sinks into a meadow pond of lilies and a swan.
She floats above an afternoon of music from the trees.
She vanishes like blood that people walk upon.
She reappears: A mad *bitch* dog that reason cannot seize;
A fever withering the river and the crops:
A lovely girl protected by her cruel/incandescent energies.

                                                    [1989]

# MARGE PIERCY, 1936–

## NOON OF THE SUNBATHER

The sun struts over the asphalt world
arching his gaudy plumes till the streets smoke
and the city sweats oil under his metal feet.
A woman nude on a rooftop lifts her arms:

"Men have swarmed like ants over my thighs,
held their Sunday picnics of gripe and crumb,
the twitch and nip of all their gristle traffic.
When will my brain pitch like a burning tower?
Lion, come down! explode the city of my bones."

The god stands on the steel blue arch and listens.
Then he strides the hills of igniting air,
straight to the roof he hastens, wings outspread.
In his first breath she blackens and curls like paper.
The limp winds of noon disperse her ashes.

But the ashes dance. Each ashfleck leaps at the sun.

[1963]

## THE FRIEND

We sat across the table.
he said, cut off your hands.
they are always poking at things.
they might touch me.
I said yes.

Food grew cold on the table.
he said, burn your body.
it is not clean and smells like sex.
it rubs my mind sore.
I said yes.
  *    *    *

I love you, I said.
that's very nice, he said
I like to be loved,
that makes me happy.
Have you cut off your hands yet?

[1964]


## THE WOMAN IN THE

The woman in the
ordinary pudgy graduate student girl
is crouching with eyes and muscles clenched.
Round and smooth as a pebble
you efface yourself
under ripples of conversation and debate.
The woman in the block of ivory soap
has massive thighs that neigh
and great breasts and strong arms that blare and trumpet.
The woman of the golden fleece
laughs from the belly uproariously
inside the girl who imitates
a Christmas card virgin with glued hands.
It is time to bust out of girlscout camp.
It is time to stop running
for most popular sweetheart of Campbell Soup.
You are still searching for yourself in others' eyes
and creeping so you wont be punished.
In you bottled up is a woman peppery as curry,
a yam of a woman of butter and brass,
compounded of acid and sweet like a pineapple,
like a hand grenade set to explode,
like goldenrod ready to bloom.

[1971]


## HOMAGE TO LUCILLE, DR. LORD-HEINSTEIN

We all wanted to go to you.
Even women who had not heard
of you, longed for you, our
cool gray mother who would

gently, carefully and slowly, using
no nurse but ministering herself,
open our thighs and our vaginas
and show us the os smiling
in the mirror like a full rising moon.

You taught us our health, our sickness
and our regimes, presiding over
the raw ends of life, a priestess eager
to initiate. Never did you tell us
we could not understand what you
understood. You made our bodies
glow transparent. You did not think
you had a license to question us
about our married state or lovers' sex.

Your language was as gentle and caring
as your hands. On the mantel
in the waiting room the clippings hung,
old battles, victories, marches.
You with your flower face, strong
in your thirties in the thirties,
were carted to prison for the crime
of prescribing birth control
for workingclass women in Lynn.

The quality of light in those quiet
rooms where we took our shoes off
before entering and the little
dog accompanied you like a familiar,
was respect: respect for life,
respect for women, respect for choice,
a mutual respect I cannot imagine
I shall feel for any other doctor,
bordering on love.

[1985]

Menopause—word used as an insult:
a menopausal woman, mind or poem
as if not to leak regularly or on the caprice
of the moon, the collision of egg and sperm,
were the curse we first learned to call that blood.

I have twisted myself to praise that bright splash.
When my womb opens its lips on the full
or dark of the moon, that connection
aligns me as it does the sea. I quiver,
a compass needle thrilling with magnetism.

Yet for every celebration there's the time
it starts on a jet with the seatbelt sign on.
Consider the trail of red amoebae
crawling onto hostess' sheets to signal
my body's disregard of calendar, clock.

How often halfway up the side of a mountain,
during a demonstration with the tactical police
force drawn up in tanks between me and a toilet;
during an endless wind machine panel with four males
I the token woman and they with iron bladders,

I have felt that wetness and wanted to strangle
my womb like a mouse. Sometimes it feels cosmic
and sometimes it feels like mud. Yes, I have prayed
to my blood on my knees in toilet stalls
simply to show its rainbow of deliverance.

My friend Penny at twelve, being handed a napkin
the size of an ironing board cover, cried out
Do I have to do this from now till I die?
No, said her mother, it stops in middle age.
Good, said Penny, there's something to look forward to.

Today supine, groaning with demon crab claws
gouging my belly, I tell you I will secretly dance

and pour out a cup of wine on the earth
when time stops that leak permanently;
I will burn my last tampons as votive candles.          [1988]


## THE BOOK OF RUTH AND NAOMI

When you pick up the Tanakh and read
the Book of Ruth, it is a shock
how little it resembles memory.
It's concerned with inheritance,
lands, men's names, how women
must wiggle and wobble to live.

Yet women have kept it dear
for the beloved elder who
cherished Ruth, more friend than
daughter. Daughters leave. Ruth
brought even the baby she made
with Boaz home as a gift.

Where you go, I will go too,
your people shall be my people,
I will be a Jew for you,
for what is yours I will love
as I love you, oh Naomi
my mother, my sister, my heart.

Show me a woman who does not dream
a double, heart's twin, a sister
of the mind in whose ear she can whisper,
whose hair she can braid as her life
twists its pleasure and pain and shame.
Show me a woman who does not hide

in the locket of bone that deep
eye beam of fiercely gentle love
she had once from mother, daughter,
sister; once like a warm moon
that radiance aligned the tides
of her blood into potent order.

* * *

At the season of first fruits we recall
two travelers, co-conspirators, scavengers
making do with leftovers and mill ends,
whose friendship was stronger than fear,
stronger than hunger, who walked together
the road of shards, hands joined.

[1992]

# ALICIA OSTRIKER, 1937–

## PROPAGANDA POEM:
## MAYBE FOR SOME YOUNG MAMAS

### I. THE VISITING POET

     (after reading the girls my old pregnancy poem
     that I thought ripe and beautiful
     after they made themselves clear it was ugly
     after telling the girls I would as soon
     go to my grave a virgin, god
     forbid, as go to my grave without
     ever bearing and rearing a child
     I laughed
     and if looks could kill I would
     have been one dead duck in that
          so-called "feminist" classroom)

Oh young girls in a classroom
with your smooth skins like paper not yet written on
your good American bodies, your breasts, your bellies
fed healthy on hamburgers and milkshakes, almost
like photographs in solution half-developed
I leaned and strained toward you, trying to understand
what you were becoming
as you sat so quietly under the winter light
that fell into our classroom
and I tried, as a teacher, to transmit information
that's my job, knowledge like currency
you have to spend it
* * *

oh young mamas
no matter what your age is you
are born when you give birth
to a baby you start over

one animal

and both gently just slightly
separated from each other
swaying, swinging
like a vine, like an oriole nest
keep returning to each other
like a little tide, like a little wave
for a little while
        better than sex, that bitter honey, maybe
        could be the connection you've been waiting for
        because no man is god, no woman is a goddess
        we are all of us spoiled by that time

        but a baby
                any baby
                        your baby is
                                the
        most perfect human thing you can ever touch
        translucent
        and I want you to think about    touching
        and the pleasure of   touching
        and being touched by this most perfect thing
                this pear tree blossom
           this mouth these leafy hands these genitals
                like petals
          a warm scalp resting against your cheek
                fruit's warmth
                beginning—

Curtains curtains you say young girls
we want to live our lives
don't want the burden the responsibility
the disgusting mess
of children
we want our freedom and we want it now

I see you shudder truly and I wonder what
                    kind of lives you want so badly
                    to live or who has cut you with what axes
                    from the sense of your
                    flowing sap or why
                    are you made of sand
young girls will you walk
out of this door and spend your substance freely
or who has shown to you the greedy mirror
the lying mirror
the desert
sand—

I am telling you and you can take me for a fool there is no
good time like the good time a whole mama
has with a whole little baby and that's
                                   where the first images
of deity came from—sister you know it's true
you know in secret how they
cut us down
                    because who can bear the joy that hurts nobody
                    the dazzling circuit of contact without dominance
                    that by the way might make you less vulnerable
                    to cancer and who knows what other diseases
                    of the body
                    because who can bear a thing that makes you happy
                    and rolls the world a little way
                                        on forward
                                   toward its destiny

                    because a woman is acceptable if she is
                    weak
                    acceptable if she is a victim
                    acceptable also if she is an angry victim ("shrew," "witch")
                    a woman's sorrow is acceptable
                    a deodorized sanitized sterilized antiperspirant
                    grinning efficient woman is certainly acceptable

but who can tolerate the power of a woman
close to a child, riding our tides
into the sand dunes of the public spaces.

## 2. POSTSCRIPT TO PROPAGANDA

That they limit your liberty, of course,
entirely. That they limit your cash. That they limit your sleep.
Your sleep is a dirty torn cloth.
That they whine until you want to murder them. That their beauty
prevents you. That their eating and excreting exactly resembles
the slime-trails of slugs. On your knees you follow, cleaning,
unstaining. That they burn themselves, lacerate themselves, bruise
themselves. That they get ill. That you sit at their bedsides
exhausted, coughing, reading dully to them, wiping their foreheads
with wet washcloths to lower the fever, your life peeling away
from you like layers of cellophane. Of course.

That you are wheels to them. That you are grease.
An iron doorway they kick open, they run out, nobody has
remembered to close it. That their demanding is a gray north wind.
That their sullenness is a damp that rots your wood, their
malice a metal that draws your blood, their disobedience the fire that
burns your sacred book, their sorrows the webbing that entraps you
like a thrashing fish. That when your child grieves, mother,
you bend and grieve. That you disentwine yourself from them, lock
the pores of your love, set them at a distance. That in this
fashion the years pass, like calendar pages flipped in a silent
movie, and you are old, you are wrinkled as tortoises.

Come on, you daughters of bitches, do you want to live forever?


## 3. WHAT ACTUALLY

What a lot of garbage we all shovel. What a lot of
self-serving, self-pitying rhetoric we splash around in.
We paint ourselves wrong. How can I, to paraphrase the
poet, say what I actually mean? What, anyway, do I mean?
About motherhood? It is the unanimity that offends me.
The ideological lockstep, that cannot permit women, humans,
simply to choose for themselves. When I was in college
everyone expected to get married and have babies, and
everyone thought this was her own idea, although from this
distance we can see that we were programmed. Presently
everyone believes motherhood is the sinister invention
of patriarchy.

*  *  *

This week in Paris I learn that the serious intellectual
women are into lesbianism, incest, armed violence and the
theory of hysteria. G. gave her slide lecture on the
re-emergence of the goddess image in women's art and was
called a Nazi. How can I be a Nazi? she said. I'm a Jew.

A friend's daughter dies of crib death. She tries to have
another, fails. Fails. Fails. She and her husband divorce,
she moves to another town, in a year she is pregnant. She
does not want to marry the nice young man. She does not
want an abortion. She keeps her job, she has the baby, she
prays. A friend crosses her fifty-year old legs in bluejeans,
swallows her vodka and says she knows that nothing but her
sobbing when at last she was alone in the airport parking lot
kept her children's jet from crashing in the Atlantic. A
friend's green-eyed son has leukemia, he plays baseball, he
collects stamps, she buys a camera and takes pictures of him
in teeshirt and shorts, as naked as she dares.

Born. I believe that some of us are born to be mamas,
nobody can know how many or which ones. We are probably
identifiable at an early age by our foolish happiness in the
presence of smaller children. Some born not to be. Some in
the middle. Were there maybe a few young mamas sitting in
that classroom in the winter light, subdued, their codes
inaudible? Were they afraid to choose? Have we not explained
to the young that choice equals risk? Wanted to tell them to
decode themselves, like unwrapping a package carefully, not to
damage it. Wanted to tell them, mamas or not mamas, we all get
damaged when put to use, we get like wornout houses, but only
the life that hoards and coffins itself is already dead.

[1975–1979]

## THE EXCHANGE

I am watching a woman swim below the surface
Of the canal, her powerful body shimmering,
Opalescent, her black hair wavering
Like weeds. She does not need to breathe. She faces

* * *

Upward, keeping abreast of our rented canoe.
Sweet, thick, white, the blossoms of the locust trees
Cast their fragrance. A redwing blackbird flies
Across the sluggish water. My children paddle.

If I dive down, if she climbs into the boat,
Wet, wordless, she will strangle my children
And throw their limp bodies into the stream.
Skin dripping, she will take my car, drive home.

When my husband answers the doorbell and sees
This magnificent naked woman, bits of sunlight
Glittering on her pubic fur, her muscular
Arm will surround his neck, once for each insult

Endured. He will see the blackbird in her eye,
Her drying mouth incapable of speech,
And I, having exchanged with her, will swim
Away, in the cool water, out of reach.

[1984]

# DIANE WAKOSKI, 1937–

## JUSTICE IS REASON ENOUGH

He, who once was my brother, is dead by his own hand.
Even now, years later, I see his thin form lying on the sand

where the sheltered sea washes against those cliffs
he chose to die from. Mother took me back there every day for
over a year and asked me, in her whining way, why it had to
    happen

over and over again—until I wanted
never to hear of David any more. How
could I tell her of his dream about the gull beating its wings
effortlessly together until they drew blood?

* * *

Would it explain anything, and how can I tell
anyone here about the great form and its beating wings. How it
swoops down and covers me, and the dark tension leaves

me with blood on my mouth and thighs. But it was that dream,
you must know, that brought my tight, sullen little

brother to my room that night and pushed his whole taut body
right over mine until I yielded, and together we yielded to the
    dark tension.
Over a thousand passing years, I will never forget
him, who was my brother, who is dead. Mother asked me why
every day for a year; and I told her justice. Justice is
reason enough for anything ugly. It balances the beauty in the
    world.

                                                            [1958]


## THE REALIZATION OF DIFFERENCE

The realization of difference comes
quietly. We are looking
at prints of Zen masters—
Chinese,
Japanese.
There is one of persimmons—
just space and persimmons.

The next was slashes of paint,
slashing trees on a slashed mountain—
two grace notes of men
climbing the white page of snow.
Your excitement,
a splatter of paint,
covered me with muddy colors.
I remembered climbing the white mountain
of ice that was your love
and feeling smaller than a grace note
on the white sheet. I remember
dying a thousand times

from the cold as I fell across the page.
I almost hated you
when, excitement rubbing off,
you said, "but,
maybe,
don't the figures stand out too much?"
A realization of difference came,
and comes and comes and comes.
When will I find a lover
who is not a blizzard of slashed feelings?
And when will the realization
of difference
come to you?

[1966]


## THANKING MY MOTHER FOR PIANO LESSONS

The relief of putting your fingers on the keyboard,
as if you were walking on the beach
and found a diamond
as big as a shoe;

as if
you had just built a wooden table
and the smell of sawdust was in the air,
your hands dry and woody;

as if
you had eluded
the man in the dark hat who had been following you
all week;

the relief
of putting your fingers on the keyboard,
playing the chords of
Beethoven,
Bach,
Chopin
      in an afternoon when I had no one to talk to,
      when the magazine advertisement forms of soft sweaters

and clean shining Republican middle-class hair
walked into carpeted houses
and left me alone
with bare floors and a few books

I want to thank my mother
for working every day
in a drab office
in garages and water companies
cutting the cream out of her coffee at 40
to lose weight, her heavy body
writing its delicate bookkeeper's ledgers
alone, with no man to look at her face,
her body, her prematurely white hair
in love
        I want to thank
my mother for working and always paying for
my piano lessons
before she paid the Bank of America loan
or bought the groceries
or had our old rattling Ford repaired.

I was a quiet child,
afraid of walking into a store alone,
afraid of the water,
the sun,
the dirty weeds in back yards,
afraid of my mother's bad breath,
and afraid of my father's occasional visits home,
knowing he would leave again;
afraid of not having any money,
afraid of my clumsy body,
that I knew
        no one would ever love

But I played my way
on the old upright piano
obtained for $10,
played my way through fear,
through ugliness,
through growing up in a world of dime-store purchases,

and a desire to love
a loveless world.

I played my way through an ugly face
and lonely afternoons, days, evenings, nights,
mornings even, empty
as a rusty coffee can,
played my way through the rustles of spring
and wanted everything around me to shimmer like the narrow tide
on a flat beach at sunset in Southern California,
I played my way through
an empty father's hat in my mother's closet
and a bed she slept on only one side of,
never wrinkling an inch of
the other side,
waiting,
waiting,

I played my way through honors in school,
the only place I could
talk
      the classroom,
      or at my piano lessons, Mrs. Hillhouse's canary always
      singing the most for my talents,
      as if I had thrown some part of my body away upon entering
      her house
      and was now searching every ivory case
      of the keyboard, slipping my fingers over black
      ridges and around smooth rocks,
      wondering where I had lost my bloody organs,
      or my mouth which sometimes opened
      like a California poppy,
      wide and with contrasts
      beautiful in sweeping fields,
      entirely closed morning and night,

I played my way from age to age,
but they all seemed ageless
or perhaps always
old and lonely,
wanting only one thing, surrounded by the dusty bitter-smelling

leaves of orange trees,
wanting only to be touched by a man who loved me,
who would be there every night
to put his large strong hand over my shoulder,
whose hips I would wake up against in the morning,
whose mustaches might brush a face asleep,
dreaming of pianos that made the sound of Mozart
and Schubert without demanding
that life suck everything
out of you each day,
without demanding the emptiness
of a timid little life.

I want to thank my mother
for letting me wake her up sometimes at 6 in the morning
when I practiced my lessons
and for making sure I had a piano
to lay my school books down on, every afternoon.
I haven't touched the piano in 10 years,
perhaps in fear that what little love I've been able to
pick, like lint, out of the corners of pockets,
will get lost,
slide away,
into the terribly empty cavern of me
if I ever open it all the way up again.
Love is a man
with a mustache
gently holding me every night,
always being there when I need to touch him;
he could not know the painfully loud
music from the past that
his loving stops from pounding, banging,
battering through my brain,
which does its best to destroy the precarious gray matter when I
am alone;
he does not hear Mrs. Hillhouse's canary singing for me,
liking the sound of my lesson this week,
telling me,
confirming what my teacher says,
that I have a gift for the piano
few of her other pupils had.

\* \* \*

When I touch the man
I love,
I want to thank my mother for giving me
piano lessons
all those years,
keeping the memory of Beethoven,
a deaf tortured man,
in mind;
      of the beauty that can come
from even an ugly
past.

                                          [1970]


## THE GIRLS
*for Margaret Atwood & Cathy Davidson*

I never understood the girls
who had the sweaters
and the latest hairdos copied out of magazines
and who were not afraid of snakes.
They were the thin-hipped ones who looked good
in straight skirts, like exclamation points
behind phrases like "Wow," and "Gee whiz."

I envied their lemon-scented hands
raised to answer almost as many questions
as I, the ugly duckling class brain, did,
with my fat ankles,
and ass as soft as a sofa pillow.
Valerie Twadell who was Miss La Habra
at our August Corn Festival
chased me with worms.

Cathy, with her Zelda-ish bob,
and slimness that even her sorority girl students envy
tells of a snake they ritually put in the 8th grade teacher's
    desk;
and now you, Peggy, as I heard someone nice
call you, slender and chic as Jane Fonda,

tell of your own simple connection with snakes,
wearing them as electric tight bracelets,
wound on a willow wrist,
the delight you took in scaring others,
even men, or women like me,
who would have died had we found even a harmless little
        black
fellow
curled in the grass.

I have never been
one of the girls:
smart without being labeled with derogatory titles like
            "the encyclopedia"
            "the brain,"
graceful without watching calories,
followed by men who adored me even when I turned them
        away,
slow-voiced,
quiet,
with ankles like colts,
and at complete ease with snakes.
I have never been
one of the girls.
At 47, I still envy your cool acceptance
of all these gifts.
                Some part of me
was denied
what all women have,
or are supposed to have, an ease
with the fatly coiled Python whose skin
is like milky underwear,
the thread-like green mamba who slips past
your fingers like mountain water,
the cobra who sits on the family radio
in Sri Lanka,
the cottonmouth who swims next to you all night
in muddy fertile loving water,
or the magic necklace Denise imagines
around her throat.
*   *   *

Men see me as the Medusa,
with vipers hissing around my hair.
How ironic/ I have always been so afraid
of snakes that when I was six
I couldn't turn to the SNAKE page
in my Golden Encyclopedia.

I have never been one of the girls,
comfortable wearing a blacksnake as a belt.
Had I been Lawrence,
near his well in Sicily,
I would have turned and run. He knew
snakes were
the Lords of Life,
but I know you pretty girl women,
who handle them like hula hoops,
or jump ropes,
or pet kittens,
are the real Gods, and your ease with snakes
is proof.
In your presence I am neither man
nor woman. I am simply the one
afraid of snakes; who knows
that in this life
it is the one thing
not allowed.

[1986]

## MONEYLIGHT

Last night I danced alone
in my darkened living room.
Usually when I do this
I am rock 'n rolling, in a way I'd be
embarrassed to do
in public. I dance alone
because that kind of dancing doesn't
require a partner, anyway. But
last night, when I danced, I
held my hands as if they were on the
shoulder and holding the hand

of a man, a partner.
I dipped and swayed and pretended
my cheek was against his, that I was
at a dance.
That I was a different
person.
I was not happy with the thought of single dancing,
but I was almost happy, dancing with a shadow
man. This is
The King of Spain, I thought.

My husband was upstairs in his room,
working on some project or watching sports
TV. He came down once for a Coke
and smiled at me. "Poor Diane," he said.
Didn't offer to dance. Went back upstairs
and left me with my teenage music
and shadow man.

What middle age brings
is the knowledge you can never
be young again. Oddly satisfying,
once you stop being sad. You
can dance with the shadow partner
and not feel you have failed. You can
dance alone and not think it's because
there's something wrong with you. You
can invent a lover and not think
you are crazy. You can make him say all the things
your husband or lovers never said, and he'll dance
when you want to dance, and when you are tired,
you can retire to bed with your book, drink a last cup of tea,
and fall asleep next to your kind husband who whispers,
"Poor Diane," and pulls you closer like a child
to assuage you, to hold you, to love you securely, as no
        father,
as no lover, even the invisible one,
ever has.

[1991]

292

# ELEANOR WILNER, 1937—

## EMIGRATION

There are always, in each of us,
these two: the one who stays,
the one who goes away—
Charlotte, who stayed in the rectory
and helped her sisters die in England;
Mary Taylor who went off to Australia
and set up shop with a woman friend.
"Charlotte," Mary said to her, "you are all
like potatoes growing in the dark."
And Charlotte got a plaque in Westminster
Abbey; Mary we get a glimpse of
for a moment, waving her kerchief
on the packet boat, and disappearing.
No pseudonym for her, and nothing
left behind, no trace
but a wide wake closing.

Charlotte stayed, and paid and paid—
the little governess with the ungovernable
heart, that she put on the altar.
She paid the long indemnity of all
who work for what will never wish them well,
who never set a limit to what's owed
and cannot risk foreclosure. So London
gave her fame, though it could never
sit comfortably with her at dinner—
how intensity palls when it is
plain and small and has no fortune.
When she died with her unborn child
the stars turned east
to shine in the gum trees of Australia,
watching over what has sidetracked evolution,
where Mary Taylor lived
to a great old age, Charlotte's letters in a box
beside her bed, to keep her anger hot.
*   *   *

God bless us everyone until we sicken,
until the soul is like a little child
stricken in its corner by the wall; so there is
one who always sits there under lamplight
writing, staying on, and one
who walks the strange hills of Australia,
far too defiant of convention for the novels
drawn daily from the pen's "if only"—
if only Emily had lived,
if only they'd had money, if only
there had been a man who'd loved them truly . . .
when all the time there had been
Mary Taylor, whom no one would remember
except she had a famous friend named Charlotte
with whom she was so loving-angry,
who up and left to be a woman
in that godforsaken outpost past
the reach of fantasy, or fiction.

[1984]


## CODA, OVERTURE

She stepped out of the framing circle of the dark.
We thought, as she approached, to see her
clearly, but her features only grew more indistinct
as she drew nearer, like those of statues
long submerged in water. We couldn't name her,
she who can't be seen

except in spaces between wars, brief intervals

when history relents, reflection
intervenes, returning home
becomes the epic moment—not the everyday event
postponed in bars; or when you finally reach
the other side of the mountain
and all the paths lead down. As if
an ancient spell had been read backwards:
though what we'd seen—the burning cities
at our backs—had stopped us

in our tracks, a frozen chorus, colonnade
of salt, pillars like the wife of Lot,
the sight of her restored us
to ourselves. How else explain it? The way
she walked among us as we lined her path,
her gaze intent on us till we returned
her look, and then, like embers caught
in a sudden draft, our hope blazed up
again, the flush of blood crept up
reviving limbs . . . we laughed, embraced
and were so natural, so like old friends
picking up where we'd left off, it was as if
the interval of stone had gone
from memory, or it had never been.

But the cities *had* burned, the worst
had all been done, was, even now, being done
again—and yet, perhaps . . .
the one word not at our command: *perhaps*
to learn to live
in the dissolving grip of that green gaze,
put down the shield
emblazoned with the face
of Medusa, the mouth forever open
in a howl. The same face
Goya painted as the rifles were raised
and cocked, *Der Schrei* of Munch
at the vortex where one century of war plunged
into the next; the Pantheon
with its single vacant eye, Cyclops
cramming nations in his mouth—
an emptiness that nothing can assuage
creates its mirror image in
the gaping mouth, unfinished cry
as the head and the body are severed—the horror
on the hero's shield, the sound
of hoofs trampling the wind.

[1989]

## SARAH'S CHOICE

A little late rain                                   *The testing*
the desert in the beauty of its winter              *of Sarah*
bloom, the cactus ablaze
with yellow flowers that glow
even at night in the reflected light
of moon and the shattered crystal of sand
when time was so new
that God still walked
among the tents, leaving no prints
in the sand, but a brand burned into
the heart—on such a night
it must have been, although
it is not written in the Book
how God spoke to Sarah
what he demanded of her
how many questions came of it
how a certain faith was
fractured, as a stone is split
by its own fault, a climate of extremes
and one last drastic change
in the temperature.

"Go!" said the Voice. "Take your son,
your only son, whom you love,
take him to the mountain, bind him
and make of him a burnt offering."
Now Isaac was the son of Sarah's age,
a gift, so she thought, from God. And how
could he ask her even to imagine such a thing—
to take the knife
of the butcher and thrust it
into such a trusting heart, then
light the pyre on which tomorrow burns.
What fear could be more holy
than the fear of *that?*

"Go!" said the Voice, Authority's own.
And Sarah rose to her feet, stepped out
of the tent of Abraham to stand between

the desert and the distant sky, holding its stars
like tears it was too cold to shed.
Perhaps she was afraid the firmament
would shudder and give way, crushing her
like a line of ants who, watching
the ants ahead marching safe under the arch,
are suddenly smashed by the heel
they never suspected. For Sarah,
with her desert-dwelling mind, could
see the grander scale in which the heel
might simply be the underside of some Divine
intention. On such a scale, what is
a human son? So there she stood, absurd
in the cosmic scene, an old woman bent
as a question mark, a mote in the eye
of God. And then it was that Sarah spoke
in a soft voice, a speech
the canon does not record.

"No," said Sarah to the Voice.                               *The*
"I will not be chosen. Nor shall my son—                    *teachings*
if I can help it. You have promised Abraham,                *of Sarah*
through this boy, a great nation. So either
this sacrifice is sham, or else it is a sin.
Shame," she said, for such is the presumption
of mothers, "for thinking me a fool,
for asking such a thing. You must have known
I would choose Isaac. What use have I
for History—an arrow already bent
when it is fired from the bow?"

Saying that, Sarah went into the tent
and found her restless son awake, as if
he'd grown aware of the narrow bed in which he lay.
And Sarah spoke out of the silence
she had herself created, or that had been there
all along. "Tomorrow you will be
a man. Tonight, then, I must tell you
the little that I know. You can be chosen
or you can choose. Not both.
*   *   *

The voice of the prophet grows shrill.
He will read even defeat as a sign
of distinction, until pain itself
becomes holy. In that day, how shall we tell
the victims from the saints,
the torturers from the agents of God?"

"But mother," said Isaac, "if we were not God's
chosen people, what then should we be? I am afraid
of being nothing." And Sarah laughed.

Then she reached out her hand. "Isaac,          *The*
I am going now, before Abraham awakes, before   *unbinding*
the sun, to find Hagar the Egyptian and her son *of Isaac*
whom I cast out, drunk on pride,
God's promises, the seed of Abraham
in my own late-blooming loins."

"But Ishmael," said Isaac, "how should I greet him?"
"As you greet yourself," she said, "when you bend
over the well to draw water and see your image,
not knowing it reversed. You must know your brother
now, or you will see your own face looking back
the day you're at each other's throats."

She wrapped herself in a thick dark cloak
against the desert's enmity, and tying up
her stylus, bowl, some dates, a gourd
for water—she swung her bundle on her back,
reached out once more toward Isaac.
"It's time," she said. "Choose now."

"But what will happen if we go?" the boy
Isaac asked. "I don't know," Sarah said.
"But it is written    what will happen    if you stay."

[1989]

# WANDA COLEMAN, 1938–

## WOMEN OF MY COLOR

i follow the curve of his penis
and go down

there is a peculiar light in which women
of my color are regarded by men

being on the bottom where pressures
are greatest is least desirable
would be better to be dead i
sometimes think

there is a peculiar light in which women
of my race are regarded by black men

as saints
as mothers
as sisters
as whores

but mostly as the enemy

it's not our fault    we are victims
who have chosen to struggle and stay alive

there is a peculiar light in which women
of my race are regarded by white men

as exotic
as enemy

but mostly as whores

it's enough to make me cry
but i don't

following the curve of his penis
i go down

will i ever see
the sun?

[1979]

# DEAR MAMA (2)

*she say that's what*
*mama's for*

you don't know or maybe you do
time you couldn't buy us shoes and asked grandpa
for money. he sent you one dollar
i remember your eyes scanning the letter. the tears
you got us shoes somehow by the good grace of a friend
maybe you are hip in your old-fashioned oklahoma cornspun way

or the time we sat in the dark with no electricity
eating peaches and cold toast
wondering where you'd gone to get the money
for light

grandma named you lewana. it sounds hawaiian
not that bastard mix of white black and red you are
not that bitter cast of negro staged to play to
rowdy crowds on the off broadway of american poor

and she added mae—to make it sound *country*
like jemima or butterfly mc queen or bobbi jo
it's you. and you named us and fed us and
i can't love you enuff for it

you don't know or maybe you do
it hurts being a grown working black woman
branded strong
hurts being unable to get over
in this filthy white world
hurts to ask your parents for help
hurts to swallow those old beaten borrowed green backs
whole
hurts to know
it'll hurt worse if you don't

[1983]

# PAULA GUNN ALLEN, 1939–

## NIGHT VISION

I am standing
on the balcony
of a gold Chinese pavilion
watching the sun
smear shadows
over the pool below.
A girl in a white mask
brings dripping shells
holding shining pearls
to the women at the side.
The water where she dives
is dark; her white clothes
give it some light, but not
enough. When she emerges
with my pearl, she removes her mask.
I see she is a man.
She dives once more
ruffling the shadows for the sun to sweep.
I watch until the water is still
and walk on.

[1982]


## LOS ANGELES, 1980

The death culture swarms
over the land bringing
honeysuckle   eucalyptus   palm
ivy   brick   and unfinished wood
torn from forests to satisfy organic
craving. The death society walks
hypnotized by its silent knowledge
nor does it hear the drum quiet
to the core.
The trees know.
Look.
They are dying.

The small birds who walk heedless
of the people swarming around them
know: they peck at sesame seeds trucked
from factories far away and crumbs
dropped from Rainbow buns. They
do not fly at human approach. They
act as if we are not there.

The dying generation does not know.
Boys offer me papers that shriek
of impending death: *Klan and Nazis Unite!*
the headlines proclaim. I must be aware, be
ware. The rally forming on the steps
beyond the plaza swirls with belief
that protest can change something, a
transformation needed, longed for,
that does not ever seem to come.
"It's getting worse," the young beard
assures me. His hair, teeth, skin
gleam with assured elegance.
"I know," I reply.

The dying generation moves purposefully:
well-dressed in Jantzen and Wrangler
Gucci and Adidas, clothes, bodies,
smiles gleaming, cool in the practiced
superiority of well-cut, natural fiber
clothes and vitamin-drenched consciousness,
they live their truth. They cannot count
the cost. But their silent hearts beat
slow with knowledge their bodies share
with the birds.

On my way to this New Jerusalem
on a smog-shrouded hill, I passed
fine stores filled with hidden omen,
dedicated to health and cleanliness,
luxury and the One True Path.
I could see they were there to save
my life. One brick-front shop's
bronze-tasteful sign announced:

Weight and Smoking Control Center.
In its smoky glass I saw
my own reflection:
short, fat, a black cigarette
in my hand, my self-cut hair
greying, my worn clothes mocking
the expensive, seductive sign.
I could see how I am
neither healthy nor wealthy.
But I am wise
enough to know
that death comes in pretty packages too,
and all around me
the dying air agreed.

The death people do not know
what they create, or how they hide
from the consequences of their dreams.
Wanting the good they slide
into an unforgiving destiny.
Alfalfa sprout, sesame seed,
no meat, no cigarettes: what will change
the inexorable dying we are facing?
No rally, no headline, no designer jean
can do more than hasten it.

We are related, after all,
the beautiful
wealthy
sun children and I.
We wander together into a smoky tomorrow,
seeing the clouds of darkness gather
on the surrounding hills,
shroud the sea, cover and oppose our
brightest dreams.
The dying grows silent
around us
and we walk
still believing it need not be.

[1982]

# EVE THE FOX

Eve the fox swung
her hips appetizingly, she
sauntered over to Adam the hunk
who was twiddling his toes and
devising an elaborate scheme
for renaming the beasts: Adam
was bored, but not Eve for she
knew the joy of swivelhips
and the taste of honey on her lips.
She was serpent wise and snake foolish,
and she knew all the tricks of the trade
that foxy lady, and she used them
to wile away the time: bite into this,
my hunky mate, she said, bending
tantalizingly low so her warm breasts
hung like peaches in the air. You
will know a thing or two when I get
through to you, she said, and gazed
deep with promise into his squinted eyes.
She admired the glisten of sweat and light
on his ropey arms, that hunky man of mine,
she sighed inside and wiggled deliciously
while he bit deep into the white fleshy
fruit she held to his lips. And wham-bam,
the change arose, it rose up in Adam
as it had in Eve and let me tell you
right then they knew all
they ever wanted to know about knowing,
and he discovered the perfect curve of her
breasts, the sweet gentle halfmoon of her belly,
the perfect valentine of her vulva,
the rose that curled within the garden
of her loins, that he would enter like bees,
and she discovered the tender power
of his sweat, the strong center of his
muscled arms, she worshipped the dark hair
that fell over his chest in waves.

And together riding the current of this
altogether new knowing they had found,
they bit and chewed, bit and chewed.

[1989]

# PART III

*Loving in the War Years*
—CHERRIE MORAGA

# LORNA DEE CERVANTES, 1940–

## BENEATH THE SHADOW OF THE FREEWAY

I

Across the street—the freeway,
blind worm, wrapping the valley up
from Los Altos to Sal Si Puedes.
I watched it from my porch
unwinding. Every day at dusk
as Grandma watered geraniums
the shadow of the freeway lengthened.

2

We were a woman family:
Grandma, our innocent Queen;
Mama, the Swift Knight, Fearless Warrior.
Mama wanted to be Princess instead.
I know that. Even now she dreams of taffeta
and foot-high tiaras.

Myself: I could never decide.
So I turned to books, those staunch, upright men.
I became Scribe: Translator of Foreign Mail,
interpreting letters from the government, notices
of dissolved marriages and Welfare stipulations.
I paid the bills, did light man-work, fixed faucets,
insured everything
against all leaks.

3

Before rain I notice seagulls.
They walk in flocks,
cautious across lawns: splayed toes,
indecisive beaks. Grandma says
seagulls mean storm.

In California in the summer,
mockingbirds sing all night.
Grandma says they are singing for their nesting wives.
"They don't leave their families
borrachando."

She likes the ways of birds,
respects how they show themselves
for toast and a whistle.

She believes in myths and birds.
She trusts only what she builds
with her own hands.

4

She built her house,
cocky, disheveled carpentry,
after living twenty-five years
with a man who tried to kill her.

Grandma, from the hills of Santa Barbara,
I would open my eyes to see her stir mush
in the morning, her hair in loose braids,
tucked close around her head
with a yellow scarf.

Mama said, "It's her own fault,
getting screwed by a man for that long.
Sure as shit wasn't hard."
Soft, she was soft

5

in the night I would hear it
glass bottles shattering the street
words cracked into shrill screams
inside my throat    a cold fear
as it entered the house in hard
unsteady steps    stopping at my door
my name    bathrobe    slippers
outside a 3 A.M. mist heavy
as a breath full of whiskey
stop it    go home    come inside
Mama if he comes here again
I'll call the police

inside
a gray kitten    a touchstone
purring beneath the quilts
grandma stitched
from his suits
the patchwork singing
of mockingbirds


6

"You're too soft . . . always were.
You'll get nothing but shit.
Baby, don't count on nobody"
—a mother's wisdom.
Soft. I haven't changed,
maybe grown more silent, cynical
on the outside.

"Oh Mama, with what's inside of me
I could wash that all away. I could."

"But Mama, if you're good to them
they'll be good to you back."
*    *    *

Back. The freeway is across the street.
It's summer now. Every night I sleep with a gentle man
to the hymn of mockingbirds,

and in time, I plant geraniums.
I tie up my hair into loose braids,
and trust only what I have built
with my own hands.

[1981]


POEM FOR THE YOUNG WHITE MAN
WHO ASKED ME HOW I, AN INTELLIGENT,
WELL-READ PERSON COULD BELIEVE
IN THE WAR BETWEEN RACES

In my land there are no distinctions.
The barbed wire politics of oppression
have been torn down long ago. The only reminder
of past battles, lost or won, is a slight
rutting in the fertile fields.

In my land
people write poems about love,
full of nothing but contented childlike syllables.
Everyone reads Russian short stories and weeps.
There are no boundaries.
There is no hunger, no
complicated famine or greed.

I am not a revolutionary.
I don't even like political poems.
Do you think I can believe in a war between races?
I can deny it. I can forget about it
when I'm safe,
living on my own continent of harmony
and home, but I am not
there.

I believe in revolution
because everywhere the crosses are burning,
sharp-shooting goose-steppers round every corner,

there are snipers in the schools . . .
(I know you don't believe this.
You think this is nothing
but faddish exaggeration. But they
are not shooting at you.)

I'm marked by the color of my skin.
The bullets are discrete and designed to kill slowly.
They are aiming at my children.
These are facts.
Let me show you my wounds: my stumbling mind, my
"excuse me" tongue, and this
nagging preoccupation
with the feeling of not being good enough.

These bullets bury deeper than logic.
Racism is not intellectual.
I can not reason these scars away.

Outside my door
there is a real enemy
who hates me.

I am a poet
who yearns to dance on rooftops,
to whisper delicate lines about joy
and the blessings of human understanding.
I try. I go to my land, my tower of words, and
bolt the door, but the typewriter doesn't fade out
the sounds of blasting and muffled outrage.
My own days bring me slaps on the face.
Every day I am deluged with reminders
that this is not
my land
and this is my land.

I do not believe in the war between races

but in this country
there is war.

[1981]

313

# JUDY GRAHN, 1940–

### ELLA, IN A SQUARE APRON, ALONG HIGHWAY 80
from *The Common Woman*

She's a copperheaded waitress,
tired and sharp-worded, she hides
her bad brown tooth behind a wicked
smile, and flicks her ass
out of habit, to fend off the pass
that passes for affection.
She keeps her mind the way men
keep a knife—keen to strip the game
down to her size. She has a thin spine,
swallows her eggs cold, and tells lies.
She slaps a wet rag at the truck drivers
if they should complain. She understands
the necessity for pain, turns away
the smaller tips, out of pride, and
keeps a flask under the counter. Once,
she shot a lover who misused her child.
Before she got out of jail, the courts had pounced
and given the child away. Like some isolated lake,
her flat blue eyes take care of their own stark
bottoms. Her hands are nervous, curled, ready
to scrape.
The common woman is as common
as a rattlesnake.

[1970]

### MY NAME IS JUDITH

My name is Judith, meaning
She Who Is Praised
I do not want to be called praised
I want to be called The Power of Love.

if Love means protect then whenever I do not
defend you

314

I cannot call my name Love.
if Love means rebirth then when I see us
dead on our feet
I cannot call my name Love.
if Love means provide & I cannot
provide for you
why would you call my name Love?

do not mistake my breasts
for mounds of potatoes
or my belly for a great roast duck.
do not take my lips for a streak of luck
nor my neck for an appletree,
do not believe my eyes are a warm swarm of bees;
do not get Love mixed up with me.

Don't misunderstand my hands
for a church with a steeple,
open the fingers & out come the people;
nor take my feet to be acres of solid brown earth,
or anything else of infinite worth
to you, my brawny turtledove;
do not get me mixed up with Love.

not until we have ground we call our own
to stand on
& weapons of our own in hand
& some kind of friends around us
will anyone ever call our name Love,
& then when we do we will all call ourselves
grand, muscley names:
the Protection of Love,
the Provision of Love & the
Power of Love.
until then, my sweethearts,
let us speak simply of
romance, which is so much
easier and so much less
than any of us deserve.

[1978]

## HANNAH
from *Helen You Always Were/The Factory*

Flames were already eating
at my skirts,
and I heard one of the girls
behind me screaming just how much
burning hurts. I could see the
people gathered on the sidewalk.
Eight stories high
I stood on the ledge
of the Triangle building
and exclaimed out loud.
Then I took my hat
with its white and yellow flowers
and flung it out, and opening
my purse, I scattered the coins
I had earned
to the shocked crowd.
Then, I took Angelina's hand in mine.
I thought we should go down
in style, heads high
as we had been during the strike
to end this kind of fire.
I grabbed Ellie's fingers to my right;
her clothes were smoking
like a cigarette; my little sister,
so serious, seventeen,
actually gave me a clenched smile
just as we leaped, all three
into the concrete sea.
We fell so far.
We're probably falling still.

They say a hundred twenty
thousand workers
marched on our behalf;
they say our eulogy
was delivered in a whisper;
they say our bodies

landed under the earth,
so heavy we became,
so weighted as we spun down;
they say safety conditions changed
after we were killed.
Because we fell so hard
and caused such pain.
Because we fell so far.
We're falling still.

[1982]


# TOI DERRICOTTE, 1941–

## THE FEEDING

My grandmother
haunted the halls
above Webster's Funeral
Home like a red-
gowned ghost. Till dawn
I'd see her spectral
form—henna-hair
blown back,
green eyes:
tameless.

She was proud.
Like God,
I swore I'd love her.
At night we whispered
how we hated mother
and wished that I could
live with *her*.

In the morning while she slept,
I'd pluck
costume diamonds

from a heart-shaped chest,
try her tortoise combs
and hairpins in my hair.
She'd wake
and take me to her bed.

Maroon-quilted, eider-downed,
I drowned.
Rocking on her wasted breast,
I'd hear her tell me
how she nursed my father
till he was old enough to ask.

Then, she'd draw me
to her—ask me
if she still had milk.
Yes. I said, yes.
Feeding on the sapless
lie,
even now
the taste of emptiness
weights my mouth.

[1978]


## ON THE TURNING UP OF UNIDENTIFIED
## BLACK FEMALE CORPSES

Mowing his three acres with a tractor,
a man notices something ahead—a mannequin—
he thinks someone threw it from a car. Closer
he sees it is the body of a black woman.

The medics come and turn her with pitchforks.
Her gaze shoots past him to nothing. Nothing
is explained. How many black women
have been turned up to stare at us blankly,

in weedy fields, off highways,
pushed out in plastic bags,

shot, knifed, unclothed partially, raped,
their wounds sealed with a powdery crust.

Last week on TV, a gruesome face, eyes bloated shut.
No one will say, "She looks like she's sleeping," ropes
of blue-black slashes at the mouth. Does anybody
know this woman? Will anyone come forth? Silence

like a backwave rushes into that field
where, just the week before, four other black girls
had been found. The gritty image hangs in the air
just a few seconds, but it strikes me,

a black woman, there is a question being asked
about my life. How can I
protect myself? Even if I lock my doors,
walk only in the light, someone wants me dead.

Am I wrong to think
if five white women had been stripped,
broken, the sirens would wail until
someone was named?

Is it any wonder I walk over these bodies
pretending they are not mine, that I do not know
the killer, that I am just like any woman—
if not wanted, at least tolerated.

Part of me wants to disappear, to pull
the earth on top of me. Then there is this part
that digs me up with this pen
and turns my sad black face to the light.

[1989]


POEM FOR MY FATHER

You closed the door.
I was on the other side,
screaming.

\* \* \*

It was black in your mind.
Blacker than burned-out fire.
Blacker than poison.

Outside everything looked the same.
You looked the same.
You walked in your body like a living man.
But you were not.

would you not speak to me for weeks
would you hang your coat in the closet without saying hello
would you find a shoe out of place and beat me
would you come home late
would i lose the key
would you find my glasses in the garbage
would you put me on your knee
would you read the bible to me in your smoking jacket after your
      mother died
would you come home drunk and snore
would you beat me on the legs
would you carry me up the stairs by my hair so that my feet never
      touch bottom
would you make everything worse
to make everything better

i believe in god, the father almighty,
the maker of heaven, the maker
of my heaven and my hell.

would you beat my mother
would you beat her till she cries like a rabbit
would you beat her in a corner of the kitchen
while i am in the bathroom trying to bury my head underwater
would you carry her to the bed
would you put cotton and alcohol on her swollen head
would you make love to her hair
would you caress her hair
would you rub her breasts with ben gay until she stinks
would you sleep in the other room in the bed next to me while
      she sleeps on the pull-out cot

would you come on the sheet while i am sleeping, later i look
        for the spot
would you go to embalming school with the last of my mother's
        money
would i see your picture in the book with all the other
        black boys you were the handsomest
would you make the dead look beautiful
would the men at the elks club
would the rich ladies at funerals
would the ugly drunk winos on the street
know ben
pretty ben
regular ben

would your father leave you when you were three with a mother
        who threw butcher knives at you
would he leave you with her screaming red hair
would he leave you to be smothered by a pillow she put
        over your head
would he send for you during the summer like a rich uncle
would you come in pretty corduroys until you were nine and
        never heard from him again

would you hate him
would you hate him every time you dragged hundred pound
        cartons of soap down the stairs into white ladies' basements
would you hate him for fucking the woman who gave birth to you
hate him flying by her house in the red truck so that the
        other father threw down his hat in the street and stomped
        on it angry like we never saw him

(bye bye
to the will of grandpa
bye bye to the family fortune
bye bye when he stomped that hat,
to the gold watch,
embalmer's palace,
grandbaby's college)
mother crying silently, making floating island
sending it up to the old man's ulcer
*   *   *

would grandmother's diamonds
close their heartsparks
in the corner of the closet
like the yellow eyes of cockroaches?

Old man whose sperm swims in my veins,

come back in love, come back in pain.

[1989]


# IRENA KLEPFISZ, 1941–

## ABOUT MY FATHER

—he became a teetotaler out of his socialist convictions; during
      the war he began to drink again
—he was casual; he kept his tie in his pocket till the last minute
      before oral exams
—he left me on the street to be picked up by the the nuns from the
      orphanage; he watched me from a distant doorway
—once he refused to hit me; he told my mother his hand was
      too large
—he wrote to his aunt that he hoped the baby would be a boy
—when he was a student, jews were not permitted to sit in the
      front rows of lecture halls; he made it a point to
      stand through the lectures; ultimately, jews were
      allowed to sit
—he was a discus thrower
—according to some, he got along with everyone: jews, goyim,
      children
—he was caught a couple of times by the germans; they thought
      he was a polish smuggler
—once he was put on a train for treblinka; he jumped, was shot at
      and wounded, but got back to warsaw alive
—he believed in resistance

[1975]

# I

it is a terror
in the closet     her knees
are limp   eyes straining to see
every object glows with a
private halo   pulling down
her skirt     the trickle
of urine along her thigh and calf
she wipes it carelessly with her hand
biting her lips she fixates on
pebbles and rusty nails along
the path to the truck     it is an oblivion
seen in matter-of-fact gestures
wiping the child's nose with her fingers
she says   blow       his eyes shine     as she
feels the pressure of the doorknob     palms
wet slipping out of her grasp     she whispers
not now     not yet     we've been so careful
he's a good child     just a little more time
she pleads with them     we will not be
careless anymore     this time the knob falls
into the glare of lights     voices scream
orders she does not understand     but obeys
blow     she tells him pulling down her skirt
and wiping his nose with her fingers     later
it is still over     has been over
since the knob slipped from her hand
like the wet fish that jumped while she tried
to scale it     later after the not yet
not now     the walk nude across the yard
she glimpses the meaning of the order
allows her eyes to widen for one
moment and see the path     it is a coldness
never before felt or imagined     she clutches
her hands tearing at her thighs     wailing
to the others she tries to lean on them
to explain the mistake     the small error
nothing is irrevocable     she screams     nothing

to them trying to lean     they push her away
and her hands cup the knob     for a better hold
to keep out the light    her world is cement
stone    iron

II
listening to conversations     over brandy
i am always amazed at their certainty
about the past    how it could have been
different     could have been     turned around
with what ease     they transport themselves
to another time/place     taking the comfort
confidence of an after dinner drink

                 it would be too impolite
of me to say     my mother hid with me
for two years among ignorant peasants     who
would have turned us in     almost at once     had
they known who we were     who would have watched
with glee while we were carted off    even though
grandad had bounced me on his knees and fed me
from his own spoon     and my mother is a frightened
woman

            it would be too impolite
to say    you do not know yourselves    you do not know
others

                                       [1975]

*Der mames shabosim/*
MY MOTHER'S SABBATH DAYS
                    Inspired by Vella Grade in Chaim Grade's memoir

*Bay undz is es geven andersh.* I knew nothing
of the 613 *mitsves*    which did not bind me    nor
of the 3 which did    though I am sure my grandmother
Rikla Perczykow    knew them all     and I have a vague
image    of her covering her eyes    and swaying.

Shoshana     Różka     Lodzia    Mamma Lo     and more recently
Rose    in short: my mother     in all her reincarnations

did not pass on     such things.
She'd given them up     even before she'd ever claimed them.
She was more modern      and besides     there were other matters
to teach     so by age 11     *kh'bin shoyn geven a brenendike sotsyalistke*
I was a passionate socialist     impatient     so impatient
to grow     into my knowledge     never guessing
there was no choice     for work     and rest     wrestled
in every human life     with work     inevitably
the unbeatable winner.


So for us it was different. *Erev shabes*     was plain     *fraytik*
or more precisely: *piontek*.     I remember     summer evenings
I'd wait for her     at the Mosholu stop of the Lexington line.
Bright heat and light     at 6 o'clock.     She was full
of tales     of Miss Kant     the designer     a career woman
longing for home and family     in love with a handsome pilot
of Scottie     the model     who married smart     a wealthy buyer
and now sat brazenly chic     in a reform synagogue.
I listened     eager     to understand these widow tales     of romance
amid the rush     of each season's showing     and once     even
saw     on a page of the *Times*     a mannequin     dressed in
the very gown     Mamma Lo had made.


All the way up Jerome Avenue     we'd walk     past the Jewish deli
where we never ate     (what was the point if you could make it at home?)
past the pizza place     where occasionally     while shopping     she'd buy me
a slice     past the outdoor groceries     fruit stands     fabric     shoes
lingerie     and stationery stores—till Gun Hill Road     and Jade Gardens.
Perhaps I knew it was *treyf*.     She certainly did
but was not concerned.     We'd order     the salty wonton soup
chow mein     or pepper steak     and though she mocked the food
she never resisted.
It was Friday.  The shop was closed.  We'd eat dinner and like the rich
lean leisurely back in our booth.  I didn't know it was *erev shabes*.
Still—she rested.

[1990]

# Robin Morgan, 1941–

## THE INVISIBLE WOMAN

The invisible woman in the asylum corridor
sees others quite clearly,
including the doctor who patiently tells her
she isn't invisible,
and pities the doctor, who must be mad
to stand there in the asylum corridor,
talking and gesturing
to nothing at all.

The invisible woman has great compassion.
So, after a while, she pulls on her body
like a rumpled glove, and switches on her voice
to comfort the elated doctor with words.
Better to suffer this prominence
than for the poor young doctor to learn
he himself is insane.
Only the strong can know that.

                                                    [1970]

## HEIRLOOM

For weeks now certain hours of every day
have been wiped sterile by the visit
to her hospital room where semi-privately
she semi-lives. For weeks
I've sourly reveled in the duty
while loathing its victim—my philanthropy
about as gracious as the bestowal of a poison cup
on a thirsty beggar who embodies a convenient excuse
but with a regrettable smell.

For days I've watched her reason fracturing
faster even than her body's fragmentation, as each
cell gradually detaches itself and shudders off
via the Parkinson method of interentropic travel.
For days the medication has made her more intense

than usual: cantankerous, weepy, domineering, sentimental,
and and and repetitive, a record that will not break
but always seems about to—the scratch on her soul itself.
No wonder she's abrasive. The wonder is,
since nothing will help her anyway,
that I can still be so ungenerous.

But then this afternoon we took each other
by surprise at the quite unexpected intersection
of Insanity and Humor—La Place de la Hallucination.
Forget that she frequently remembers I'm her sister,
or her mother, or her niece, or myself—her own child
but four years old again. Today she had some style.
Or something in me finally recognized whose style it was
I thought I'd made my own.

The patent-leather shoe with the round white buckle
had no business being up there on the night-table, even
if it did ring so insistently. The fly that walked the track
on which the room-partitioning curtain could be pulled
was going to get run over but he refused to listen to advice.
The teensy lady who perched cross-legged on the windowsill
while wearing the whole poinsettia plant right in her hat
really should have left much earlier—but people just don't
realize how visitors can tire a popular patient out.
And whoever had sent the basket of Florida newborn babies' heads
certainly had weird taste.

And I, who should know better, who at a younger age and chemistry
than she have heard radio static stutter in strict rhyme,
flinched from a Navajo blanket that snapped its teeth at me,
watched beloved faces leer with helpful malice—
I find myself explaining to her
What Is Really There. Except she's caught me
as suddenly as I catch her, and in astonishment
I shrug and say, "You seeing 'em again, huh? Well,
whatthehell, why not. What else is there to see?"

—and miracle of bitter miracle, she laughs.
And helpless I am laughing and the semi-roommate laughs
and the invisible lady in the poinsettia hat

can be heard distinctly laughing
and in this space of semi-dying there is life
and magic and shared paranoia thicker than water
and more clear than blood and we are laughing
while the bright shoe rings
and the fly dares death
and the oranges clamor to be fed
and all the thousand spear-carrying extras
direct from Central Casting come scurrying in
got up in white to hustle us apart—
as if our waving to each other weren't a sign
beyond their understanding;
as if the giggly last whisper, "Try to get through
the night any old way you can, Love. See you
in the morning," weren't a hiccuped message
encoded too deep in each of all our lonely cells
for any deciphering.

                                            [1982]


DAMN YOU, LADY
              (The Funky Double Sonnet Tragicomic
              Lesbian Feminist Blues)


Damn you, lady, get out of my blood for good.
Your eyes, hair, laugh, your politics—erase
them—how your body's swift lewd grace once stood
beside me, how love lit your falcon face.

          Damn you, lady, I refuse to wail
          one moment longer so uncritically
          over you—as if I were a fool
          (or even incorrect politically).

Your gestures in quickliquid flow,
your voice, indigo as a violin's—
get out. Go, let my dreams sleep free
of you, your fragrance, words, songs, silences . . .

          Lovesick morons fail the revolution,
          mooning about while work needs to be done,

and feminism's surely the solution
to everything—except your being gone.

. . . the way you slept, woke, moved at midnight,
your antic grin that struck and blazed me glad
to be alive, the way you loved a fight
in a just cause. The way you drove me mad.

      Damn you, lady, I will not obsess
      one second more. Love's just a masquerade
      at which we women, like men, can oppress
      (an awkward truth we'd rather not parade).

but see I have regained myself entire,
immune to you, asbestos to your fire.

      Damn you, lady, I will yet live through
      this memory, everywhere I turn, of you.

                            [1988]

# ALTA, 1942–

BITTER HERBS

NATURAL PUSSY
25¢ in a dispenser
*Gulf* station, pinole

J Douglas says prisoners
use cardboard rolls, filled
with a greasy baggie,
surrounded by a hot wet
                   washcloth
"sure feels like pussy"
\*   \*   \*

Playboy bunnies twitch their tails
bouncing squashedup titties
and grinning.

if you come in me
a child is likely to
come back out.
my name is Alta.
I am a woman.

[1969]

## EUCH, ARE YOU HAVING YOUR PERIOD?

euch, are you having your period?
why didn't you tell me?
i shoulda fucked him ina dark.
he coulda thot bloody sheets
look ma a virgin

[1970]

## FIRST PREGNANCY

lonely and big
a couple of times i cried
hearing you
beating off under covers

[1970]

## PENUS ENVY

penus envy, they call it
think how handy to have a thing
that poked out; you could just shove
it in any body, whang whang & come,
wouldn't have to give a shit.
you *know* you'd come!
wouldn't have to love that person,
trust that person.
whang, whang & come.
if you couldn't get relief for free,

pay a little $, whang whang & come.
you wouldn't have to keep, or abort,
wouldn't have to care about the kid.
wouldn't fear sexual violation.
penus envy, they call it.
the man is sick in his heart.
that's what I call it.

[1970]


EURIDICE

all the male poets write of orpheus
as if they look back & expect
to find me walking patiently
behind them. they claim i fell into hell.
damn them, i say.
i stand in my own pain
& sing my own song.

[1975]

from *Theme & Variations*


6.

(for pat parker)

yr eyes dark & aware.
was i afraid of yr touch
me in san lorenzo, you
in the filmore. were we re-
strained by the no trespassing signs.
afraid to cross into enemy territory:
someone else caused us to fear: my neighbors
dangerous behind their curtains or yr neighbors loud
on their porches.

why did we never close our eyes
in a kiss. the colors so bright. magenta,
green, blue.
*   *   *

i scratch my head until it bleeds then
i scratch the protective scab until it bleeds.
i will have my wounds; you cannot
take them from me. thief. you
cannot have it all.

racism makes my speech
stupid. i constantly have to retract.
tracks. retrace my steps. tired of the
red carpet they've bled for me,
i eat my words & wait her forgiveness.

why remain friends? it's not like we never
hurt each other.

: we must love each other more than we fear each other.
we must share a personal love greater than political stupidity.

[1980]


# MARILYN HACKER, 1942–


## THE MUSES

*C'est Vénus toute entière à sa proie attachée . . .*
—Racine, PHÈDRE


Don't think I haven't noticed you
waiting in the other room to kill me.
She came too close to the root, my sister,
rooting in the coals for a pristine
death, wishing, oh, wishing
it wasn't so flabby,
the skin creases gone livid and all
those sensual surfaces puckering
like a plucked chicken
(and that was what she

thought of seeing a
limp cock for the
first time: a
turkey neck).
Now I stand in front of the
oven, warming
my hands. At my desk
after sundown, my nails turn blue.
And you are waiting in
one of the other
rooms. Sometimes you are a
middle-aged woman, your skin
flabby, bluish, your hair
frizzed out in filaments, picking up
whispers of plots to Do You In
you can almost hear. You pat your face
feeling the puckers and creases, knowing
it is already Too Late, even
if it is only Tuesday, when you dreamed
it was Friday.
        Sometimes
you are a Beautiful Boy, out of a
pederast's fantasy, dark-curled
golden and edible, mouth
curved in a snarl or a lie. Rage
wrinkles your cheeks in a newborn's imperative howl
and to placate you, I can only say Yes
I will curl my hair, lend you twenty dollars, Yes
the world is ending, fashion is all, if
I were honest I would starve myself to death.

And one of you
will tear out chunks of my hair, and one
of you will slap me across the eyes, and
one of you will hit my head with a rock
at the top of the stairs and
one of you will kick me in the stomach
and one of you will smash at my nails
with a lead paperweight. Oh lying
at the foot of the stairs, my legs

wedged against the door, fingers
sticky against my eyelids, listening
to you tear up the rest of the house, I
will not be convinced
by your onyx
identical eyes.

[1968]

## SONNET FOR IVA

The bathroom tiles are very pink and new.
Out the window, a sixty-foot willow
tree forks, droops. Planted eighteen years ago,
its huge roots choke the drains. The very blue
sky is impenetrable. I hear you
whine outside the locked door. You're going to cry.
If I open the door, I'll slap you. I've
hit you six times this morning. I threw
you on the rug and smacked your bottom. Slapped
your face. Slapped your hands. I sit on the floor.
We're both scared. I picked you up, held you, lov-
ing your cheek's curve. Yelled, shook you. I want to stop
this day. I cringe on the warm pink tiles of
a strange house. We cry on both sides of the door.

[1976; 1980]

## MOTHER II

No one is "Woman" to another
woman, except her mother.
Her breasts were unmysterious
naked: limp, small. But I thought pus
must ooze from them: her underwear
like bandages. Blood came from where
I came from, stanched with pads between
her legs, under the girdle, seen
through gaping bathroom doors. Around
her waist, all sorts of rubber. Bound
to stop the milk, my milk, her breasts
stayed flat. I watched my round self, guessed
a future where I'd droop and leak.

But dry and cool against her cheek
I'd lean my cheek. I stroked the lace
and serge she sheathed her carapace
with: straight skirts, close cuffs, full sleeves;
was, wordless, catechized; believed:
nude, she was gaunt; dressed, she was slim;
nude, she was flabby; dressed, her firm
body matched her brisk, precise
mid-continental teacher's voice,
which she had molded, dry, perfect-
ed from a swamp of dialect.
Naked or clad, for me, she wore
her gender, perpetual *chador,*
her individual complex
history curtained off by sex.
Child, I determined that I would
not be subsumed in womanhood.
Whatever she was, I was not.
Whoever she was, I forgot
to ask, and she forgot to tell,
muffled in costumes she as well
rejected as a girl, resumed
—on my account? Are women doomed,
beasts that repeat ourselves, to rage
in youth against our own old age,
in age to circumscribe our youth
with self-despisal dressed as truth?
Am I "Woman" to my water-
dwelling brown loquacious daughter,
corporeal exemplar of
her thirst for what she would not love?

[1985]


BALLAD OF LADIES LOST AND FOUND

*for Julia Alvarez*


Where are the women who, *entre deux guerres,*
came out on college-graduation trips,
came to New York on football scholarships,
came to town meeting in a decorous pair?
Where are the expatriate *salonnières,*

the gym teacher, the math-department head?
Do nieces follow where their odd aunts led?
The elephants die off in Cagnes-sur-Mer.
H.D., whose "nature was bisexual,"
and plain old Margaret Fuller died as well.

Where are the single-combat champions:
the Chevalier d'Eon with curled peruke,
Big Sweet who ran with Zora in the jook,
open-handed Winifred Ellerman,
Colette, who hedged her bets and always won?
Sojourner's sojourned where she need not pack
decades of whitegirl conscience on her back.
The spirit gave up Zora; she lay down
under a weed-field miles from Eatonville,
and plain old Margaret Fuller died as well.

Where's Stevie, with her pleated schoolgirl dresses,
and Rosa, with her permit to wear pants?
Who snuffed Clara's *mestiza* flamboyance
and bled Frida onto her canvases?
Where are the Niggerati hostesses,
the kohl-eyed ivory poets with severe
chignons, the rebels who grew out their hair,
the bulldaggers with marcelled processes?
Conglomerates co-opted Sugar Hill,
and plain old Margaret Fuller died as well.

Anne Hutchinson, called witch, termagant, whore,
fell to the long knives, having tricked the noose.
Carolina Maria de Jesús'
tale from the slagheaps of the landless poor
ended on a straw mat on a dirt floor.

In action thirteen years after fifteen
in prison, Eleanor of Aquitaine
accomplished half of Europe and fourscore
anniversaries for good or ill,
and plain old Margaret Fuller died as well.
*   *   *

Has Ida B. persuaded Susan B.
to pool resources for a joint campaign?
(Two Harriets act a pageant by Lorraine,
cheered by the butch drunk on the IRT
who used to watch me watch her watching me;
We've notes by Angelina Grimké Weld
for choral settings drawn from the *Compiled*
*Poems* of Angelina Weld Grimké.)
There's no such tense as Past Conditional,
and plain old Margaret Fuller died as well.

Who was Sappho's protégée, and when did
we lose Hrotsvitha, dramaturge and nun?
What did bibulous Suzanne Valadon
think about Artemisia, who tended
to make a life-size murderess look splendid?
Where's Aphra, fond of dalliance and the pun?
Where's Jane, who didn't indulge in either one?
Whoever knows how Ende, Pintrix, ended
is not teaching Art History at Yale,
and plain old Margaret Fuller died as well.

Is Beruliah upstairs behind the curtain
debating Juana Inés de La Cruz?
Where's *savante* Anabella, Augusta-Goose,
Fanny, Maude, Lidian, Freda and Caitlin,
"without whom this could never have been written"?
Louisa who wrote, scrimped, saved, sewed, and nursed,
Malinche, who's, like all translators, cursed,
Bessie, whose voice was hemp and steel and satin,
outside a segregated hospital,
and plain old Margaret Fuller died as well.

Where's Amy, who kept Ada in cigars
and love, requited, both country and courtly,
although quinquagenarian and portly?
Where's Emily? It's very still upstairs.
Where's Billie, whose strange fruit ripened in bars?
Where's the street-scavenging Little Sparrow?
Too poor, too mean, too weird, too wide, too narrow:

Marie Curie, examining her scars,
was not particularly beautiful;
and plain old Margaret Fuller died as well.

Who was the grandmother of Frankenstein?
The Vindicatrix of the Rights of Woman.
Madame de Sévigné said prayers to summon
the postman just as eloquent as mine,
though my Madame de Grignan's only nine.
But Mary Wollstonecraft had never known
that daughter, nor did Paula Modersohn.
The three-day infants blinked in the sunshine.
The mothers turned their faces to the wall;
and plain old Margaret Fuller died as well.

Tomorrow night the harvest moon will wane
that's floodlighting the silhouetted wood.
Make your own footnotes; it will do you good.
Emeritae have nothing to explain.
She wasn't very old, or really plain—
my age exactly, volumes incomplete.
"The life, the life, will it never be sweet?"
She wrote it once; I quote it once again
midlife at midnight when the moon is full
and I can almost hear the warning bell
offshore, sounding through starlight like a stain
on waves that heaved over what she began
and truncated a woman's chronicle,
and plain old Margaret Fuller died as well.

                                                [1985]


NEARLY A VALEDICTION

You happened to me. I was happened to
like an abandoned building by a bull-
dozer, like the van that missed my skull
happened a two-inch gash across my chin.
You were as deep down as I've ever been.
You were inside me like my pulse. A new-
born flailing toward maternal heartbeat through

338

the shock of cold and glare: when you were gone,
swaddled in strange air I was that alone
again, inventing life left after you.

I don't want to remember you as that
four o'clock in the morning eight months long
after you happened to me like a wrong
number at midnight that blew up the phone
bill to an astronomical unknown
quantity in a foreign currency.
The U.S. dollar dived since you happened to me.
You've grown into your skin since then; you've grown
into the space you measure with someone
you can love back without a caveat.

While I love somebody I learn to live
with through the downpulled winter days' routine
wakings and sleepings, half-and-half caffeine-
assisted mornings, laundry, stock-pots, dust-
balls in the hallway, lists instead of lust
sometimes, sometimes, instead of longing, trust
that what comes next comes after what came first.
She'll never be a story I make up.
You were the one I didn't know where to stop.
If I had blamed you, now I could forgive
you, but what made my cold hand, back in prox-
imity to your hair, your mouth, your mind,
want where it no way ought to be, defined
by where it was, and was and was until
the whole globed swelling liquefied and spilled
through one cheek's nap, a syllable, a tear,
was never blame, whatever I wished it were.
You were the weather in my neighborhood.
You were the epic in the episode.
You were the year poised on the equinox.

[1990]

339

# JANICE MIRIKITANI, 1942–

## SOUL FOOD
*For Cecil*

We prepare
the meal together.
I complain,
hurt, reduced to fury
again by their
subtle insults
insinuations
because I am married to you.
Impossible autonomy, no mind
of my own.

You like your fish
crisp, coated with cornmeal,
fried deep,
sliced mangos to sweeten
the tang of lemons.
My fish is raw,
on shredded lettuce,
lemon slices thin as skin,
wasabe burning like green fire.
You bake the cornbread flat
and dip it in
the thick soup
I've brewed from
turkey carcass, rice gruel,
sesame oil and chervil.
We laugh over watermelon
and bubbling cobbler.

You say,
there are few men
who can stand
to have a woman equal,
upright.

This meal,
unsurpassed.                                    [1987]

# BREAKING TRADITION

*For my daughter*

My daughter denies she is like me,
her secretive eyes avoid mine.
    She reveals the hatreds of womanhood
    already veiled behind music and smoke and telephones.
I want to tell her about the empty room
    of myself.
    This room we lock ourselves in
    where whispers live like fungus,
    giggles about small breasts and cellulite,
    where we confine ourselves to jealousies,
    bedridden by menstruation.
    This waiting room where we feel our hands
    are useless, dead speechless clamps
    that need hospitals and forceps and kitchens
    and plugs and ironing boards to make them useful.
I deny I am like my mother.    I remember why:
    She kept her room neat with silence,
    defiance smothered in requirements to be otonashii,
    passion and loudness wrapped in an obi,
    her steps confined to ceremony,
    the weight of her sacrifice she carried like
    a foetus. Guilt passed on in our bones.
I want to break tradition—unlock this room
    where women dress in the dark.
    Discover the lies my mother told me.
    The lies that we are small and powerless
    that our possibilities must be compressed
    to the size of pearls, displayed only as
    passive chokers, charms around our neck.
Break Tradition.
    I want to tell my daughter of this room
    of myself
    filled with tears of shakuhachi,
    the light in my hands,
    poems about madness,
    the music of yellow guitars,
    sounds shaken from barbed wire and
    goodbyes and miracles of survival.

\* \* \*

My daughter denies she is like me
     her secretive eyes are walls of smoke
     and music and telephones.
     her pouting ruby lips, her skirts
     swaying to salsa, Madonna and the Stones.
     her thighs displayed in carnivals of color.
     I do not know the contents of her room.
She mirrors my aging.

She is breaking tradition.

                                       [1987]


# SHARON OLDS, 1942–


## SOLITARY

*for Muriel Rukeyser*

I keep thinking of you standing in Korea, in the courtyard
of the prison where the poet is in solitary.
Someone asked you why not in the street
where you could be seen. You said you wanted
to be as close to him as you could.
You stood in the empty courtyard. You thought
it was probably doing no good. You have written
a poem about it. This is not that poem.
This is another—there may be details
wrong, the way variations come in
when you pass on a story. This is a poem
about a woman, a poet, standing in a courtyard,
feeling she is probably doing no good.
Pass it on: a poet, a woman,
a witness, standing
alone
in a prison
courtyard
in Korea.

                                       [1980]

## THAT YEAR

The year of the mask of blood, my father
hammering on the glass door to get in

was the year they found her body in the hills,
in a shallow grave, naked, white as
mushroom, partially decomposed,
raped, murdered, the girl from my class.

That was the year my mother took us and
hid us so he could not get at us
when she told him to leave; so there were no more
tyings by the wrist to the chair,
no more denial of food
or the forcing of foods, the head held back,
down the throat at the restaurant,
the shame of vomited buttermilk
down the sweater with its shame of new breasts.

That was the year
I started to bleed,
crossing over that border in the night,

and in Social Studies, we came at last
to Auschwitz. I recognized it
like my father's face, the face of the guard
turning away—or worse yet
turning toward me.

The symmetrical piles of white bodies,
the round white breast-shapes of the heaps,
the smell of the smoke, the dogs the wires the
rope the hunger. It had happened to others.
There was a word for us. I was:   a Jew.

It had happened to six million.
And there was another word that was not
for the six million, but was a word for me
and for many others. I was:
a survivor.

[1980]

## THE LANGUAGE OF THE BRAG

I have wanted excellence in the knife-throw,
I have wanted to use my exceptionally strong and accurate arms
and my straight posture and quick electric muscles
to achieve something at the center of a crowd,
the blade piercing the bark deep,
the haft slowly and heavily vibrating like the cock.

I have wanted some epic use for my excellent body,
some heroism, some American achievement
beyond the ordinary for my extraordinary self,
magnetic and tensile, I have stood by the sandlot
and watched the boys play.

I have wanted courage, I have thought about fire
and the crossing of waterfalls, I have dragged around

my belly big with cowardice and safety,
my stool black with iron pills,
my huge breasts oozing mucus,
my legs swelling, my hands swelling,
my face swelling and darkening, my hair
falling out, my inner sex
stabbed again and again with terrible pain like a knife.
I have lain down.

I have lain down and sweated and shaken
and passed blood and feces and water and
slowly alone in the center of a circle I have
passed the new person out
and they have lifted the new person free of the act
and wiped the new person free of that
language of blood like praise all over the body.

\* \* \*

I have done what you wanted to do, Walt Whitman,
Allen Ginsberg, I have done this thing,
I and the other women this exceptional
act with the exceptional heroic body,
this giving birth, this glistening verb,
and I am putting my proud American boast
right here with the others.

[1980]

## PAJAMAS

My daughter's pajamas lie on the floor
inside out, thin and wrinkled as
peeled skins of peaches when you ease the
whole skin off at once.
You can see where her waist emerged, and her legs,
her arms, and head, the fine material
gathered in rumples like skin the caterpillar
ramped out of and left to shrivel.
You can see, there at the center of the bottoms,
the raised cotton seam like the line
down the center of fruit, where the skin first splits
and curls back. You can almost see the hard
halves of her young buttocks, the precise
stem-mark of her sex. Her shed
skin shines at my feet, and in the air there is a
sharp fragrance like peach brandy—
the birth-room pungence of her released life.

[1984]

## WHAT IF GOD

And what if God had been watching, when my mother
came into my room, at night, to lie down on me
and pray and cry? What did He do when her
long adult body rolled on me
like lava from the top of the mountain
and the magma popped from her ducts, and my bed
shook from the tremors, the cracking of my nature
across? What was He? Was He a bison

to lower His partly extinct head
and suck His Puritan phallus while we cried
and prayed to Him, or was He a squirrel
reaching through her hole in my shell, His arm
up to the elbow in the yolk of my soul
stirring, stirring the gold? Or was He
a kid in Biology, dissecting me
while she held my split carapace apart
so He could firk out the eggs, or was He a man
entering me while she pried my spirit
open in the starry dark—
she said that all we did was done in His sight
so He must have seen her weep, into my
hair, and slip my soul from between my
ribs like a tiny hotel soap, He
washed His hands of me as I washed my
hands of Him. Is there a God in the house?
Is there a God in the house? Then reach down
and take that woman off that child's body,
take that woman by the nape of the neck like a young cat
and lift her up, and deliver her over to me.

[1988; 1992]

## THE GIRL

They chased her and her friend through the woods
and caught them in a small clearing, broken
random bracken, a couple of old mattresses,
the dry ochre of foam rubber,
as if the place had been prepared.
The thin one with black hair
started raping her best friend,
and the blond one stood above her,
thrust his thumbs back inside her jaws, she was 12,
stuck his penis in her mouth and throat
faster and faster and faster.
Then the black-haired one stood up—
they lay like pulled-up roots at his feet,
two naked 12-year-old girls, he said
*Now you're going to know what it's like*
*to be shot 5 times and slaughtered like a pig,*

and they switched mattresses,
the blond was raping and stabbing her friend,
the black-haired one sticking inside her
in one place and then another,
the point of his gun pressed deep into her waist,
she felt a little click in her spine and a
sting like 7-Up in her head and then he
pulled the tree-branch across her throat
and everything went dark,
the gym went dark, and her mother's kitchen,
even the globes of light on the rounded
lips of her mother's nesting bowls went dark.

When she woke up she was lying on the cold
iron-smelling earth, she was under the mattress,
pulled up over her like a
blanket at night,
she saw the body of her best friend
and she began to run,
she came to the edge of the woods and she stepped
out from the trees, like a wound debriding,
she walked across the field to the tracks
and said to the railway brakeman *Please, sir. Please, sir.*

At the trial she had to say everything—
her big sister taught her the words—
she had to sit in the room with them and
point to them. Now she goes to parties
but does not smoke, she is a cheerleader,
she throws her body up in the air
and kicks her legs and comes home and does the dishes
and her homework, she has to work hard in math,
the night over the roof of her bed
filled with white planets. Every night she
prays for the soul of her best friend and
then thanks God for life. She knows
what all of us want never to know
and she does a cartwheel, the splits, she shakes the
shredded pom-poms in her fists.

[1988]

## FIRST SEX
### (for J.)

I knew little, and what I knew
I did not believe—they had lied to me
so many times, so I just took it as it
came, his naked body on the sheet,
the tiny hairs curling on his legs like
fine, gold shells, his sex
harder and harder under my palm
and yet not hard as a rock his face cocked
back as if in terror, the sweat
jumping out of his pores like sudden
trails from the tiny snails when his knees
locked with little clicks and under my
hand he gathered and shook and the actual
flood like milk came out of his body, I
saw it glow on his belly, all they had
said and more, I rubbed it into my
hands like lotion, I signed on for the duration.

[1988]

# CAROLYN M. RODGERS, 1942–

### U NAME THIS ONE

let uh revolution come, uh
state of peace is not known to me
anyway
since I grew uhround in chi town
where
howlin wolf howled in the tavern on 47th st.
and muddy waters made u cry the salty nigger blues,
    where pee wee cut Lonnell fuh fuckin wid
    his sistuh and blood baptized the street
    at least twice ev'ry week and judy got
    kicked out grammar school fuh bein pregnant
    and died tryin to ungrow the seed

we was all up in there and
	just livin was guerilla warfare, yeah.

let uh revolution come.
couldn't be no action like what
	i dun already seen.

[1969]


SOME ME OF BEAUTY

		the fact is
that i don't hate any body any more
		i went through my mean period
		if you remember i spit out nails
			chewed tobacco on the paper
and dipped some bad snuff.
		but in one year
just like i woke up one morning and
		saw my mother's head gray
and i asked myself/could it have turned
			overnight?
knowing full well the grayness had been
		coming and had even been there
			awhile
just like that i woke up one morning
	and looked at my self
		and what i saw was
					carolyn
		not imani ma jua or soul sister poetess of
			the moment
		i saw more than a "sister" . . .
		i saw a Woman. human.
					and black.
		i felt a spiritual transformation
			a root revival of love
		and i knew that many things
			were over
		and some me of—beauty—
				was about to begin. . . .

[1976]

our mothers,
when asked
may speak of us
in terms of our accomplishments.
my daughter is a flower
shedding buds of brown babies.
she holds two diplomas in
her fists as she shows her
obliqueness to a world that
only cares for credentials.
what is your claim to fame?
what is your claim to life—
when there are no diplomas
to be lauded,
no husband to be pillared upon,
no buds to be babied.
when does the wind blow on your face
and in what direction do you turn
when it rains?

[1978]

# TESS GALLAGHER, 1943–

## INSTRUCTIONS TO THE DOUBLE

So now it's your turn,
little mother of silences, little
father of half-belief. Take up
this face, these daily rounds
with a cabbage under each arm
convincing the multitudes
that a well-made-anything
could save them. Take up
most of all, these hands

trained to an ornate piano
in a house on the other side
of the country.

I'm staying here
without music, without
applause. I'm not going
to wait up for you. Take
your time. Take mine
too. Get into some trouble
I'll have to account for. Walk
into some bars alone
with a slit in your skirt. Let
the men follow you on the street
with their clumsy propositions, their
loud hatreds of this and that. Keep
walking. Keep your head
up. They are calling to you—slut, mother,
virgin, whore, daughter, adultress, lover,
mistress, bitch, wife, cunt, harlot,
betrothed, Jezebel, Messalina, Diana,
Bethsheba, Rebecca, Lucretia, Mary,
Magdelena, Ruth, you—Niobe,
woman of the tombs.

Don't stop for anything, not
a caress or a promise. Go
to the temple of the poets, not
the one like a run-down country club,
but the one on fire
with so much it wants
to be done with. Say all the last words
and the first: hello, goodbye, yes,
I, no, please, always, never.

If anyone from the country club
asks if you write poems, say
your name is Lizzie Borden.
Show him your axe, the one
they gave you with a silver

blade, your name engraved there
like a whisper of their own.

If anyone calls you a witch,
burn for him; if anyone calls you
less or more than you are
let him burn for you.

It's a dangerous mission. You
could die out there. You
could live forever.

[1976]


## ON YOUR OWN

How quickly the postures shift.
Just moments ago we seemed human
or in the Toledo of my past
I made out I was emotionally illiterate
so as not to feel a pain I deserved.

Here at the Great Southern
some of the boys have made it
into gray suits and pocket calculators.
I'm feeling end-of-season, like a somebody
who's hung around the church
between a series of double weddings.

Friend, what you said about the terror
of American Womanhood,
I forget it already, but I know
what you mean. I'm so scary some days
I'd run from myself. It's hard work
having your way, even
half the time, and having it,
know what not to do with it. Who
hasn't thrown away a life or two
at the mercy of another's passion,
spite or industry.
*    *    *

It's like this on your own: the charms
unlucky, the employment
solitary, the best love always
the benefit of a strenuous doubt.

SPACIOUS ENCOUNTER

What they cut away in braids from childhood
returns. I use it. With my body's nearest silk
I cover you in the dream-homage, attend and revive
by attending. I know very little of what to do
without you. Friends say, "Go on with your life."
But who's assigned this complicitous extension,
these word-caressings? this night-river
full of dead star-tremors, amazed floatings, this
chaotic laboratory of broken approaches?

Your unwritten pages lift an ongoing dusk in me.
Maybe this makes me your only reader now. The one
you were writing towards all along, who can't put down
her double memory pressed to shape
your one bodiless body. Book I am wearing in my night-rushing
to overtake these kneelings and contritions of daylight. Book
that would be a soul's reprisal
if souls could abandon their secret missions
so necessary to our unbelief. No,
the embrace hasn't ended.
Though everyone's grief-clock
runs down. Even mine sweeps
the room and goes forth with a blank face
more suited each day to enduring.

Ours is the compressed altitude
of two beings who share one retina
with the no-world seared onto it, and
the night-river rushing through, one-sided,
and able to carry what is one-sidedly felt
when there is no surface to what
flows into you. Embrace

I can't empty. Embrace I would know with my arms
cut away on no street in no universe
to which we address so much unprofound silence.
I unshelter you—my vanishing
dialogue, my remnant, my provision.

[1992]

## I STOP WRITING THE POEM

to fold the clothes. No matter who lives
or who dies, I'm still a woman.
I'll always have plenty to do.
I bring the arms of his shirt
together. Nothing can stop
our tenderness. I'll get back
to the poem. I'll get back to being
a woman. But for now
there's a shirt, a giant shirt
in my hands, and somewhere a small girl
standing next to her mother
watching to see how it's done.

[1992]

# NIKKI GIOVANNI, 1943–

## SEDUCTION

one day
you gonna walk in this house
and i'm gonna have on a long African
gown
you'll sit down and say "The Black . . . "
and i'm gonna take one arm out
then you—not noticing me at all—will say "What about
this brother . . . "
and i'm going to be slipping it over my head
and you'll rap on about "The revolution . . . "
while i rest your hand against my stomach

you'll go on—as you always do—saying
"I just can't dig . . . "
while i'm moving your hand up and down
and i'll be taking your dashiki off
then you'll say "What we really need . . . "
and i'll be licking your arm
and "The way I see it we ought to . . . "
and unbuckling your pants
"And what about the situation . . . "
and taking your shorts off
then you'll notice
your state of undress
and knowing you you'll just say
"Nikki,
isn't this counterrevolutionary . . . ?"

[1968]


ADULTHOOD
        (for claudia)

i usta wonder who i'd be
when i was a little girl in indianapolis
sitting on doctors porches with post-dawn pre-debs
(wondering would my aunt drag me to church sunday)
i was meaningless
and i wondered if life
would give me a chance to mean

i found a new life in the withdrawal from all things
not like my image

when i was a teen-ager i usta sit
on front steps conversing
the gym teachers son with embryonic eyes
about the essential essence of the universe
(and other bullshit stuff)
recognizing the basic powerlessness of me

but then i went to college where i learned
that just because everything i was was unreal
i could be real and not just real through withdrawal

355

into emotional crosshairs or colored bourgeoisie intellectual pretensions
but from involvement with things approaching reality
i could possibly have a life

so catatonic emotions and time wasting sex games
were replaced with functioning commitments to logic
and
necessity and the gray area was slowly darkened into
a Black thing

for a while progress was being made along with a certain
degree of happiness cause i wrote a book and found a love
and organized a theatre and even gave some lectures on
Black history
and began to believe all good people could get
together and win without bloodshed
then
hammarskjöld was killed
and lumumba was killed
and diem was killed
and kennedy was killed
and malcolm was killed
and evers was killed
and schwerner, chaney and goodman were killed
and liuzzo was killed
and stokely fled the country
and le roi was arrested
and rap was arrested
and pollard, thompson and cooper were killed
and king was killed
and kennedy was killed
and i sometimes wonder why i didn't become a
debutante sitting on porches, going to church all the time,
wondering is my eye make-up on straight
or a withdrawn discoursing on the stars and moon
instead of a for real Black person who must now feel
and inflict
pain

[1968]

her grandmother called her from the playground
      "yes, ma'am"
      "i want chu to learn how to make rolls" said the old
woman proudly
but the little girl didn't want
to learn how because she knew
even if she couldn't say it that
that would mean when the old one died she would be less
dependent on her spirit so
she said
      "i don't want to know how to make no rolls"
with her lips poked out
and the old woman wiped her hands on
her apron saying "lord
      these children"
and neither of them ever
said what they meant
and i guess nobody ever does

[1973]


# LOUISE GLUCK, 1943–

## POMEGRANATE

First he gave me
his heart. It was
red fruit containing
many seeds, the skin
leathery, unlikely.
I preferred
to starve, bearing
out my training.
Then he said Behold
how the world looks, minding
your mother. I
peered under his arm:

What had she done
with color & odor?
Whereupon he said Now *there*
is a woman who loves
with a vengeance, adding
Consider she is in her element:
the trees turning to her, whole
villages going under
although in hell
the bushes are still
burning with pomegranates.
At which
he cut one open & began
to suck. When he looked up at last
it was to say My dear
you are your own
woman, finally, but examine
this grief your mother
parades over our heads
remembering
that she is one to whom
these depths were not offered.

[1975]


## MYTHIC FRAGMENT

When the stern god
approached me with his gift
my fear enchanted him
so that he ran more quickly
through the wet grass, as he insisted,
to praise me. I saw captivity
in praise; against the lyre,
I begged my father in the sea
to save me. When
the god arrived, I was nowhere,
I was in a tree forever. Reader,
pity Apollo: at the water's edge,
I turned from him, I summoned
my invisible father—as
I stiffened in the god's arms,

of his encompassing love
my father made
no other sign from the water.

[1985]

BROWN CIRCLE

My mother wants to know
why, if I hate
family so much,
I went ahead and
had one. I don't
answer my mother.
What I hated
was being a child,
having no choice about
what people I loved.

I don't love my son
the way I meant to love him.
I thought I'd be
the lover of orchids who finds
red trillium growing
in the pine shade, and doesn't
touch it, doesn't need
to possess it. What I am
is the scientist,
who comes to that flower
with a magnifying glass
and doesn't leave, though
the sun burns a brown
circle of grass around
the flower. Which is
more or less the way
my mother loved me.

I must learn
to forgive my mother,
now that I'm helpless
to spare my son.

[1990]

# SUSAN GRIFFIN, 1943–

## I LIKE TO THINK OF HARRIET TUBMAN

I like to think of Harriet Tubman.
Harriet Tubman who carried a revolver,
who had a scar on her head from a rock thrown
by a slave-master (because she
talked back), and who
had a ransom on her head
of thousands of dollars and who
was never caught, and who
had no use for the law
when the law was wrong,
who defied the law. I like
to think of her.
I like to think of her especially
when I think of the problem of
feeding children.

The legal answer
to the problem of feeding children
is ten free lunches every month,
being equal, in the child's real life,
to eating lunch every other day.
Monday but not Tuesday.
I like to think of the President
eating lunch Monday, but not
Tuesday.
And when I think of the President
and the law, and the problem of
feeding children, I like to
think of Harriet Tubman
and her revolver.

And then sometimes
I think of the President
and other men,
men who practice the law,
who revere the law,

who make the law,
who enforce the law
who live behind
and operate through
and feed themselves
at the expense of
starving children
because of the law,
men who sit in paneled offices
and think about vacations
and tell women
whose care it is
to feed children
not to be hysterical
not to be hysterical as in the word
hysterikos, the greek for
womb suffering,
not to suffer in their
wombs,
not to care,
not to bother the men
because they want to think
of other things
and do not want
to take the women seriously.
I want them
to take women seriously.
I want them to think about Harriet Tubman,
and remember,
remember she was beat by a white man
and she lived
and she lived to redress her grievances,
and she lived in swamps
and wore the clothes of a man
bringing hundreds of fugitives from
slavery, and was never caught,
and led an army,
and won a battle,
and defied the laws
because the laws were wrong, I want men
to take us seriously.

I am tired wanting them to think
about right and wrong.
I want them to fear.
I want them to feel fear now
as I have felt suffering in the womb, and
I want them
to know
that there is always a time
there is always a time to make right
what is wrong,
there is always a time
for retribution
and that time
is beginning.

[1970]


SONG MY

(Oh God, she said.)

It began a beautiful day by the sun up
And we sat in our grove of trees of smiles
Of morning eggs and toast and jam
and long talks, and baby babble
Becky sitting in her chair
spreading goo in her hair.

(Oh God, she said, look at the baby)

saying "hi" "ho" "ha" hi hi, goggydoggymamadada HI
and the light was coming through the window
through the handprints on the glass
making shadow patterns, and the cold day
was orange outside and they were muddling
in their underwear, getting dressed,
putting diapers on the baby,
slipping sandals on her feet.

(Oh God, she said, look at the baby
He has blood all over, she cried,)

Then the postman came,
And she went out on the steps
and got her magazine. They stood
by the stairs and looked, the baby
tugging at her skirt saying
mamamamama upupup mememe
and they looked at the pictures of Song My.

(Oh God, she said, look at the baby
He has blood all over, she cried,
Look at that woman's face, my God,
She knows she's going to get it.)

Going to get it, they knew
they were going to get it,
and it was a beautiful day,
the day that began in the fields
with the golden grain against the blue sky
the babies singing as if there were not
soldiers in the air.

[1971]


## AN ANSWER TO A MAN'S QUESTION, "WHAT CAN I DO ABOUT WOMEN'S LIBERATION?"

Wear a dress.
Wear a dress that you made yourself, or bought in a dress store.
Wear a dress and underneath the dress wear elastic, around
your hips, and underneath your nipples.
Wear a dress and underneath the dress wear a sanitary napkin.
Wear a dress and wear sling-back, high-heeled shoes.
Wear a dress, with elastic and a sanitary napkin underneath,
and sling-back shoes on your feet, and walk down Telegraph Avenue.
Wear a dress, with elastic and a sanitary napkin and sling-
back shoes on Telegraph Avenue and try to run.

Find a man.
Find a nice man who you would like to ask you for a date.
Find a nice man who *will* ask you for a date.

Keep your dress on.
Ask the nice man who asks you for a date to come to dinner.
Cook the nice man a nice dinner so the dinner is ready before
he comes and your dress is nice and clean and wear a smile.
Tell the nice man you're a virgin, or you don't have
birth control, or you would like to get to know him better.
Keep your dress on.
Go to the movies by yourself.

Find a job.
Iron your dress.
Wear your ironed dress and promise the boss you won't get
pregnant (which in your case is predictable) and you like to
type, and be sincere and wear your smile.
Find a job or get on welfare.
Borrow a child and get on welfare.
Borrow a child and stay in the house all day with the child,
or go to the public park with the child, and take the child
to the welfare office and cry and say your man left you and
be humble and wear your dress and your smile, and don't talk
back, keep your dress on, cook more nice dinners, stay
away from Telegraph Avenue, and still, you won't know the
half of it, not in a million years.

[1976]

## SUNDAY MORNING
### for Barbara Deming

It is a Sunday morning a few minutes before noon and
the sun has come out, you have eaten a melon of a
perfect ripeness, you have written a letter describing as
best you could the nuance of a certain feeling, what kept
you awake seems to have vanished, you listen as a
woman's voice sings, it is something in her voice, like a
bowl filling, you look into the face of a friend, it is her
likeness, her image, an aspect of her soul, a smile that
enters you and makes you love, and you know, miles
away, she is dying, and you are dared even so by this
morning, you are dared to feel happiness burst in you.
*   *   *

You know that what keeps waking you is still there. You will cry again. You will see the hair of women cut off because they were consigned to die, you will see very thin children with a look in the eye that enters your heart like coldness, you will find yourself shaking with grief over someone you never knew. And you think, I cannot bear for the world to be without this woman, and the sunlight graces the stack of old weeds out your window, and you remember the scent of the soil, and you are dared to feel joy.

And the joy has a rim which turns over like a somersault into ash, into cinder, into the trees planted, the flowers put in the soil so rich with the bodies of those who suffered what is beyond reason to imagine except that you have somehow understood it happened, the sense-lessness, they call it murder, and in the space of empti-ness left void by the ones who had lived there you reach out your hand, longingly, longingly, and your heart is pulled like a thread of cloth unwinding until you dis-solve in wanting what you cannot even name but life as you look up into the trees at this moment is so dazzling that you cherish the air.

You turn over the record. You want to hear that voice again. What is she saying? She is not ignorant of what has happened on this earth. And now you hear that as she calls out her song about love, she is shouting. And you know why. Secretly, you make a promise that from now on you too will shout. Both of you have had a certain grief make its way like an old refugee tired beyond speaking deep into your breath. You came to recognize this foreigner as one of your own family. As the lost one. Without this one nothing ever made sense. Only you never knew it was senseless. You just felt a vague ache. But now that you have heard this story, the ache has turned into a pillar of tears.

Do you want to know why she shouts? She wants your attention. And now when you are listening her low

voice speaks in the gentlest of tones with the softest
of sounds, like a kiss whispering to you tenderness,
whispering beauty until once more you are broken,
until once more you dare to love this world.

[1987]


# LINDA McCARRISTON, 1943–


## A CASTLE IN LYNN

In the hometown tonight,
in the quiet before sleep,
a man strokes himself in the darkened
theater of memory. Best old

remembrance, he gets to play it
as slow as he needs, as his hand,
savvy tart of a million reruns,
plays the tune, plays the parts:

now hand is the hard bottom
of the girl. Now hand is full
of the full new breast. Now hand
—square hand, cruel as a spade—

splits the green girlwood of her body.
No one can take this from him now
ever, though she is for years a mother
and worn, and he is too old

to force any again. His cap hangs
on a peg by the door—plaid wool
of an elderly workingman's park-bench
decline. *I got there before*

*the boys did,* he knows, hearing
back to her pleading, back to her

sobbing, to his own voice-over
like his body over hers: laughter,

mocking, the elemental voice
of the cock, unhearted, in its own
quarter. *A man is king in his own
castle,* he can still say, having got

what he wanted: in a lifetime
of used ones, second-hand, one girl
he could spill like a shot of whiskey,
the whore only he could call *daughter.*

[1991]

## HOTEL NIGHTS WITH MY MOTHER

The hometown flophouse
was what she could afford
the nights he came after us
with a knife. I'd grab my books,
already dreading the next day's
explanations of homework undone
—*I ran out of paper*—the lies
I'd invent standing in front of
the nuns in the clothes I'd lain in
full-bladdered all night, a flimsy
chair-braced door between us
and the hallway's impersonal riot.

Years later, then, in the next
city, standing before my first class,
I scanned the rows of faces,
their cumulative skill in the
brilliant adolescent dances
of self-presentation, of hiding.
New teacher, looking young, seeming
gullible, I know, I let them
give me any excuse and took it.
I was watching them all
*   *   *

for the dark-circled eyes,
yesterday's crumpled costume, the marks
—the sorrowful coloring of marks—
the cuticles flaming and torn.
I made of myself each day a chink
a few might pass through unscathed.

[1991]


REVISION

Absorbed in the work, final touches
to a poem that rings true, she is stopped.
She lifts her head but does not turn to see
whose eyes are on her, have her in a locking
beam, the eyes of a tiger. She knows. It is
herself, the first time coming, a drink
in her hand, her face at midnight blotched
and swollen with crying. At the desk she sits
erect to let the other see her.
The house around the two of them is order
and light and quiet. The writer faces
a window, and from outside, snow and
the light on it, backlight her shape,
silhouette it, making of a woman typing
a page a faceless, mythic figure. Then,
she was the two of them, as she is now,
and she sits a long time still to be
apprehended, deeply, her happiness
in the small—her own—that surrounds her.
And she leans unsteady on the doorframe
appraising the woman at abysmal distance
as a longing streams between them across
the room of years, a tenderness exchanged
in the common body.

[1991]

# Sandra McPherson, 1943–

## PREGNANCY

It is the best thing.
I should always like to be pregnant,

Tummy thickening like a yoghurt,
Unbelievable flower.

A queen is always pregnant with her country.
Sheba of questions

Or briny siren
At her difficult passage,

One is the mountain that moves
Toward the earliest gods.

Who started this?
An axis, a quake, a perimeter,

I have no decisions to master
That could change my frame

Or honor.
Immaculate. Or if it was not, perfect.

Pregnant, I'm highly explosive—
You can feel it, long before

Your seed will run back to hug you—
Squaring and cubing

Into reckless bones, bouncing odd ways
Like a football.

The heart sloshes through the microphone
Like falls in a box canyon.

\* \* \*

The queen's only a figurehead.
Nine months pulled by nine

Planets, the moon slooping
Through its amnion sea,

Trapped, stone-mad . . . and three
Beings' lives gel in my womb.

[1970]


## FOR ELIZABETH BISHOP

The child I left your class to have
Later had a habit of sleeping
With her arms around a globe
She'd unscrewed, dropped, and dented.
I always felt she *could* possess it,
The pink countries and the mauve
And the ocean which got to keep its blue.
Coming from the Southern Hemisphere to teach,
Which you had never had to do, you took
A bare-walled room, alone, its northern
Windowscapes as gray as walls.
To decorate, you'd only brought a black madonna.
I thought you must have skipped summer that year,
Southern winter, southern spring, then north
For winter over again. Still, it pleased you
To take credit for introducing us,
And later to bring our daughter a small flipbook
Of partners dancing, and a ring
With a secret whistle.—All are
Broken now like her globe, but she remembers
Them as I recall the black madonna
Facing you across the room so that
In a way you had the dark fertile life
You were always giving gifts to.
Your smaller admirer off to school,
I take the globe and roll it away: where
On it now is someone like you?

[1982]

# AT THE GRAVE OF HAZEL HALL

*NOTE: Hazel Hall (1886–1924) was author of three books of poetry. In a wheelchair since age twelve, she lived in Portland, Oregon, with her mother and sister. Her poems were published in such magazines as* Poetry *and* Harper's. *Until she lost her eyesight, she made her living by doing needlework. Her urn is housed in a mausoleum a mile from my former home.*

From the first tap on the deep stairway,
I could hear your chamber sounding nearer,
chaste studio like a shower or a swimming pool
in winter, scrubbed, swabbed, tiered with glass flower-cones
for your mourners who died long ago.

Echo of your abstemious self-descriptions,
this white-mosaicked room holds no more
important vacancy than yours. But yours was a world
in which *important* had no opposite—
a stitch pulled gravity.

Not the grand male slabs, marbled conversation of the "great
and talkative"; not those, Unvisited Vase.
Famous people may have died into the unknown
in their clubby joinery, but you
are still unknown and twin of all that mystery.

Today the messy sunlight strews
itself through bevels and brasses of your tight mausoleum.
You are drafting "Hand in Sunlight"
(you write with the other hand)
and find your thirtyish skin flushed, yellow-grooved, and pale
    blue.

The palm is gathered at the thumb.
"I am not," you conclude, "one of those too frail to sin."
Your unwalking feet are stasis; your hands, motion,
"mutually interested" in embroidering, earlier today,
the "wicked, yellow-lidded eye" of a cross-stitched peacock.

It is blinding you. To see what you still can,
you ride your chair toward the second-story window,
hold a mirror out like an insect net

for passers-by to step into.
Nainsook, linen in your lap; patricians, leaf-kickers

in your glass, with the "disputed tread"
of a too-modest woman hesitating, slowly burning through. . . .
I was thinking: Here you are,
still in your window,
in that roly-poly copper urn, a handle on each side

(for whom to hold?),
and listening for "footfalls."
I should be dancing across the tiles,
should scuff and click for you at last. Right here.
I've only brought some pussy willows to be your flower,

animal paws for the blind,
knobby twigs cut from the swan marsh.
Feel them, silvergray lanugo, cold stems clammy with memorial
        tapwater,
a bud at each twig's end the double of a deer's hoof.
Sniff the catkins—it's very faint. An aura of skunk.

"To live with Hazel
is to make one disappointed in almost everyone else,"
your sister says. She brings, at your request,
more prose than poetry. Some Frost,
Millay, and Dickinson. A lot of Katherine Mansfield,

James Stephen's *Crock of Gold* (over and over,
it is your favorite). *Jacob's Room.*
A history of philosophy that weighs your body down
so your soul can escape alone.
In these Twenties tiers and niches

many urns are books,
so many volumes with women's names,
Drusilla Salomon, a Helen Meredith.
They hoped now they were dead someone would read them.
A cinderellan library, archives of burned diaries!
\*   \*   \*

But you—your turnable, unwasted pages
on death—you chose that pregnant vessel.
Chose "forcing death to approach in the rhythms of poetry,"
spurring it with your needle,
its "moving gleam like chips of ice in a heated seam,"
fusing toward this cold room of fatal fevers.

> "My room?" you wrote. "Its sill
> is brown, its wall is gray,
> curtains of dull, sticky gold
> smother hours in their fold.
> The floor is not mine: always
> I must waive my rights to feet."

Your feet uttered nothing. You sewed loose syllables together.
Needlework covered every surface.
"A crocus must be made so subtly as to seem afraid
of lifting colour from the ground."
But after all that keeping within lines,

you craved in language incongruity:
"a raging thread," "the glitter of sterility,"
the rip and stab among the dainty, fine
commissions from the growing families up the hill.
Liked "despair . . . brilliantly unrepressed"

and "hours of light about to thrust themselves into me
like omnivorous needles into listless cloth."
Boldly you entered the crematorium, smoky tavern
of eternal nightlife. "I am seeing so far tonight
that I am blinded by the space between me
and the inevitable. Logical smug death
takes me. The body lies unhumorous at length. The moon
bleeds gray light on the meadow
and I am weary as a sheep. I have broken with myself,
but I lie down with all the tired women,

every woman's sorrow is my own. I have given,
I have given all my hands."
                    And on my second visit

I bring a rose. "A fibre of rain" spins down.
A bloodless electric organ eternally in sickness and in tune
plays music to another funeral. Whoever came

to yours, you never met another writer.
Your mother came to study the two urns, your father's, yours.
If she left willows, she saw within a week how catkins pushed
peroxide yellow between the gray, a moppy blossom
which, so slightly jarred, now pollinates the columbarium.

Like us she died. Like us she burned and chose to mix herself with you.

[1988]


# PAT PARKER, 1944–1989


## FOR WILLYCE

When i make love to you
  i try
    with each stroke of my tongue
      to say   i love you
      to tease   i love you
      to hammer   i love you
      to melt   i love you

  & your sounds drift down
    oh god!
        oh jesus!
    and I think—
here it is, some dude's
getting credit for what
      a woman
      has done,
        again.

[1973; 1978]

# THERE IS A WOMAN IN THIS TOWN

there is a woman in this town

she goes to different bars
sits in the remotest place
watches the other people
drinks til 2 & goes home—alone

some say she is lonely
some say she is an agent
none of us speak to her

Is she our sister?

there is a woman in this town

she lives with her husband
she raises her children
she says she is happy
& is not a women's libber

some say she is misguided
some say she is an enemy
none of us know her

Is she our sister?

there is a woman in this town

she carries a lot of weight
her flesh triples on her frame
she comes to all the dances
dances a lot; goes home—alone

some say she's a lot of fun
some say she is too fat
none of us have loved her

Is she our sister?

there is a woman in this town

she owns her own business
she goes to work in the day
she goes home at night
she does not come to the dances

some say she is a capitalist
some say she has no consciousness
none of us trust her

Is she our sister?

there is a woman in this town

she comes to all the parties
wears the latest men's fashions
calls the women mama
& invites them to her home

some say she's into roles
some say she hates herself
none of us go out with her

Is she our sister?

there is a woman in this town

she was locked up

she comes to many meetings
she volunteers for everything
she cries when she gets upset

some say she makes them nervous
some say she's too pushy
none of us invite her home

Is she our sister?


there is a woman in this town

she fills her veins with dope
goes from house to house to sleep
borrows money whenever she can
she pays it back if she must

some say she is a thief
some say she drains their energy
none of us have trusted her

Is she our sister?

once upon a time, there was a dream
a dream of women. a dream of women
coming together and turning the world
around. turning the world around and making it over.
a dream of women, all women being sisters.
a dream of caring; a dream of protection, a dream
of peace.
once upon a time there was a dream
a dream of women. for the women who rejected the
dream, there had only been a reassurance. for the women
who believed the dream—there is dying, women,
sisters dying
once upon a time there was a dream, a dream of women
turning the world all over and it still lives—
it lives for those who would be sisters

it lives for those who need a sister
it lives for those who once upon a time had a dream.

[1973; 1978]

## LOVE ISN'T

I wish I could be
the lover you want
come joyful
bear brightness
like summer sun

Instead
I come cloudy
bring pregnant women
with no money
bring angry comrades
with no shelter

I wish I could take you
run over beaches
lay you in sand
and make love to you

Instead
I come rage
bring city streets
with wine and blood
bring cops and guns
with dead bodies and prison

I wish I could take you
travel to new lives
kiss ninos on tourist buses
sip tequila at sunrise

Instead
I come sad
bring lesbians
without lovers
bring sick folk
without doctors
bring children
without families
*   *   *

I wish I could be
your warmth
your blanket

All I can give
is my love.

I care for you
I care for our world
if I stop
caring about one
it would be only
a matter of time
before I stop
loving
the other.

[1985]


# MINNIE BRUCE PRATT, 1944–

## MOTIONLESS ON THE DARK SIDE OF THE LIGHT

When I try to get back to my mother
at first I don't want to see the child
on her knees by the bed who is praying
against her hands, face and hands placed
flat and cool on the rough blue-and-white
woven bedspread that burns wet, hot, wet
after a while in the half-darkness.   Light
slices by her from the cracked kitchen
door, voices fall through into her room.

Motionless on the dark side of the light,
she kneels and listens to her mother talk
to her father, her mother's voice slurred,
desperate, a voice she's never heard before.
His reeks of whiskey, pills, death.   Reckless,
the mother threatens to kill herself too.

Is that what he wants?   In the lighted room
one of them decides.   All the child can do is pray.
Her knees hurt from the rug, nubby as gravel.
She prays her mother will not leave her.
She prays in the dark room rimmed with light.
She prays to someone there, but who is there?
Does she ask out loud?   Does she ask, silent?

The white fluorescence by her slowly widens.
Her mother has come to ask why she is crying.
Her mother says she will stay, promises to live.

The child begins to pray nights by the window.
Some nights the moon opens its full mouth and
takes her   silently kneeling   inside   fearless.

[1989]


## POEM FOR MY SONS

When you were born, all the poets I knew
were men, dads eloquent on their sleeping
babes and the future:   Coleridge at midnight,
Yeats' prayer that his daughter lack opinions,
his son be high and mighty, think and act.
You've read the new father's loud eloquence,
fiery sparks written in a silent house
breathing with the mother's exhausted sleep.

When you were born, my first, what I thought was
milk:   my breasts sore, engorged, but not enough
when you woke.   With you, my youngest, I did not
think:   my head unraised for three days, mind-dead
from waist-down anesthetic labor, saddle
block, no walking either.
                              Your father was then
the poet I'd ceased to be when I got married.
It's taken me years to write this to you.

I had to make a future, willful, voluble,
lascivious, a thinker, a long walker,
unstruck transgressor, furious, shouting,

379

voluptuous, a lover, a smeller of blood,
milk, a woman mean as she can be some nights,
existence I could pray to, capable of
poetry.
          Now here we are.   You are men,
and I am not the woman who rocked you
in the sweet reek of penicillin, sour milk,
the girl who could not imagine herself
or a future more than a warm walled room,
had no words but the pap of the expected,
and so, those nights, could not wish for you.

But now I have spoken, my self, I can ask
for you:    that you'll know evil when you smell it;
that you'll know good and do it, and see how both
run loose through your lives; that then you'll remember
you come from dirt and history; that you'll choose
memory, not anesthesia; that you'll have work
you love, hindering no one, a path crossing
at boundary markers where you question power;
that your loves will match you thought for thought
in the long heat of blood and fact of bone.

Words not so romantic nor so grandly tossed
as if I'd summoned the universe to be
at your disposal.
                    I can only pray:

That you'll never ask for the weather, earth,
angels, women, or other lives to obey you;

that you'll remember me, who crossed, recrossed
you,
      as a woman making slowly toward
an unknown place where you could be with me,
like a woman on foot, in a long stepping out.

                                        [1989]

# ALMA LUZ VILLANUEVA, 1944–

## TO JESUS VILLANUEVA, WITH LOVE

my first vivid memory of you
mamacita,
we made tortillas together
yours, perfect and round
mine, irregular and fat
we laughed
and named them: oso, pajarito, gatito.
my last vivid memory of you
          (except for the very last
          sacred memory
          i won't share)
mamacita,
beautiful, thick, long, gray hair
the eyes gone sad
with flashes of fury
when they wouldn't let you
have your chilis, your onions, your peppers
          —what do these damned gringos
          know of MY stomach?—*
so when I came to comb
your beautiful, thick, long, gray hair
as we sat for hours
(it soothed you
my hand
on your hair)
I brought you your chilis, your onions,
          your peppers.
and they'd always catch you
because you'd forget
and leave it lying open.
they'd scold you like a child
and be embarrassed like a child
silent, repentant, angry
and secretly waiting for my visit, the new
          supplies
we laughed at our secret
we always laughed
          you and I

you never could understand
the rules
at clinics, welfare offices, schools
any of it.
I did.
you lie. you push. you get.
I learned to do all this by
the third clinic day of being persistent
     ly
sent to the back of the line by 5 in the
      afternoon
and being so close to done by 8 in the
      morning
so my lungs grew larger
and my voice got louder
and a doctor consented
to see an old lady,
and the welfare would give you the money
and the landlady would remember to spray
     for cockroaches
and the store would charge the food till
     the check came
and the bank might cash the check if I got
     the nice man this time
and I'd order hot dogs and Cokes for us
at the old "Ice Palace" on Market Street
and we'd sit on the steps
by the rear exit, laughing
          you and I

mamacita,
I remember you proudly at Christmas
time, church at midnight services:
you wear a plain black dress
your hair down, straight and silver
(you always wore it up
tied in a handkerchief,
knotted to the side)
your face shining, your eyes clear,
your vision intact.
you play Death.

you are Death
you quote long stanzas from a poem I've
        long forgotten;
even fitful babies hush
such is the power of your voice,
your presence
fills us all.
the special, pregnant
silence.
eyes and hands lifted up
imploringly and passionately
the vision and power
offered to us,—
eyes and hands cast down
it flows through you
to us,
a gift.

your daughter, my mother
told me a story I'd never
heard before:
            you were leaving Mexico
            with your husband and two
            older children, pregnant
            with my mother.
            the U.S. customs officer
            undid everything you so
            preciously packed, you
            took a sack, blew it up
            and when he asked about
            the contents of the sack,
            well, you popped it with
            your hand and shouted
            MEXICAN AIR!*

aiiiiiiiiiii mamacita, Jesus,
I won't forget my visions and reality
to lie, to push, to get
just isn't
enough.

*Translated from Spanish; she refused and pretended to be unable to speak English.        [1977]

383

power of my blood, your secret
wrapped in ancient tongues
spoken by men who claimed themselves
gods and priests and oracles—they
made elaborate rituals
secret chants and extolled the cycles,
calling women unclean.
men have killed
made war
for blood to flow, as naturally
as a woman's
once a month—
men have roamed the earth to find
the patience of pregnancy
the joy of birth—

the renewal of blood.
      (the awful, bloody secret: O woman
         you dare birth
yourself)

        call me witch
        call me hag
        call me sorceress
        call me mad
        call me woman.   do not
        call me goddess.
        I do not want the position.

        I prefer to gaze in wonder, once
        a month, at my
        witches' blood.

                                      [1977]

# ALICE WALKER, 1944–

## WOMEN

They were women then
My mama's generation
Husky of voice—Stout of
Step
With fists as well as
Hands
How they battered down
Doors
And ironed
Starched white
Shirts
How they led
Armies
Headragged Generals
Across mined
Fields
Booby-trapped
Ditches
To discover books
Desks
A place for us
How they knew what we
*Must* know
Without knowing a page
Of it
Themselves.

[1973]

## THE THING ITSELF

Now I am going
to rape you,
you joked;
after a pleasure
wrung
from me.

*  *  *
With playful roughness
you dragged my body
to meet yours;
on your face
the look of
mock
lust
you think
all real women
like

As all "real" women
really
like rape.

Lying
barely breathing
beneath
your heaving
heaviness
I fancied I saw
my great-great-grandmother's
small hands
encircle
your pale neck.

There was no
pornography
in her world
from which to learn
to relish the pain.

(She was the thing
itself.)

Oh, you who seemed
the best of them,
my own sad
Wasichu;

in what gibberish
was our freedom
engraved on
our chains.

[1984]

# INGRID WENDT, 1944–

## THE NEWEST BANANA PLANT LEAF

unfurls in rain
outside the window as
between the lips
of my cunt you
have just spoken
centuries
of promises
names like stars
on a flag someone
still believes in
raised at reveille
the year
the century this day
makes complete.

[1973]

## MUSSELS
### *for Ralph*

We've learned where the big ones grow,
to harvest not from the tops of rocks where shells
fill with sand

to follow the tide out to the farthest reefs we can reach
and still not get wet, where last time we found
giant anemones green-sheathed and dripping under

&ast;  &ast;  &ast;

the overhangs like the cocks of horses, we laughed, or
elephants, having each come to the same conclusion,
fresh from bed and married long enough

to say such things to each other, again
to remember the summer we first discovered mussels
big as fists protecting Sisters Rocks.

Just married and ready for anything, even
mussels were game, black as obsidian, stubbornly
clinging to rocks, to each other, their shells

so tightly together we had to force them apart
with a knife, the meat
inside a leap of orange, poppy-bright; and when

three perch in a row took the hook you'd baited
tender as liver we said we must try them ourselves
someday, if they're safe, which they weren't

all the years we lived down south: red algae in summer
tides infiltrating our chance to experiment, food without precedent,
how would we know what to do?

Counting at last on friends who had been to Europe and now
are divorced, we waded waist deep to pick some,
scraping our knuckles raw on barnacles

none of us knowing to soak our catch two hours at least
to clean out the sand; the sand we took in with butter and lemon
cleaning our teeth for a week.

Now we can't get our fill of them.
Weekend vacations you work to the last, cooking
one more batch to freeze for fritters or stew.

Now we harvest them easily, take the right tools, wear boots
we gave to each other for birthdays so we don't have
to remember to watch out for waves

to feel barnacles unavoidably crushed underfoot
like graveyards of dentures waves have exposed, although
sometimes now I find myself

passing over the biggest, maybe because
they've already survived the reach of starfish,
blindly prowling on thousands of white-tipped canes,

or they've grown extra barnacles,
limpets, snails, baby anemones,
rock crabs hiding behind. As though

age after all counts for something
and I've grown more tender-hearted,
wanting you not to know about the cluster

I found today, for the first
time in years having taken time off from job
and housework and child care, sleeping so late

my feet got wet on the incoming tide, unexpectedly
talking aloud, saying look at that one, bigger even
than Sisters Rocks: a kind of language

marriage encourages, private as memories of mussels,
anachronistic as finding I miss you
picking mussels to take home to you

not the ones you'd pick if you could but fresh
as any young lover's bouquet and far more edible,
more than enough to last us at least a week.

[1987]

## AFTER A CLASS IN SEAWEED

These names like exotic diseases—*Alaria, Porphyra,*
*Fucus*—or terms transmitted from darkrooms (try
*Iridia;* try *Laminaria*). Still, it's hard to
imagine our world's future food supply

blessed with names like Bull Whip Kelp, though
that's what it looks like, and history shows

Maiden's Hair is poisonous, leaving us
(if we stick with the representational) Sea
Palm and Lettuce—high in iron, potassium,
iodine, protein, you name it—and once you see
how good they can taste, who knows, you might
impress your friends with your daring, you might

start a new trend. Believe me, these new scientist
cooks know what they're up to. Last week I stir-fried
some kind of algae with onions, green peppers, garlic
and soy sauce. Forgot it wasn't spinach. Tried
Porphyra chips with salsa, disguising an aftertaste
clinging like limpets, like shrivelled up slug trails

that don't wash off. Anything's possible. Like
tonight, the casserole I took to the potluck
full of Sea Palms everyone took to be diced
black olives (smothered with hamburger, tucked
into a sauce of tomato and cheddar). Like finding
good intentions not only tricking the tongue, but blinding.

[1993]


# LUCHA CORPI, 1945–

## EMILY DICKINSON

Like you, I belong to yesterday,
to the bays where
day is anchored to
wait for its hour.

Like me, you belong to today,
the progression of that hour
when what is unborn
begins to throb.

\*   \*   \*

We are cultivators of
the unsayable, weavers
of singulars, migrant
workers in search of
floating gardens as yet
unsown, as yet unharvested.

[1980]


WINTER SONG
         *To Magdalena Mora*
         *(1952–1981)*

In the opening
and shutting of an eye
full
of magic
clocks
and old dreams
winter comes:

The wind murmurs melancholy
as the all's well of the night watchman
who looked after my parents' house
—I go back every winter
lest I forget who I am
or where I come from.

The rain comes down singing
toward its destiny of mineral and seed.
Between the hollow of an opening wing
and the lowering of eyelids in repose
we learn to love in instants and surrenders
and between the intimate question posed by night
and the darksweet reply given by dawn
we engender in pain a new life.

Nothing is fixed or perpetual
not rain
or seed
or you
or I

or our grief
in this world that is bleeding
because we're forever cutting paths
opening our way along unfamiliar roads
conquering the fury of oblivion verse by verse.

[1990]


# SHARON DOUBIAGO, 1946–

SELF

You walk the streets
touching, in the iodine night,
the body he no longer finds.
You lean against an old building
that shakes with every wave thrown to the beach.
He calls your name
but runs past you when you answer.
Under the harsh corner light a man curses,
*Hey! You can't be out here*
*looking like that!*

No one sees you.
You weave among the dancers
exposing your face.
They are in love with the veils on your face.
You wonder where she comes from, cinematic, bitter
celluloid. Your mind
the myth behind the face, your body
the trap to catch it.

One who has told you stories of his grandfather
driving stage up the coast, the wind
parting his red beard over each shoulder,
knocks the drink from your hand.

He sees then your mask has fallen too,
you are soft, naked.

He pays for another drink,
grabs you. It is then
you find yourself,
an unshakable building, pitifully
dwarfing his man size, his little
lust.

You are both shocked. Inside you
lives a thing
as bizarre and fierce
as anything they imagine.

[ 1977]

## FROM THE WAITRESS PAPERS

It's half over. You vow
not to look again at the clock
though the moan
spilt to the cold floor
spreading everywhere in the dark
is your own, you realize,
as you make your way back
through its echo
to the bar.

As you pass among them
a hand touches your leg.
*The curve of your thigh,* he mutters.
Your ass, another declares
is the finest he's seen in days.

Outside it rains.
Under the lamps Fort Bragg looks like a stage set.
Jewelry, laundromat, blue hardware, your car.
Even now, two months later, you pray
he'll be waiting for you
when you get off.

The man who followed you home your second night
has never looked at you since you told him
he frightened you.

Adelaid, who has money
she doesn't know what to do with
salutes the air and vows: *Never
say die.* Quigley is crying.
The doctor told him today
his wife has two months.
In the morning he'll drive to the city
bring her home. *Nobody understands*
he keeps weeping, *we're all alone.*
And you, you the waitress
here for tits and laughs
you are breaking down.

[1977]

## FATHER

I am like you, Mama always said.
Often we went fishing.
It takes patience and silence
to be a fisherman.
Most fail, you always said.

I am like you, Mama always said,
and if I reach back far enough
we are fishing again from the narrow rock ledge
that jettied the ocean at Seal Beach.
We crawled out to where crabs and unnameables crawled
out of dark seaweedy crevices, the dark holes
the ocean kept screaming up from.
We sat there, always on the dark side, for hours.
days.

It takes patience and silence
to be a fisherman.
We sat in the cold, cruel spray
of wave after wave churning to shore,
and with the contorted fishy bodies
of fishermen, old, toothless, bearded,
their awful cries above the cries of gulls
after deserted mussel.
bait.

\*   \*   \*

I am like you, Daddy, Mama always said.
Your body a great melancholy night in which I sat
beneath your heart
in terrible silence
and fished.

The old men danced as the day
moved on, those
fishers, those broken
bearded kings, those
Ahabs.
As the flaming ball fell
to the water line between my thighs
I was a drowned creature
drifting hundreds of years
in the unspeakable
foundations.

Unwarped, unarguable shapes
glided to and fro
my passive eyes.
Did I ever catch a fish?
Did I ever want to?

I wanted only
to sit there longer
on the dry landside of my father
knowing the shadow of my father is my father.
Daddy, still I wake
on that broken throne of gnarled torsos.
Daddy, the dark power you cast
I took.

Though sometimes still
the girl curls
into your humped darkness,
contorts her fishy body
into the great heartsea
beneath your ribs
\*   \*   \*

and in silence
works her way all the way back
to an old woman coming from Asia
and further than that
to an old white whale
cruising the pelvis of the world

until our story (You, the ruthless boy
so young even still
I see you outlive me)
is turning into
foam
and the great birth
from your severed and flung
genital.

[1982]


# MARILYN NELSON WANIEK, 1946–

## LEVITATION WITH BABY

The Muse bumped
against my window this morning.
No one was at home but me
and the baby. The Muse said
there was room on her back for two.
*Okay,* I said, *but first I've got to*

Pack his favorite toys.
Small ones are the best:
that way he can sit and play quietly
as the earth slides out from under our feet.
Let's see, somewhere there's
a wind-up dog with a drum
that sometimes keeps him busy
ten minutes or more.
And we'd better take some books.

\* \* \*

Disposable diapers,
pre-moistened towelettes,
plastic bags,
and I'll pack a lunch.
Peanut butter and crackers
are nutritious,
and the crumbs brush right off.

While I was packing his lunch
the baby got hungry,
so I put him in his high chair,
unpacked the crackers,
and gave him some.
He threw the third one down,
so I took him out,
wiped the high chair,
wiped the floor under and around the chair,
wiped the window next to it,
and wiped his fingers and face.
Then I took off his pants,
shook them out,
and wiped the soles of his shoes.

I filled two plastic bottles,
changed his diaper,
and got him dressed.
I washed my hands.
I sat down at my desk.
*Okay,* I said. *Now
I'm ready for takeoff.*

As he cried for a bottle
I saw my next-door neighbor,
shirtless, in the pants he wears
to work in his garden,
scribbling furiously on the back of a paper bag
as he ascended over the roof of his house
on the Muse's huge, sun-spangled wings.

[1985]

# A STRANGE BEAUTIFUL WOMAN

A strange beautiful woman
met me in the mirror
the other night.
Hey,
I said,
What you doing here?
She asked me
the same thing.

[1985]

# THE HOUSE ON MOSCOW STREET

It's the ragged source of memory,
a tarpaper-shingled bungalow
whose floors tilt toward the porch,
whose back yard ends abruptly
in a weedy ravine. Nothing special:
a chain of three bedrooms
and a long side porch turned parlor
where my great-grandfather, Pomp, smoked
every evening over the news,
a long sunny kitchen
where Annie, his wife,
measured cornmeal
dreaming through the window
across the ravine and up to Shelby Hill
where she had borne their spirited,
high-yellow brood.

In the middle bedroom's hard,
high antique double bed
the ghost of Aunt Jane,
the laundress
who bought the house in 1872,
though I call with all my voices,
does not appear.
Nor does Pomp's ghost,
with whom one of my cousins believes
she once had a long and intimate

unspoken midnight talk.
He told her, though they'd never met,
that he loved her; promised
her raw widowhood would heal
without leaving a scar.

The conveniences in an enclosed corner
of the slant-floored back side porch
were the first indoor plumbing in town.
Aunt Jane put them in,
incurring the wrath of the woman
who lived in the big house next door.
Aunt Jane left the house
to Annie, whose mother she had known
as a slave on the plantation,
so Annie and Pomp could move their children
into town, down off Shelby Hill.
My grandmother, her brother, and five sisters
watched their faces change slowly
in the oval mirror on the wall outside the door
into teachers' faces, golden with respect.
Here Geneva, the randy sister,
damned their colleges,
daubing her quicksilver breasts
with gifts of perfume.

As much as love,
as much as a visit
to the grave of a known ancestor,
the homeplace moves me not to silence
but to righteous, praise Jesus song:

Oh, catfish and turnip greens,
hot-water cornbread and grits.
Oh, musty, much-underlined Bibles;
generations lost to be found,
to be found.

[1990]

# AI, 1947–

## SHE DIDN'T EVEN WAVE
*For Marilyn Monroe*

I buried Mama in her wedding dress
and put gloves on her hands,
but I couldn't do much about her face,
blue-black and swollen,
so I covered it with a silk scarf.
I hike my dress up to my thighs
and rub them,
watching you tip the mortuary fan back and forth.
Hey. Come on over. Cover me all up
like I was never here. Just never.
Come on. I don't know why I talk like that.
It was a real nice funeral. Mama's.
I touch the rhinestone heart pinned to my blouse.
Honey, let's look at it again.
See. It's bright like the lightning that struck her.

I walked outside
and face the empty house.
You put your arms around me. Don't.
Let me wave goodbye.
Mama never got a chance to do it.
She was walking toward the barn
when it struck her. I didn't move;
I just stood at the screen door.
Her whole body was light.
I'd never seen anything so beautiful.

I remember how she cried in the kitchen
a few minutes before.
She said, *God. Married.*
*I don't believe it, Jean, I won't.*
*He takes and takes and you just give.*
At the door, she held out her arms
and I ran to her.
She squeezed me so tight:

I was all short of breath.
And she said, *don't do it.*
*In ten years, your heart will be eaten out*
*and you'll forgive him, or some other man, even that*
*and it will kill you.*
Then she walked outside.
And I kept saying, I've got to, Mama,
hug me again. Please don't go.

[1979]


## THE MAN WITH THE SAXOPHONE

New York. 5 A.M.
The sidewalks empty.
Only the steam
pouring from the manhole covers seems alive,
as I amble from shop window to shop window,
sometimes stopping to stare, sometimes not.
Last week's snow is brittle now
and unrecognizable as the soft, white hair
that bearded the face of the city.
I head further down Fifth Avenue
toward the thirties,
my mind empty
like the Buddhists tell you is possible
if only you don't try.
If only I could
turn myself into a bird
like the shaman I was meant to be,
but I can't.
I'm earthbound
and solitude is my companion,
the only one you can count on.
Don't, don't try to tell me otherwise.
I've had it all and lost it
and I never want it back,
only give me this morning to keep,
the city asleep
and there on the corner of 34th and Fifth,
the man with the saxophone,
his fingerless gloves caked with grime,

his face also,
the layers of clothes welded to his skin.
I set down my case;
he steps backwards
to let me know I'm welcome
and we stand a few minutes
in the silence so complete,
I think I must be somewhere else, not here,
not in this city, this heartland of pure noise.
Then he puts the sax to his lips again
and I raise mine,
I suck the air up my diaphragm
and bend over into the cold, golden reed,
waiting for the notes to come,
and when they do,
for that one moment,
I'm the unencumbered bird of my imagination,
rising only to fall back
toward concrete,
each note a black flower,
opening, mercifully opening
into the unforgiving new day.

[1985]

# Ellen Bass, 1947–

### IN CELEBRATION

Last night I licked
your love, you love,
like a cat. And
I watched you rise like
bread baking, like
a helium balloon, rise
with the skill of a soufflé,
your love, waving like
passengers on a boat coming in.

My cheek resting on your belly,
moist like a bathroom mirror, resting
in your hair like
dew grass, I drew
your love out like
the head of a turtle, like
an accordion, like
an expandable drinking glass.
I licked
you love, your love,
hard as a lollipop, plump
and tender as a plum.
I held you
like a mitten, like a cup,
and, like the crowds in the spray of a Yellowstone geyser,
like kids splashing in a July fire hydrant,
like a dinner guest biting in a whole tomato,
I gasped,
I laughed,
I feasted on your vintage.

[1973]


VAGINAS OF WOMEN

Vaginas of women, all the clusters
of vulva, clitoris, labia,
all the shades of coral and persimmon
peach, tulip, and carnelian,
the evening sky as the sun goes down
when clouds illuminate in underwater colors,
and the shapes, orchid and iris
butterfly and lotus blossom
flower and bud opening like morning glories.
Oh petals, fluted and smooth,
pink pearl, sweet pea, pulsing like stars
rising like dunes, pouring forth
sweet melon juice, singing
singing, singing to each other like wild birds.

[1977]

# TAMPONS

My periods have changed. It is years
since I have swallowed pink and gray darvons, round
chalky midols from the bottle with the smiling girl.
Now I plan a quiet space,
protect myself those first few days when my uterus lets
go and I am an open anemone. I know
when my flow will come. I watch my mucous pace
changes like a dancer, follow the fall
and rise of my body heat. All this
and yet I never questioned them, those slim white handies.

It took me years to learn to use them
starting with pursettes and a jar of vaseline.
I didn't know where the hole was.
I didn't even know enough
to try to find one. I pushed until
only a little stuck out and hoped
that was far enough.
I tried every month through high school.

And now that I can change it in a moving car—
like Audrey Hepburn changing dresses in the taxi
in the last scene of *Breakfast at Tiffany's*—
I've got to give them up.

Tampons, I read, are
bleached, are
chemically treated to
compress better,
contain asbestos.
Good old asbestos. Once we learned not to shake it—
Johnson & Johnson's—on our babies or diaphragms,
we thought we had it licked.

So what do we do? They're universal.
Even macrobiotics and lesbian separatists are hooked on them.

Go back to sanitary napkins?

Junior high, double napkins
on the heavy days, walking home damp underpants
chafing thighs. It's been a full twelve years
since I have worn one, since Spain when Marjorie pierced my ears
and I unloaded half a suitcase of the big gauze pads in the hotel trash.

Someone in my workshop suggested tassaways, little
cups that catch the flow.

> They've stopped making them,
> we're told. Women found they could reuse them
> and the company couldn't make enough
> money that way. Besides,
> the suction pulled the cervix out of shape.

Then diaphragms.

> It presses on me, one woman says.
> So swollen these days. Too tender.

Menstrual extraction, a young woman says.
I heard about that. Ten minutes
and it's done.

> But I do not trust putting tubes into my uterus each month.
> We're told everything is safe
> in the beginning.

Mosses.
The Indians used mosses.

> I live in Aptos. We grow
> succulents and pine.
> I will buy mosses
> when they sell them at the co-op.

Okay. It's like the whole birth control schmeer.
There just isn't a good way. Women bleed.
We bleed.
The blood flows out of us. So we will bleed.
Blood paintings on our thighs, patterns
like river beds, blood on the chairs in
insurance offices, blood on Greyhound buses
and 747's, blood blots, flower forms

on the blue skirts of the stewardesses.
Blood on restaurant floors, supermarket aisles, the steps of government
buildings. Sidewalks

                                    Gretel's bread
             will have
                         like
                blood trails,

crumbs. We can always find our way.

We will ease into rhythm together, it happens
when women live closely—African tribes, college sororities—
our blood flowing on the same days. The first day
of our heaviest flow we will gather in Palmer, Massachusetts
on the steps of Tampax, Inc. We'll have a bleed-in.
We'll smear the blood on our faces. Max Factor
will join OB in bankruptcy. The perfume industry
will collapse, who needs
whale sperm, turtle oil, when we have free blood?
For a little while cleaning products will boom,
409, Lysol, Windex. But
the executives will give up. The cleaning woman is leaving a
red wet rivulet, as she scrubs down the previous stains.
It's no use. The men would have to
do it themselves, and that will never come up
for a vote at the Board. Women's clothing manufacturers, fancy
furniture, plush carpet, all will phase out. It's just not
practical. We will live the old ways.

Simple floors, dirt or concrete, can be hosed down
or straw, can be cycled through the compost.
Simple clothes, none in summer. No more swimming pools.
Swim in the river. Yes, swim in the river.
Dogs will fall in love with us.
We'll feed the fish with our blood. Our blood
will neutralize the chemicals and dissolve the old car parts.
Our blood will detoxify the phosphates and the
PCB's. Our blood will feed the depleted soils.
Our blood will water the dry, tired surface of the earth.
We will bleed. We will bleed. We will

bleed until we bathe her in our blood and she turns
slippery new like a baby birthing.

[1977]

## I DIDN'T KNOW
### *for Florence Howe*

Ten years ago I sat in a classroom next to my teacher.
We sat in a circle at half desks. She, on my right
read a poem by Denise Levertov, *Life at War*
and she choked back tears.

I was a beginning poet.
I wrote of love and jacaranda trees.
Once I tried to write about the war,
but the poem was not one that would make anyone
choke back tears.

I wished, as I heard her read, and afterward,
I wished I could write that way
about those things.

I didn't know I would have to
wake with the taste of them thick in my saliva,
to wake with the sweat of them, with low groans,
to hear my husband grind his teeth with dreams of them.

I didn't know I would have visions of my baby's skin
sloughing off from radiation burn,
that in the sweetest times, especially
the sweetest times, pink dusk, my baby sucking,
patting my breast, or after she's in her small wicker bed
when Alan lights orange candles and incense
and we turn to our own loving,
I didn't know I'd come to where there is no joy
without that pale underbelly of what is to come.

I didn't know
what I wished for.

[1978]

## FOR BARBARA, WHO SAID SHE COULDN'T
## VISUALIZE TWO WOMEN TOGETHER

Picture lilacs.
Picture armfuls of lilacs, wet
with rain. Nuzzle your whole face
into the bouquet. Feel the cool drops
on your lips. Inhale.

Picture the ocean
from a cliff.
Stand at the edge, see
how the foam tumbles in
and disperses,
watch this heavy water
undulate until you're dizzy.
Lie down.

With one fingertip
touch the flat petal
of a California poppy. Lightly
travel the entire surface.
Close your eyes.

Imagine sun on your eyelids.
Recall the smell of wild mint
and the taste of wild blueberries
and the grace of coming upon a doe
at dusk by a river
and she does not bolt.
She lifts her gaze to you
before she goes on drinking.

Imagine damp seeds sending out blind roots
            into the generous soil.
Picture the root hairs absorbing the mineral-rich drink.
Feel the turgid green push up
            with a force that splits rock.
Hear the laughter.
*   *   *

Barbara, open your eyes.
Look at these women. You can visualize
any two
together.

[1984]

# CHERYL CLARKE, 1947–

## HAIR: A NARRATIVE

it is passing strange to be in the company
of black women
and be the only one who does not worry about
not being with a man
and even more passing strange
is to be among black women
and be the only one wearing her hair natural
or be the only one who has used a straightening
iron.

An early childhood memory:

me: sitting in the kitchen
holding down onto my chair
shoulders hunching
toes curling in my sneakers.

my mother: standing behind me
bracing herself against the stove
greasing the edges of my scalp
and the roots of my hair violently
heating the straightening comb alternately
and asking between jerking and pulling:

    "why couldn't you have *good* hair?"
    \*   \*   \*

by the time mother finished pressing my virgin wool
to patent leather,
I was asking why I had to have hair at all.

(the first time I heard a straightening iron crackle
through my greased kitchen, I thought a rattlesnake
had got loose.)

so much pain to be black, heterosexual, and female
to be trained for some *Ebony* magazine mail order man
wanting a woman with long hair, big legs, and able
to bear him five sons.
hardly any man came to be worth the risk of nappy edges.

the straightening iron: sado-masochistic artifact
salvaged from some chamber of the Inquisition
and given new purpose in the new world.

what was there
about straight hair
that made me want to suffer
the mythical anguish of hell
to have it?
made me a recluse
on any rainy, snowy, windy, hot, or humid day,
away from any activity that produced the least
moisture to the scalp.
most of all sex.
(keeping the moisture from my scalp
always meant more to me
than fucking some dude.)

there was not
a bergamot
or a plastic cap
that could stop
water
from undoing
in a matter of minutes
what it had taken hours of torture

to *almost* perfect.
I learned to hate water.

I am virgo and pragmatic
at fifteen I made up my mind
if I had to sweat my hair back with anyone
it would be my beautician.
she made the pretense bearable.

once a month I would wait several hours
in that realm of intimacy
for my turn in her magical chair
for my four vigorous shampoos
for her nimble fingers to massage
my hair follicles to arousal
for her full bosom to embrace
my willing head
against the war of tangles
against the burning metamorphosis
she touched me naked
taught me art
gave me good advice
gave me language
made me love something bout myself.

Willie Mays' wife thought integration
meant she could get a permanent in a
white woman's beauty salon.
and my beautician telling me to love myself
applying the chemical
careful of the time
soothing me with endearments
and cool water to stop the burning
then the bristle rollers
to let me dry forever
under stacks of *Jet, Tan,* and *Sepia.*
and then the magnificence of the comb-out.

"au naturel" and the promise of
black revolutionary cock à la fanon

made our relationship suspect.
I asked for tight curls.
my beautician gave me a pick
and told me no cock was worth so drastic a change.
I struggled to be liberated from the supremacy
of straight hair,
stopped hating water
gave up the desire for the convertible sports coupe
and applied the lessons of my beautician
who never agreed with my choice
and who nevertheless still gives me language, art,
intimacy, good advice,
and four vigorous shampoos per visit.

[1983]


## WEARING MY CAP BACKWARDS

poets are among the first witches
so suffer none to live
or suffer none to be heard
and watch them burn before your eyes
less they recant and speak their verse
in latin.

i'm a poet.
i speaks in pig latin.
i eats pigs feet—a shonuff sign
of satan
to those whose ears are trained to
dactyls and iambs
who resolve all conflicts in couplets.

i run from mice.
mistake dead, brown leaves
scurried by sharp quick breezes
for rats
and write at stop lights
listening to duke ellington
at the cotton club.
*  *  *

an atavistic witch am i.
wearing beads of tarot
searching for wiccas
burning old drafts
chasing dreaded women
covering their locks
till sheba's return.

[1986]


# LINDA HOGAN, 1947–

## DAYBREAK

Daybreak.
My daughter sitting at the table,
strong arms,
my face in her eyes
staring at her innocence
of what is dark
her fear at night of nothing
we have created
light as a weapon against.
Dust floats
small prisms
red
blue
in her hair.
Light in her eyes, fireworks,
the smell of powder on her
is lilac
scenting narrow arms, thighs.
The cobalt light of her eyes
where yesterday a colt's thin legs
walked in a field
of energy.
Matter is transformed.

Her innocence is my guilt.
In her dark eyes
the children of Hiroshima
are screaming
and her skin is
their skin
falling off.
How quickly we could vanish,
your skin nothing.
How soft
you disappear confused
daughter
daughters
I love you.

[1983]


FRIDAY NIGHT

Sometimes I see a light in her kitchen
that almost touches mine,
and her shadow falls straight
through trees and peppermint
and lies down at my door
like it wants to come in.

Never mind that on Friday nights
she slumps out her own torn screen
and lies down crying on the stoop.
And don't ask about the reasons;
she pays her penalties for weeping.
Emergency Room:
Eighty dollars to knock a woman out.
And there are laughing red-faced neighbor men
who put down their hammers
to phone the county.
Her crying tries them all.
Don't ask for reasons
why they do not collapse
outside their own tight jawbones
or the rooms they build
a tooth and nail at a time.

\* \* \*

Never mind she's Mexican
and I'm Indian
and we have both replaced the words
to the national anthem with our own.
Or that her house smells of fried tortillas
and mine of Itchko and sassafras.

Tonight she was weeping in the safety of moonlight
and red maples.
I took her a cup of peppermint tea,
and honey,
it was fine blue china
with marigolds growing inside the curves.
In the dark, under the praying mimosa
we sat smoking little caves of tobacco light,
me and the *Señora of Hysteria,* who said
Peppermint is every bit as good as the ambulance.
And I said, Yes. It is home grown.

[1985]

## THE TRUTH IS

In my left pocket a Chickasaw hand
rests on the bone of the pelvis.
In my right pocket
a white hand. Don't worry. It's mine
and not some thief's.
It belongs to a woman who sleeps in a twin bed
even though she falls in love too easily,
and walks along with hands
in her own empty pockets
even though she has put them in others
for love not money.

About the hands, I'd like to say
I am a tree, grafted branches
bearing two kinds of fruit,
apricots maybe and pit cherries.
It's not that way. The truth is
we are crowded together

and knock against each other at night.
We want amnesty.

Linda, girl, I keep telling you
this is nonsense
about who loved who
and who killed who.

Here I am, taped together
like some old Civilian Conservation Corps
passed by from the Great Depression
and my pockets are empty.
It's just as well since they are masks
for the soul, and since coins and keys
both have the sharp teeth of property.

Girl, I say,
it is dangerous to be a woman of two countries.
You've got your hands in the dark
of two empty pockets. Even though
you walk and whistle like you aren't afraid
you know which pocket the enemy lives in
and you remember how to fight
so you better keep right on walking.
And you remember who killed who.
For this you want amnesty,
and there's that knocking on the door
in the middle of the night.

Relax, there are other things to think about.
Shoes for instance.
Now those are the true masks of the soul.
The left shoe
and the right one with its white foot.

[1985]

# MOLLY PEACOCK, 1947–

## SO, WHEN I SWIM TO THE SHORE

Living alone is like floating on blue
waters, arms out, legs down, in a wide bay
face to the sun on a brilliant white day,
the buildings of the city all around one,
millions of people doing what is done
in yellow buildings ringing a turquoise bay
in which one floats, in a lazy K
arms out, head back, legs spread beneath the brew
the clouds will make later on. One is
at the center of something of which one is
no more a part.
                        So, when I swim to the shore
and go home and lie down, lips blue, cunt cold,
yet clitoris hard and blue and I am still
alone—never again your finger or lip
or knuckle or two fingers or tongue tip—
what do you think I will do? Send you a bill
for my service as a shill in the carney game
you played with your wife? Hell, let's tame
our own monsters. There's this in being out of love:
I own every blue day I'm not a part of.

[1984]

## OUR ROOM

I tell the children in school sometimes
why I hate alcoholics: my father was one.
"Alcohol" and "disease" I use, and shun
the word "drunk" or even "drinking," since one time
the kids burst out laughing when I told them.
I felt as though they were laughing at me.
I waited for them, wounded, remem-
bering how I imagined they'd howl at me
when I was in grade 5. Acting drunk
is a guaranteed screamer, especially
for boys. I'm quiet when I sort the junk
of my childhood for them, quiet so we

for boys. I'm quiet when I sort the junk
of my childhood for them, quiet so we
will all be quiet, and they can ask what
questions they have to and tell about what
happened to them, too. The classroom becomes
oddly lonely when we talk about our homes.

[1984]


SMELL

The smoky smell of menses—Ma always
left the bathroom door open—smote the hall
the way the elephant-house smell dazed
the crowd in the vestibule at the zoo, all
holding their noses yet pushing toward it.
The warm smell of kept blood and the tinny
smell of fresh blood would make any child quit
playing and wander in toward the skinny
feet, bulldog calves, and doe moose flanks planted
on either side of the porcelain bowl
below the blurry mons. The oxblood napkin landed
in the wastecan. The wise eyes of elephants roll
above their flanks, bellies, and rag-tear ears
in a permeable enormity of smell's
majesty and pungency; and benignity. Years
of months roll away what each month tells:
God, what animals we are, huge of haunch,
bloody and wise in the stench of bosk.

[1984]


# NTOZAKE SHANGE, 1948–


ITS HAPPENIN/BUT YOU DONT KNOW ABT IT
                                        *(for david)*

these kisses are clandestine
no one can see them
i hold them in my hand
shd i be discovered/

i stick them in my hair & my head gets hot
so i haveta excuse myself

under no circumstances
can the legs that slip over my hips
leave tellin marks/ scents
of love/ this wd be unpardonable
so i am all the time
rubbin my arms/ exposin myself
to river mists/ to mask the sweetness
you leave me swillin in

i cant allow you to look at me
how you do so i am naked & wantin
to be explored like a honeysuckle patch
when you look at me how you do so
i am all lips & thigh/
my cover is blown & the kisses
run free/ only to hover sulkin over
yr cheek/ while i pretend
they are not mine
cuz its happenin/ but you dont know abt it

the kisses they take a slow blues walk
back to me
in the palm of my hand
they spread out/ scratch kick curse & punch
till my skin cries/
kisses raisin hell/ in my fists/
they fly out mad & eager
they'll fly out mad & eager
if you look at me how you do so i am naked
& wantin/ if you look at me how you do so
i am all lips & thigh/
they gonna fly out mad & eager
they fly out & climb on you
the kisses/ they
flyin
if you look at me
how you do so

[1978]

people keep tellin me to put my feet on the ground
i get mad & scream/ there is no ground
only shit pieces from dogs horses & men who dont live
anywhere/ they tell me think straight & make myself
somethin/ i shout & sigh/ i am a poet/ i write poems/
i make words/ cartwheel & somersault down pages
outta my mouth come visions distilled like bootleg
whiskey/ i am like a radio but i am a channel of my own
i keep sayin i do this/ & people keep askin what am i gonna do/
what in the hell is goin on?

did somebody roll over the library witta atomic truck
did hitler really burn all the books/ it's true
nobody in the united states can read or understand
english anymore/ i must have been the last survivor of
a crew from mars/ this is where someone in brown cacky comes
to arrest me & green x-ray lights come outta my eyes & i
can leap over skyscrapers & fly into the night/ i can be
sure no one will find me cuz i am invisible to
ordinary human beings in the u.s.a./ there are no poets
who go to their unemployment officer/ sayin i wanna put
down my profession as "poet"/ they are sure to send you to
another office/ the one for aid to totally dependent persons/

people keep tellin me these are hard times/ what are you gonna be
doin ten years from now/ what in the hell do you think/ i
am gonna be writin poems/ i will have poems/ inchin up the
walls of the lincoln tunnel/ i am gonna feed my children poems on
rye bread with horseradish/ i am gonna send my mailman off
with a poem for his wagon/ give my doctor a poem for his heart/
i am a poet/ i am not a part-time poet/ i am not an amateur
poet/ i dont even know what that person cd be/ whoever that
is authorizing poetry as an avocation/ is a fraud/
put yr own feet on the ground/ writers dont have to plan
another existence forever to live schizophrenically/ to
be jane doe & medea in one body/
i have had it/ i am not goin to grow up to be somethin else
i am goin to be ol & grey wizened & wise as aunt mamie/
i am gonna write poems til i die & when i have gotten outta

this body i am gonna hang round in the wind & knock over
everybody who got their feet on the ground/ i'ma let you
run wild/ & leave a poem or two with king kong
in his aeroplane to drop pieces of poems
so you all will haveta come together/ just to figure out/
how you got so far away/ so far away from words
however/ did you capture language/ is a free thing.

[1978]


# OLGA BROUMAS, 1949–

### EYE OF HEART

Because I was whipped as a child
frequently by a mother so bewildered
by her passion
her generous hunger she would freak
at the swell of her
even her love for me
alone in the small house
of our room by the Metropolis and fling me
the frantic flap of her hand as if some power
in me to say I want brought the unbearable
also to her lips

and as it didn't hurt
nearly as much as her distress
imagined it and set the set I grew up longing
for consummation as she did
beyond endurance
tenderness acceptance of the large
insatiable that grows so small
and grateful if allowed
its portion of sun

so that the images that led me down
the spiral of forgetting self and listing
like a phenomenon in the grip of its weather

dazzling or threatening but free
of civilization were the links
whereby her terror
made good its promise to annihilate
my will her will I couldn't tell
the difference then as now

when making love I can
breathe in forever on that rise
indefinite plateau whose briefness
like an eye is unselfconscious and the sphere
of the horizon its known line.

[1989]


TOUCHED

       Cold
December nights I'd go
and lie down in the shallows
and breathe the brackish tide till light

broke me from dream. Days I kept busy
with fractured angels' client masquerades.
One had a tumor
recently removed, the scar

a zipper down his skull, his neck
a corset laced with suture.
I held, and did my tricks, two
palms, ten fingers, each a mouth

suctioning off the untold harm
parsed with the body's violent grief
at being cut. Later a woman
whose teenage children passed on in a crash

let me massage her deathmask
belly till the stretch
marks gleamed again, pearls
on a blushing rise. A nurse of women HIV
*   *   *

positives in the City
came, her strong young body filled
my hands. Fear grips her only
late at night, at home, her job

a risk on TV. It was calm, my palm
on her belly and her heart
said Breathe. I did. Her smile
could feed. Nights I'd go down

again and lie down on the gritty
shale and breathe the earth's salt
tears till the sun
stole me from sleep and when you

died I didn't
weep nor dream but knew you
like a god breathe in
each healing we begin.

[1989]

# RACHEL HADAS, 1949–

YES, BUT

It is irrevocable. Not like marriage
or buying a house or being merely
happy or unhappy.

> Yes, but to come home after some boring concert
> or party, everybody sweating, aging
> and here is this whole other little life
> asleep and floating, waves of possibility

Yes, but it wakes you from the silky or salty
dream-dark you need, you too, your life, your age,
it wakes you with its life   I'M ME   I'M ME
* * *

Yes, but the icons of regeneration
life stamped deep in the loins and come again
here and caressable: a miracle

Yes, but the cold prepackaged
duck whose preslit innards
I tugged and scooped this morning
packed in so tight    socked in
the flesh, the cavity, the sealed-in blood

Yes, but this is backasswards. Birth is not
through throat or anus, not through eyes or finger

Yes, but it is downward

Yes, but down, roots, rain, the pull of earth
making from nothing and they pull it out

Yes, but then the toys strewn over the floor
the magnets stuck to the refrigerator
door that recapitulate our A
BC for Civilization all to be learned again,
Lamarck was wrong, I was born bare of Greek
nasty and brutish    small and ignorant

Yes, but primary colors dragged with a loaded
paintbrush over paper rich and dripping
rich smell of fingerpaints loamlike    edible

Yes, culture, nurture, but the world
is lurching toward its close.
Not simply life, this life: mortality
is true, is sometimes easy:
this world, our precious earth, the only one we live in

Yes, but all ages gutter, limp, and falter
children bring hope, they push the darkness back

Not this time, not this twilight.
No Yes, no But, just No: it is the end.

We walk its daily weight so dark upon us
unspeakable    we never speak of it
each little future flickers
doomed precious    it goes on but not forever
not long now    oh not long.

        and lights across the river,
        a barge passes under a bridge
        bearing its black message:
        the poetry reading falters
        in the darkened amphitheater
        sirens scream END    THE END
        we scream too, friends together
        we put our heads in one another's laps
        wailing and waiting

Yes, and we look like mothers turned to children
children to mothers    one another's needs
even in the last hour desperate, human
I do not know the end
the clock hands moving    moving
the child's cry in the night
hushes it for a little

        that mortal ticking

                                    [1987]


PASS IT ON, II

I grope to find the phrases for two thoughts.
One, everything is new—
butterfly    doorknob    toothbrush
        clap your hands
look at the light    the light—

and two, I'm starting to run out of words
for private use. You'd think
that one could give and keep at the same time,
        take through giving,
twin gestures, teaching/mothering: two tasks

* * *

you give your blood and brains to and they thank you
by passing plates for more. Okay, okay,
I didn't do it to be thanked. And yet
        the bottom of the barrel
feels perilously close to glinting up.

Crusty tongue. Cups that once held milk.
A mouth begins as organ of ingestion,
then gets its teeth in talk and never stops.
        Cup breast tongue
all provided courtesy of mother.

I never thought of thanking mine for years.
She never made those velvet vocables,
smooth secret treasures, taffy to the palate,
        mine to keep,
in fact my own invention, I knew,

not some old heirloom. Later I let go.
They fell from my open mouth and I live on
to tell the tale again.
        Pass it on.
Keep words and eat them. Don't your eyes light up

equally at *cookie* or any other noun
you recognize?—all goodies you'll hand down,
as the phrase goes, we hope, to your own children.
        A body passes
through a body, changing it forever.

*Carry on the torch* was what they told me
in high school, i.e. teach; be like your father.
Knowledge, it seemed, was like a relay race.
        I didn't know
the torch would have to pass through my own body.

                            [1989]

What starts as one more Monday morning class
merges to a collective Dickinson,
separate vessels pooling some huge truth
sampled bit by bit by each of us.

She sings the pain of loneliness for one.
Another sees a life of wasted youth;
then one long flinching from what lay beneath
green earth; last, pallid peerings at the stone

she too now knows the secret of.

                         Alone,
together, we'd decipher BIRD  SOUL   BEE
dialect humdrum only until heard
with the rapt nervy patience, Emily,
you showed us that we owed you. One small bird
opens its wings. They spread. They cover us:
myriad lives foreshortened into Word.

                                      [1989]

# CAROLYN FORCHÉ, 1950–

## BURNING THE TOMATO WORMS

*That from which these things are born*
*That by which they live*
*That to which they return at death*
*Try to know that*

I

Now pines lift
Linking their dark spines
Weak clouds fly the breaks like pelicans
                        over ploughed land

\* \* \*

During thick fields of American wind
Between apples and the first snow
In horse-breath weather I remember her

2

Before I was born, my body as snowfat
Crept over Wakhan
As grandfathers spat into fires and thawed
Their tarpaulin
Sending crackled paths of blood
Down into my birth

Their few logs were sleeves of fire
Twists of smoke still brush
Out of the ice where they died

3

Anna's hands were like wheat rolls
Shelling snow peas, Anna's hands
Are both dead, they were Uzbek,
Uzbek hands known for weaving fine rugs

Eat Bread and Salt and Speak the Truth

She was asking me to go with her
To the confrontation of something
That was sacred and eternal
It was a timeless, timeless thing
Nothing of her old age or my childhood
Came between us

4

Her footsteps bloodied snow
Smoke from her bread fire crept
From the house
The wood grew white in her stove
\* \* \*

*When time come*
*We go quick*
*I think*
*What to take*

On her back ground wheat and straw dolls
In the sack white cheese, duck blood

*Mother of God*
*I tell you this*
*Dushenka*
*You work your life*
*You have nothing*


5

I came down from her in south Michigan
Picture the resemblance

Now I squint out over the same fields scraped in sun
And now I burn tomato worms and string useless gourds

She had drawn apple skin
Tightly bent feet
Pulled babushkas and rosary beads
On which she paid for all of us

She knew how much grease
How deep to seed
That cukes were crawlers

Every morning at five she would market
Or wake me to pick and hoe, crows
Cackling between us, Slovakia swear words
Whenever I stopped to feed them

This is the way we have it
Light a glass of candles
Heavy sweatered winter woman
Buried the October before I was grown

**6**

She would take gladiolas to the priest
Like sword sprouts they fumed near her bed

After raising my father and nine others
In a foreign country
*Find yourself a good man*
*Get married*
*There is nothing left*

*Before we have a village*
*Across the Slovakian border*
*Now*
*There is no Slovakia*

*Before we dance like gypsies*
*Listen*
*You—young yet*


**7**

Still the china Virgin
Plugs in below the mantelpiece, lights up
Pointing at her own heart
Big as a fist and full of daggers

I get down on my knees with every other Slavic woman
And we speak the language


**8**

She took up against her hoe stick, watched the moon
She could hear snow touch chopped wood
Her room smelled of advent candles
Cake flour clung to her face


**9**

Between apples and first snow
In horse-breath weather

Birds shape the wind
Dogs chained to the ground
Leave their dung
Where the ditches have burned

And I wish she were alive
But she is big under the ground, dead
I walk to the Eastern market
A half block under October suns that move away
Women still there selling summer squash
But always more die

10

Moons fill with blood nights
Crab-walking northeast
My father has left the garden
To seed, first frost
We lug tomatoes in worms and all

11

Stiff air, same color as a child's vein
Rigid against the freezing curls of birch bark
The snow's round thaw at fence-post bases
Snow deep across the yard
Ice grunting with boot heels
And a small sun an inch across like blood
On the frost when some trap
Chomps down a rabbit whose dark eyes
Wait for dogs

12

I chew up my gloves on the way to the barn
I wait in the pony stall for a boy
To come, circle his tongue
In my mouth while the stud horse
Muds floorboards beside us
*   *   *

Bales of feed split beneath
Our bellies, we wait like nothing
For tires to grind past beside us
Over a new fall in the road

All day snapping knives to the back side of the shed
He waits for me
Winter light spreading out in our houses
His own father downing a shot of Four Roses
Playing songs on combs and kleenex

*When you hear them hoot owls hollerin'*
*It's a sign a rain*


13

*I want to ask you why I live*
And we go back apart across the field
*Why I am here and will have to feel the way I die*

It was all over my face
Grandma flipped kolačy rolls
Dunked her hands in bowls of water
Looked at me
Wrung the rags into the stoop
Kept it from me
Whatever she saw

[1976]


THE ISLAND
                    *for Claribel Alegría*


I

In Deya when the mist
rises out of the rocks it comes
so close to her hands she could
tear it to pieces like bread.
She holds her drink and motions
with one hand to describe this:

what she would do with so many
baskets of bread.

*Mi prieta,* Asturias called her,
my dark little one. Neruda
used the word *negrita,* and it is
true: her eyes, her hair,
both violent, as black
as certain mornings have been
for the last fourteen years.
She wears a white cotton dress.
Tiny mirrors have been stitched
to it—when I look for myself
in her, I see the same face
over and over.

I have the fatty eyelids
of a Slavic factory girl,
the pale hair of mixed blood.
Although José Martí has said
we have lived our lives in the heart
of the beast, I have never heard
it pounding. When I have seen
an animal, I have never reached
for a knife. It is like
Americans to say it is only a bear
looking for something to eat
in the garbage.

But we are not unalike.
When we look at someone, we are seeing
someone else. When we listen
we hear something taking place
in the past. When I talk to her
I know what I will be saying
twenty years from now.

**2**

Last summer she returned
to Salvador again. It had been
ten years since *Ashes of Izalco*
was burned in a public place,
ten years without bushes
of coffee, since her eyes
crossed the finca like black
scattering birds.

It was simple. She was
there to embrace her mother.
As she walked through her village
the sight of her opened its windows.
It was simple. She had come
to flesh out the memory of a poet
whose body was never found.
Had it changed? It was different.
In Salvador nothing is changed.

**3**

Deya? A cluster of the teeth,
the bones of the world, greener
than Corsica. In English
you have no word for this. I can't
help you. I am safe here. I have
everything I could want.
In the morning I watch the peak
of the Teix knife into the clouds.
To my country I ship poetry instead
of bread, so I cut through nothing.
I give nothing, so you see I have
nothing, according to myself.

Deya has seven different shawls
of wind. The sky holds them
out to her, helps her into them.
I am *xaloc*, a wind
from the southwest as far away

as my country and there is nothing
to help me in or out of it.

Carolina, do you know how long it takes
any one voice to reach another?

[1976–1978; 1981]


# JORIE GRAHAM, 1951 —


## THE WAY THINGS WORK

is by admitting
or opening away.
This is the simplest form
of current: Blue
moving through blue;
blue through purple;
the objects of desire
opening upon themselves
without us;
the objects of faith.
The way things work
is by solution,
resistance lessened or
increased and taken
advantage of.
The way things work
is that we finally believe
they are there,
common and able
to illustrate themselves.
Wheel, kinetic flow,
rising and falling water,
ingots, levers and keys,
I believe in you,
cylinder lock, pulley,
lifting tackle and
Crane lift your small head—

I believe in you—
your head is the horizon to
my hand. I believe
forever in the hooks.
The way things work
is that eventually
something catches.

[1980]

## FROM THE NEW WORLD

Has to do with the story about the girl who didn't die
    in the gas chamber, who came back out asking
for her mother. Then the moment—the next coil—where the guard,
    Ivan, since the 50's an autoworker in Cleveland,
orders a man on his way in to rape her.
    Then the narrowing, the tightening, but not in hunger, no,—the
                                        witness

recollecting this on the stand somewhere in Israel in
    February 87 should You be keeping
track. Has to do with her coming back out? Asking for her mother?
    Can you help me in this?
Are you there in your stillness? Is it a real place?
    God knows I too want the poem to continue,

want the silky swerve into shapeliness
    and then the click shut
and then the issue of sincerity, the glossy diamond-backed
    skin—will you buy me, will you take me home. . . . About the one
who didn't die, her face still there on the new stalk of her body as the
    doors open,

the one who didn't like a relentless treble coming back out
    right here into the thing we call
daylight but which is what now, unmoored?
    The one time I knew something about us
though I couldn't say what

my grandmother then already ill
    took me by the hand asking to be introduced.

And then *no, you are not Jorie—but thank you for*
    *saying you are. No. I'm sure. I know her you*
*see.* I went into the bathroom, locked the door.
    Stood in front of the mirrored wall—

not so much to see in, not looking up at all in fact,
    but to be held in it as by a gas,
the thing which was me there in its chamber. Reader,
    they were all in there, I didn't look up,
they were all in there, the coiling and uncoiling
    billions,

the about-to-be-seized,
    the about to be held down,

the about to be held down, bit clean, shaped,
    and the others, too, the ones gone back out, the ending
wrapped round them,
    hands up to their faces why I don't know,

and the about-to-be stepping in,
    one form at a time stepping in as if to stay clean,
stepping over something to get into here,
    something there on the floor now dissolving,
not looking down but stepping up to clear it,

and clearing it,
    stepping in.
Without existence and then with existence.
    Then into the clearing as it clamps down
all round.
    Then into the fable as it clamps down.

    We put her in a Home, mother paid.
We put him in a Home, mother paid.
    There wasn't one that would take both of them we
could afford.
    We were right we put him down the road it's all
there was,
    there was a marriage of fifty years, you know this
*   *   *

already don't you fill in the blanks,
  they never saw each other again,
paralyzed on his back the last few years
  he bribed himself a private line, he rigged the phone so he

could talk, etcetera, you know this,
  we put her in X, she'd fallen out we put her back in,
there in her diaper sitting with her purse in her hands all day every
  day, asking can I go now,
meaning him, meaning the
  apartment by then long since let go you know this

don't you, shifting wind sorting and re-sorting the stuff, flesh,
  now the sunstruck field beyond her window,
now her hands on the forties sunburst silver
  clasp, the white patent-leather pocketbook—
I stood there. Let the silver down all over my shoulders.

  The sink. The goldspeck Formica. The water
uncoiling.
  Then the click like a lock being tried.
Then the hollow caressing the back of my neck.
  Then the whole thing like a benediction you can't
shake off,

and the eyes unfastening, nervous, as if they smelled something up
                                                    there
  and had to go (don't wait for me), the
eyes lifting, up into the decoration, the eyes
  looking. Poor thing.
As if real. As if *in* the place.
  The twitch where the eyes meet the eyes.
A blush.
  You see it's not the matter of her coming back out

alive, is it?
  It's the asking-for. The please.
Isn't it?
  Then the man standing up, the witness, screaming it's him it's him
I'm sure your Honor I'm sure. Then Ivan coming up to him
  and Ivan (you saw this) offering his hand, click, whoever

he is, and the old man getting a dial-tone, friend,
   and old whoever clicking and unclicking the clasp the
silver knobs,
   shall we end on them? a tracking shot? a

close-up on the clasp a two-headed beast it turns out
   made of silvery
leaves? Where would you go now? *Where*
   screaming it's him it's
him? At the point where she comes back out something begins, yes,
   something new, something completely
new, but what—there underneath the screaming—what?

*Like* what, I wonder, to make the bodies come on, to make
   room,

*like what,* I whisper,

*like* which is the last new world, *like, like,* which is the thin

young body (before it's made to go back in) whispering *please.*

                                                        [1991]


# JOY HARJO, 1951–


## ANCHORAGE
### *for Audre Lorde*

This city is made of stone, of blood, and fish.
There are Chugatch Mountains to the east
and whale and seal to the west.
It hasn't always been this way, because glaciers
who are ice ghosts create oceans, carve earth
and shape this city here, by the sound.
They swim backwards in time.

Once a storm of boiling earth cracked open
the streets, threw open the town.

It's quiet now, but underneath the concrete
is the cooking earth,
                          and above that, air
which is another ocean, where spirits we can't see
are dancing            joking         getting full
on roasted caribou, and the praying
goes on, extends out.

Nora and I go walking down 4th Avenue
and know it is all happening.
On a park bench we see someone's Athabascan
grandmother, folded up, smelling like 200 years
of blood and piss, her eyes closed against some
unimagined darkness, where she is buried in an ache
in which nothing makes
                          sense.

We keep on breathing, walking, but softer now,
the clouds whirling in the air above us.
What can we say that would make us understand
better than we do already?
Except to speak of her home and claim her
as our own history, and know that our dreams
don't end here, two blocks away from the ocean
where our hearts still batter away at the muddy shore.

And I think of the 6th Avenue jail, of mostly Native
and Black men, where Henry told about being shot at
eight times outside a liquor store in L.A., but when
the car sped away he was surprised he was alive,
no bullet holes, man, and eight cartridges strewn
on the sidewalk
                          all around him.

Everyone laughed at the impossibility of it,
but also the truth. Because who would believe
the fantastic and terrible story of all of our survival
those who were never meant
                          to survive?

[1983]

# THE BOOK OF MYTHS

When I entered the book of myths
                 in your sandalwood room on the granite island,
  I did not ask for a way out.
This is not the century for false pregnancy
              in these times when myths
                         have taken to the streets.
There is no more imagination; we are in it now, girl.
  We traveled the stolen island of Manhattan
             in a tongue of wind off the Atlantic
       shaking our shells, in our mad skins.
I did not tell you when I saw Rabbit sobbing and laughing
                  as he shook his dangerous bag of tricks
     into the mutiny world on that street outside Hunter.
Out came you and I blinking our eyes once more, entwined in our loves
      and hates as we set off to recognize the sweet
and bitter gods who walk beside us, whisper madness
in our invisible ears any ordinary day.
  I have fallen in love a thousand times over; every day is a common
miracle of salt roses, of fire in the prophecy wind, and now and then
              I taste the newborn blood in my daughter's
         silk hair, as if she were not nearly a woman
    brown and electric in her nearly womanly self.
There is a Helen in every language; in American her name is Marilyn
              but in my subversive country,
     she is dark earth and round and full of names
dressed in bodies of women
    who enter and leave the knife wounds of this terrifyingly
beautiful land;
             we call ourselves ripe, and pine tree, and woman.
     In the book of myths that fell open in your room of unicorns
I did not imagine the fiery goddess in the middle of the island.
She is a sweet trick of flame,
           had everyone dancing, laughing and telling the stories
that unglue the talking spirit from the pages.
When the dawn light came on through the windows,
          I understood how my bones would one day
      stand up, brush off the lovely skin like a satin blouse
and dance with foolish grace to heaven.

                                    [1990]

# RITA DOVE, 1952–

## THE GREAT PALACES OF VERSAILLES

*Nothing nastier than a white person!*
She mutters as she irons alterations
in the back room of Charlotte's Dress Shoppe.
The steam rising from a cranberry wool
comes alive with perspiration
and stale Evening of Paris.
*Swamp she born from, swamp*
*she swallow, swamp she got to sink again.*

The iron shoves gently
into a gusset, waits until
the puckers bloom away. Beyond
the curtain, the white girls are all
wearing shoulder pads to make their faces
delicate. That laugh would be Autumn,
tossing her hair in imitation of Bacall.

Beulah had read in the library
how French ladies at court would tuck
their fans in a sleeve
and walk in the gardens for air. Swaying
among lilies, lifting shy layers of silk,
they dropped excrement as daintily
as handkerchieves. Against all rules

she had saved the lining from a botched coat
to face last year's gray skirt. She knows
whenever she lifts a knee
she flashes crimson. That seems legitimate;
but in the book she had read
how the *cavaliere* amused themselves
wearing powder and perfume and spraying
yellow borders knee-high on the stucco
of the *Orangerie.*
\*   \*   \*

A hanger clatters
in the front of the shoppe.
Beulah remembers how
even Autumn could lean into a settee
with her ankles crossed, sighing
*I need a man who'll protect me*
while smoking her cigarette down to the very end.

[1986]


AFTER READING *Mickey in the Night Kitchen*
FOR THE THIRD TIME BEFORE BED
> *I'm in the milk and the milk's in me! . . . I'm Mickey!*

My daughter spreads her legs
to find her vagina:
hairless, this mistaken
bit of nomenclature
is what a stranger cannot touch
without her yelling. She demands
to see mine and momentarily
we're a lopsided star
among the spilled toys,
my prodigious scallops
exposed to her neat cameo.

And yet the same glazed
tunnel, layered sequences.
She is three; that makes this
innocent. *We're pink!*
she shrieks, and bounds off.

Every month she wants
to know where it hurts
and what the wrinkled string means
between my legs. *This is good blood*
I say, but that's wrong, too.
How to tell her that it's what makes us—
black mother, cream child.
That we're in the pink
and the pink's in us.

[1989]

## ARROW

The eminent scholar "took the bull by the horns,"
substituting urban black speech for the voice
of an illiterate cop in Aristophanes' *Thesmophoriazusae.*
And we sat there.
Dana's purple eyes deepened, Becky
twitched to her hairtips
and Janice in her red shoes
scribbled *he's an arschloch; do you want*
*to leave? He's a model product of his*
*education,* I scribbled back; *we can learn from this.*

So we sat through the applause
and my chest flashed hot, a void
sucking at my guts until I was all
flamed surface. I would have to speak up.
Then the scholar progressed

to his prize-winning translations of
the Italian Nobel Laureate. He explained the poet
to us: immense difficulty
with human relationships; sensitive;
women were a scrim through which he could see
heaven.
We sat through it. Quite lovely, these poems.
We could learn from them although they were saying
*you women are nothing, nothing at all.*

When the moment came I raised my hand,
phrased my question as I had to: sardonic,
eminently civil my condemnation
phrased in the language of fathers—
felt the room freeze behind me.
And the answer came as it had to:
*humanity—celebrate our differences—*
*the virility of ethnicity.* My students
sat there already devising

their different ways of coping:
Dana knowing it best to have
the migraine at once, get the poison out quickly
Becky holding it back for five hours    and Janice
making it to the evening reading and
party afterwards
in black pants and tunic with silver mirrors
her shoes pointed and studded, wicked witch shoes:
Janice who will wear red for three days or
yellow brighter
than her hair so she can't be
seen    at all

[1989]

# CHERRIE MORAGA, 1952–

## FOR THE COLOR OF MY MOTHER

*I am a white girl gone brown to the blood color of my mother*
*speaking to her through the unnamed part of the mouth*
*the wide-arched muzzle of brown women*

at two
my upper lip split open
clear to the tip of my nose
it spilled forth a cry that would not yield
that traveled down six floors of hospital
where doctors wound me into white bandages
only the screaming mouth exposed

the gash sewn back into a snarl
would last for years

*I am a white girl gone brown to the blood color of my mother*
*speaking for her*
\*   \*   \*

at five, *her* mouth
pressed into a seam
a fine blue child's line drawn across her face
her mouth, pressed into mouthing english
mouthing yes yes yes
mouthing stoop lift carry
(sweating wet sighs into the field
her red bandana comes loose from under the huge brimmed hat
moving across her upper lip)

at fourteen, her mouth
painted, the ends drawn up
the mole in the corner colored in darker larger mouthing yes
she praying no no no
lips pursed and moving

at forty-five, her mouth
bleeding into her stomach
the hole gaping growing redder
deepening with my father's pallor
finally stitched shut from hip to breastbone
      an inverted V
      *Vera*
      *Elvira*

*I am a white girl gone brown to the blood color of my mother*
*speaking for her*

as it should be,
dark women come to me
                        sitting in circles
I pass thru their hands
the head of my mother
painted in clay colors

        touching each carved feature swollen eyes and mouth
*   *   *

they understand the explosion, the splitting
open    contained within the fixed expression

they cradle her silence

                    nodding to me

[1983]


## LOVING IN THE WAR YEARS

Loving you is like living
in the war years.
I *do* think of Bogart & Bergman
not clear who's who
but still singin a long smoky
mood into the piano bar
drinks straight up
the last bottle in the house
while bombs split
outside, a broken
world.

A world war going on
but you and I still insisting
in each our own heads
still thinkin how
*if I could only make some contact*
*with that woman across the keyboard*
we size each other up
        *yes . . .*

Loving you has this kind of desperation
to it, like do or die, I
having eyed you from the first
time you made the decision to move
from your stool
to live dangerously.

All on the hunch
that in our exchange of photos
of old girlfriends, names

of cities and memories
back in the states
the fronts we've manned
out here on the continent
all this on the hunch
that *this* time there'll be
no need for resistance.

Loving in the war years
calls for this kind of risking
without a home to call our own
I've got to take you as you come
to me, each time like a stranger
all over again. Not knowing
what deaths you saw today
I've got to take you
as you come, battle bruised
refusing our enemy, fear.

We're all we've got. You and I

maintaining
this wartime morality
where being queer
and female is as rude
as we can get.

[1983]

# Naomi Shihab Nye, 1952–

## HUGGING THE JUKEBOX

On an island the soft hue of memory,
moss green, kerosene yellow, drifting, mingling
in the Caribbean Sea,
a six-year-old named Alfred
learns all the words to all the songs
on his grandparents' jukebox, and sings them.

To learn the words is not so hard.
Many barmaids and teenagers have done as well.
But to sing as Alfred sings—
how can a giant whale live in the small pool of his chest?
How can there be breakers this high, notes crashing
at the beach of the throat,
and a reef of coral so enormous only the fishes know its size?

The grandparents watch. They can't sing.
They don't know who this voice is, trapped in their grandson's body.
The boy whose parents sent him back to the island
to chatter mango-talk and scrap with chickens—
at age three he didn't know the word "sad"!
Now he strings a hundred passionate sentences on a single line.
He bangs his fist so they will raise the volume.

What will they do together in their old age?
It is hard enough keeping yourself alive.
And this wild boy, loving nothing but music—
he'll sing all night, hugging the jukebox.
When a record pauses, that live second before dropping down,
Alfred hugs tighter, arms stretched wide,
head pressed on the luminous belly. "Now!" he yells.
A half-smile when the needle breathes again.

They've tried putting him to bed, but he sings in bed.
Even in Spanish—and he doesn't speak Spanish!
Sings and screams, wants to go back to the jukebox.
*O mama I was born with a trumpet in my throat*
     *spent all these years tryin' to cough it up . . .*

He can't even read yet. He can't *tell time.*
But he sings, and the chairs in this old dance hall jerk to attention.
The grandparents lean on the counter, shaking their heads.
The customers stop talking and stare, goosey bumps surfacing on their arms.
His voice carries out to the water where boats are tied
and sings for all of them, *a wave.*
For the hens, now roosting in trees,
for the mute boy next door, his second-best friend.
And for the hurricane, now brewing near Barbados—
a week forward neighbors will be hammering boards over their windows,

rounding up dogs and fishing lines,
the generators will quit with solemn clicks in every yard.

But Alfred, hugging a sleeping jukebox, the names of the tunes gone dark,
will still be singing, doubly loud now, teasing his grandmother,
"Put a coin in my mouth!" and believing what she wants to believe;
this is not the end of the island, or the tablets this life has been
scribbled on, or the song.

[1980; 1982]

## BLOOD

"A true Arab knows how to catch a fly in his hands,"
my father would say. And he'd prove it,
cupping the buzzer instantly
while the host with the swatter stared.

In the spring our palms peeled like snakes.
True Arabs believed watermelon could heal fifty ways.
I changed these to fit the occasion.

Years before, a girl knocked,
wanted to see the Arab.
I said we didn't have one.
After that, my father told me who he was,
"Shihab"—"shooting star"—
a good name, borrowed from the sky.
Once I said, "When we die, we give it back?"
He said that's what a true Arab would say.

Today the headlines clot in my blood.
A little Palestinian dangles a truck on the front page.
Homeless fig, this tragedy with a terrible root
is too big for us. What flag can we wave?
I wave the flag of stone and seed,
table mat stitched in blue.

I call my father, we talk around the news.
It is too much for him,
neither of his two languages can reach it.
I drive into the country to find sheep, cows,

to plead with the air:
Who calls anyone *civilized?*
Where can the crying heart graze?
What does a true Arab do now?

[1986]


# MARY JO SALTER, 1954–


## WELCOME TO HIROSHIMA

is what you first see, stepping off the train:
a billboard brought to you in living English
by Toshiba Electric. While a channel
silent in the TV of the brain

projects those flickering re-runs of a cloud
that brims its risen columnful like beer
and, spilling over, hangs its foamy head,
you feel a thirst for history: what year

it started to be safe to breathe the air,
and when to drink the blood and scum afloat
on the Ohta River. But no, the water's clear,
they pour it for your morning cup of tea

in one of the countless sunny coffee shops
whose plastic dioramas advertise
mutations of cuisine behind the glass:
a pancake sandwich; a pizza someone tops

with a maraschino cherry. Passing by
the Peace Park's floral hypocenter (where
how bravely, or with what mistaken cheer,
humanity erased its own erasure),

you enter the memorial museum
and through more glass are served, as on a dish

of blistered grass, three mannequins. Like gloves
a mother clips to coatsleeves, strings of flesh

hang from their fingertips; or as if tied
to recall a duty for us, *Reverence*
*the dead whose mourners too shall soon be dead,*
but all commemoration's swallowed up

in questions of bad taste, how re-created
horror mocks the grim original,
and thinking at last *They should have left it all*
you stop. This is the wristwatch of a child.

Jammed on the moment's impact, resolute
to communicate some message, although mute,
it gestures with its hands at eight-fifteen
and eight-fifteen and eight-fifteen again

while tables of statistics on the wall
update the news by calling on a roll
of tape, death gummed on death, and in the case
adjacent, an exhibit under glass

is glass itself: a shard the bomb slammed in
a woman's arm at eight-fifteen, but some
three decades on—as if to make it plain
hope's only as renewable as pain,

and as if all the unsung
debasements of the past may one day come
rising to the surface once again—
worked its filthy way out like a tongue.

[1985]


EMILY WANTS TO PLAY

    That alarming cry—
and before I even understand
I'm up, I've stumbled down the hall
    to where she lies in wait on her back,
    smiling. She's fooled me again.

        By the digital clock
it's 2:53 in the morning, and
    Emily wants to play.

        She rustles in
sheer happiness, under quilts I peel
back to take her up, up,
    and into the crook of my arm,
    where she's far too thrilled to settle.
    She wants no bottle,
shrugs off my gentle rocking—no,
    she'd rather squirm

        to face those two
red eyes dividing hour from minute,
staring at hers as if they know
    how blue they'll grow by day.
    As she turns to me
        I look away,
with a heavy nod to illustrate
    *We're sleeping now, see?*

        But see she does,
her eyes a magnifying glass
to burn my eyes in shame: she's had
    time already to learn
that nighttime is for love.
        Wakefulness
touches me gladly now, the thought
    of the giant yellow moon

        the night she was born,
and later, come winter, how
I nursed her by the light of snow
    ticking against this window.
    Having won me at last,
        she yawns; she's been vigilant
as this memory of her that can't
    rest until set down.

                                        [1989]

## CHERNOBYL

Once upon a time,
the word alone was scary.
Now, quainter than this rhyme,
it's the headline of a story

long yellowed in the news.
The streets were hosed in Kiev,
and Poles took more shampoos.
The evacuees were brave.

Under the gay striped awning
of Europe's common market,
half-empty booths were yawning
at the small change in the pocket.

As far away as Rome,
unseen through weeks of sun,
the cloud kept children home.
Milk gurgled down the drain.

In Wales, spring lambs were painted
blue, not to be eaten
till next spring when . . . Still tainted,
they'd grown into blue mutton.

Then we had had enough.
Fear's harder to retain
than hope or indifference. Safe
and innocent, the rain

fell all night as we slept,
and the story at last was dead—
all traces of it swept
under the earth's green bed.

[1989]

# THYLIAS MOSS, 1955–

## THERE WILL BE ANIMALS

There will be animals to teach us
what we can't teach ourselves.

There will be a baboon who is neither stupid nor clumsy
as he paints his mandrill face for the war being waged
against his jungle.

There will be egrets in a few thousand years
who will have evolved without plumes so we cannot take them.

There will be ewes giving and giving their wool
compensating for what we lack in humility.

There will be macaws with short arched bills
that stay short because they talk without telling lies.

Mackerel will continue to appear near Cape Hatteras each spring
and swim north into Canadian waters so there can be continuity.

There will be penguins keeping alive Hollywood's golden era.

The chaparral cock will continue to outdistance man
twisting and turning on a path unconcerned with shortcuts.

Coffinfly dun will leave the Shawsheen River
heading for the lights of Lawrence. What they see in 48 hours
makes them adults who will fast for the rest of their short lives,
mating once during the next hour and understanding everything
as they drop into a communal grave three feet thick with family
reaching the same conclusions.

The coast horned lizard still won't be found
without a bag of tricks; it will inflate and the first
of six million Jewfish will emerge from its mouth.
We will all be richer.
\* \* \*

John Dory will replace John Doe
so the nameless among us will have Peter's thumbmark on their
  cheek
and the coin the saint pulled from their mouths in their pockets.
Then once and for all we will know it is no illusion:
the lion lying with the lamb, the grandmother and Little Red
  Riding Hood
walking out of a wolf named Dachau.

[1989]

## THE PARTY TO WHICH WOLVES ARE INVITED

I'm five years old.
My parents tell me I'll turn into a boy
if I kiss my elbow.
(I have a mustache because I almost
succeeded).

I like to hear them at night
trying to kiss their own elbows
and turn into each other,
she thinking to show him
what a husband should be,
he intending to teach her
a thing or two about wives.

When the moon gets full of itself
my parents do not make love.
We live in an attic. We make do.

The lightning flashes as night is executed.

I'd rather kiss toads.

Stormtrooping thunder arrives. Anne is doomed.

See Anne. See Anne run. Run, Anne, run to
Burundi, 95 of every 100 adults (and all of the
children) can't read or write or draw swastikas.
*   *   *

I knew it; I'm dreaming I lift violets to her nose.
She pots the scent in beer steins.

I go to summer camp in a Radio Flyer wagon.
I lift the violets to her nose. I've botched my
memory. I kiss her elbow. She's in my cabin.
She can't swim either. We kiss toads in the swamp.

The graves are muddy. The rain mistakes them for
bathtubs. The toads turn into paterollers, sell
us. From the frying pan, Anne, into the fire.
My parents do not make love. The moon is full of
itself. Look at that yellow skin; bet my bottom
dollar the baby will be mulatto. No one's on bottom,
no one's on top, my parents do not make love.
*Runagate, runagate.* Keep moving. Women and children
first. Every man for himself. Kiss the blood off my
elbow, please. I'm homesick. I send letters
with no return address. I don't know where I
am, where the attic is. All I know is that I smell
violets. I must be near the woods. Near wolves.
They have no elbows. I can kiss them all
day long and they won't turn into something else.

Now I want my parents to step out and yell
*surprise.* Otherwise, anything that moves
is a wolf.

[1990]

# CHITRA DIVAKARUNI, 1956–

## MAKING SAMOSAS

We sift salt into *chapati* flour, pour oil
and skin-warm water. *Punch it
more, more,* my mother says. *The trick
is to get all the kinks out
before you start.* The filling

is already cooling, spread on
the round tin tray on the counter
where this winter day the late sun
catches it briefly, the warm yellow
potatoes, the green glint of peas. She
rolls out the dough that I have made
into little balls, her circles perfect

as in my childhood. *The doctor said*
*he wasn't to have any,* she says.
*But what rages he would fly into*
*if we tried to stop him. Remember*
*that time on your birthday*
*when he threw the chutney bowl*
*clear across the room?*
My father, whom we have not seen
these seven years
who hung up each time we called

even after his stroke. I stir
tamarind into the chutney and see him
as she does,
in his kitchen 1500 miles away,
his left leg dragging a little.
He peers into the leached white light
of a refrigerator, reaches for
a carton, a bottle. Around him
a city of silent, falling snow.
*Stuff carefully,* she says, *press too hard*
*and they'll fall apart.* The oil ready,

she slides the samosas in, one by one.
They puff up crisp and golden,
hissing. I lift them
with a slotted spoon and drain them
on newspapers. Her back to me
my mother washes her hands,
letting the water run and run. The kitchen
fills with the old brown smell
of roasted cumin, crushed cilantro leaves.

[1991]

## VISIT

I peel off your plastic underwear,
wipe the damp crud crusting folds of skin.
My fingers probe where a daughter
should never go. I try
to gentle them but you flinch away
and will not look at me. Your shame
fills the room, rusty odor
of urine, the stains
down the front of your robe.

The bathing takes so long, wrinkle
by wrinkle, hair by matted hair.
Your breasts sagging into tepid water.
The large circles of washcloth
on armpit and thigh. You close
your eyes and mouth, pale
tight slits, against me. When
I lift you out, porous, weightless,
and wrap you in towels,
you cannot stop the shaking.

Through the meal I talk and talk
to fill the hollows of your bones
with my futile voice. You part
your lips, obedient to my spoon:
mashed potatoes, strained carrot soup,
soaked bread. Perhaps a boiled egg
tonight, I ask, apples chopped fine,
cooked soft. I show you pictures
of my daughters—birthdays, visits
to the zoo. You smile
at the bright shapes, then look
through me. The skin around your eyes
creases in concentration
at something I cannot see.

If I told you that tonight
I must pack your things, that tomorrow
they will take you to Sunnyside Manor,

would you know to weep?
To remember how at Gorakhpur
when your father broke his hip,
you kept him with you? Year after year
cleaned the bedsores opening their mouths
like red flowers?
To ask why I cannot?

There is so much I have no answers for:
why the cloudless afternoon
outside your window is jagged
by lightning and a sound so fierce
you hold your head and moan.
Why I bend into the floor's grime
and scrub, teeth clamped, until I ache,
jaw and nail and knee. Why
seeing again the forgotten blue tiles
of your kitchen, your eyes fill
in this phenol air, raw stinging whiff
of cadaver labs. Why as the dark
seeps around your bed you at last
grip my hand hard, not letting go,
as though forever were a possible truth.

[1991]

# FINAL NOTATIONS

it will not be simple, it will not be long
it will take little time, it will take all your thought
it will take all your heart, it will take all your breath
it will be short, it will not be simple

it will touch through your ribs, it will take all your heart
it will not be long, it will occupy your thought
as a city is occupied, as a bed is occupied
it will take all your flesh, it will not be simple

You are coming into us who cannot withstand you
you are coming into us who never wanted to withstand you
you are taking parts of us into places never planned
you are going far away with pieces of our lives

it will be short, it will take all your breath
it will not be simple, it will become your will

—ADRIENNE RICH, 1991

# BIOGRAPHIES

AI (1947) is a native of Tucson, Arizona. Her father was Japanese and her mother was born in Texas of African-American, Choctaw Indian, Irish, and German descent. She has published four volumes of poetry, the second of which, *Killing Floor,* was the Lamont Poetry Selection of the Academy of American Poets. Her most recent book is *Fate* (Houghton Mifflin, 1991). She lives in New York City. See page 400.

PAULA GUNN ALLEN (1939) was born in New Mexico of Laguna-Sioux-Lebanese parents. She is the author of a novel, two critical studies, and eight volumes of poetry, the most recent of which is *Skins and Bones: Poems* 1979–87 (West End Press, 1988). She is professor of Native American Studies and Ethnic Studies at the University of California/Berkeley. See page 301.

In 1969, ALTA (1942) founded Shameless Hussy Press, the United States' first feminist publishing house. She has published more than a dozen volumes of poems and stories, including *The Shameless Hussy: Selected Stories, Essays and Poetry* (The Crossing Press, 1980). She recently founded Dancing Cane Productions to produce videos. See page 329.

ELLEN BASS (1947) was coeditor of the first edition of *No More Masks!* (Anchor, 1973). Since that date, she has published four volumes of poetry, the most recent of which was *Our Stunning Harvest* (New Society Publishers, 1985). She has spent the past decade working with survivors of child sexual abuse, and is coauthor of *The Courage to Heal* (Harper & Row, 1988). She lives in California. See page 402.

LOUISE BOGAN (1897–1970) was born in Maine and lived most of her life in New York City, working as an editor and writer for *The New Yorker.* She held the Chair of Poetry at the Library of Congress (1946–67), and was a recipient of the Bollingen Prize, and an award from the Academy of American Poets. In addition to two volumes of criticism, she published six volumes of poems, the last of which was *The Blue Estuaries: Poems* 1923–1968 (Farrar Strauss & Giroux,1968). See page 50.

Born in St. Paul, Minnesota, KAY BOYLE (1903–1992) lived in Europe for most of the twenties, thirties,and forties,writing as foreign correspondent for *The New Yorker* from 1946 to 1953. She is the author of more than thirty books, among them six volumes of poetry, the most recent of which, *The Collected Poems* (Copper Canyon Press, 1991) contains all previous poems plus those written since 1985. See page 53.

GWENDOLYN BROOKS (1917) was born in Kansas, graduated from Wilson Junior College in 1936, and has always lived in Chicago. Among her awards are the American Academy of Arts and Letters Award, the Pulitzer Prize, and two Guggenheim Fellowships. She is Poet Laureate of Illinois, succeeding Carl Sandburg. In addition to a novel and an autobiography, she has published more than thirteen volumes of poetry. See page 95.

A native of Greece, OLGA BROUMAS (1949) holds degrees from the University of Pennsylvania (B.A.) and the University of Oregon (M.F.A.). She has published five volumes of poems, the first of which, *Beginning with O,* won the Yale Series of Younger Poets award in 1977. Her most recent volume is *Perpetua* (Copper Canyon Press, 1989). She lives in Provincetown, Massachusetts, where she is a bodywork therapist. She teaches in the Creative Writing Program at Boston University. See page 421.

LORNA DEE CERVANTES (1940) has published two volumes of poems, *Emplumada* (University of Pittsburgh Press, 1981), and *From the Cables of Genocide: Poems on Love and Hunger* (Arte Publico Press, 1991). She lives in Boulder, Colorado. See page 309.

Iowan AMY CLAMPITT (1920) was an undergraduate at Grinnell College. Since 1983, she has published four volumes of poems, the most recent of which is *Westward* (Alfred A. Knopf, 1990). She holds a Lila Wallace-Reader's Digest Writer's Award and a fellowship from the John D. and Catherine T. MacArthur Foundation. She lives in New York City and teaches at Smith College. See page 111.

Born in Washington, D.C., CHERYL CLARKE (1947) has published three volumes of poetry, the two most recent of which are *Living As A Lesbian* (1986) and *Humid Pitch: Narrative Poetry* (1989), both published by Firebrand Books. See page 409.

LUCILLE CLIFTON (1936) is the author of seven volumes of poems, the most recent of which is *Quilting: Poems 1987–1990 (Boa Editions Ltd., 1991).* A new volume will be called *Book of Light* (Copper Canyon Press, 1993). She is also the author of more than a dozen books of fiction and poetry for children. She is now distinguished Professor of Humanities at St. Mary's College in Maryland. In 1992 she won the Shelley Memorial Award from the Poetry Society of America. See page 254.

A native of Los Angeles, WANDA COLEMAN (1938) presently works as a medical secretary. Her sixth book, *African Sleeping Sickness: Stories and Poems* (Black Sparrow Press, 1990) contains a revision of *Mad Dog Black Lady,* first published in 1979. She has had literary fellowships from the Guggenheim Foundation and the California Arts Council. See page 299.

JANE COOPER's (1924) first published book, *The Weather of Six Mornings* (Macmillan, 1968) was the Lamont selection of the Academy of American Poets. Her most recent volume, *Scaffolding: New and Selected Poems* (Anvil Press Poetry, 1984), was reissued in 1993 by Tilbury House. A new collection *Green Notebook, Winter Road.* will be issued by Tilbury House in 1994. Recently, she retired from teaching at Sarah Lawrence College to enjoy writing fulltime. See page 161.

LUCHA CORPI (1945) is a teacher in the Oakland Public Schools and the author of two novels and two collections of poetry, *Palabras de mediodia/Noon Words* (El Fuego de Atzlán Publications, 1980) and *Variaciones sobre una tempestad/Variations on the Storm* (Third Woman Press, 1990). In 1990 she was awarded a Creative Artists Fellowship by the City of Oakland and was named Poet Laureate at Indiana University Northwest. Her poems, written in Spanish, are translated into English by Catherine Rodriguez-Nieto. See page 390.

JAYNE CORTEZ (1936) was born in Arizona, grew up in California, and lives in New York City. She has published seven volumes of poetry, the most recent of which are *Coagulations: New and Selected Poems* (Thunder's Mouth Press, 1984) and *Poetic Magnetic (Bola Press. 1991)*. See page 261.

TOI DERRICOTTE (1941) was born in Hamtramck, Michigan, and holds degrees from Wayne State University (B.A.) and New York University (M.A.). She has published three volumes of poetry, the most recent of which is *Captivity* (University of Pittsburgh Press, 1989). She now lives in Maryland. See page 317.

DIANE DI PRIMA (1934) has published more than a dozen volumes of poems, in addition to fiction, a play, a memoir, and several volumes of criticism. *Pieces of a Song: Selected Poems* (City Lights Books, 1990) and *Seminary Poems* (Floating Island, 1991) are her most recent volumes. She writes and teaches at San Francisco Institute of Magical and Healing Arts. See page 229.

CHITRA DIVAKARUNI (1956) recently won the Gerbode Award for Poetry, which will give her time for writing. She has published three volumes of poems, the most recent of which was *Black Candle* (Calyx Books, 1991). She holds degrees from Calcutta University (B.A.) and the University of California/Berkeley (Ph.D.). Since 1989, she has taught English and creative writing at Foothill College in California. See page 457.

HILDA DOOLITTLE, known as H.D. (1886–1961), was born in Pennsylvania and attended Bryn Mawr College. In 1911, she went abroad for a visit and never returned to live in the United States. Her first volume appeared in 1916, and seven other volumes in the next several decades followed, in addition to four novels, a memoir, and several critical works. Her work is accessible today in modern volumes, including *Collected Poems 1912–1944* (New Directions, 1983) and *Trilogy* (New Directions, 1973). See page 28.

SHARON DOUBIAGO (1946) received the 1991 Hazel Hall Oregon Book Award for Poetry for *Psyche Drives the Coast: Poems 1974–87* (Empty Bowl, 1990). She is the author of five volumes of poetry, including the epic poems *Hard Country* (West End Press, 1992) and *South America Mi Hija* (University of Pittsburgh Press, 1992). She has also published two collections of short fiction and is at work on more. See page 392.

Ohioan RITA DOVE (1952) holds degrees from Miami University (B.A.) and from the Iowa Writer's Workshop (M.F.A.). She is the author of a novel, a volume of short stories, and four collections of poetry, among them *Thomas and Beulah* (Carnegie-Mellon University Press, 1986), which won the Pulitzer Prize. Her most recent volume is *Grace Notes* (W.W. Norton, 1989). She is professor of English at the University of Virginia, and has just been named Poet Laureate of the United States. See page 442.

ALICE RUTH MOORE DUNBAR-NELSON (1875–1935) was born in New Orleans, and worked as a teacher much of her life. She published two collections of short fiction but no volume of poetry in her lifetime. Gloria T. Hull's edited two volumes of *The Works of Alice Dunbar-Nelson* (Oxford University Press, 1988) makes available a slim collection of poems, much of which was published in periodicals and anthologies. See page 15.

CAROLYN FORCHÉ'S (1950) first volume of poems *Gathering the Tribes* (Yale University Press, 1976) won the Yale Series of Younger Poets Award. Her second volume, *The Country between Us* (Harper & Row, 1981), was the Lamont Poetry Selection for 1981. She has also published a translation of the El Salvadorian poet Claribel Allegria. She teaches at George Mason University. See page 427.

TESS GALLAGHER (1943) grew up in Northwestern Washington and attended the University of Washington where she studied with Theodore Roethke. She has published a volume of stories, another of essays, and five volumes of poems, the most recent of which is *Moon Crossing Bridge* (Graywolf Press, 1992). See page 350.

In the last twenty-five years of her life, JEAN GARRIGUE (1912–1972) published seven volumes of poems, a novella, short stories, and critical studies, all out of print. A volume of *Selected Poems,* with an introduction by J. D. McClatchy, was published by the University of Illinois Press in 1992. See page 73.

NIKKI GIOVANNI (1943) was born in Knoxville Tennessee. She has published eight volumes of poetry, the most recent of which is *Those Who Ride the Night Winds* (William Morrow, 1983). She teaches at Virginia Polytechnic Institute and State University, and in a creative writing program for senior citizens. See page 354.

LOUISE GLUCK (1943) was born in New York City. She has published six volumes of poems, the most recent of which, *Ararat* (The Ecco Press, 1990), which focused on the death of her father, won the Pulitzer Prize. She lives in Vermont. See page 357.

PATRICIA GOEDICKE (1931) has published ten volumes of poetry, the most recent of which is *Paul Bunyan's Bearskin* (Milkweed Editions, 1992). For the past ten years she has taught in the creative writing program of the University of Montana in Missoula. See page 206.

JORIE GRAHAM (1951) grew up in Italy. She has published four volumes of poems beginning with *Hybrids of Plants and of Ghosts* (Princeton University Press, 1980), and most recently *Region of Unlikeness* (The Ecco Press, 1991). She is currently on the permanent faculty of the University of Iowa's Writer's Workshop and was recently awarded the John D. and Catherine T. MacArthur Fellowship and a Peter I. B. Lavan Younger Poet Award from the Academy of American Poets. See page 435.

JUDY GRAHN (1940) grew up in New Mexico. She has worked as a waitress, fry-cook, meat wrapper, WAF, maid, typist, medical secretary, file-clerk, lab technician, social service worker, sandwich maker, barmaid, poet, and barbarian. She has published four volumes of poetry, the most recent of which is *The Queen of Swords* (The Crossing Press, 1987). See page 314.

Californian SUSAN GRIFFIN (1943) is the author of an award-winning play, and several volumes of nonfiction, among them the ground-breaking *Woman And Nature: The Roaring Inside* (Harper & Row, 1978) and the recent *Chorus of Stones: The Private Life of War* (Doubleday, 1992) She has published three volumes of poetry, the most recent of which is *Unremembered Country* (Copper Canyon Press, 1987). See page 360.

Boston-born ANGELINA WELD GRIMKÉ (1880–1958) published youthful poems in the *Boston Globe* in the 1890s, and later, her poems appeared in African-American anthologies and in the African-American journals *Opportunity* and *Crisis*. But she published no volume of poems in her lifetime. She spent much of her life as a high school teacher in Washington, D.C. Her three-act play *Rachel* was published in 1920. A volume of *Selected Works,* edited by Carolivia Herron, was published by Oxford University Press in 1991. See page 18.

MARILYN HACKER (1942) is the author of seven books of poetry, including *Presentation Piece* (Viking Press, 1974), which was a Lamont Poetry Selection and received the National Book Award in 1975, and *Going Back to the River* (Vintage Books, 1990) which received a Lambda Literary Award from the Gay and Lesbian Publishers and Booksellers Association in 1991. She is editor of the *Kenyon Review. Against Elegies: New and Selected Poems* will be published by Copper Canyon Press in 1994. See page 332.

RACHEL HADAS (1949) has published four volumes of poetry, the most recent of which is *Pass It On* (Princeton University Press, 1989). Her most recent books are *Unending Dialogue: Voices from an AIDS Poetry Workshop* (1991) and a memoir, *Mirrors of Astonishment* (1992). She is professor of English at the Newark campus of Rutgers University. See page 423.

HAZEL HALL (1886–1924) lived her thirty-eight years in Portland, Oregon, from age twelve forward, confined to a single room and in a wheelchair. She earned her living through fine sewing and wrote poetry for pleasure. Two volumes were published in her lifetime—*Curtains* (John Lane Co, 1921) and *Walkers* (Dodd, Mead Co., 1923)—and one, *Cry of Time,* posthumously in 1928 by Dutton. A volume of *Selected Poems* was published by Ahsahta Press in 1980. See page 32.

ANNE HALLEY (1928) has published two volumes of poems, the most recent of which is *The Bearded Mother* (University of Massachusetts Press, 1979). She has also published fiction and translation, and two major critical Afterwords—to Mary

Doyle Curran's *The Parish and the Hill* and to Jo Sinclair's *Anna Teller,* both reprinted by The Feminist Press at CUNY. See page 182.

JOY HARJO (1951) was born in Tulsa, Oklahoma, of Creek decent. She has published three volumes of poetry, the most recent of which is *In Mad Love and War* (Wesleyan University Press, 1990). She teaches at the University of Colorado at Boulder. See page 439.

LINDA HOGAN (1947) is a Chickasaw writer. Her work includes five volumes of poetry, the most recent of which is *Savings* (Coffee House Press, 1988). A new volume, *The Book of Medicines,* will be published in 1993 by Coffee House Press. See page 413.

COLETTE INEZ (1931) grew up in a Catholic orphanage in Brussels, and later in foster homes, the daughter of a priest and a scholar. She is the author of four volumes of poetry, the most recent of which is *Family Life* (Story Line Press, 1988). She is on the faculty of Columbia University's Writing Program. Her *New and Selected Poems* will be published by Story Line Press in 1993. See page 212.

JOSEPHINE JACOBSEN (1908) is the author of six volumes of poetry, the most recent of which are *The Chinese Insomniacs: New Poems* (University of Pennsylvania Press, 1981) and *The Sisters: New and Selected Poems* (The Bench Press, 1987). She served as Poetry Consultant to the Library of Congress, 1971–1973. Her awards include those from the National Institute of Arts and Letters, the Academy of American Poets, and the Lenore Marshall Award. See page 68.

GEORGIA DOUGLAS JOHNSON (1886–1966) was born in Atlanta, Georgia, attended Atlanta University and Oberlin Conservatory, and later taught school. She published four volumes of poems: *The Heart of a Woman* (1918; reprinted by Books for Libraries, 1971); *Bronze,* (1922; reprinted by AMS, 1975); *An Autumn Love Cycle* (1928; reprinted by Books for Libraries, 1971); and *Share My World* (privately printed, 1962). See page 34.

JUNE JORDAN (1936) was born in Harlem and studied at Barnard College and the University of Chicago. She has published twenty-one books, most recently the political essay *Technical Difficulties,* in 1992. Her most recent collection of poems is *Naming Our Destiny: New and Selected Poems* (Thunder's Mouth Press, 1989). She is professor of African-American Studies and Women's Studies at the University of California/Berkeley. See page 264.

SHIRLEY KAUFMAN (1923) has published five volumes of poems and several books of translations of Israeli poets. Her most recent volume of poems is *Rivers of Salt* (Copper Canyon Press, 1993). Among her many awards is the Shelley Memorial Award (1991) of the Poetry Society of America. She now lives in Jerusalem. See page 135.

CAROLYN KIZER (1925) is a life-long feminist. She was born in Spokane, Washington, and educated at Sarah Lawrence College. From 1966 to 1970 she served as the first Director of the literature program at the National Endowment for the Arts. She has published seven books of poems, including *Mermaids in the Basement: Poems for Women* (Copper Canyon Press, 1984). In 1985 she won the Pulitzer Prize for *Yin* (Boa Editions, 1984). Her most recent volume is *The Nearness of You* (Copper Canyon Press, 1987). She lives in California. See page 167.

IRENA KLEPFISZ (1941) was born Warsaw, Poland and emigrated to the United States in 1949. She is the author of five volumes of poems, the most recent of which is *A Few Words in the Mother Tongue: Poems Selected and New, 1971–1990* (Eighth Mountain Press, 1990). A volume of prose, *Dreams of an Insomniac: Jewish Feminist Essays, Speeches, and Diatribes* was also published by Eighth Mountain Press in 1990. A founder of *Conditions,* she is currently contributing editor to *Sinister Wisdom* and a consultant on Yiddish language and literature to *Bridges.* See page 322.

MAXINE KUMIN (1925) received her B.A. and M.A. from Radcliff College. She has published five volumes of fiction, two of essays, and nine volumes of poems, the most recent of which is *Looking for Luck* (W.W. Norton, 1992). In 1973 she won the Pulitzer Prize for *Up Country: Poems of New England: New & Selected Poems* (Viking, 1974); she won the Levinson Award from *Poetry* in 1986. She lives in New Hampshire. See page 176.

DENISE LEVERTOV (1923) was born in England and educated privately. She came to the United States in 1948, and since then has published nineteen volumes of poetry, in addition to several volumes of translation and others of essays. Her most recent volume of poems is *A Door in the Hive* (New Directions, 1989). See page 142.

A member of the illustrious Lowell family, AMY LOWELL (1874–1925) was born in Brookline, Massachusetts, and educated privately at home and abroad. She did not publish her first volume until she was 38 in 1912, and then published seven others before her death in 1925. *What's O'Clock,* published posthumously, received the Pulitzer Prize for 1925. She also published several volumes of critical essays and a two-volume biography of John Keats in the last year of her life. See page 6.

AUDRE LORDE (1934–1993) published four volumes of prose, including *The Cancer Journals* (Spinsters, Inc, 1980) and *Sister Outsider* (The Crossing Press, 1984); and nine volumes of poetry, the most recent of which is *Our Dead Behind Us* (W.W. Norton, 1986). A new volume of poems will be published posthumously. See page 234.

CYNTHIA MACDONALD'S (1928) most recent volume is *Living Wills: New and Selected Poems* (1991). A psychoanalyst as well as a poet and a mother, she has held many awards, including a Guggenheim. A former New Yorker, twelve years ago she founded the creative writing program at the University of Houston. See page 188.

LINDA MCCARRISTON (1943) grew up in a working class tenement in Lynn, Massachusetts. She has published two volumes of poems, the second of which, *Eva-Mary* (TriQuarterly Books, 1991), won the Terrence Des Pres Prize for Poetry and was nominated for the National Book Award. She lives in Cambridge. See page 366.

COLLEEN J. McELROY (1935) is the author of two works of fiction and six volumes of poems, the most recent of which is *What Madness Brought Me Here: New and Selected Poems, 1968-1988* (Wesleyan University Press, 1990). She has had both an American Book Award (1984) and the Washington State Governer's Award (1987). She is professor of English at the University of Washington. See page 248.

PHYLLIS McGINLEY (1905–1978) grew up in Oregon, went to college at the University of Utah, and later moved east. She published many books for children, a volume of essays, and nine volumes of poetry, including *Times Three: Selected Verse* (Curtis Publishing Company, 1960), which won the Pulitzer Prize in 1961. See page 66.

SANDRA McPHERSON (1943) has published ten volumes of poetry, the most recent of which are *Streamers* (The Ecco Press, 1988) and *The God of Indeterminacy* (University of Illinois Press, 1993). She is professor of English at the University of California at Davis. See page 369.

Activist MAUDE MEEHAN (1920) has taught writing workshops and courses in poetry. She has published two volumes of poems: *Chipping Bone* (1985) and *Before the Snow* (1991). She lives in Santa Cruz, California. See page 116.

EDNA ST. VINCENT MILLAY (1892–1950) grew up in Maine and then went to Vassar College. She published fiction and plays—and acted in them—as well as twelve volumes of poems in her lifetme. *The Collected Poems* (Harper, 1952) was published posthumously. She won the Pulitzer Prize in 1924 for *The Harp-Weaver and Other Poems* (Harper, 1923). See page 43.

Texan VASSAR MILLER (1924) has published eleven volumes of poems, the most recent of which is *If I Had Wheels Or Love: Collected Poems* (Southern Methodist University Press, 1991). She has had multiple awards from the Texas Institute of Letters. She writes, "I hope to keep writing till I die." See page 164.

JANICE MIRIKITANI (1942) is a *Sansei* (third generation Japanese-American), and the author of two volumes of poems, the most recent of which is *Shedding Silence* (Celestial Arts, 1988). She lives in San Francisco, where, in addition to writing poetry, she is a choreographer, editor, and community activist. See page 340.

Missouri-born MARIANNE MOORE (1887–1972) was educated ar Bryn Mawr College, then worked for nearly two decades as a teacher of stenography to American Indians, and then as a librarian in New York City. She published thirteen volumes of poems, including *The Complete Poems* (Viking, 1967). In 1951, she won the Pulitzer Prize for *Collected Poems* (Macmillan), the Bollingen Prize, and National Book Award. See page 35.

CHERRIE MORAGA (1952) is co-editor of the ground-breaking anthology, *This Bridge Called My Back: Writings by Radical Women of Color* (Persephone, 1981). She has published two volumes of poetry: *Loving in the War Years: Lo Que Nunca Paso Por Sus Labios* (South End Press, 1983) and *Giving Up the Ghost: Teatro* (West End Press, 1986). She teaches Chicano/a Studies at the University of California/Berkeley. See page 445.

ROBIN MORGAN (1941), prize-winning author or editor of nine books of prose—including the ground-breaking *Sisterhood Is Powerful* (Random House, 1970)—and five volumes of poetry, is editor-in-chief of *Ms.* Magazine. Her most recent volume of poems is *Upstairs in the Garden: Poems Selected and New*, 1968-1988 (W.W. Norton, 1990). See page 326.

THYLIAS MOSS (1955) has published four collections of poetry, the most recent of which are *At Redbones* (Cleveland State University Poetry Center, 1990) and *Small Congregations: New and Selected Poems* (Ecco Press, 1993). She is the recipient of a 1987 Artist's Fellowship from the Artist's Foundation of Massachusetts. She teaches at Phillips Academy in Andover. See page 455.

LORINE NIEDECKER (1903–1970) lived most of her life in a small cabin on Black Hawk Island on Lake Koshkonong, near Fort Atkinson, Wisconsin, mainly isolated from poets and the publishing world. Six volumes of her poems were published in her lifetime, and several collections posthumously, including *The Granite Pail: Selected Poems* (North Point Press, 1985). See page 63.

NAOMI SHIHAB NYE (1952) has published three volumes of poems, the most recent of which is *Yellow Glove* (Breitenbush Books, 1986). *Hugging the Jukebox* (E.P. Dutton, 1982) won the National Poetry Series Award and the Voertman Award, Texas Institute of Letters. She has also edited an international collection of poems, *This Same Sky* (Macmillan, 1992). See page 448.

SHARON OLDS (1942) teaches at New York University and at Goldwater Hospital, a public city hospital for the physically challenged. She has published four volumes of poems, the most recent of which is *The Father* (Knopf, 1992). In 1993 she received a Lila-Wallace Reader's Digest Writer's Award. See page 342.

ALICIA OSTRIKER (1937) is the author of seven volumes of poetry, the most recent of which are *The Imaginary Lover* (University of Pittsburgh Press, 1986), and *Green Age* (University of Pittsburgh Press, 1989). She has also published several volumes of literary criticism, including *Stealing the Language: The Emergence of Women's Poetry in America* (Beacon Press, 1986). She is professor of English at Rutgers University. See page 278.

New Yorker GRACE PALEY (1922) describes herself as "a cooperative anarchist and combative pacifist." She has published three volumes of short stories and three collections of poems, the most recent of which is *New and Collected Poems* (Tilbury House, 1992). She teaches at Sarah Lawrence College and at City College/CUNY. She was the first official New York State Author. See page 132.

PAT PARKER (1944–1989) published five volumes of poems, the last of which was *Jonestown & Other Madness* (Firebrand Books, 1985). In the late eighties, she was the Director of the Oakland Feminist Women's Health Center. *Movement in Black: The Collected Poetry, 1961-1978* was reissued posthumously by Firebrand Books in 1989. See page 374.

LINDA PASTAN (1932) has published eight volumes of poems, the most recent of which is *Heroes in Disguise* (W.W. Norton, 1991). She has won the Dylan Thomas

Award, the Di Castagnola Award, the Bess Hokin Prize of *Poetry* Magazine, and the Maurice English Award. She is Poet Laureate of Maryland. See page 215.

MOLLY PEACOCK (1947) is the author of three books of poems, the most recent of which is *Take Heart* (Random House, 1989). She lives in New York City where she works as a learning specialist at Friends Seminary and serves as President of the Poetry Society of America. See page 417.

MARGE PIERCY (1936) is the author of twelve collections of poetry, the most recent of which, *Mars and Her Children,* was published in 1992. She has also written eleven novels, all still in print, the most recent of which is *He, She and It* (Knopf, 1991). She is also the editor of *Early Ripening: American Women's Poetry Now* (Pandora, 1987). See page 273.

SYLVIA PLATH (1932–1963) was born in Boston, attended Smith College, and moved eventually to England, where she studied at Newnham College, Cambridge. She published but one volume of poetry in her lifetime, *The Colossus and Other Poems* (William Heineman, 1960), and a novel *The Bell Jar* (Faber & Faber, 1963) appeared a month before her death. Seven volumes have been published posthumously. See page 220.

New Yorker MARIE PONSOT (1921) is the translator of thirty-two books, most of them children's books, from the French. She has published three volumes of poems, the most recent of which is *The Green Dark* (Knopf, 1988). Among her awards are the Eunice Tietjens Prize from *Poetry* and the Modern Language Association's Shaughnessy Medal. She teaches in the department of English at Queens College/CUNY. See page 118.

MINNIE BRUCE PRATT (1944) was born in Selma, Alabama. She has published two volumes of poetry, the second of which, *Crime Against Nature* (Firebrand Books, 1990) was the Lamont Poetry Selection for 1990. She teaches at George Washington University and the University of Maryland/College Park. See page 378.

JULIA RANDALL (1923) has published five volumes of poems, the most recent of which is *Moving in Memory* (Louisiana State University Press, 1987). She holds degrees from Bennington College (B.A.) and Johns Hopkins University (M.A.) and teaches at Hollins College. See page 153.

NAOMI REPLANSKY (1918) was born in the Bronx. Her first book, *Ring Song* (Scribners, 1952), was nominated for the National Book Award; her second volume was a chapbook, *Twenty-One Poems, Old and New* (Gingko Press, 1988). Her not-yet-published volume, *The Dangerous World,* contains poems written since 1952. See page 98.

ADRIENNE RICH (1929) has published three volumes of prose, including the ground-breaking *Of Woman Born: Motherhood as Experience and Institution* (W.W. Norton, 1976), and thirteen volumes of poetry, the most recent of which is *An Atlas of the Difficult World: Poems 1988-1991* (W.W. Norton, 1991). Her first book of poems received the Yale Younger Poets Award in 1951. Among her many honors and awards are the recent 1991 Common Wealth Award in Literature, the 1992 William Whitehead Award for lifetime achievement, and the Academy of American Poets' 1992 fellowship for "distinguished poetic achievement." See page 196.

LOLA RIDGE (1873–1941) was born in Dublin, reared in Australia and New Zealand, and came to the United States under an assumed name in 1907 to escape an unhappy marriage. In New York, she lived as a writer and militant socialist feminist, a member of the Ferrar Association from 1910 forward, a close associate of Emma Goldman. Ridge published five volumes of poems, the first of which was *The Ghetto and Other Poems* (B.W. Huebsch, 1918), and the last, *Dance of Fire* (Smith, 1935). None of her work is easily available today. See page 3.

Chicagoan CAROLYN M. RODGERS (1942) has published three volumes of poems, the most recent of which is *The Heart As Ever Green* (Anchor Press/Doubleday, 1978). Her previous volume, *how i got ovah; new and selected poems* (Anchor Press/Doubleday, 1976) was nominated for the National Book Award. See page 348.

MURIEL RUKEYSER (1913–1980) published four volumes of translation, one of fiction, one of criticism, two biographies, and eighteen volumes of poetry, the first of which, *Theory of Flight* won the Yale Younger Poets Award in 1935, and the last of which was *The Collected Poems* (McGraw Hill, 1978). Her life was rich in political engagement, from the Scottsboro Trial, to the Vietnam War, to work on behalf of imprisoned South Korean poet Kim Chi-Ha. Her work is now available in *Out of Silence: Selected Poems* (TriQuarterly Books, 1992). See page 76.

MARY JO SALTER (1954) is the author of two volumes of poems, *Henry Purcell in Japan* (Knopf, 1985) and *Unfinished Painting* (Knopf, 1989). She teaches at Mount Holyoke College. See page 451.

SONIA SANCHEZ (1934) was born in Birmingham, Alabama, and holds a B.A. from Hunter College/CUNY. She is the author of thirteen books, among them *Black Fire* (William Morrow, 1968) and *Under A Soprano Sky* (Africa World Press, Inc., 1987). Her collection *Homegirls and Handgrenades* (Thunder's Mouth Press, 1984) won the 1985 American Book Award. She holds the Laura Carnell Chair in English at Temple University where she is professor of English. See page 238.

ANNE SEXTON (1928–1974) oversaw the publication of eight volumes of poems in her lifetime, the last two *The Death Notebooks* (Houghton Mifflin, 1974) and *The Awful Rowing Toward God* (Houghton Mifflin, 1975). Her third volume, *Live or Die* (Houghton Mifflin, 1966), won the Pulitzer Prize in 1966. Three more volumes of poems have been published since her death, the most recent, *The Complete Poems* (Houghton Mifflin, 1981). See page 191.

NTOZAKE SHANGE (1948) has published two volumes of fiction, two of drama, and four volumes of poetry. She is best known as the author of a poetic drama, *for colored girls who have considered suicide/when the rainbow is enuf.* Her most recent volume of poetry is *The Love*

*Space Demands: A Continuing Saga* (St. Martin's Press, 1992). In 1993 she received a Lila Wallace-Reader's Digest Writer's award. See page 418.

ANNE SPENCER'S (1882–1975) home in Lynchberg, Virginia, is now an historical landmark, and she is beginning to be honored for her fearless assertion of the rights of Black people. She published no volume of poems in her lifetime, though some of her lyrics appeared in anthologies of Harlem Renaissance poets in the twenties. *Time's Unfading Garden: Anne Spencer's Life and Poetry* by J. Lee Greene (Louisiana State University Press, 1977) contains forty-two of her poems, most of them never before published. See page 21.

GERTRUDE STEIN (1874–1946) was born in Pennsylvania, studied psychology at Radcliffe College and medicine at Johns Hopkins University. In 1903 she left the United States for Paris where, with brother Leo and companion Alice B. Toklas, she was a central and controversial figure in the art and literary world for the rest of her life. She published nine volumes of prose, two operas—on women's lives—and an early volume of poetry, *Tender Buttons* (1913). Much of her poetry was published in volumes posthumously. She is rarely included in anthologies of poetry, and her work is not easy to find, though the new *Really Reading Gertrude Stein: A Selected Anthology with Essays* by Judy Grahn (The Crossing Press, 1989) is helpful. See page 13.

ANNE STEVENSON (1933) is an American poet who has lived in Great Britain since 1972. She has published six volumes of poems, the most recent of which is *The Other House* (Oxford, 1990). Forthcoming is *Four and a Half Dancing Men* (Oxford, 1993). See page 227.

RUTH STONE (1915) has published five volumes of poems, the most recent pair *Second-Hand Coat: Poems New and Selected* (David R. Godine, 1987—now republished by Yellow Moon Press, 1991) and *Who Is the Widow's Muse?* (Yellow Moon Press, 1991). She received the Delmore Schwartz Award for Poetry in 1984 and, in 1986, one of the second annual Whiting Writers' Awards. She teaches creative writing at the State University of New York/Binghamton and spends summers on a mountain in Vermont. See page 89.

MAY SWENSON (1919–1989) was the author of ten books of poems, including *Another Animal* (1954), chosen by John Wheelock as the first in his Scribner Series Poets of Today. Her last collections were *In Other Words,* (Knopf, 1987), and a posthumous volume, *The Love Poems of May Swenson* (Houghton Mifflin, 1991). Among many honors and awards, she held the Bollingen Prize in Poetry and a John D. and Catherine T. MacArthur Fellowship. See page 100.

GENEVIEVE TAGGARD (1894–1948) grew up in multiracial Hawaii, went to college at the University of California/Berkeley, where she knew Josephine Herbst, and then moved to New York where she began to publish her poems in the twenties, as well as three anthologies and a major prose work, *The Life and Mind of Emily Dickinson* (Knopf, 1930). Eleven volumes of poems appeared in her lifetime, the last of which was *Slow Music* (Harper, 1946). *To the Natural World* (Ahsahta Press, Boise State University, 1980) contains a selection of her poems. See page 46.

SARA TEASDALE (1884–1933) left a conventional life in St. Louis, Missouri for New York's glittering twenties. She edited two anthologies and published eight volumes of poetry in her lifetime, the last of which, *Strange Victory* (Macmillan, 1933) appeared posthumously. *Mirror of the Heart: Selected Poems* (Macmillan, 1984) also includes previously unpublished poems. See page 23.

JEAN VALENTINE (1934) is the author of six books of poetry, the most recent of which is *The River at Wolf* (alicejamesbooks, 1992). Her first book, *Dream Barker* (Yale University Press, 1965), won the Yale Younger Poets Award. She has lived and taught in New York most of her life; now she lives in County Sligo, Ireland. See page 241.

MONA VAN DUYN (1921) is the author of seven volumes of poetry, the most recent of which is *Near Changes* (Knopf, 1990) which won the Pulitzer Prize in 1991. *To See, To Take* (Atheneum, 1970) won the National Book Award in 1971. Among her many other awards and honors are The Bollingen Prize (1970), the Loines Prize from the National Institute of Arts and Letters (1976), and a Fellowship of the Academy of American Poets (1980). She was Poet Laureate of the United States, 1992–1993. See page 123.

ALMA LUZ VILLANUEVA (1944) is the author of five volumes of poetry, the most recent of which is *Planet, with Mother, May 1?* (Bilingual Press, Arizona State University, 1992). She is also the author of three novels, one of which, *The Ultraviolet Sky,* won an American Book Award in 1989, and it will be republished by Doubleday in 1993. See page 381.

DIANE WAKOSKI (1937) has published sixteen volumes of poems, the most recent of which are *Emerald Ice: Selected Poems 1962-1987* (1988) and *Medea the Sorceress* (1991), both by Black Sparrow Press. She has also published considerable prose, some of which has been collected in *Toward a New Poetry* (University of Michigan Press, 1980). She is writer in residence and University Distinguished Professor at Michigan State University. Se page 283.

ALICE WALKER (1944) is the author of five novels, two collections of short stories, two essay collections, and five volumes of poetry, the most recent of which collects published and unpublished poems into a single volume called *Her Blue Body Everything We Know* (1991). She was born in Eatonton, Georgia, received a B.A. from Sarah Lawrence College in New York, and makes her home in northern California. See page 385.

Mississippian MARGARET WALKER (1915) grew up in the segregated South, and won the Yale Young Poets Award for her first volume, *For My People* (Yale University Press, 1942). She holds an M.A (1940) and a Ph.D. (1965) from the University of Iowa. She is best known as the author of *Jubilee,* a novel. In addition to a biography of Richard Wright and a volume called *How I Wrote Jubilee and Other Essays on Literature and Life* (The Feminist Press, 1990), she has published five volumes of poems collected recently in *This Is My Century: New and Collected Poems* (University of Georgia Press, 1989). See page 92.

MARILYN NELSON WANIEK (1946) is the author of three volumes of poems, the most recent of which is *The Homeplace* (Louisiana State University Press, 1990), which won the 1992 Annisfield-Wolf Award, and was also a finalist for the 1991 National Book Award. She teaches at the University of Connecticut. See page 396.

INGRID WENDT (1944), born and reared in Aurora, Illinois, has been a resident of Oregon since 1971. She is the author of two books of poems, the second of which, *Singing the Mozart Requiem* (Breitenbush Books, 1987), won the Oregon Book Award for Poetry. With Elaine Hedges, she coedited *In Her Own Image: Women Working in the Arts* (The Feminist Press, 1981); and with Primus St. John, *From Here We Speak* (Oregon State University Press, 1993), an anthology of Oregon poetry. See page 387.

ELEANOR WILNER (1937) is the author of four books of poems, the first of which, *maya* (University of Massachusetts Press, 1979) won the Juniper Prize. Her most recent book of poetry is *Otherwise* (University of Chicago Press, 1993). She holds a Fellowship from the John D. and Catherine T. MacArthur Foundation, teaches at the Warren Wilson MFA Program for Writers, and is a contributing editor for *Calyx, A Journal of Art and Literature by Women.* See page 293.

ELINOR WYLIE (1885–1928) was born in New Jersey of a socially-prominent Pennsylvania family and reared in Washington, D.C. Her unusual private life has received more attention than her poetry. Between 1921 and 1928, she published four novels and four volumes of poetry, including *Nets to Catch the Wind* (Harcourt, 1921), her first and most acclaimed volume. *Collected Poems* (Knopf, 1932) was published posthumously. See page 25.

NELLIE WONG (1934) has published two volumes of poems, *Dreams in Harrison Railroad Park* (Kelsey Street Press, 1977) and *The Death of Long Steam Lady* (West End Press, 1984). She lives in San Francisco. See page 245.

MITSUYE YAMADA's (1923) writings are heavily focused on her bicultural heritage, women, and issues of human rights. She is founder of MultiCultural Women Writers. Her first volume of poems, *Camp Notes and Other Poems* (Shameless Hussy Press, 1976), was reissued by Kitchen Table: Women of Color Press in 1992. Her second volume is *Desert Run: Poems and Stories* (Kitchen Table: Women of Color Press, 1988). She teaches creative writing at Cypress College in southern California. See page 156.

# PERMISSIONS

"The Garden by Moonlight," "Interlude," "Autumn," "The Sisters," reprinted with permission from *Pictures of the Floating World*, in *The Complete Poetical Works of Amy Lowell*. Copyright © 1955 by Houghton Mifflin Co., © renewed 1983 by Houghton Mifflin Co., Brinton P. Roberts, and G. D'Andelot Belin, Esquire.

"Patriarchal Poetry," reprinted with permission of Yale University Press from *Bee Time Vine and Other Pieces* by Gertrude Stein (New Haven: Yale University Press, 1953).

"At April" (Collection 33-10; Folder #162); "The Garden Seat" (Collection 33-10; Folder #170); "Caprichosa" (Collection 33-10; Folder #174), by Angelina Grimke, reprinted with permission of Moorland-Spingarn Research Center, Howard University.

"Lady, Lady," "Creed," "Letter to My Sister," "1975," reprinted from *Times Unfading Garden: Anne Spencer's Life and Poetry* by J. Lee Greene, with permission and from the Anne Spencer Foundation.

"Water Lilies," reprinted with permission of Macmillan Publishing Company from *Mirror of the Heart: Poems of Sara Teasdale*, edited by William Drake, copyright © 1920 by Macmillan Publishing Company, renewed 1948 by Mamie T. Wheless. "I might have sung of the world," and "Hide and Seek," reprinted with permission of Macmillan Publishing Company from *Mirror of the Heart: Poems of Sara Teasdale*, edited by William Drake, copyright © 1984 by Morgan Guaranty Trust Company of New York; these poems are in the Collection of American Literature, the Beinecke Rare Book and Manuscript Library, Yale University. "The Kiss," and "The Wind," reprinted with permission of Macmillan Publishing Company from *Mirror of the Heart: Poems of Sara Teasdale*, edited by William Drake (New York: Macmillan, 1984).

"Let No Charitable Hope," and "Little Eclogue," from *Collected Poems* by Elinor Wylie. Copyright © 1932 by Alfred A. Knopf, Inc., and renewed 1960 by Edwina C. Rubenstein. Reprinted by permission of the publisher.

"Sheltered Garden" from Sea Garden, "I, V, VII" from Euridice, and "Helen" from Heliodora, from *H.D.: Collected Poems, 1912–1944*. Copyright © 1982 by The Estate of Hilda Doolittle. Reprinted by permission of New Directions Publishing Corporation.

"Marriage," reprinted with permission of Macmillan Publishing Company from *Collected Poems of Marianne Moore*, copyright © 1935 by Marianne Moore, renewed

a Protest Parade," from *New and Selected Poems* (New York: Macmillan Publishing Company, 1967).

Grateful acknowledgement to William Rukeyser for permission to reprint the following poems by Muriel Rukeyser: "More of a Corpse Than a Woman," "Poem Out of Childhood," "The Conjugation of the Paramecium," "Käthe Kollwitz," "The Poem as Mask," "Despisals," "To Be A Jew in the Twentieth Century," and "Resurrection of the Right Side," from *Out of Silence* by Muriel Rukeyser (Evanston, IL: TriQuarterly Books, 1992), copyright © 1992 by William L. Rukeyser. "Night Feeding," and "For Kay Boyle," from *The Collected Poems* by Muriel Rukeyser (New York: McGraw-Hill, 1978); copyright © 1978 by Muriel Rukeyser.

Grateful acknowledgment to Ruth Stone for permission to reprint her poems "In An Iridescent Time," from *In An Iridescent Time* (Orlando, FL: Harcourt, Brace and Company, 1959); and "Advice," "How to Catch Aunt Harriette," "Pokeberries," and "Father's Day," from *Second-Hand Coat, Poems New and Selected* (Cambridge, MA: Yellow Moon Press, 1991).

Grateful acknowledgement to Margaret Walker for permission to reprint "Lineage" and "Molly Means," copyright © 1942 *For My People* (New Haven, CT: Yale University Press); and "For Gwen," copyright © 1973 *October Journey* (Detroit, MI: Broadside Press).These poems now appear in *This Is My Century: New and Collected Poems* (Athens, GA: University of Georgia Press, 1989).

Grateful acknowledgment to Gwendolyn Brooks for permission to reprint her poems "The Mother," and "Jessie Mitchell's Mother," from *The World of Gwendolyn Brooks* (New York: Harper & Row Publishers, 1960); and "To Those of My Sisters Who Kept Their Naturals," from *Blacks* (Chicago: The David Company, 1987).

Grateful acknowledgment to Naomi Replansky for permission to reprint her poems "Housing Shortage," and "Two Women," from *The Ring Song* (New York: Macmillan Publishers, 1952); and "I Met My Solitude," from *Twenty-one Poems, Old and New* (New York: The Gingko Press, 1988).

Grateful acknowledgement to Rozanne Knudson and the Literary Estate of May Swenson for permission to reprint the following poems: "The Centaur," from *To Mix with Time* (New York: Macmillan Publishing Company, 1956); "Women," from *Iconograph* (New York: Macmillan Publishing Company, 1968); "A Dream" copyright © 1954 and renewed 1982; "Feel Me," copyright © 1968 (first appeared in *The New Yorker*); "In Love Made Visible," from *The Love Poems of May Swenson* (Boston: Houghton Mifflin Company, 1991). "In the Bodies of Words," from *In Other Words* (New York: Alfred A. Knopf, 1987), reprinted by permission of Alfred A. Knopf, Inc.

"The Burning Child," from *The Kingfisher*, copyright © 1983 by Amy Clampitt; "Written in Water," from *What the Light Was Like*, copyright © 1985 by Amy Clampitt; "Medusa," from *Archaic Figures*, copyright © 1987 by Amy Clampitt; "Amherst," from *Westward*, copyright © 1987 by Amy Clampitt: all reprinted by permission of Alfred A. Knopf, Inc. and Faber & Faber.

Grateful acknowledgment to Maude Meehan for permission to reprint her poems "Is There Life After Feminism," from *Chipping Bone Collected Poems:* (Santa Cruz, CA: Embers Press, 1985); and "Gift for My Mother's 90th Birthday," from *Before the Snow* (Santa Cruz, CA: Moving Parts Press, 1991).

"Among Women" and "Residual Paralysis," from *Admit Impediment*, copyright © 1981 by Marie Ponsot; "'Love Is Not Love,'" from *The Green Dark*, copyright © 1988 by Marie Ponsot: all reprinted by permission of Alfred A. Knopf, Inc.

479

Grateful acknowledgement to Maxine Kumin for permission to reprint "A Voice from the Roses," from *The Privilege* (New York: Harper & Row, 1965), and "After Love," from *The Nightmare Factory* (New York: Harper & Row, 1970). Also, "The Chain" and "Louise Bourgeois Exhibit," both from *The Long Approach*, copyright © 1984 by Maxine Kumin, both used by permission of Viking Penguin, a division of Penguin Books USA Inc. Also, "Credo" and "The Rendezvous," reprinted from *Looking for Luck: Poems by Maxine Kumin*, by permission of the author and W.W. Norton & Company, Inc. Copyright © 1992 by Maxine Kumin.

"Housewife's letter: to Mary" and "Against Dark's Harm," reprinted from *Between Wars and Other Poems* by Anne Halley (Amherst: University of Massachusetts Press, 1965), copyright © 1965 by University of Massachusetts Press. "I'd Rather See Than Be One, But . . . ," reprinted from *The Bearded Mother* by Anne Halley (Amherst: University of Massachusetts Press, 1979), copyright © 1979 by Anne Halley.

Grateful acknowledgment to Cynthia Macdonald for permission to reprint her poems "Instructions from Bly" and "Objects d'Art," from *Amputations* (New York: George Braziller, Inc., 1973); and "Inheritance," from *Transplants* (New York: George Braziller, Inc., 1976).

"Housewife" and "The Abortion," from *All My Pretty Ones*, copyright © 1962 by Anne Sexton, © renewed 1990 by Linda G. Sexton; "Consorting with Angels," from *Live or Die*, copyright © 1966 by Anne Sexton; "For My Love, Returning to His Wife," from *Love Poems*, copyright © 1967, 1968, 1969 by Anne Sexton: All poems reprinted by permission of Houghton Mifflin Co., and Sterling Lord Literistic, Inc.

Grateful acknowledgement to Adrienne Rich and W.W. Norton & Company, Inc. for permission to reprint the following poems: "Snapshots of a Daughter-in-Law," "Women," "Hunger," "Frame," "(The Floating Poem Unnumbered)" from *The Fact of a Doorframe: Poems Selected and New, 1950–1984*, copyright © 1984 by Adrienne Rich, copyright © 1975, 1978 by W.W. Norton & Company, Inc., copyright © 1981 by Adrienne Rich; "XIII (Dedications)" and "Final Notations," reprinted from *An Atlas of the Difficult World: Poems 1988-1991*, copyright © 1991 by Adrienne Rich.

Grateful acknowledgment to Patricia Goedicke for permission to reprint her poems "In the Ocean," from *Crossing the Same River* (Amherst, MA: University of Massachusetts Press, 1980); "In the Waiting Room," from *The Tongues We Speak* (Minneapolis, MN: Milkweed Editions, 1989); "Lucky," from *Listen, Love* (Daleville, IN: The Barnwood Press, 1986); and "Without Looking," from *Paul Bunyan's Bearskin* (Daleville, IN: Milkweed Editions, 1989).

Grateful acknowledgment to Colette Inez for permission to reprint her poems: "The Woman Who Loved Worms," from *The Woman Who Loved Worms* (New York: Doubleday & Company, 1972); "Warrior Daughters," from *Eight Minutes from The Sun* (Montclair, NJ: Saturday Press, 1983); and "Absolving You," from *Family Life* (Santa Cruz, CA: Storyline Press, 1988).

Grateful acknowledgement to Linda Pastan and W.W. Norton & Company, Inc., for permission to reprint the following poems: "Notes from the Delivery Room," "After Reading Nelly Sachs," and "Passover," from *PM/AM: New and Selected Poems*, copyright © 1982 by Linda Pastan; and "Duet for One Voice," from *A Fraction of Darkness*, copyright © 1985 by Linda Pastan.

Grateful acknowledgement to HarperCollins for permission to reprint the following poems by Sylvia Plath, from *The Collected Poems of Sylvia Plath*: "Candles," copyright © 1971 by Ted Hughes; "Daddy" and "Wintering," both copyright © 1963 by Ted Hughes. And to Alfred A. Knopf, Inc., for permission to reprint "The Disquieting Muses," from *The Colossus and Other Poems*, copyright © 1960 by Sylvia Plath. Also, permission granted by Faber & Faber.

"The Suburb," from Anne Stevenson's *Selected Poems, 1956-1986* (1987); and "Poem to My Daughter," from Anne Stevenson's *Minute by Glass Minute* (1982), both reprinted by permission of Oxford University Press.

Grateful acknowledgement to Diane di Prima for permission to reprint "The Quarrel," from *Dinners and Nightmares* (Corinth Books, 1961); "April Fool Birthday Poem for Granpa," and "Narrow Path into the Back Country," from *Selected Poems, 1956–1975* (Plainfield, VT: North Atlantic Books, 1975); and "Poem in Praise of My Husband (Taos)," from *Pieces of a Song, Selected Poems* (San Francisco: City Lights Bookstore, 1990).

Grateful acknowledgement to Charlotte Sheedy Literary Agency, responsible for the Estate of Audre Lorde, and to W.W. Norton and Company, Inc., for permission to reprint the following poems: "The Woman Thing," from *Undersong: Chosen Poems Old and New, Revised Edition,* copyright © 1992, 1982, 1976, 1974, 1973, 1970, 1968 by Audre Lorde; "Hanging Fire," from *The Black Unicorn,* copyright © 1978 by Audre Lorde; "Sisters in Arms," from *Our Dead Behind Us*, copyright © 1986 by Audre Lorde.

Grateful acknowledgment to Sonia Sanchez for permission to reprint her poems "poem at thirty," from *Black Fire* (New York: William Morrow & Company, 1968); and "A Poem for My Most Intelligent 10:30 AM Class," and "A poem for my brother (reflections on his death . . . )," from *Under a Soprano Sky* (Trenton, NJ: Africa World Press, Inc., 1987).

Grateful acknowledgement to Jean Valentine and publishers for permission to reprint the following poems: "First Love," from *Dream Barker and Other Poems* (New Haven: Yale University Press, 1965); "The Forgiveness Dream: Man From the Warsaw Ghetto," from *The Messenger* (New York: Farrar, Straus & Giroux, Inc., 1979), copyright © 1979 by Jean Valentine; "Snow Landscape, in a Glass Globe," "My Mother's Body, My Professor, My Bower," and "X," from *The River at Wolf* (Cambridge: alicejamesbooks, 1992).

Grateful acknowledgment to Nellie Wong for permission to reprint her poems "Relining Shelves," from *Dreams in Harrison Railroad Park* (Berkeley, CA: Kelsey Street Press, 1977); and "Toward a 44th Birthday," from *The Death of Long Steam Lady* (West End Press, 1984).

Grateful acknowledgement to Colleen McElroy for permission to reprint "Gra'ma," from *The Mules Done Long Since Gone*, copyright © 1972. Also, "In My Mother's Room," "This Is the Poem I Never Meant to Write," and "Queen of the Ebony Isles," from *Queen of the Ebony Isles*, copyright © 1984 by Colleen J. McElroy; and "Foul Line—1987," from *What Madness Brought Me Here*, copyright © 1990 by Colleen J. McElroy, both volumes published by Wesleyan University Press.

The following poems by Lucille Clifton are reprinted with the permission of BOA Editions, Ltd., 92 Park Ave., Brockport, NY 14420: "miss rosie," "admonitions," "the way it was," "turning," "the thirty-eighth year," and "the coming of Kali," from *good woman: poems and a memoir, 1969-1980,* copyright © 1987 by

Lucille Clifton; also, "to my friend, Jerina," and "wishes for sons," from *quilting: poems 1987-1990*, copyright © 1991 by Lucille Clifton. Further, "there is a girl inside," from *two headed woman*, copyright © 1980 by Lucille Clifton, is reprinted with the permission of Curtis Brown Ltd.

Grateful acknowledgement to Jayne Cortez for permission to reprint "Rape" and "Stockpiling," from *Coagulations: New & Selected Poems* (New York: Thunder's Mouth Press, 1984), copyright © 1993 by Jayne Cortez.

"What Would I Do White?" "If You Saw a Negro Lady," "Case in Point," "Poem About My Rights," "1977: Poem for Mrs. Fannie Lou Hamer," "Some People," and "The Female and the Silence of a Man," from *Naming Our Destiny* by June Jordan. Copyright © 1989 by June Jordan. Used by permission of the publisher, Thunder's Mouth Press.

Grateful acknowledgement to Marge Piercy, her agent, and her publishers for permission to reprint the following poems: "The Friend" and "Noon of the Sun-bather," from *Hard Loving*, copyright © 1969 by Marge Piercy, Wesleyan University Press, by permission of University Press of New England. "The Woman in the Ordinary," copyright © 1971, 1982 by Marge Piercy and Middlemarsh Inc., published in *Circles on the Water: Selected Poems of Marge Piercy*, reprinted by permission of Alfred A. Knopf, Inc. and the Wallace Literary Agency, Inc. "The Book of Ruth and Naomi," copyright ©1990, 1992 by Marge Piercy and Middlemarsh, Inc., published in *Mars and Her Children*, reprinted by permission of Alfred A. Knopf, Inc. and the Wallace Literary Agency, Inc. "Something to Look Forward To," from *Available Light*, copyright © 1986, 1988 by Marge Piercy and Middlemarsh Inc., published in the U.S. by Alfred A. Knopf and in the U.K. by Pandora Books, reprinted by permission of Alfred A. Knopf, Inc. and the Wallace Literary Agency, Inc. "Homage to Lucille, Dr. Lore-Heinstein," from *My Mother's Body*, copyright © 1981, 1985 by Marge Piercy and Middlemarsh Inc., published in the U.S. by Alfred A. Knopf, Inc, and in the U.K. by Pandora Books, reprinted by permission of Alfred A. Knopf, Inc., and the Wallace Literary Agency, Inc.

Grateful acknowledgment to Alicia Ostriker for permission to reprint her poems "Propaganda Poem: Maybe for Some Young Mamas," from *The Mother/Child Papers* (Boston: Beacon Press, 1986); and "The Exchange," from *A Woman Under the Surface* (Princeton, NJ: Princeton University Press, 1983).

"Justice is Reason Enough," copyright © 1962, "Thanking My Mother for Piano Lessons," copyright © 1970, and "The Girls," copyright © 1986 by Diane Wakoski; reprinted from *Emerald Ice: Selected Poems 1962-1987* with the permission of Black Sparrow Press. "Moneylight," copyright © 1991 by Diane Wakoski, reprinted from *Medea the Sorceress* with the permission of Black Sparrow Press. "The Realization of Difference," copyright © 1966 by Diane Wakoski, reprinted from *Discrepancies and Apparitions* with the permission of the author.

Grateful acknowledgment to Eleanor Wilner for permission to reprint her poems, "Emigration," from *Shekhinah* (Chicago: University of Chicago Press, 1984); and "Coda, Overture," and "Sarah's Choice," from *Sarah's Choice* (Chicago: University of Chicago Press, 1989).

"Women of My Color," copyright © 1979 by Wanda Coleman, reprinted from *African Sleeping Sickness: Stories & Poems*, with the permission of Black Sparrow Press. "Dear Mama (2)," copyright © 1983 by Wanda Coleman, reprinted from *Imagoes* with the permission of Black Sparrow Press.

Grateful acknowledgment to the American Indian Studies Center of the University of California for permission to reprint "Night Vision," and "Los Angeles," from *Shadow Country* by Paula Gunn Allen (Los Angeles: American Indian Studies Center, 1982)."Eve the Fox," from *Skins and Bones: Poems 1979-1987*, copyright © 1988 by Paula Gunn Allen, reprinted with the permission of the author and West End Press.

"Beneath the Shadow of the Freeway" and "Poem for the Young White Man Who Asked Me How I, an Intelligent, Well-Read Person, Could Believe in the War Between Races," reprinted from *Emplumada*, by Lorna Dee Cervantes, by permission of the University of Pittsburgh Press, copyright © 1981 by Lorna Dee Cervantes.

Grateful acknowledgement to Judy Grahn for permission to reprint "Ella, in a square apron, along Highway 80" and "My Name is Judith," from *The Work of a Common Woman: The Collected Poetry of Judy Grahn, 1964-1977* (Oakland: Diana Press, 1978), copyright © 1978 by Judy Grahn; and "Hannah" from "Helen you always were/the Factory," from *The Queen of Wands* (Freedom, CA: The Crossing Press, 1982), copyright © 1982 by Judy Grahn.

Grateful acknowledgment to Toi Derricotte for permission to reprint her poems "The Feeding," from *Empress of the Death House* (Detroit, MI: Lotus Press, 1978); and "On The Turning Up of Unidentified Black Female Corpses," and "Poem for My Father," from *Captivity* (Pittsburgh, PA: University of Pittsburgh Press, 1989).

"About My Father," "Perspectives on the Second World War," and "My Mother's Sabbath Days," from *A Few Words in the Mother Tongue: Poems Selected and New (1971–1990)* by Irena Klepfisz (Portland, OR: The Eighth Mountain Press, 1990); reprinted by permission of the publisher.

Grateful acknowledgment to Robin Morgan for permission to reprint her poems "The Invisible Woman," "Heirloom," and "Damn You, Lady," from *Upstairs in the Garden, New and Selected Poems* (New York: W.W. Norton, 1990), copyright © 1990 by Robin Morgan.

Grateful acknowledgement to Alta for permission to reprint the following poems: "Bitter Herbs" and "Euch, are you having your period?" from *No Visible Means of Support* (San Lorenzo, CA: Shameless Hussy Press, 1971); "First Pregnancy," "Penus envy," and "Euridice," from *I Am Not A Practicing Angel* (Freedom, CA: The Crossing Press, 1975); and from "6, (For Pat Parker)," from *Theme & Variation,* from *The Shameless Hussy: Selected Stories, Essays . . .* (Freedom, CA: The Crossing Press, 1980). All copyright © 1980 by Alta.

Grateful acknowledgement to Marilyn Hacker for permission to reprint the following poems: "The Muses," copyright © 1968 by Marilyn Hacker, from *Presentation Piece* (New York: The Viking Press, 1974); "Sonnet for Iva," copyright © 1976 by Marilyn Hacker, from *Taking Notice* (New York: Alfred A. Knopf, 1980); "Mother II" and "Ballad of Ladies Lost and Found," copyright © 1985 by Marilyn Hacker, from *Assumptions* (New York: Alfred A. Knopf, 1985); and "Nearly A Valediction," from *The Hang-Glider's Daughter:* New and Selected Poems, copyright © 1990 by Marilyn Hacker (London, UK: Onlywomen Press, 1990).

Grateful acknowledgement to Janice Mirikitani for permission to reprint "Soul Food" and "Breaking Tradition," from *Shedding Silence* (Berkeley, CA: Celestial Arts, 1987).

Grateful acknowledgement to Sharon Olds for permission to reprint the new text of "What If God" (see below). "Solitary," "That Year," and "The Language of the Brag," from *Satan Says*, copyright © 1980 by Sharon Olds, reprinted by permission of the University of Pittsburgh Press. "Pajamas," from *The Dead and the Living*, copyright © 1975, 1983 by Sharon Olds, reprinted by permission of Alfred A. Knopf, Inc. "What If God," "The Girl," and "First Sex," from *The Gold Cell*, copyright © 1987 by Sharon Olds, reprinted by permission of Alfred A. Knopf.

Grateful acknowledgement to Carolyn M. Rodgers for permission to reprint three poems: "U Name This One," from *Natural Process*, copyright © 1970 by Carolyn M. Rodgers; "Some Me of Beauty," from *how i got ovah: new & selected poems* (New York: Anchor Books, 1976), copyright © 1976 by Carolyn M. Rodgers; "Feminism," from *The Heart As Ever Green* (New York: Anchor Books, 1978), copyright © 1978 by Carolyn M. Rodgers.

Grateful acknowledgement to Graywolf Press, Saint Paul, MN, for permission to reprint the following poems by Tess Gallagher: "Instructions to the Double," from *Instructions to the Double*, copyright © 1976 by Tess Gallagher; "On Your Own," from *Under Stars*, copyright © 1978 by Tess Gallagher; "Spacious Encounter" and "I Stop Writing the Poem," from *Moon Crossing Bridge*, copyright © 1992 by Tess Gallagher.

Grateful acknowledgement to Nikki Giovanni for permission to reprint the following poems: "Seduction" and "Adulthood," from *Black Feeling, Black Talk/Black Judgment* (New York: William Morrow & Company, 1970), copyright © 1968, 1970 by Nikki Giovanni; "Legacies," from *My House* (New York: William Morrow & Company, 1973), copyright © 1973 by Nikki Giovanni.

Grateful acknowledgement to The Ecco Press for permission to reprint the following poems by Louise Gluck: "Pomegranate," copyright © 1971, 1972, 1973, 1974, 1975 by Louise Gluck, from *The House on Marshland*, first published by The Ecco Press in 1975; "Mythic Fragment," copyright © 1985 by Louise Gluck, from *The Triumph of Achilles*, first published by The Ecco Press in 1985; "Brown Circle," copyright © 1990 by Louise Gluck, from *Ararat*, first published by The Ecco Press in 1990.

Grateful acknowledgment to Susan Griffin for permission to reprint her poems "I Like to Think of Harriet Tubman," "Song My," and "An Answer to a Man's Question, 'What Can I Do About . . . ',", from *Like the Iris of an Eye* (New York: Harper & Row Publishers, 1976); and "Sunday Morning," from *Unremembered Country* (Townsend, WA: Copper Canyon Press, 1987).

"A Castle in Lynn," "Hotel Nights with My Mother," and "Revision," from *Eva-Mary*, copyright © 1991 by Linda McCarriston (Evanston, IL: TriQuarterly Books, 1991).

Grateful acknowledgement to The Ecco Press for permission to reprint the following poems by Sandra McPherson: "Pregnancy," copyright © 1970 by Sandra McPherson, from *Elegies for the Hot Season*, first published by The Ecco Press in 1982; "For Elizabeth Bishop," copyright © 1979, 1980, 1981, 1982 by Sandra McPherson, from *Patron Happiness*, first published by The Ecco Press in 1983; "At the Grave of Hazel Hall," copyright © 1988 by Sandra McPherson, from *Streamers*, first published by The Ecco Press in 1988.

"For Willyce," and "There is a woman in this town," copyright © 1978 by Pat Parker, from *Movement in Black* (Ithaca, NY: Firebrand Books, 1978); and "Love isn't," copy-

Grateful acknowledgment to Cheryl Clarke for permission to reprint her poem "hair: a narrative," from *Narrative: Poems in the Tradition of Black Women* (New York: Kitchen Table: Women of Color Press, 1983); and to Firebrand Books (Ithaca, NY 14850) for permission to reprint "wearing my cap backwards," from *Living as a Lesbian* (Ithaca, NY: Firebrand Books, 1986), copyright © 1986 by Cheryl Clarke.

Grateful acknowledgment to Linda Hogan for permission to reprint her poems "Daybreak," from *Eclipse* (Los Angeles, CA: American Indian Studies Center, 1983); and "Friday Night," and "The Truth Is," from *Seeing Through the Sun* (Amherst, MA: University of Massachusetts Press, 1985).

Grateful acknowledgment to Molly Peacock for permission to reprint her poems "So, When I Swim to the Shore," "Our Room," and "Smell," from *Raw Heaven* (New York: Random House, 1984).

Grateful acknowledgment to Ntozake Shange for permission to reprint her poems "happenin/but you dont know abt it," and "Advice," from *Nappy Edges* (New York: St. Martin's Press, 1978).

"Eye of Heart" and "Touched," from *Perpetua*, copyright © 1989 by Olga Broumas, reprinted by permission of Copper Canyon Press, P.O. Box 271, Port Townsend, WA 98368.

Grateful acknowledgment to Wesleyan University by permission of University Press of New England for permission to reprint "Yes, But," from *A Son of Sleep* by Rachel Hadas (Middletown, CT: Wesleyan University Press, 1987); and to Princeton University Press for permission to reprint "Pass It On, II," and "Teaching Emily Dickinson," from *Pass it On* (Princeton, NJ: Princeton University Press, 1989).

"Burning the Tomato Worms," copyright © 1976 by Carolyn Forché, from *Gathering the Tribes* (New Haven, CT: Yale University Press, 1976), reprinted with permission of Yale University Press. "The Island," from *The Country Between Us*, copyright © 1978 by Carolyn Forché, reprinted by permission of Harper & Row Publishers.

Grateful acknowledgment to Jorie Graham for permission to reprint her poems "The Way Things Work," from *Hybrids of Plants and of Ghosts* (Princeton, NJ: Princeton University Press, 1980); and "From the New World," from *Region of Unlikeliness* (New York: The Ecco Press, 1991).

Grateful acknowledgement to Joy Harjo for permission to reprint "The Book of Myths," from *In Mad Love and War* (Middletown, CT: Wesleyan University Press, 1990), copyright © 1990 by Joy Harjo. Also to Thunder's Mouth Press, for permission to reprint "Anchorage," from *She Had Some Horses* by Joy Harjo, copyright © 1983 by Thunder's Mouth Press.

Grateful acknowledgement to Rita Dove for permission to reprint "The Great Palaces of Versailles," from *Thomas and Beulah* by Rita Dove (Pittsburgh, PA: Carnegie-Mellon University Press, 1986), copyright © 1986 by Rita Dove. "After Reading *Mickey in the Night Kitchen* for the Third Time Before Bed," and "Arrow," from *Grace Notes* by Rita Dove (New York: W.W. Norton & Company, Inc., 1989), copyright © 1989 by Rita Dove, reprinted by permission of the publisher.

Grateful acknowledgement to Cherrie Moraga and South End Press for permission to reprint "For the Color of My Mother" and "Loving in the War Years," from *Loving in the War Years* (Boston: South End Press, 1983).

Grateful acknowledgment to Naomi Shihab Nye for permission to reprint her poems "Hugging the Jukebox," from *Hugging the Jukebox* (Portland, OR: Breitenbush Books, 1982); and "Blood," from *Yellow Glove* (Portland, OR: Breitenbush Books, 1986).

"Welcome to Hiroshima," from *Henry Purcell in Japan*, copyright © 1985 by Mary Jo Salter; "Emily Wants to Play" and "Chernobyl," from *Unfinished Painting*, copyright © 1989 by Mary Jo Salter: Both poems reprinted by permission of Alfred A. Knopf, Inc.

Grateful acknowledgment to Thylias Moss for permission to reprint her poems "There Will be Animals," from *Pyramid of Bone* (Charlottesville, VA: University Press of Virginia, 1989); and "The Party to Which Wolves Are Invited," from *At Redbones* (Cleveland, OH: Cleveland State University Poetry Center, 1990).

Grateful acknowledgement to Chitra Divakaruni and CALYX Press for permission to reprint "Making Samosas" and "Visit," copyright © 1991 by Chitra Divakaruni, from *Black Candle* (Corvallis, OR: CALYX Books, 1991).